FAIRY TAILS

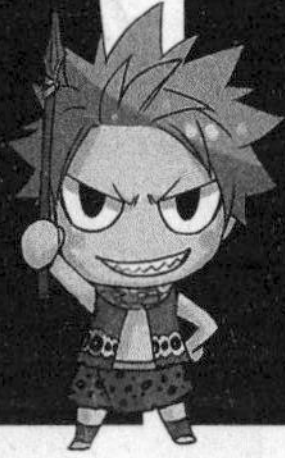

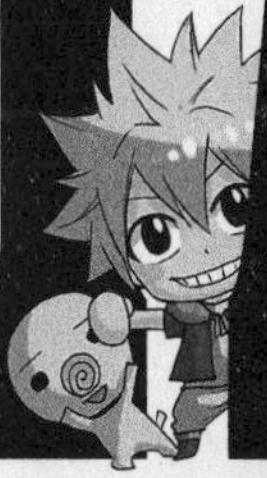

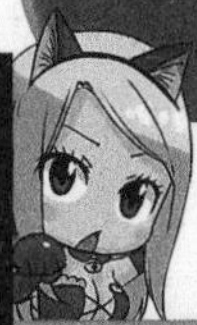

2

PRESENTED BY HIRO MASHIMA

2

CONTENTS

FAIRY TAILS

FTS2

FAIRY TAIL

FAIRY HIGH SCHOOL SIDE STORY

Gangsta Guys and Gangsta Girls

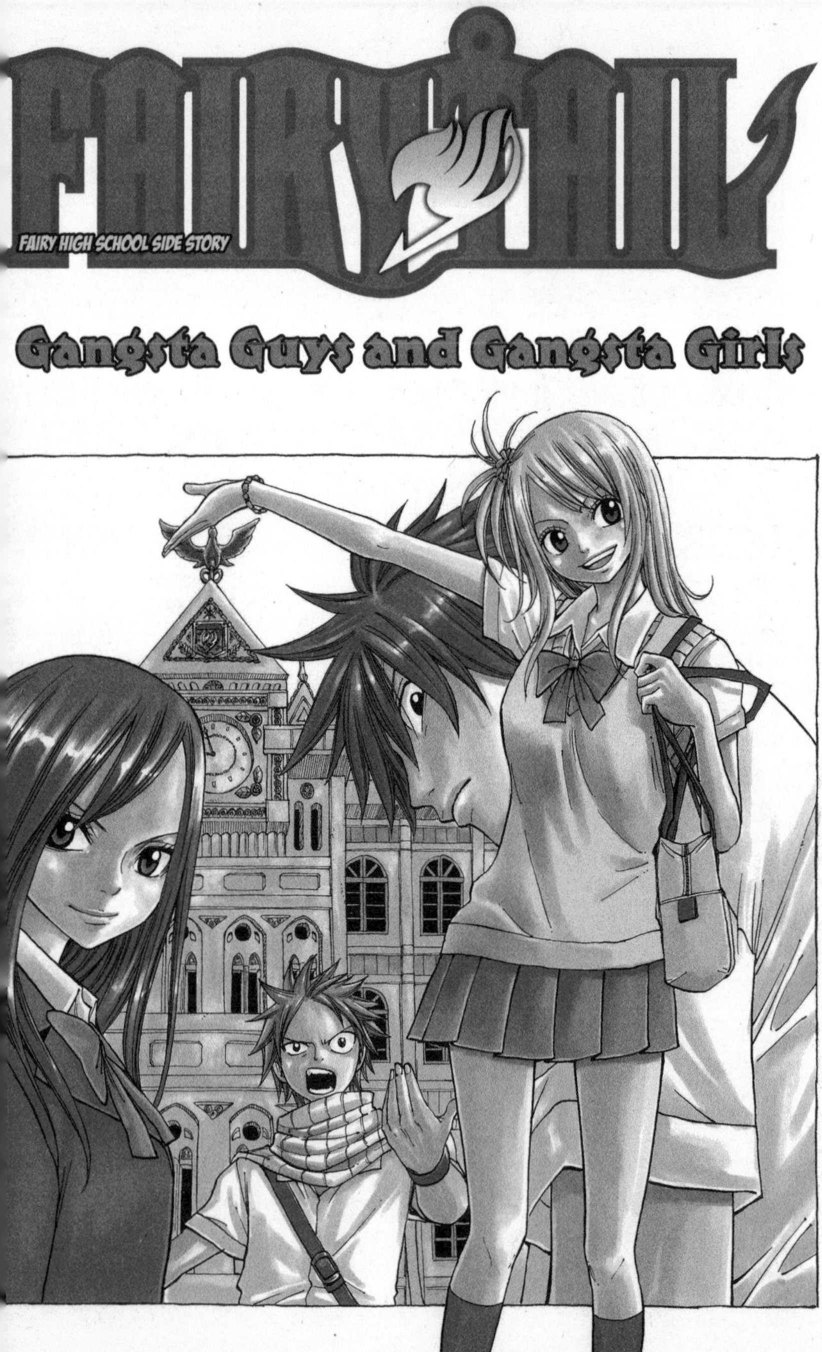

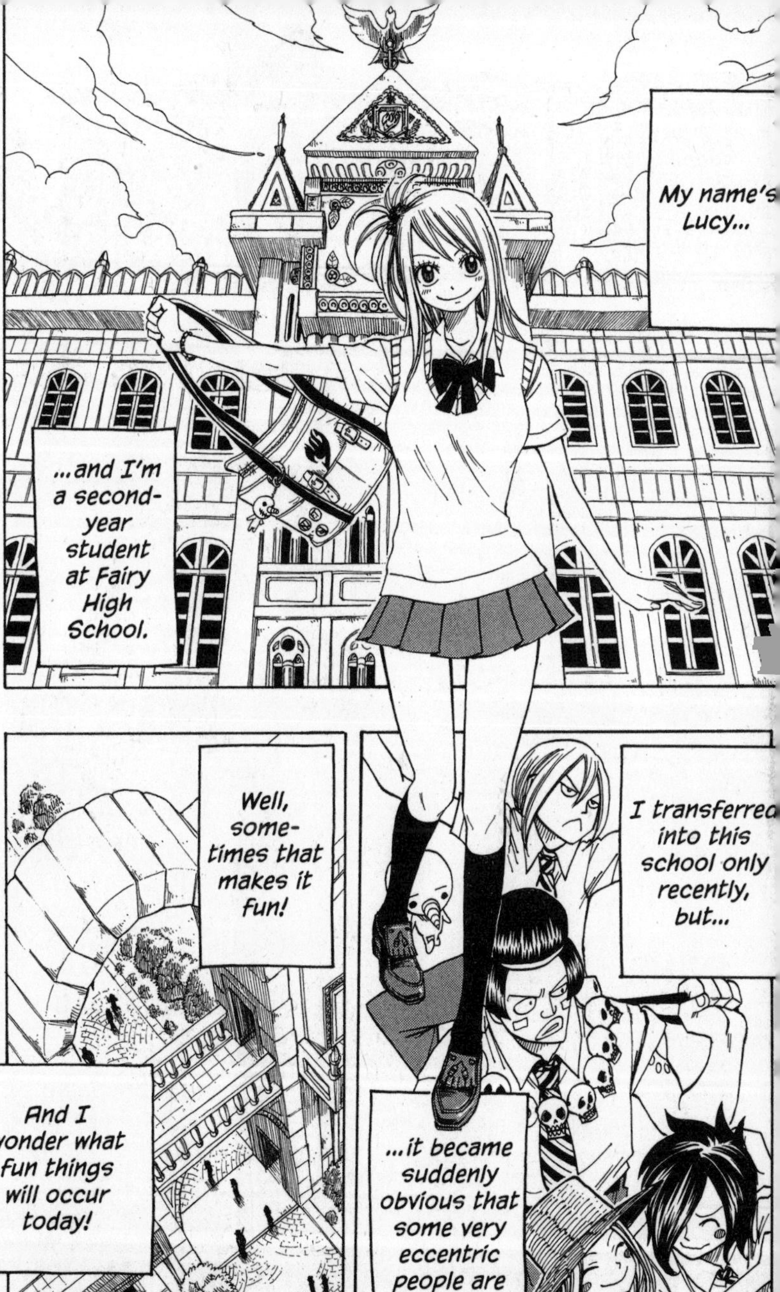
My name's Lucy...
...and I'm a second-year student at Fairy High School.
I transferre into this school only recently, but...
...it became suddenly obvious that some very eccentric people are here.
Well, sometimes that makes it fun!
And I wonder what fun things will occur today!

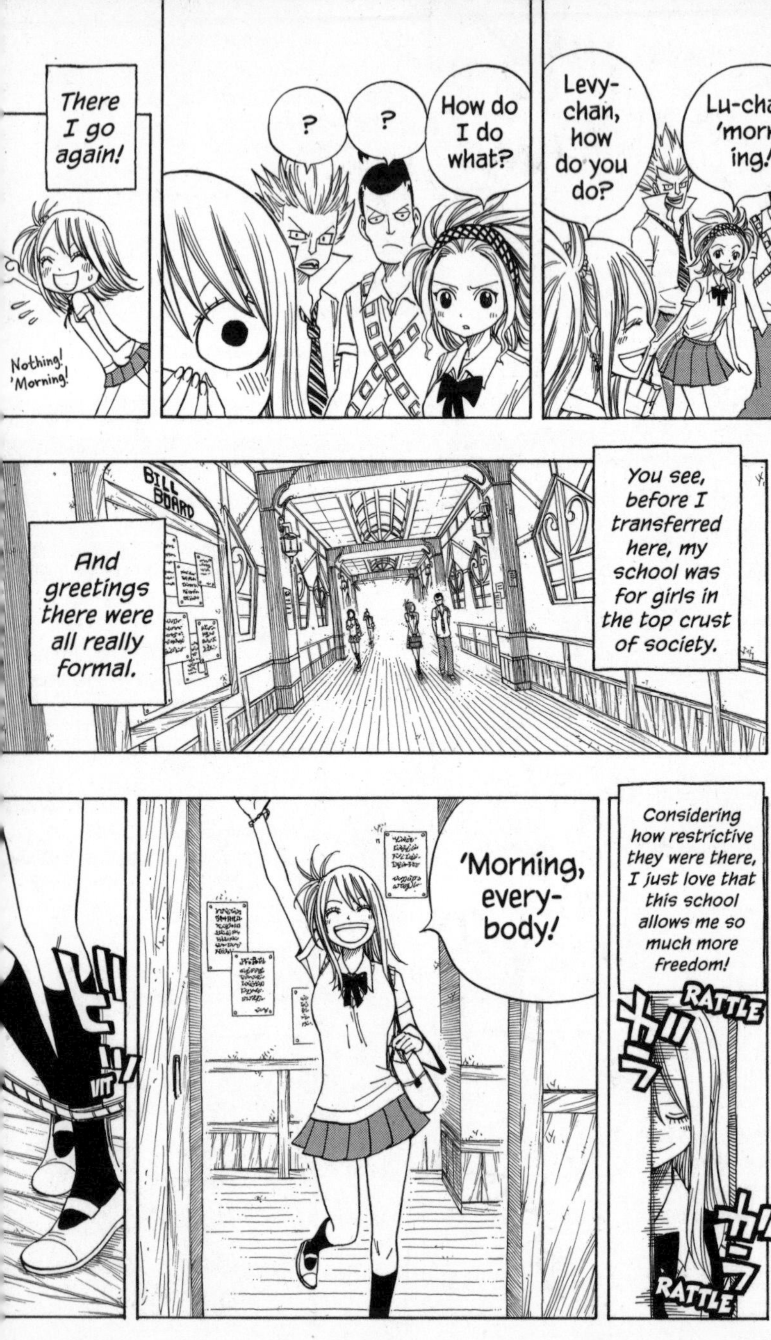
Lu-chan, 'morn-ing!
Levy-chan, how do you do?
How do I do what?
?
?
There I go again!
Nothing! 'Morning!
You see, before I transferred here, my school was for girls in the top crust of society.
And greetings there were all really formal.
BILL BOARD
Considering how restrictive they were there, I just love that this school allows me so much more freedom!
RATTLE
RATTLE
'Morning, every-body!
VIT

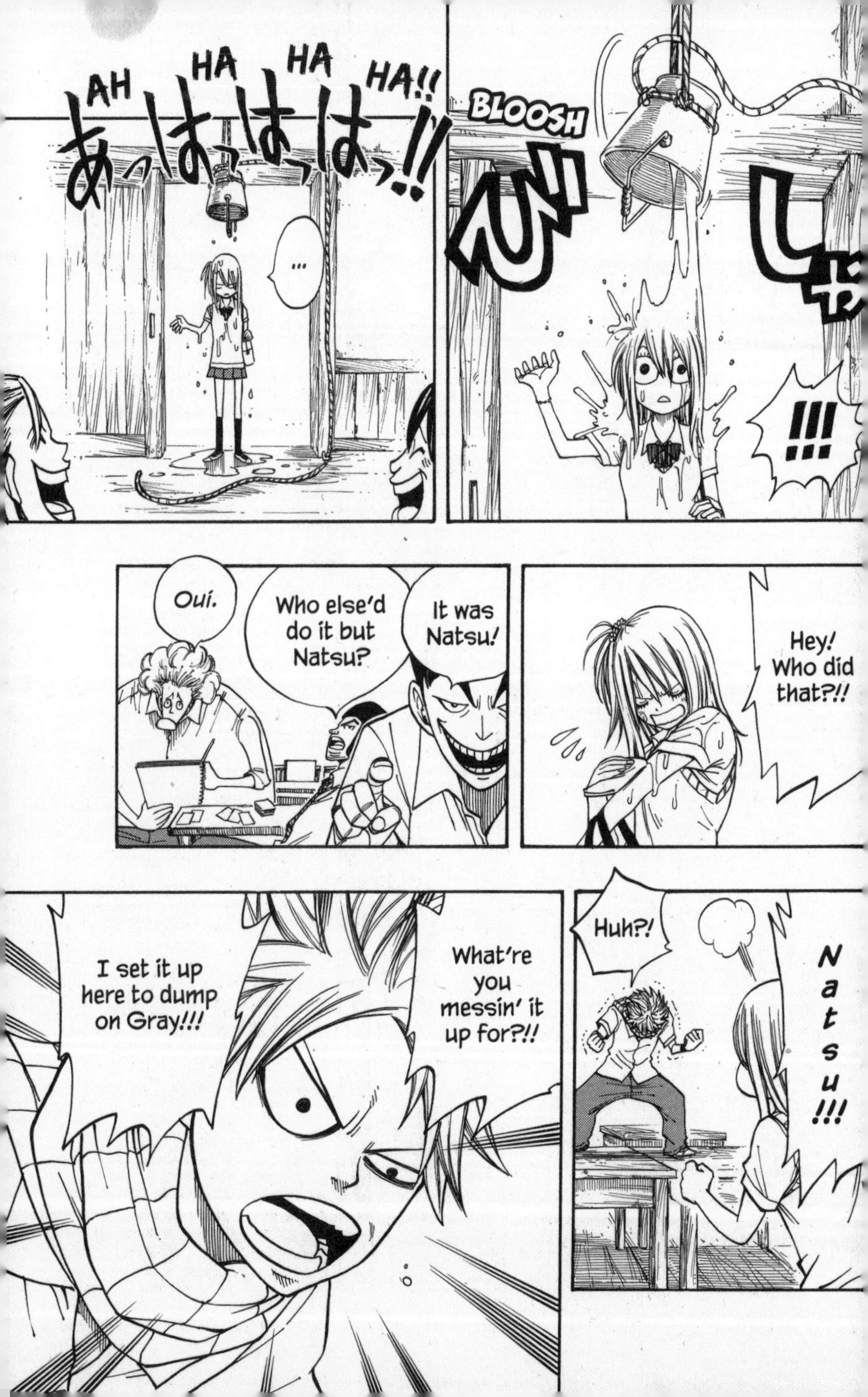
BLOOSH
びしゃ
!!!
AH HA HA HA!!
あっはっはっは!!
...
Hey! Who did that?!!
It was Natsu!
Who else'd do it but Natsu?
Oui.
Natsu!!!
Huh?!
What're you messin' it up for?!!
I set it up here to dump on Gray!!!

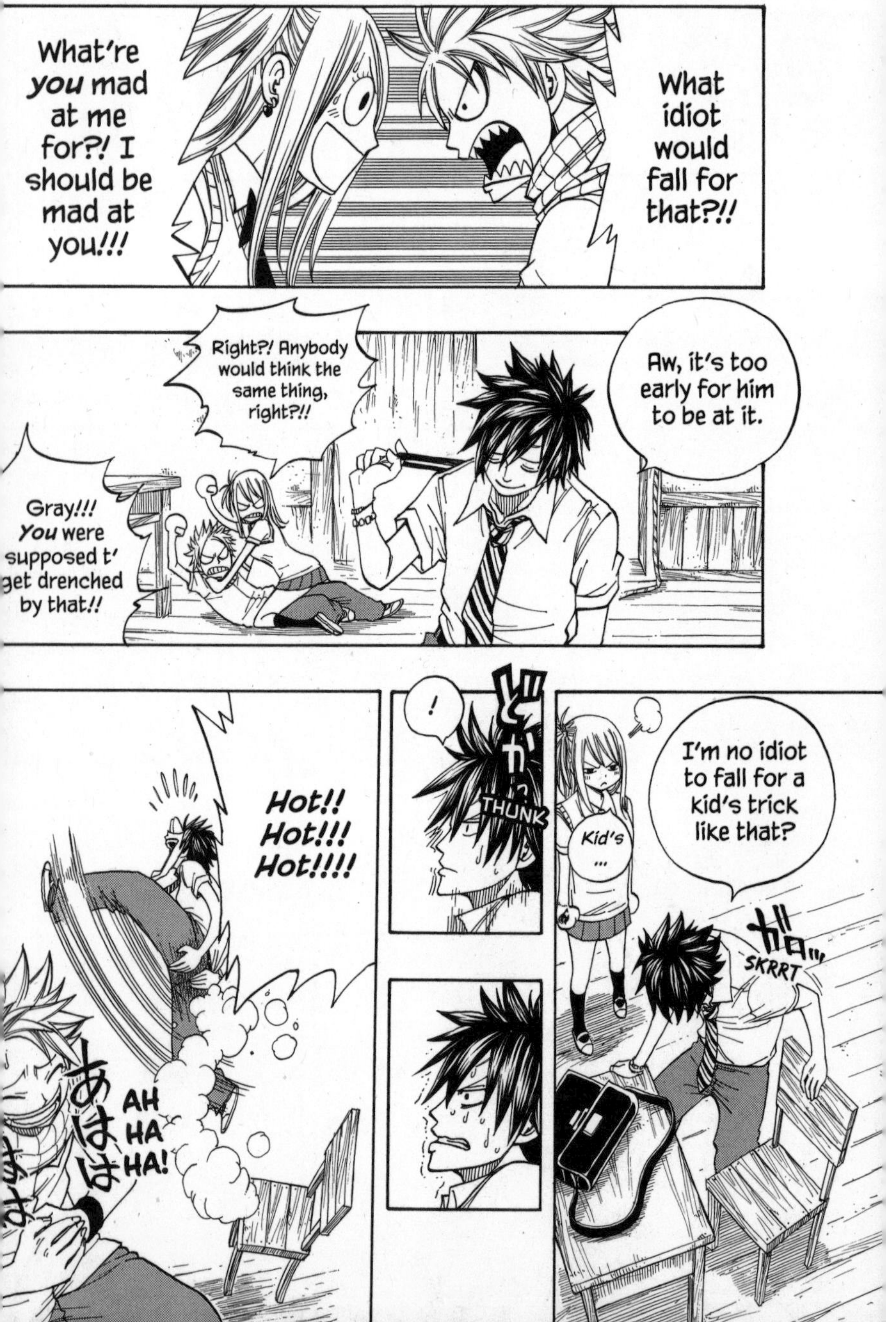
What idiot would fall for that?!!
What're *you* mad at me for?! I should be mad at you!!!
Aw, it's too early for him to be at it.
Right?! Anybody would think the same thing, right?!!
Gray!!! *You* were supposed t' get drenched by that!!
I'm no idiot to fall for a kid's trick like that?
Kid's ...
ガロッ
SKRRT
!
どかっ
THUNK
Hot!! Hot!!! Hot!!!!
あはは
AH HA HA!

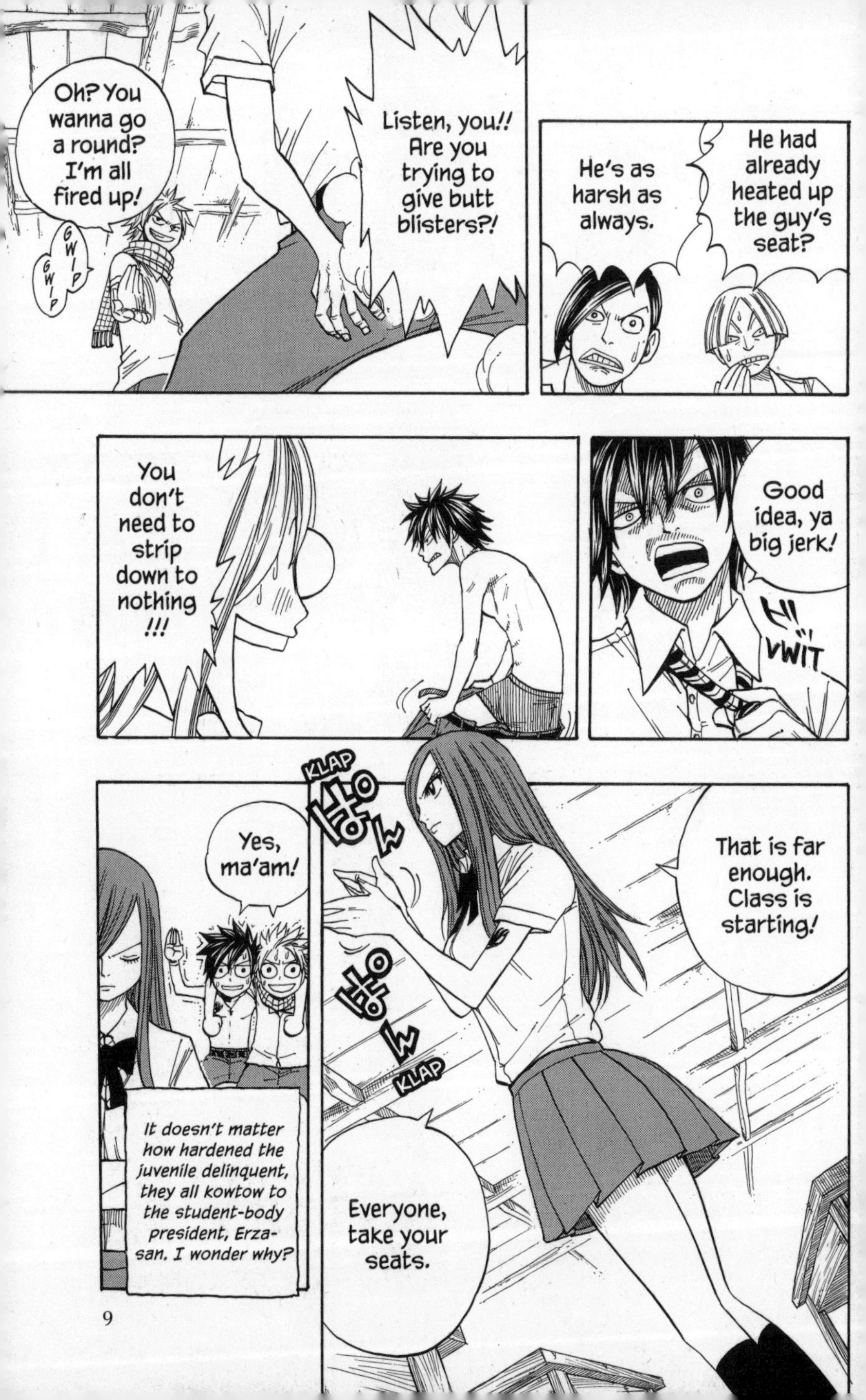
He had already heated up the guy's seat?
He's as harsh as always.
Listen, you!! Are you trying to give butt blisters?!
Oh? You wanna go a round? I'm all fired up!
GWIP
GWIP
Good idea, ya big jerk!
VWIT
You don't need to strip down to nothing!!!
KLAP
That is far enough. Class is starting!
KLAP
Everyone, take your seats.
Yes, ma'am!
It doesn't matter how hardened the juvenile delinquent, they all kowtow to the student-body president, Erza-san. I wonder why?

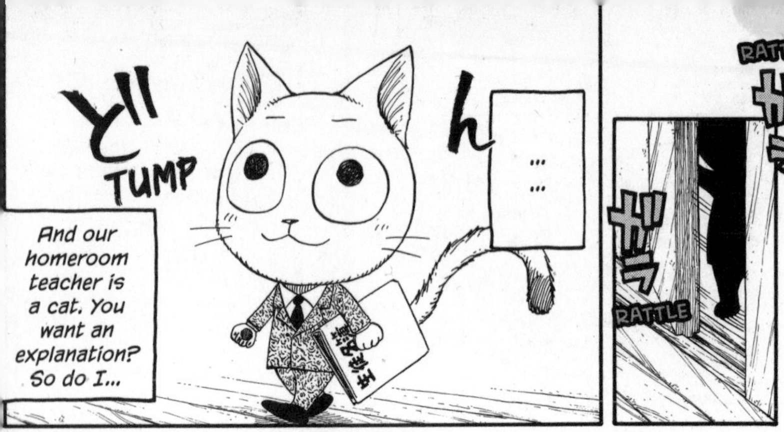
RATTLE
RATTLE
...
...
TUMP
And our homeroom teacher is a cat. You want an explanation? So do I...

Textbook: Student Rolls

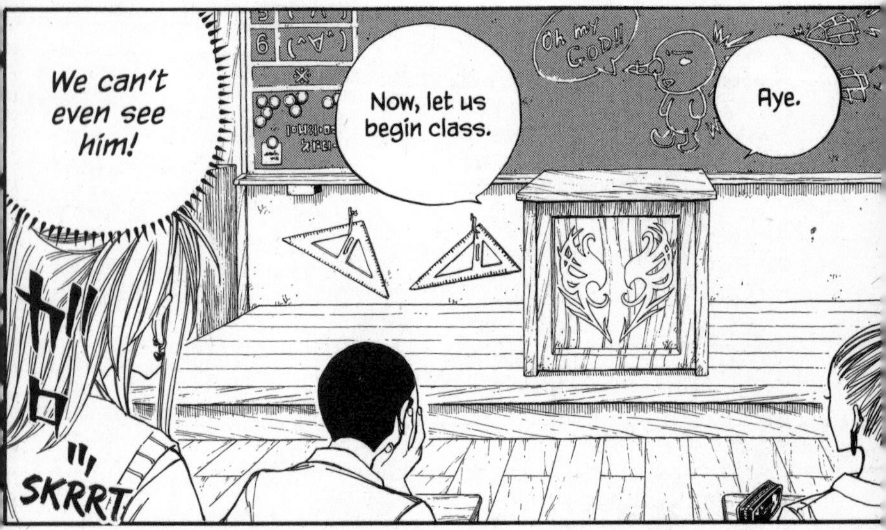
Aye.
Oh my GOD!!
Now, let us begin class.
We can't even see him!
SKRRT

Garbage can: TRASH

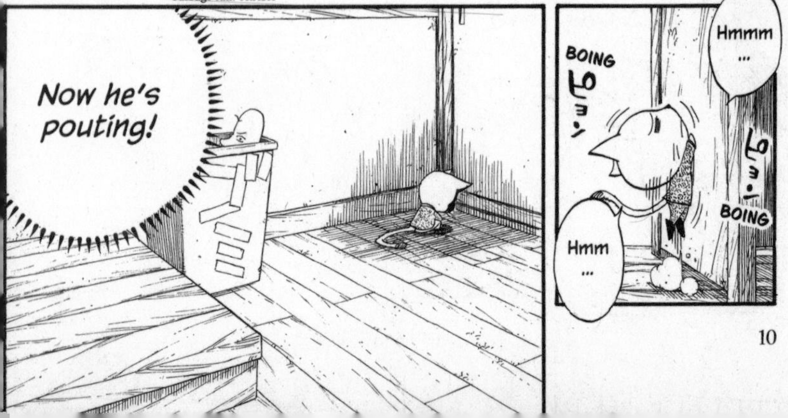
Hmmm ...
BOING
BOING
Hmm ...
Now he's pouting!

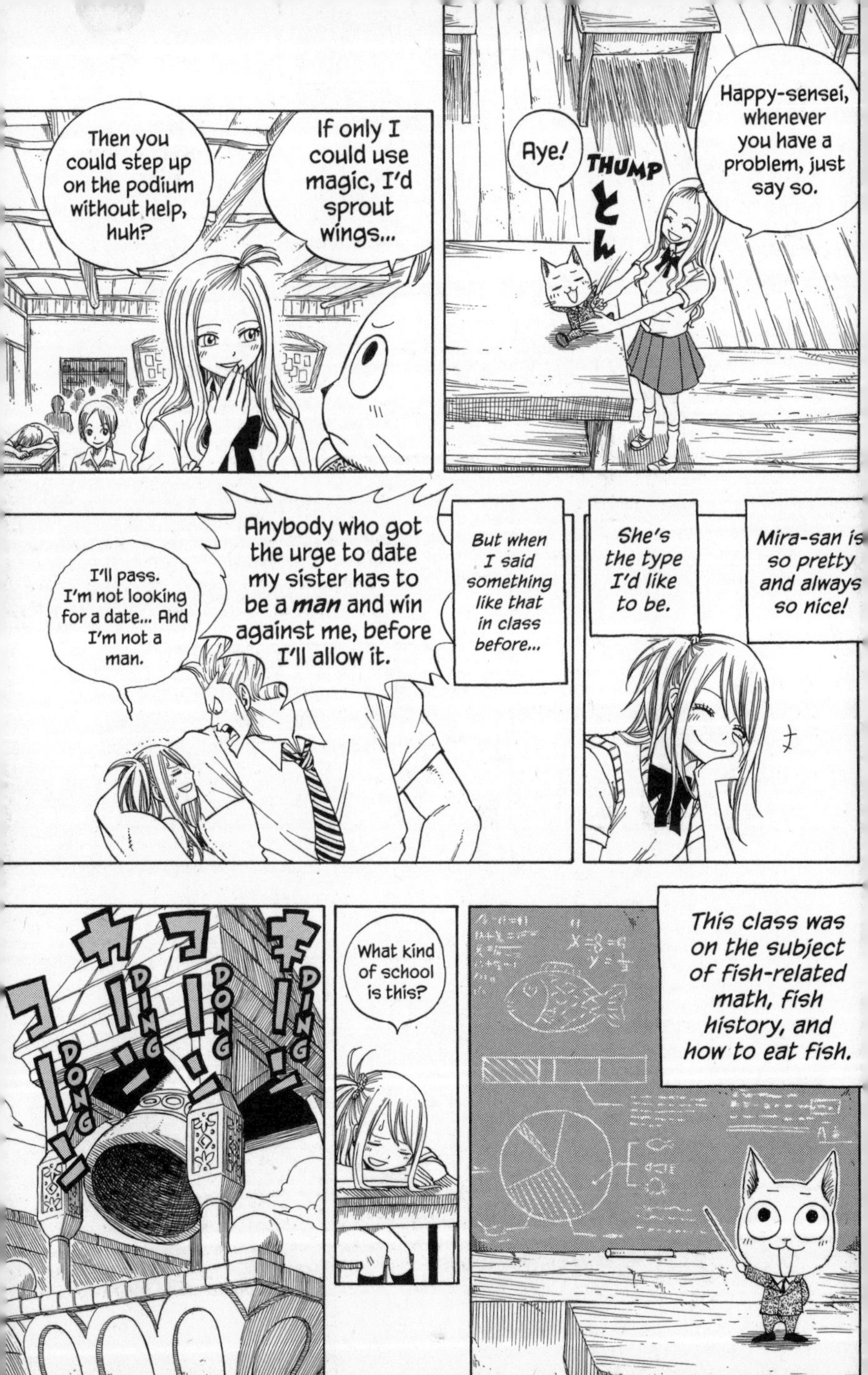

Happy-sensei, whenever you have a problem, just say so.
Aye!
THUMP
とん
If only I could use magic, I'd sprout wings...
Then you could step up on the podium without help, huh?
Mira-san is so pretty and always so nice!
She's the type I'd like to be.
But when I said something like that in class before...
Anybody who got the urge to date my sister has to be a ***man*** and win against me, before I'll allow it.
I'll pass. I'm not looking for a date... And I'm not a man.
This class was on the subject of fish-related math, fish history, and how to eat fish.
What kind of school is this?
DING
DONG
DING
DONG

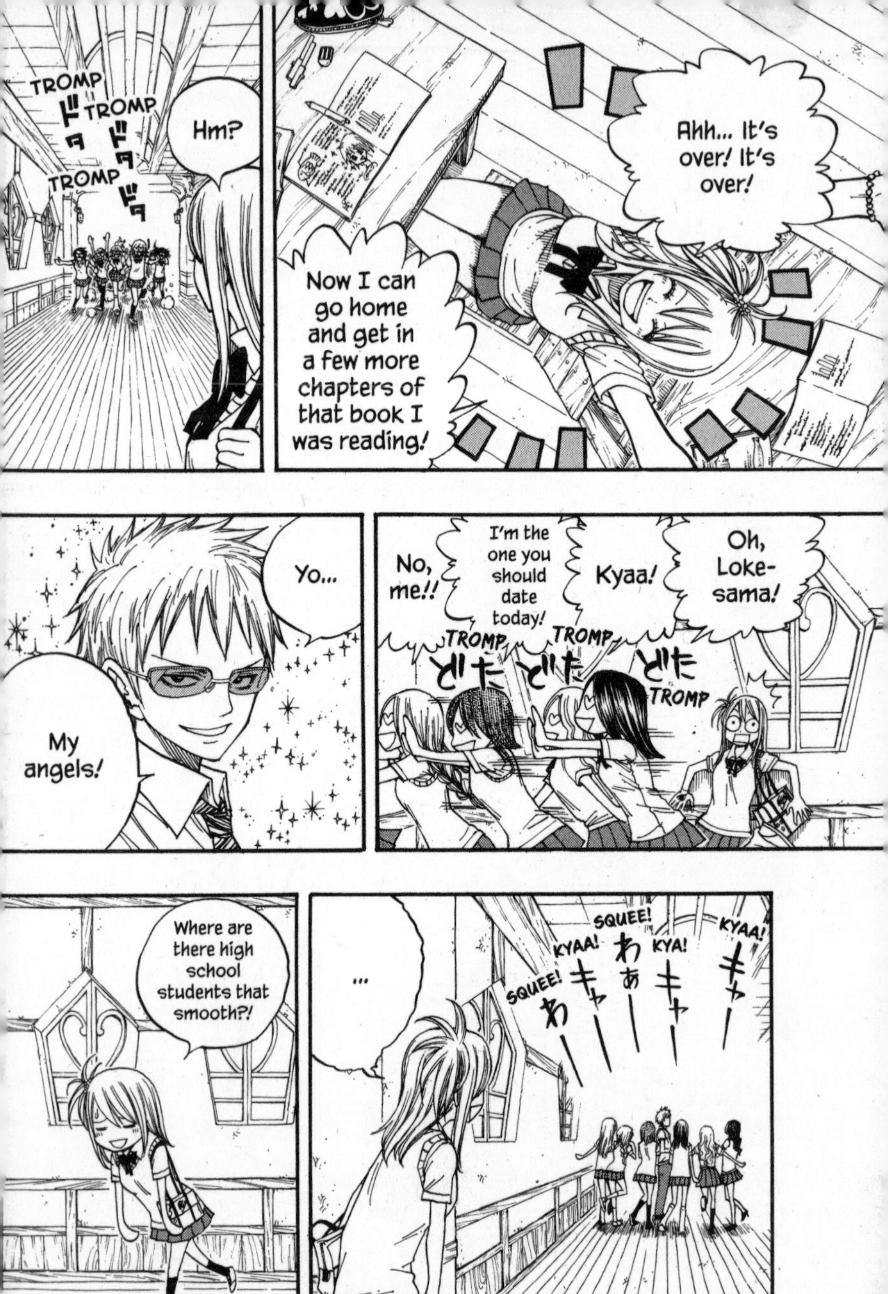
Ahh... It's over! It's over!
Now I can go home and get in a few more chapters of that book I was reading!
Hm?
TROMP ドタ
TROMP ドタ
TROMP ドタ
Oh, Loke-sama!
Kyaa!
I'm the one you should date today!
No, me!!
TROMP どた
TROMP どた
TROMP どた
Yo...
My angels!
KYAA! キャー
KYA! キャー
SQUEE! わあー
KYAA! キャー
SQUEE! わー
...
Where are there high school students that smooth?!

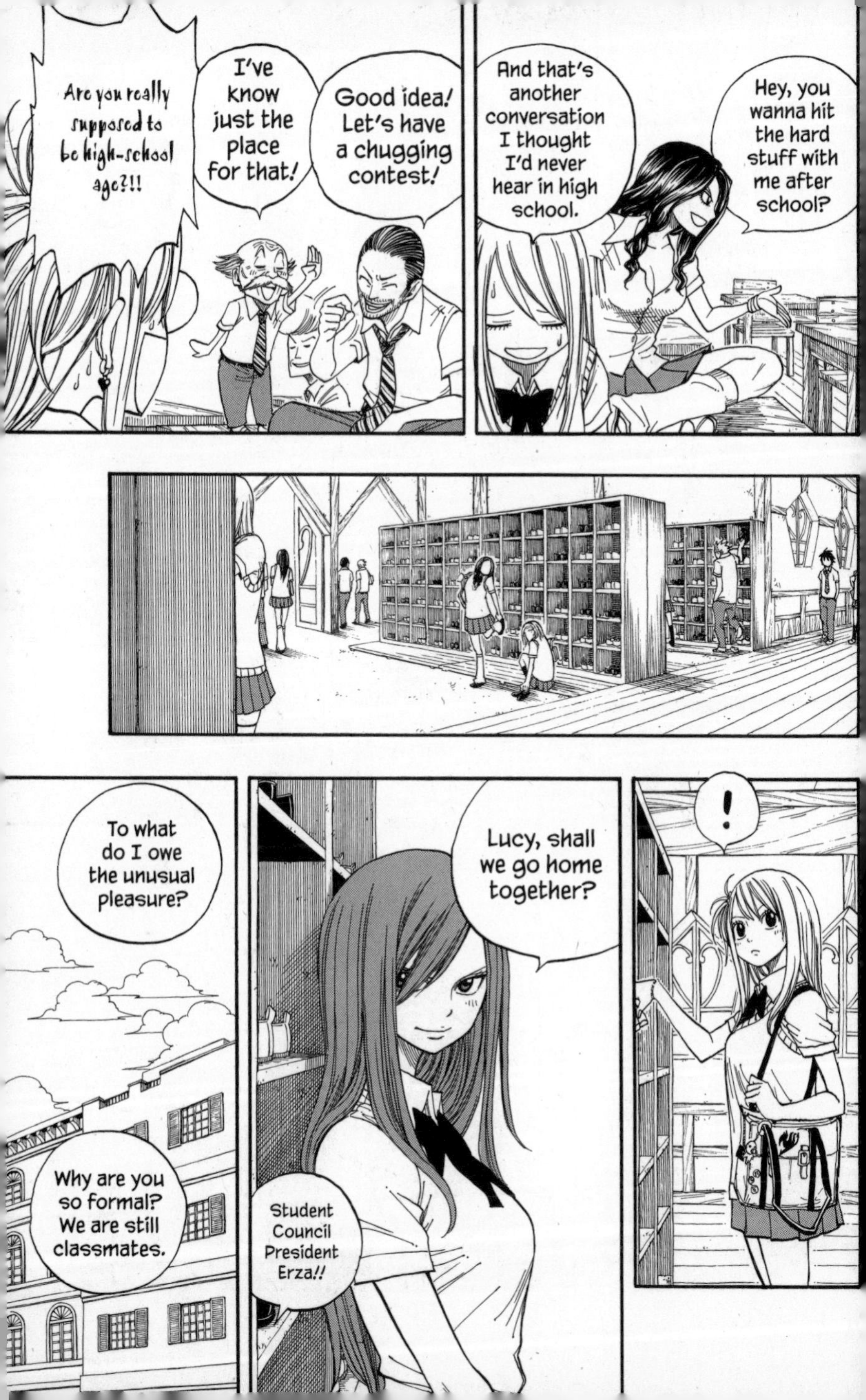
Hey, you wanna hit the hard stuff with me after school?
And that's another conversation I thought I'd never hear in high school.
Good idea! Let's have a chugging contest!
I've know just the place for that!
Are you really supposed to be high-school age?!!
!
Lucy, shall we go home together?
Student Council President Erza!!
To what do I owe the unusual pleasure?
Why are you so formal? We are still classmates.

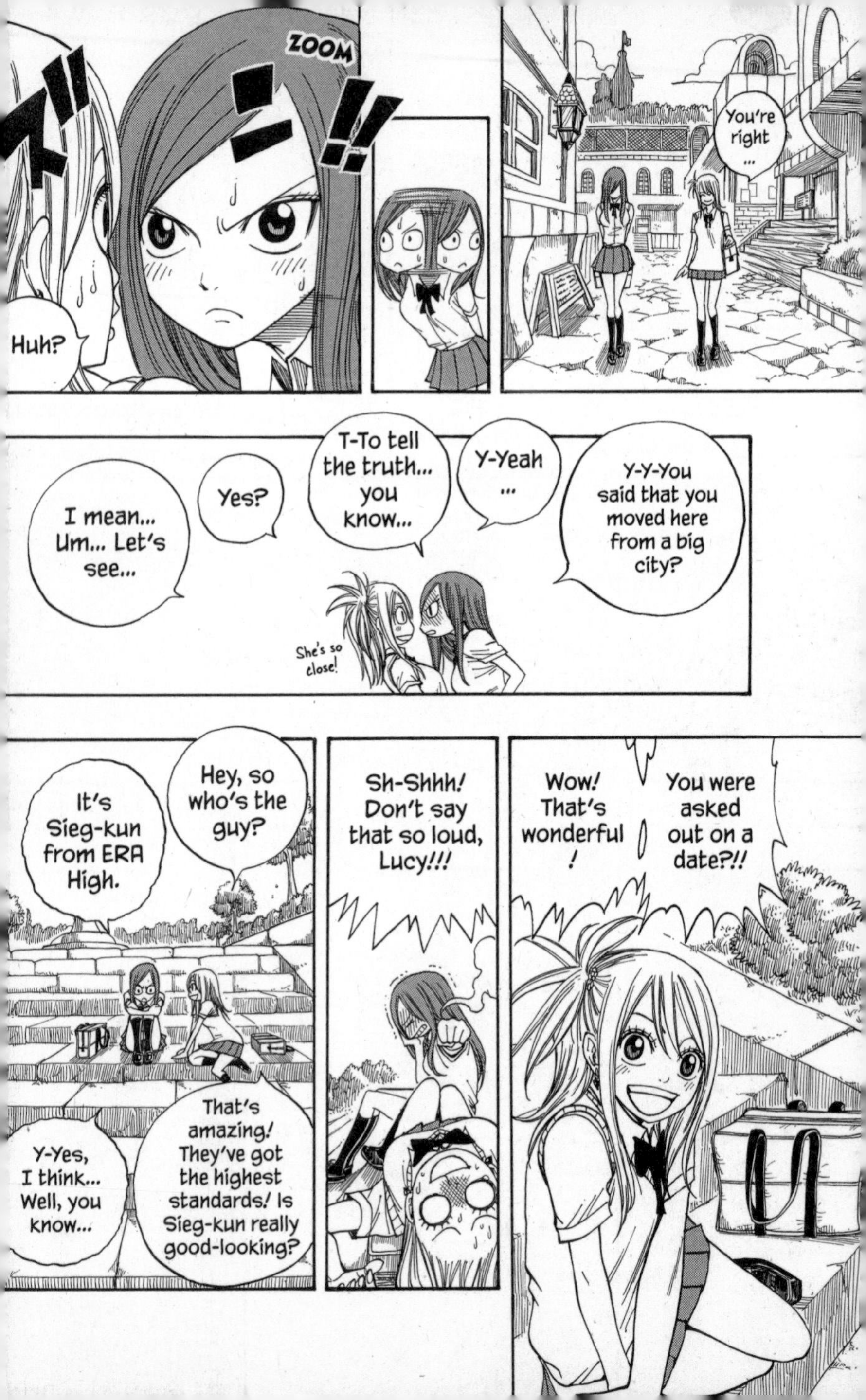
You're right ...
ZOOM
Huh?
Y-Y-You said that you moved here from a big city?
Y-Yeah ...
T-To tell the truth... you know...
Yes?
I mean... Um... Let's see...
She's so close!
You were asked out on a date?!!
Wow! That's wonderful!
Sh-Shhh! Don't say that so loud, Lucy!!!
Hey, so who's the guy?
It's Sieg-kun from ERA High.
That's amazing! They've got the highest standards! Is Sieg-kun really good-looking?
Y-Yes, I think... Well, you know...

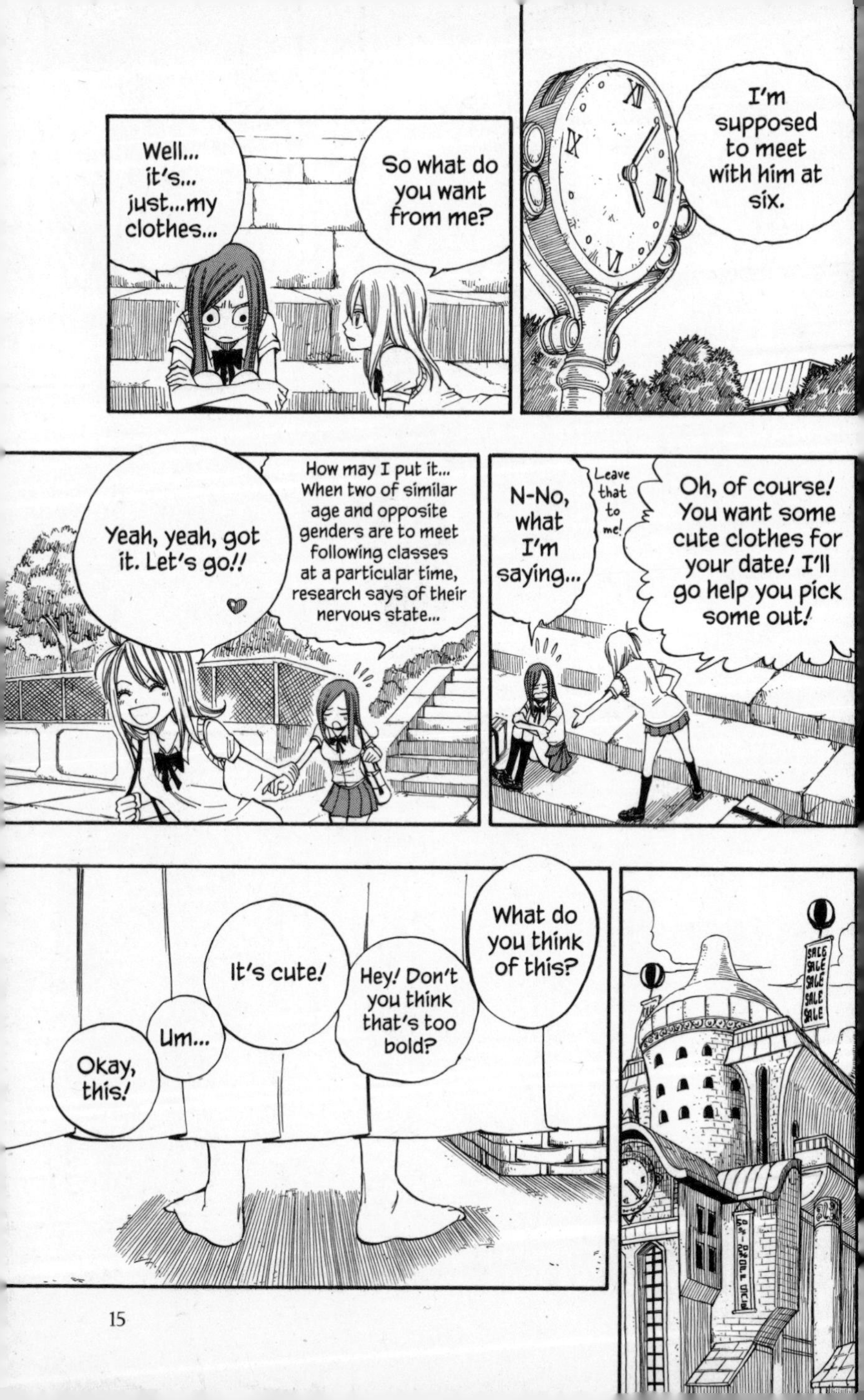
I'm supposed to meet with him at six.
So what do you want from me?
Well... it's... just...my clothes...
Oh, of course! You want some cute clothes for your date! I'll go help you pick some out!
Leave that to me!
N-No, what I'm saying...
How may I put it... When two of similar age and opposite genders are to meet following classes at a particular time, research says of their nervous state...
Yeah, yeah, got it. Let's go!!
SALE SALE SALE SALE SALE
What do you think of this?
Hey! Don't you think that's too bold?
It's cute!
Um...
Okay, this!

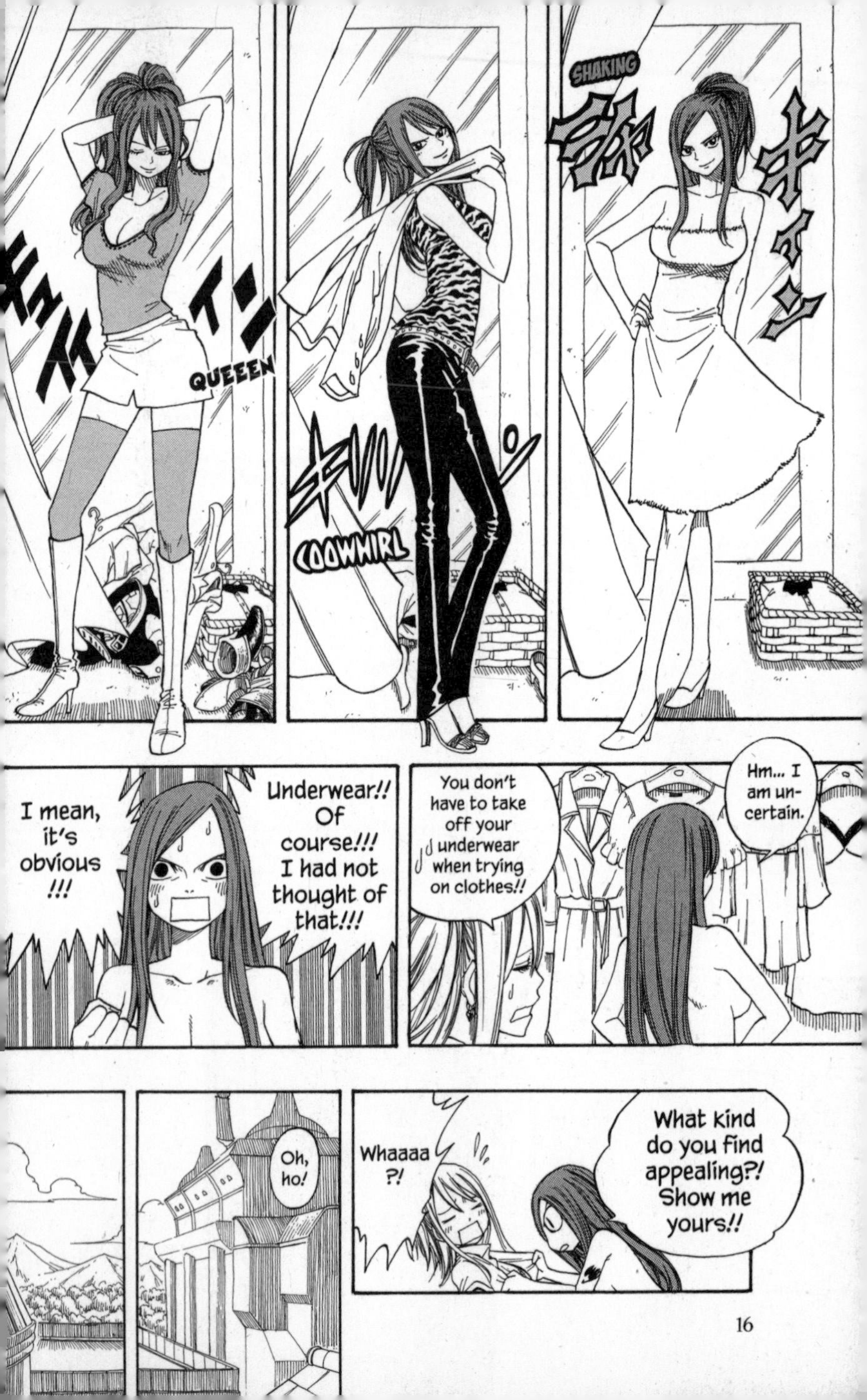
SHAKING
COOWHIRL
QUEEEN
Hm... I am un-certain.
You don't have to take off your underwear when trying on clothes!!
Underwear!! Of course!!! I had not thought of that!!!
I mean, it's obvious!!!
What kind do you find appealing?! Show me yours!!
Whaaaa?!
Oh, ho!

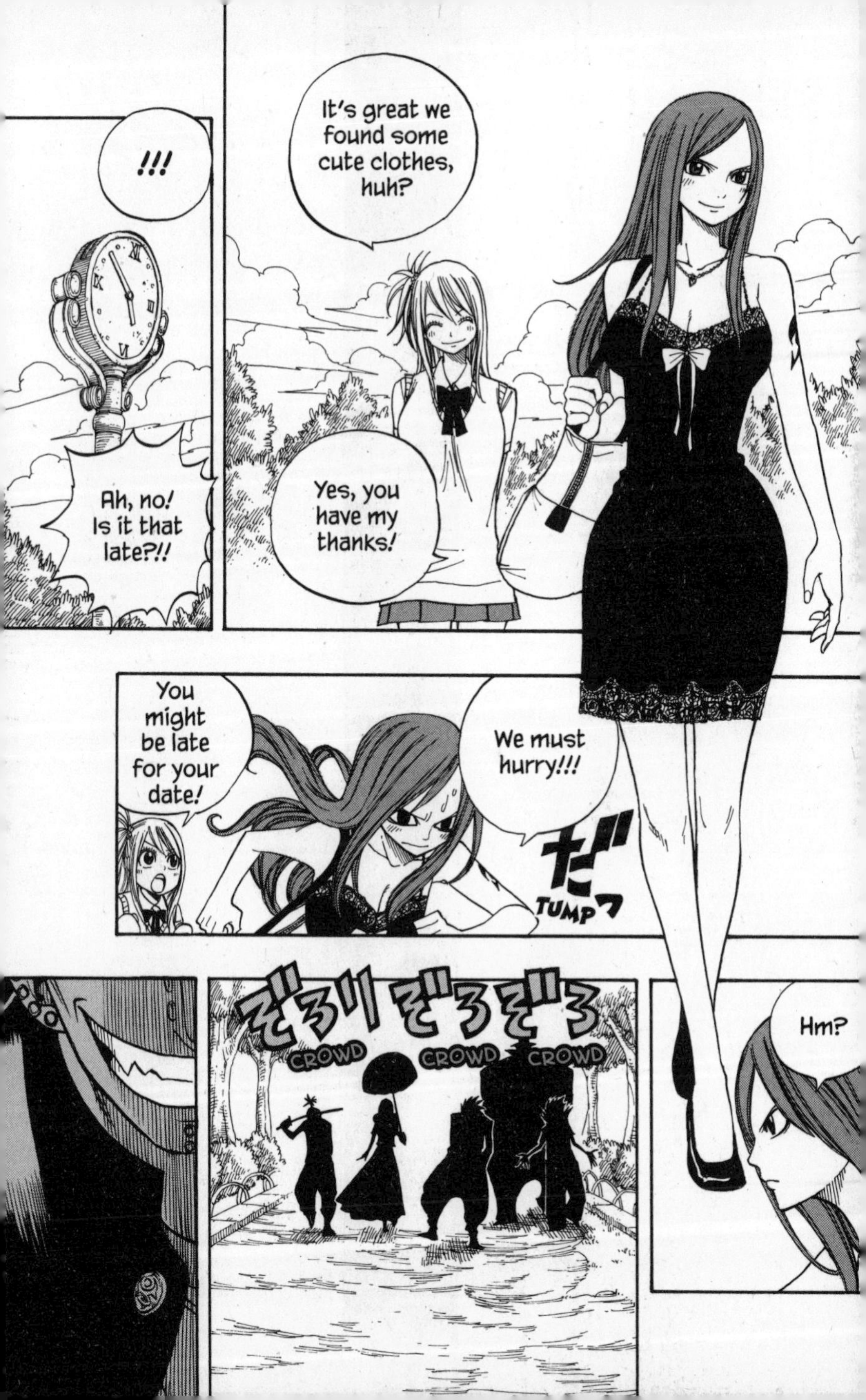

It's great we found some cute clothes, huh?
Yes, you have my thanks!
!!!
Ah, no! Is it that late?!!
You might be late for your date!
We must hurry!!!
だっ
TUMP
Hm?
ぞろり
CROWD
ぞろ
CROWD
ぞろ
CROWD

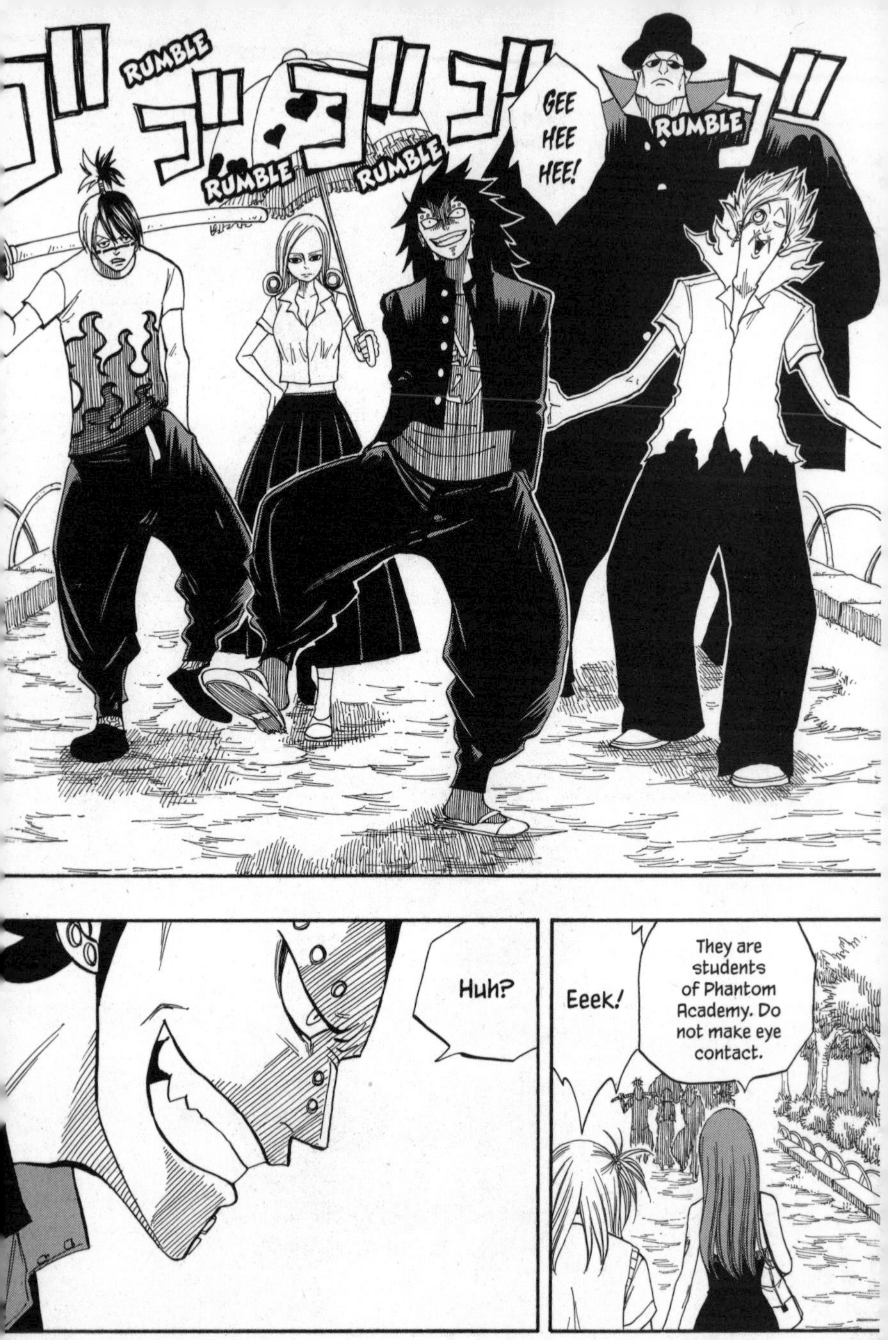
RUMBLE
GEE HEE HEE!
RUMBLE
RUMBLE
RUMBLE
They are students of Phantom Academy. Do not make eye contact.
Eeek!
Huh?

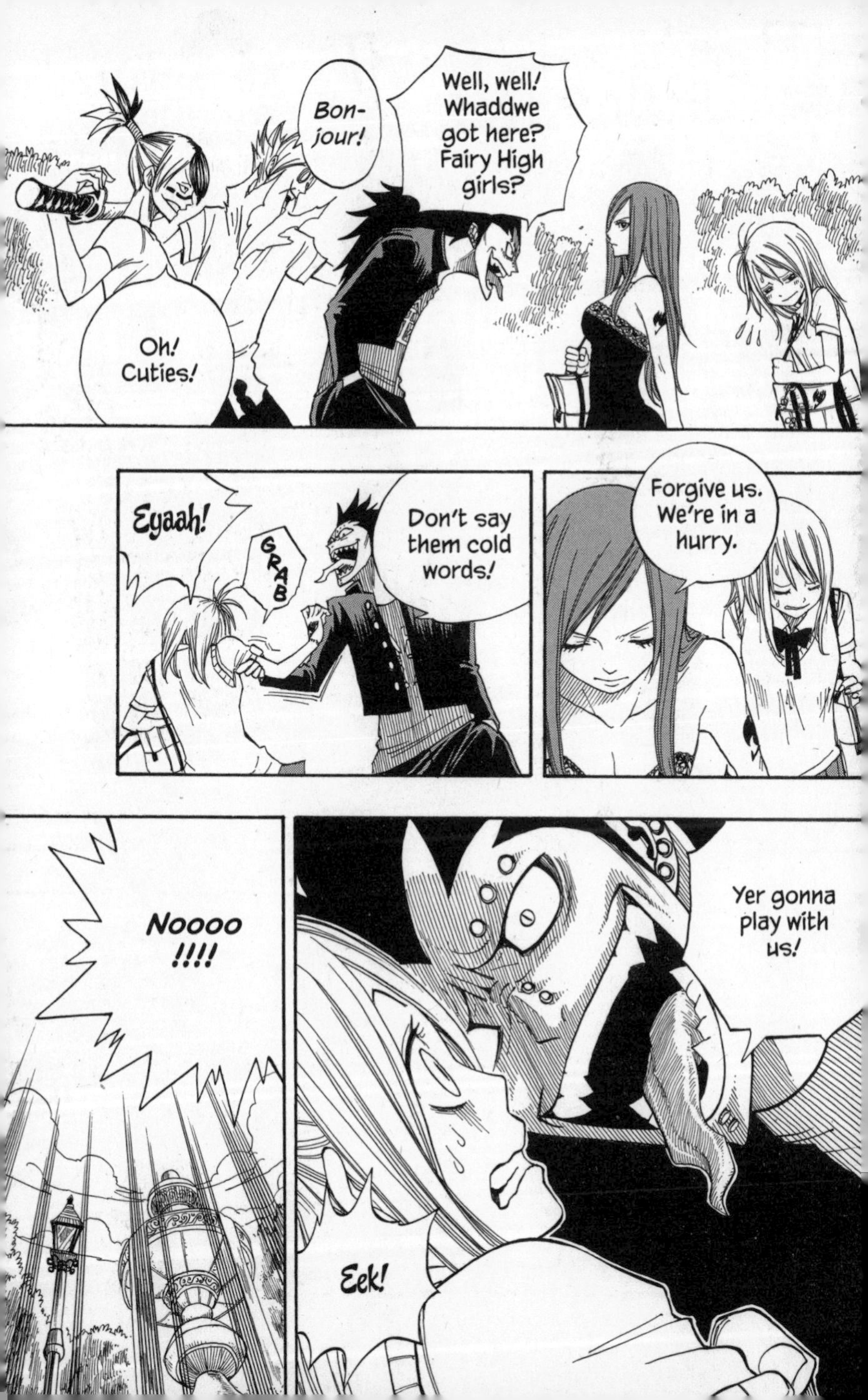
Well, well! Whaddwe got here? Fairy High girls?
Bon-jour!
Oh! Cuties!
Forgive us. We're in a hurry.
Don't say them cold words!
GRAB
Eyaah!
Yer gonna play with us!
Eek!
Noooo !!!!

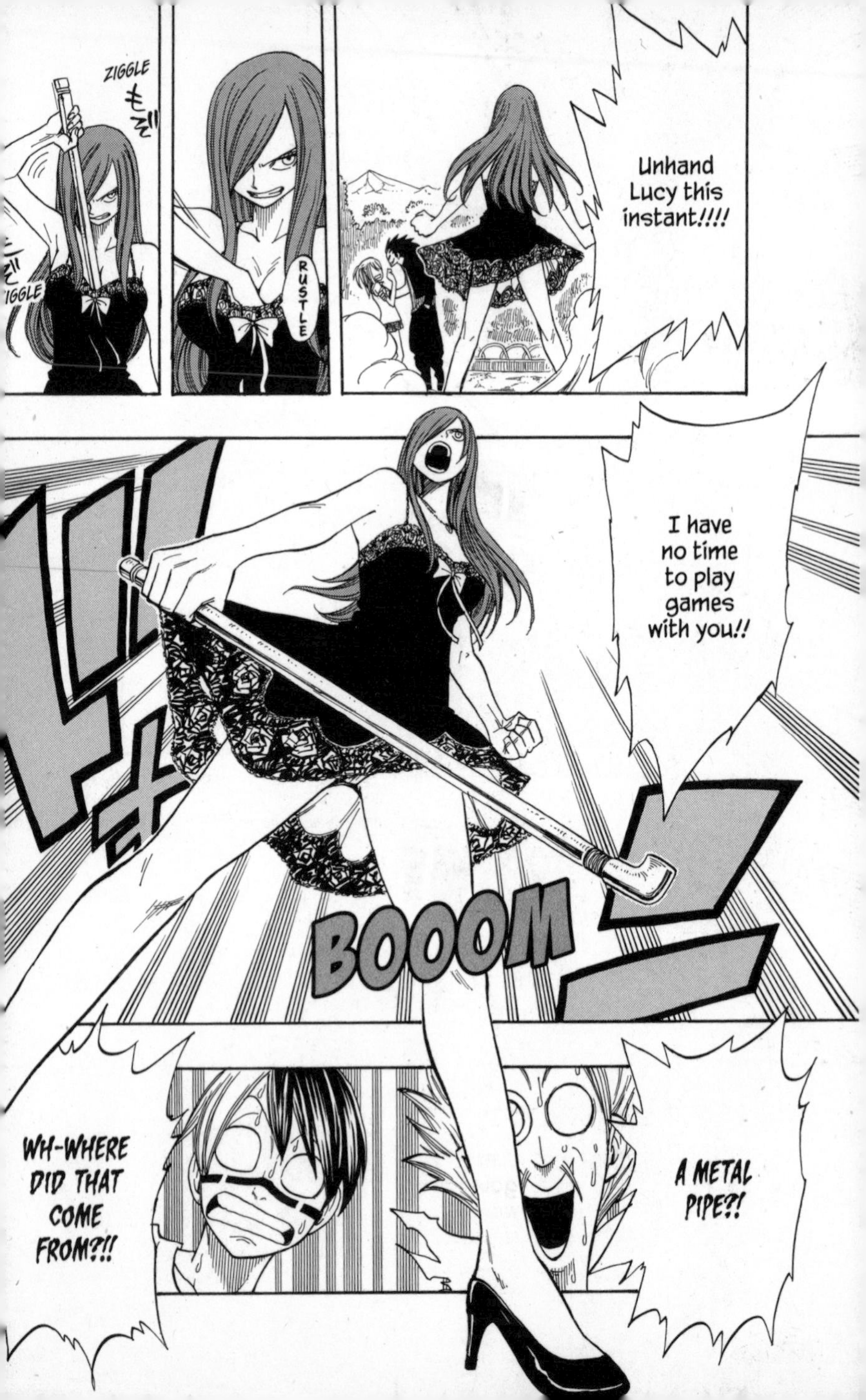
Unhand Lucy this instant!!!!
RUSTLE
ZIGGLE もぞ
ZIGGLE
I have no time to play games with you!!
BOOOM
A METAL PIPE?!
WH-WHERE DID THAT COME FROM?!!

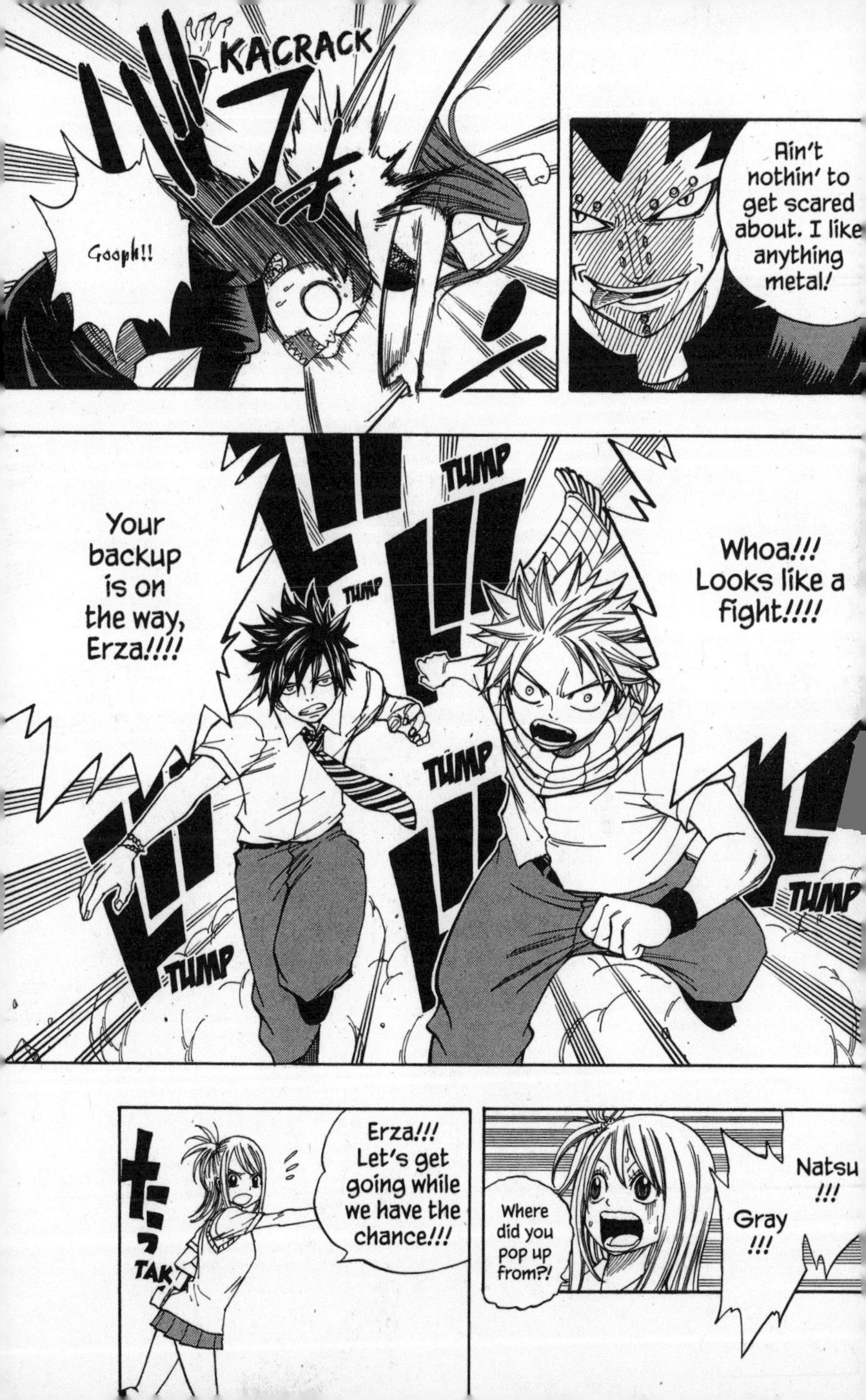
Ain't nothin' to get scared about. I like anything metal!
KACRACK
Gooph!!
Whoa!!! Looks like a fight!!!!
TUMP
TUMP
Your backup is on the way, Erza!!!!
TUMP
TUMP
TUMP
Natsu !!!
Gray !!!
Where did you pop up from?!
Erza!!! Let's get going while we have the chance!!!
TAK

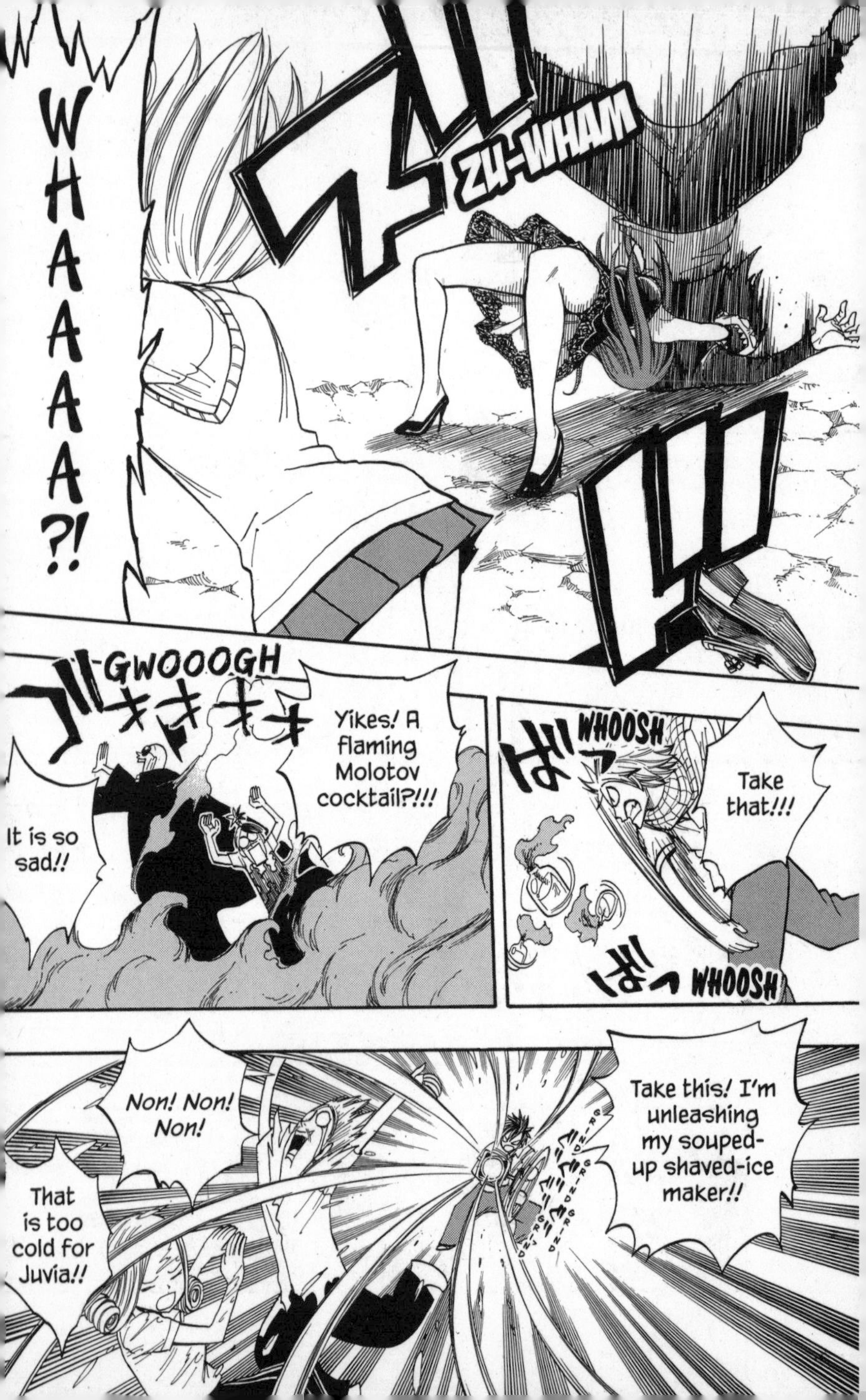
ZU-WHAM
WHAAAAAA?!
WHOOSH
Take that!!!
WHOOSH
GWOOOGH
Yikes! A flaming Molotov cocktail?!!!
It is so sad!!
Take this! I'm unleashing my souped-up shaved-ice maker!!
Non! Non! Non!
That is too cold for Juvia!!

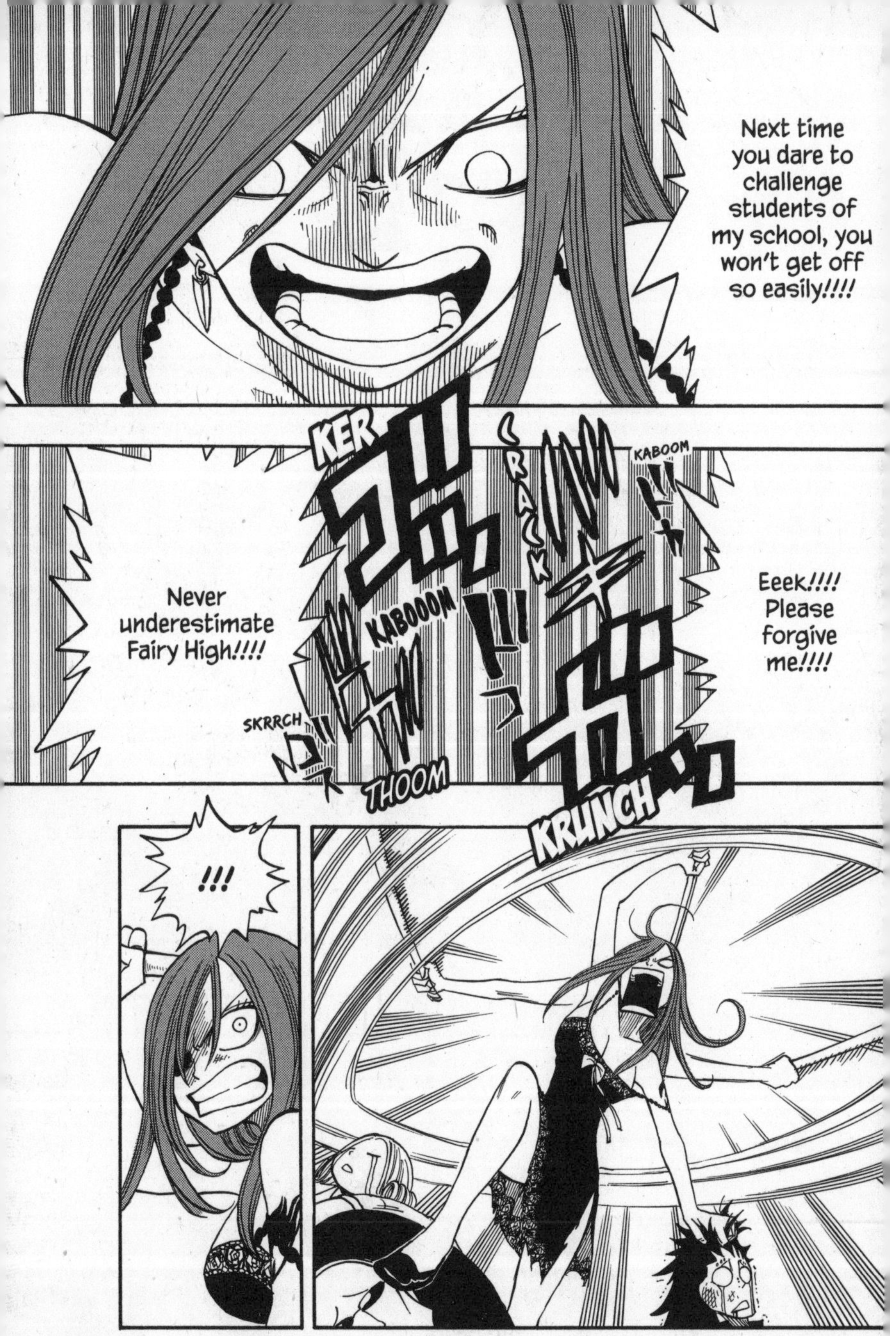
Next time you dare to challenge students of my school, you won't get off so easily!!!!
Eeek!!!! Please forgive me!!!!
KABOOM
CRACK
KER
KABOOOM
KRUNCH
THOOM
SKRRCH
Never underestimate Fairy High!!!!
!!!

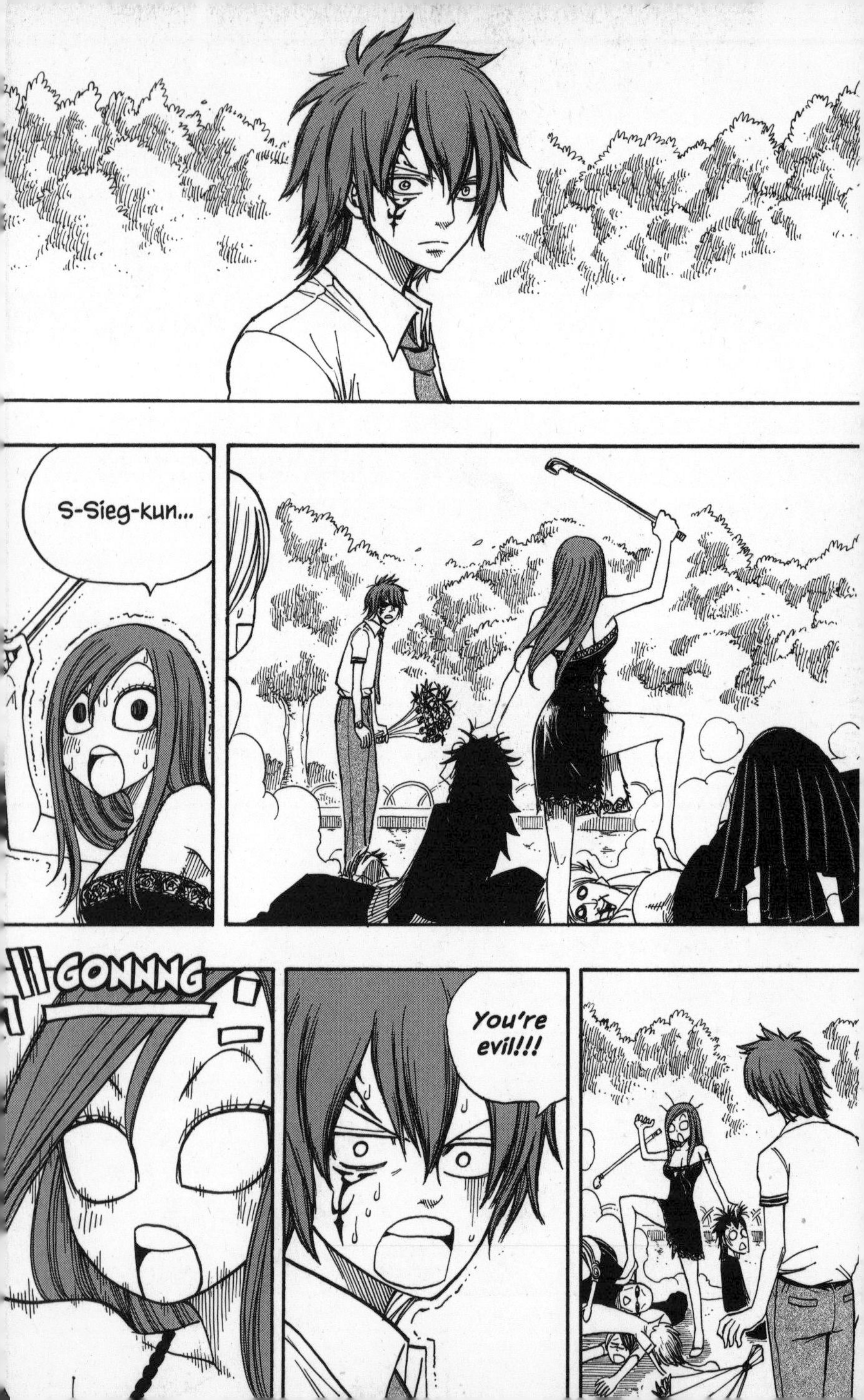
S-Sieg-kun...
You're evil!!!
GONNNG

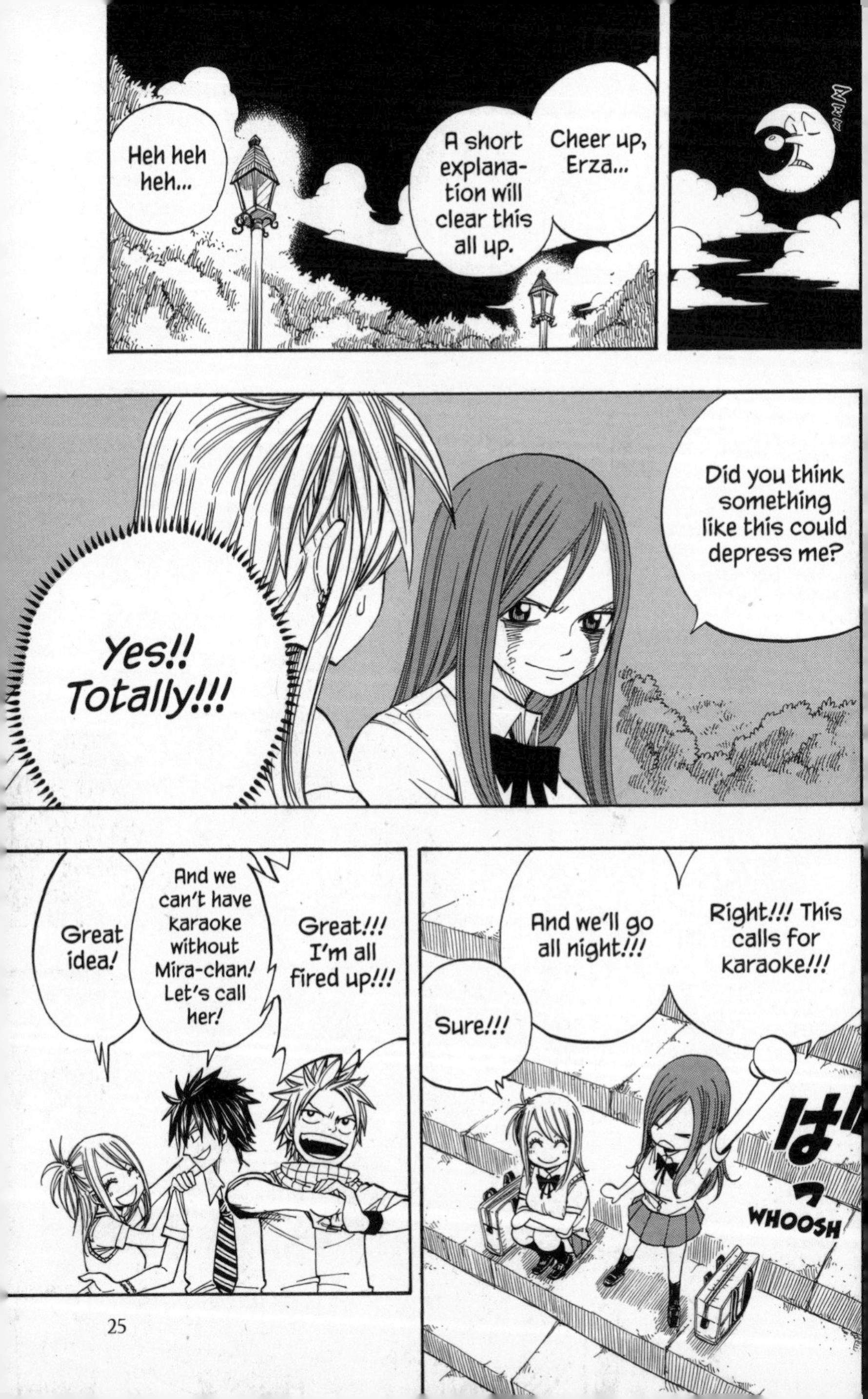
Cheer up, Erza...
A short explanation will clear this all up.
Heh heh heh...
Did you think something like this could depress me?
Yes!! Totally!!!
Right!!! This calls for karaoke!!!
And we'll go all night!!!
Sure!!!
はっ
WHOOSH
Great!!! I'm all fired up!!!
And we can't have karaoke without Mira-chan! Let's call her!
Great idea!

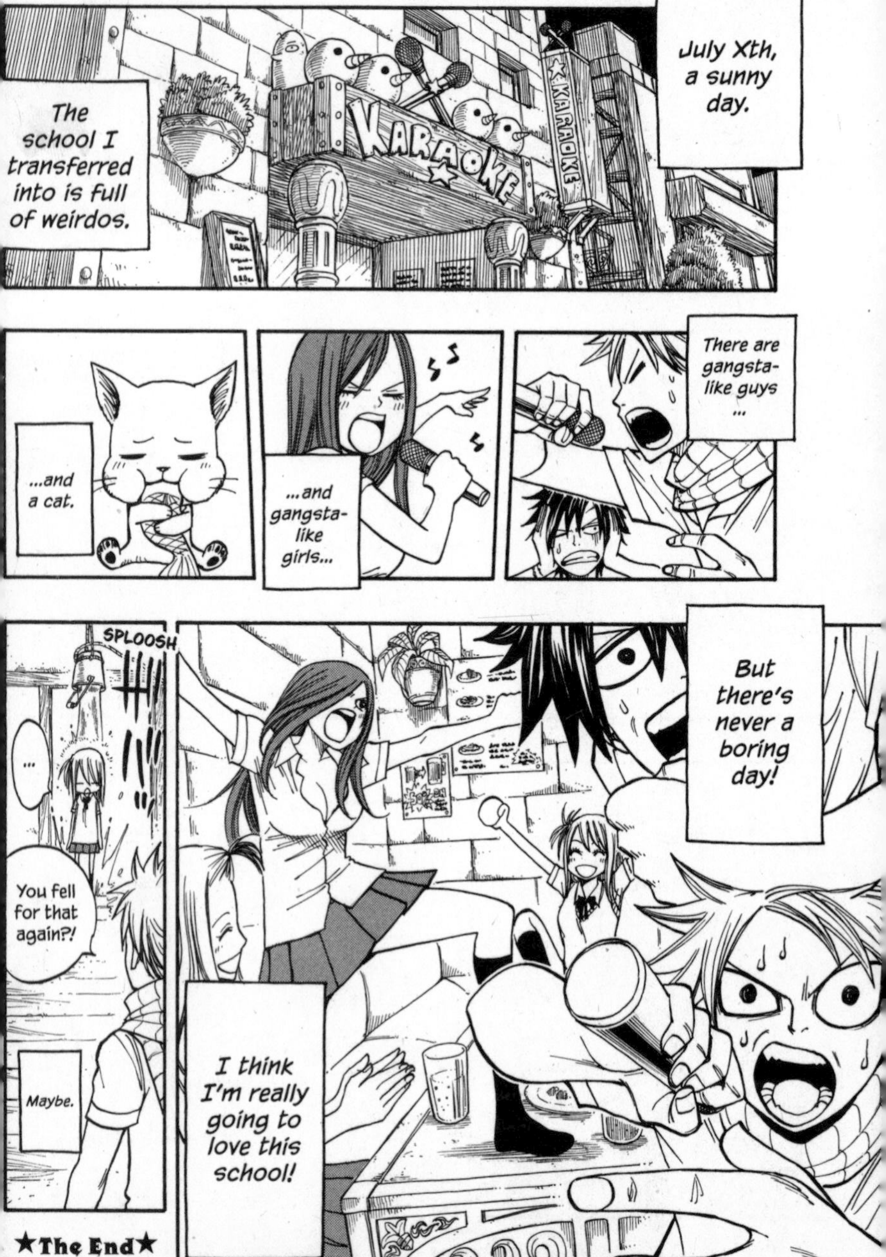
July Xth, a sunny day.
KARAOKE
KARAOKE
The school I transferred into is full of weirdos.
There are gangsta-like guys...
...and gangsta-like girls...
...and a cat.
But there's never a boring day!
I think I'm really going to love this school!
SPLOOSH
...
You fell for that again?!
Maybe.

★The End★

FT★S

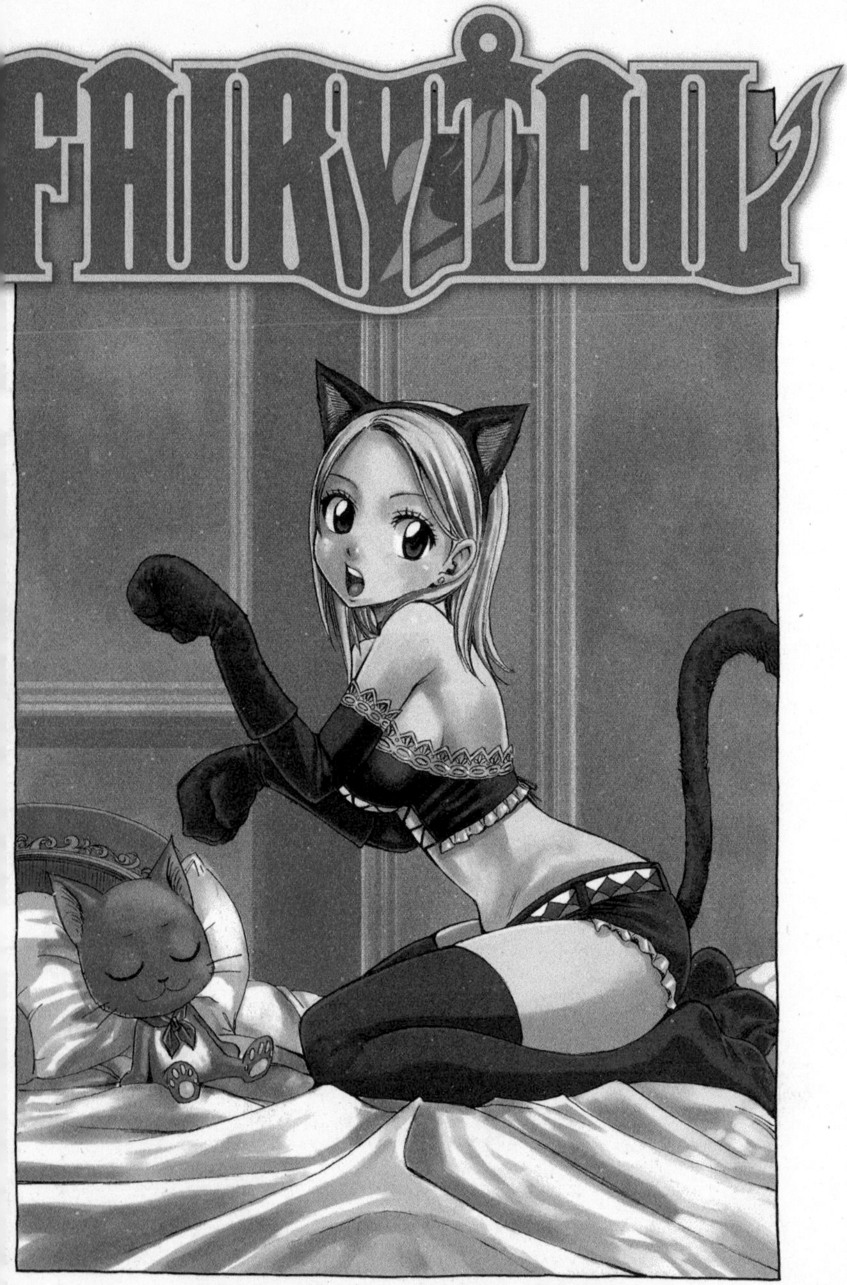
FAIRY TAIL

Welcome to Fairy Hills

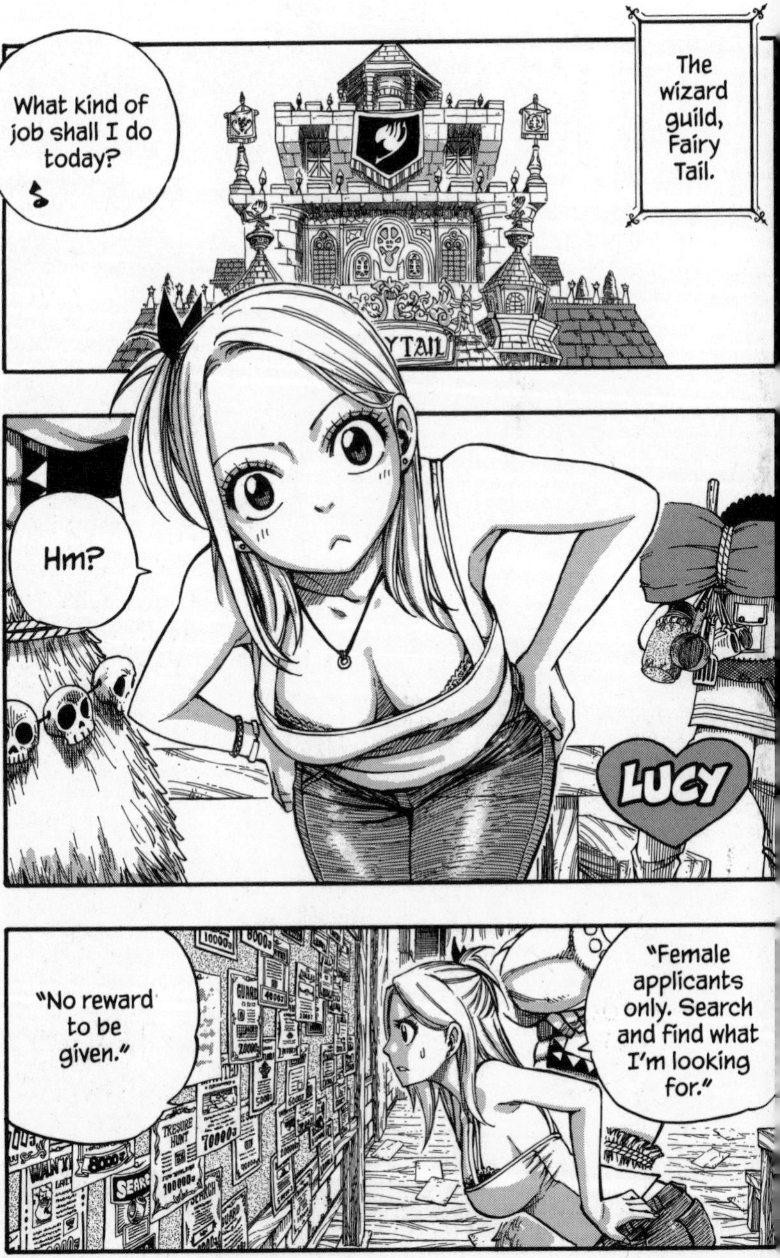
The wizard guild, Fairy Tail.
What kind of job shall I do today?
Hm?
LUCY
"Female applicants only. Search and find what I'm looking for."
"No reward to be given."

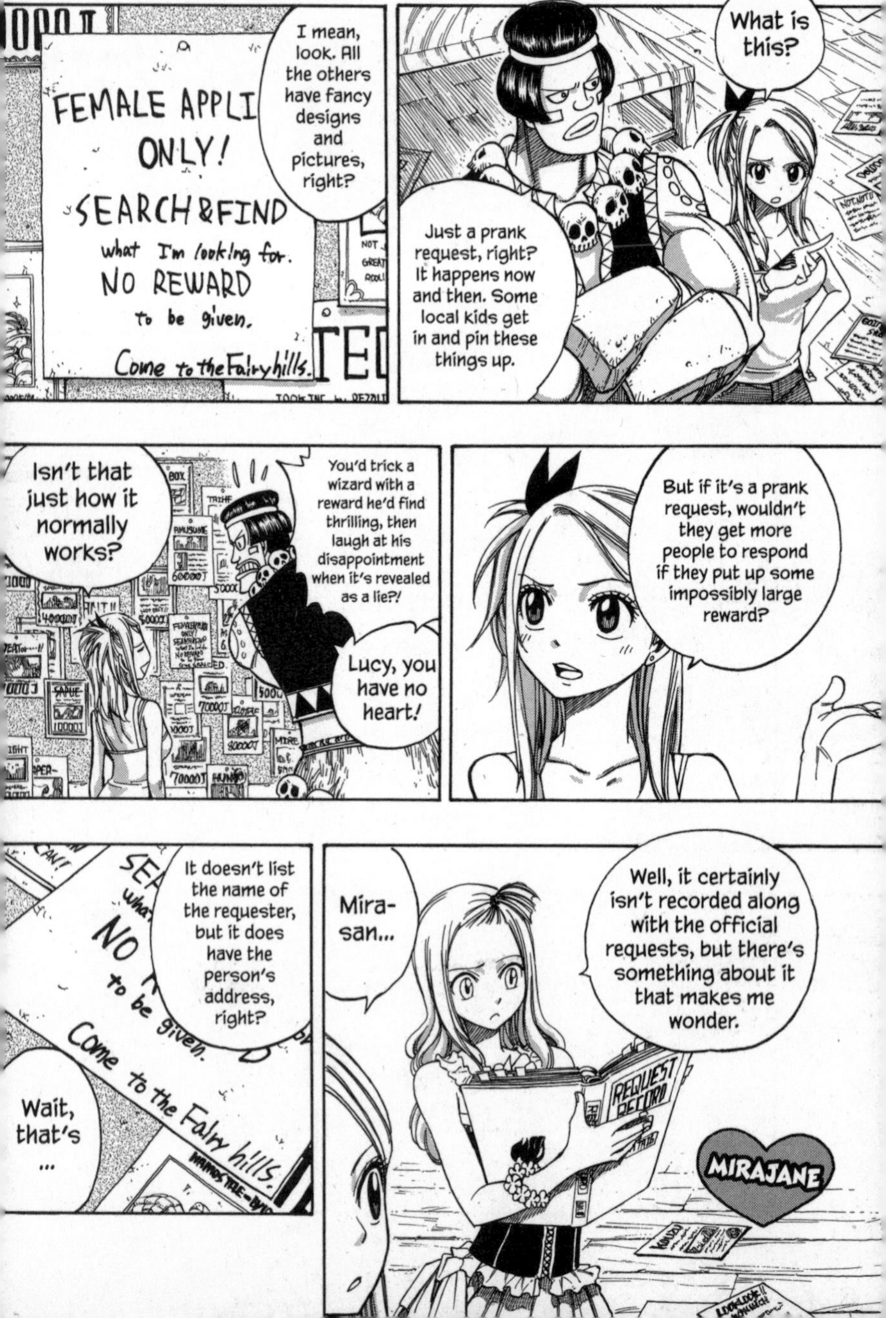
What is this?
Just a prank request, right? It happens now and then. Some local kids get in and pin these things up.
I mean, look. All the others have fancy designs and pictures, right?
FEMALE APPLI ONLY!
SEARCH&FIND what I'm looking for.
NO REWARD to be given.
Come to the Fairy hills.
But if it's a prank request, wouldn't they get more people to respond if they put up some impossibly large reward?
Isn't that just how it normally works?
You'd trick a wizard with a reward he'd find thrilling, then laugh at his disappointment when it's revealed as a lie?!
Lucy, you have no heart!
Mira-san...
Well, it certainly isn't recorded along with the official requests, but there's something about it that makes me wonder.
REQUEST RECORD
MIRAJANE
It doesn't list the name of the requester, but it does have the person's address, right?
NO
to be given.
Come to the Fairy hills.
Wait, that's ...

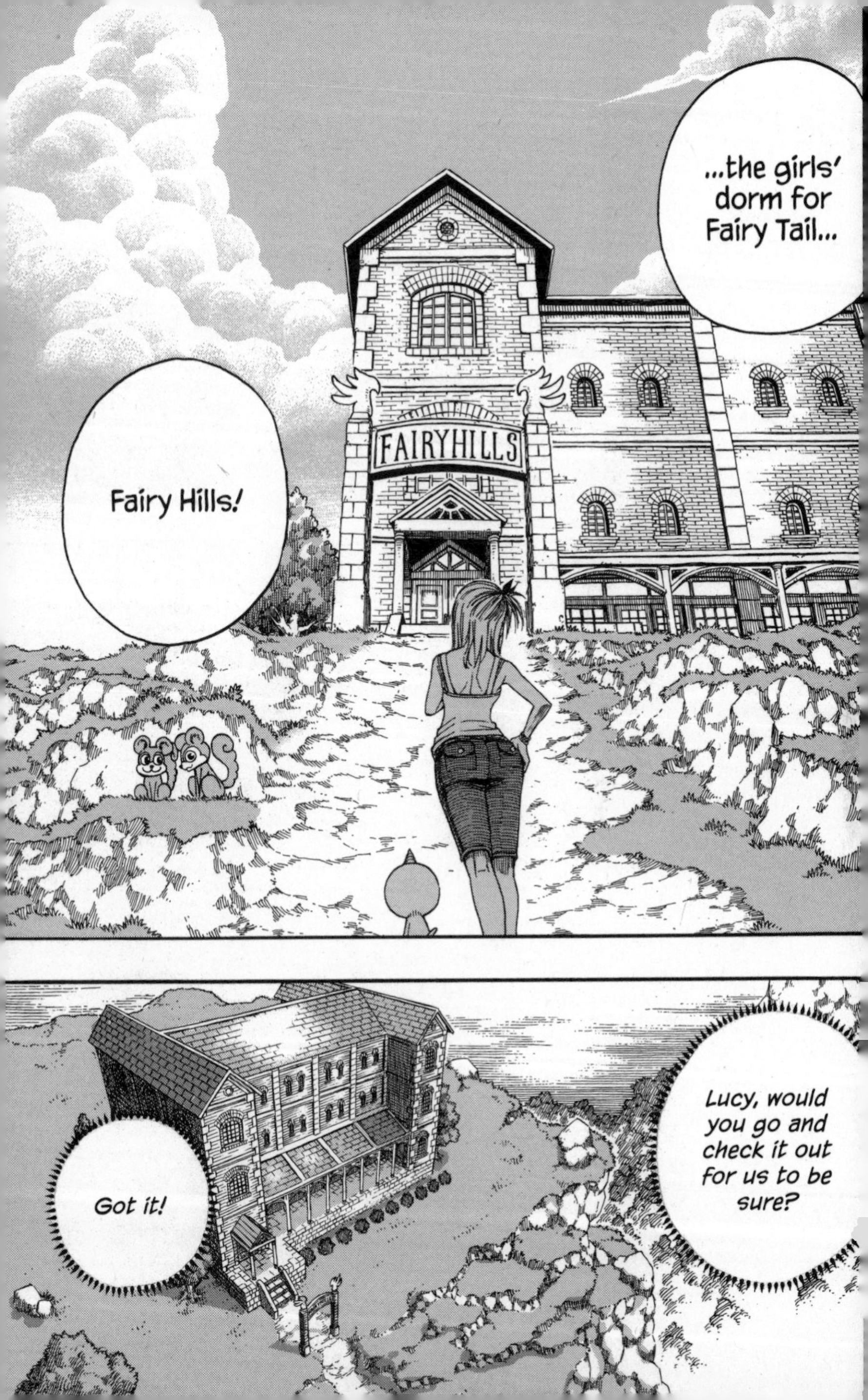
...the girls' dorm for Fairy Tail...
FAIRYHILLS
Fairy Hills!
Lucy, would you go and check it out for us to be sure?
Got it!

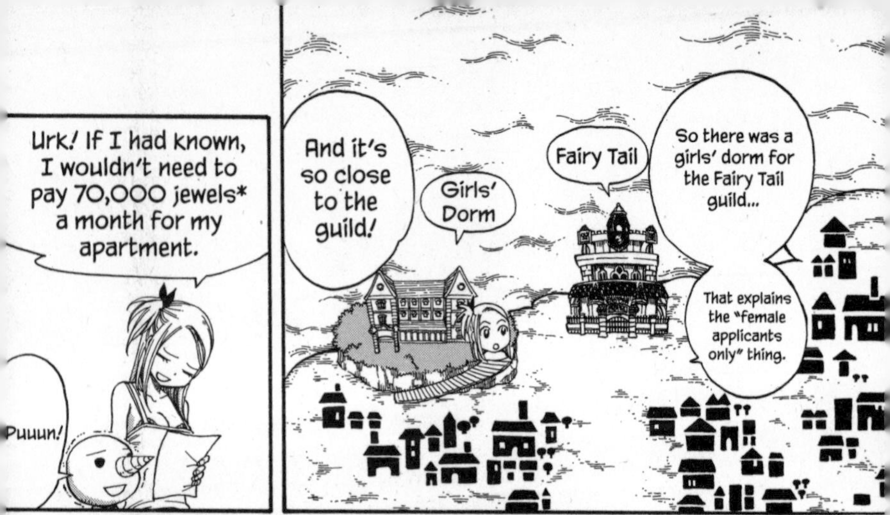
So there was a girls' dorm for the Fairy Tail guild...
That explains the "female applicants only" thing.
Fairy Tail
Girls' Dorm
And it's so close to the guild!
Urk! If I had known, I wouldn't need to pay 70,000 jewels* a month for my apartment.
Puuun!

*Jewels: The currency for this world.

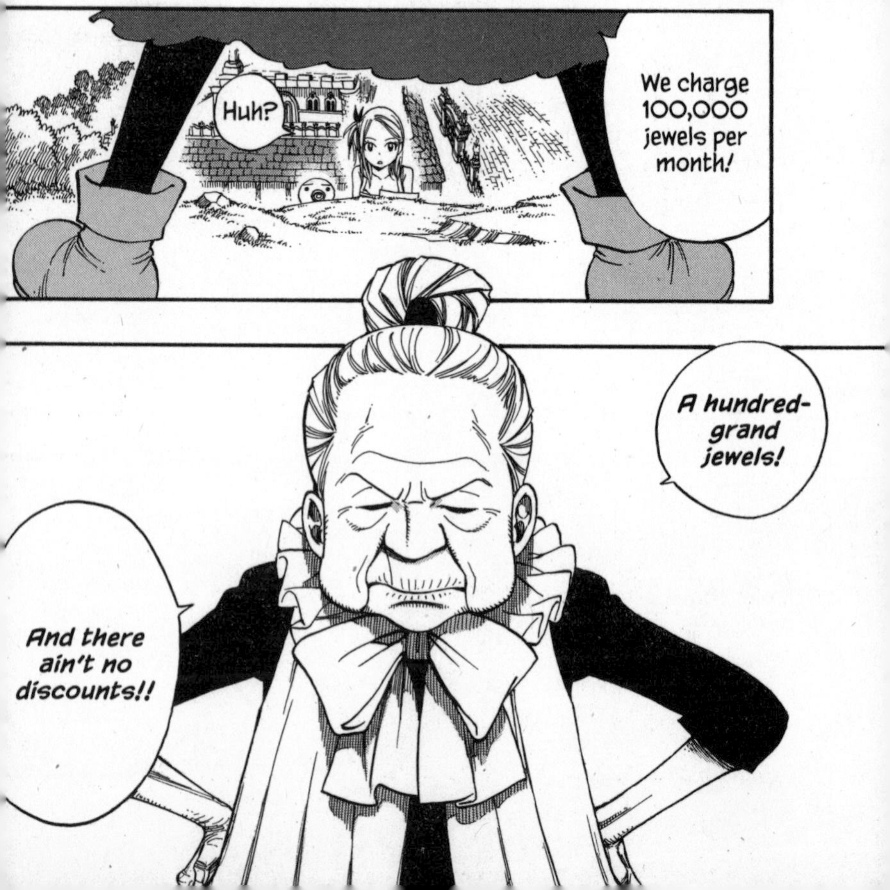
We charge 100,000 jewels per month!
Huh?
A hundred-grand jewels!
And there ain't no discounts!!

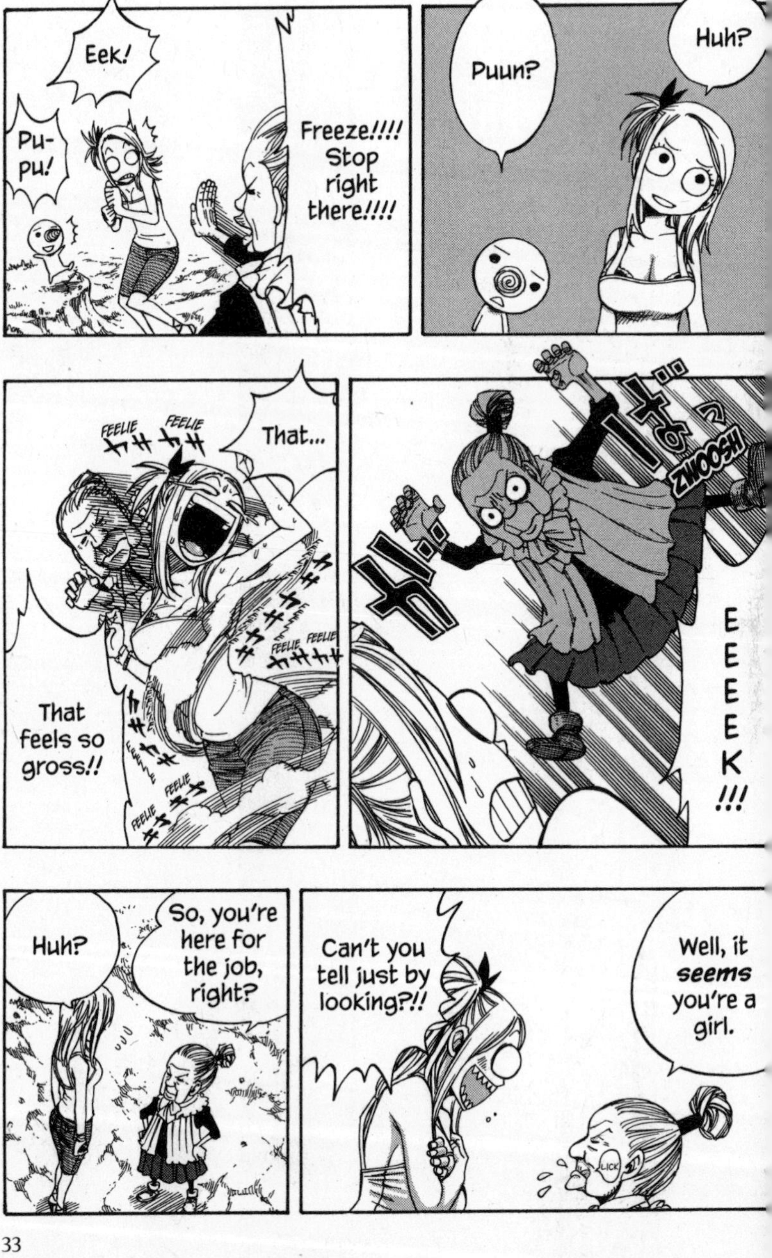
Huh?
Puun?
Freeze!!!! Stop right there!!!!
Eek!
Pu-pu!
ZWOOSH
EEEEEK!!!
That...
FEELIE FEELIE
FEELIE FEELIE
That feels so gross!!
FEELIE FEELIE
Well, it *seems* you're a girl.
LICK
Can't you tell just by looking?!!
So, you're here for the job, right?
Huh?

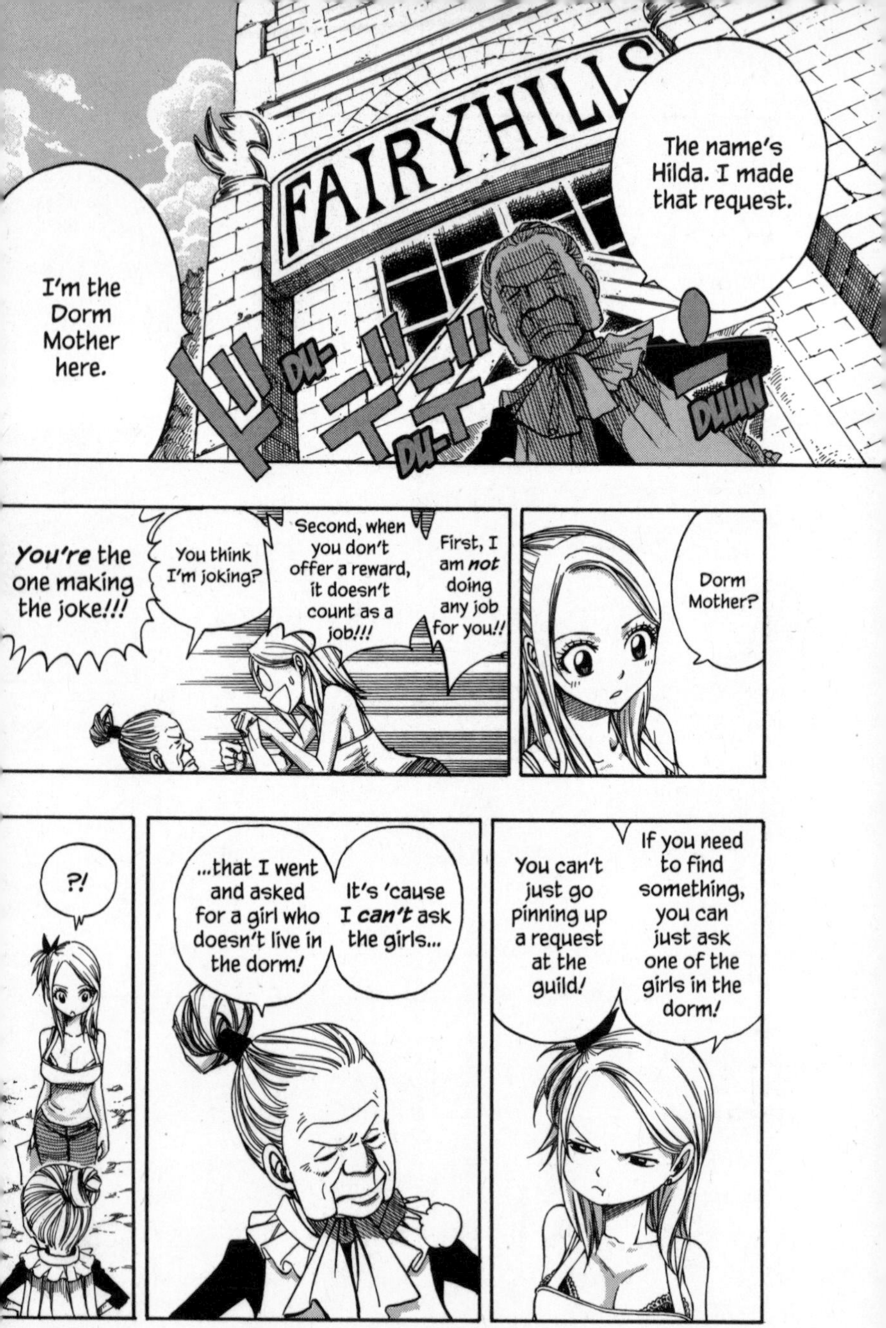
FAIRYHILLS
The name's Hilda. I made that request.
DU-
DU-
DUUN
I'm the Dorm Mother here.
Dorm Mother?
First, I am *not* doing any job for you!!
Second, when you don't offer a reward, it doesn't count as a job!!!
You think I'm joking?
You're the one making the joke!!!
If you need to find something, you can just ask one of the girls in the dorm!
You can't just go pinning up a request at the guild!
It's 'cause I *can't* ask the girls...
...that I went and asked for a girl who doesn't live in the dorm!
?!

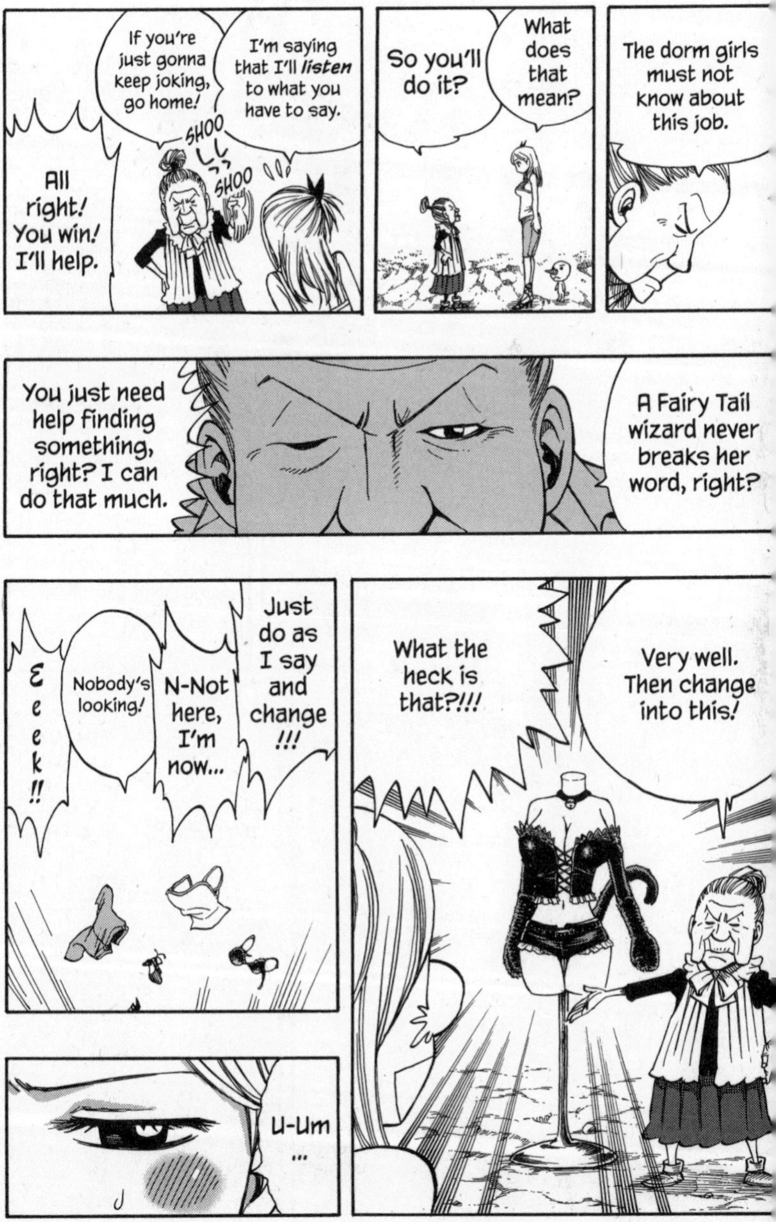

The dorm girls must not know about this job.
What does that mean?
So you'll do it?
I'm saying that I'll *listen* to what you have to say.
If you're just gonna keep joking, go home!
SHOO SHOO
All right! You win! I'll help.
A Fairy Tail wizard never breaks her word, right?
You just need help finding something, right? I can do that much.
Very well. Then change into this!
What the heck is that?!!!
Just do as I say and change!!!
N-Not here, I'm now...
Nobody's looking!
Eeek!!
U-Um ...

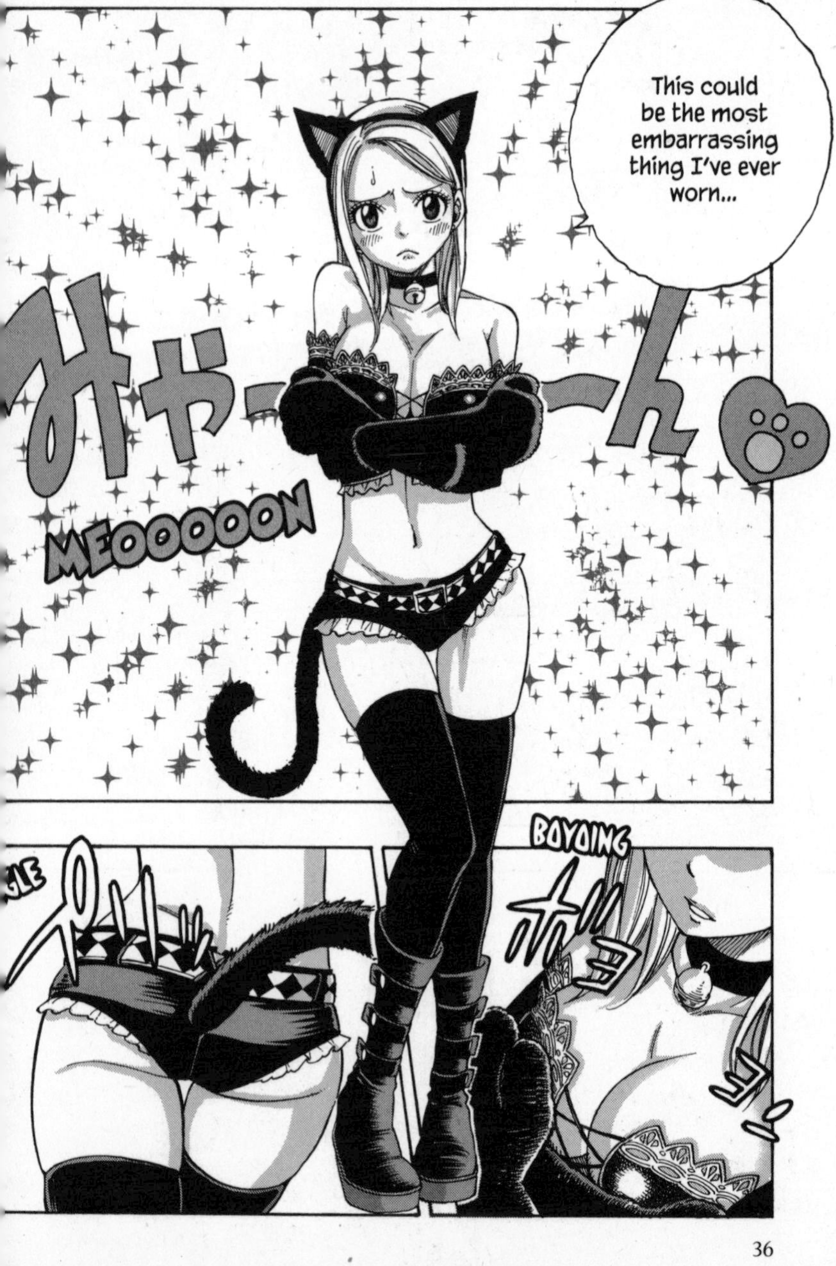
This could be the most embarrassing thing I've ever worn...
みゃーーん
MEOOOOON
BOYOING
GLE

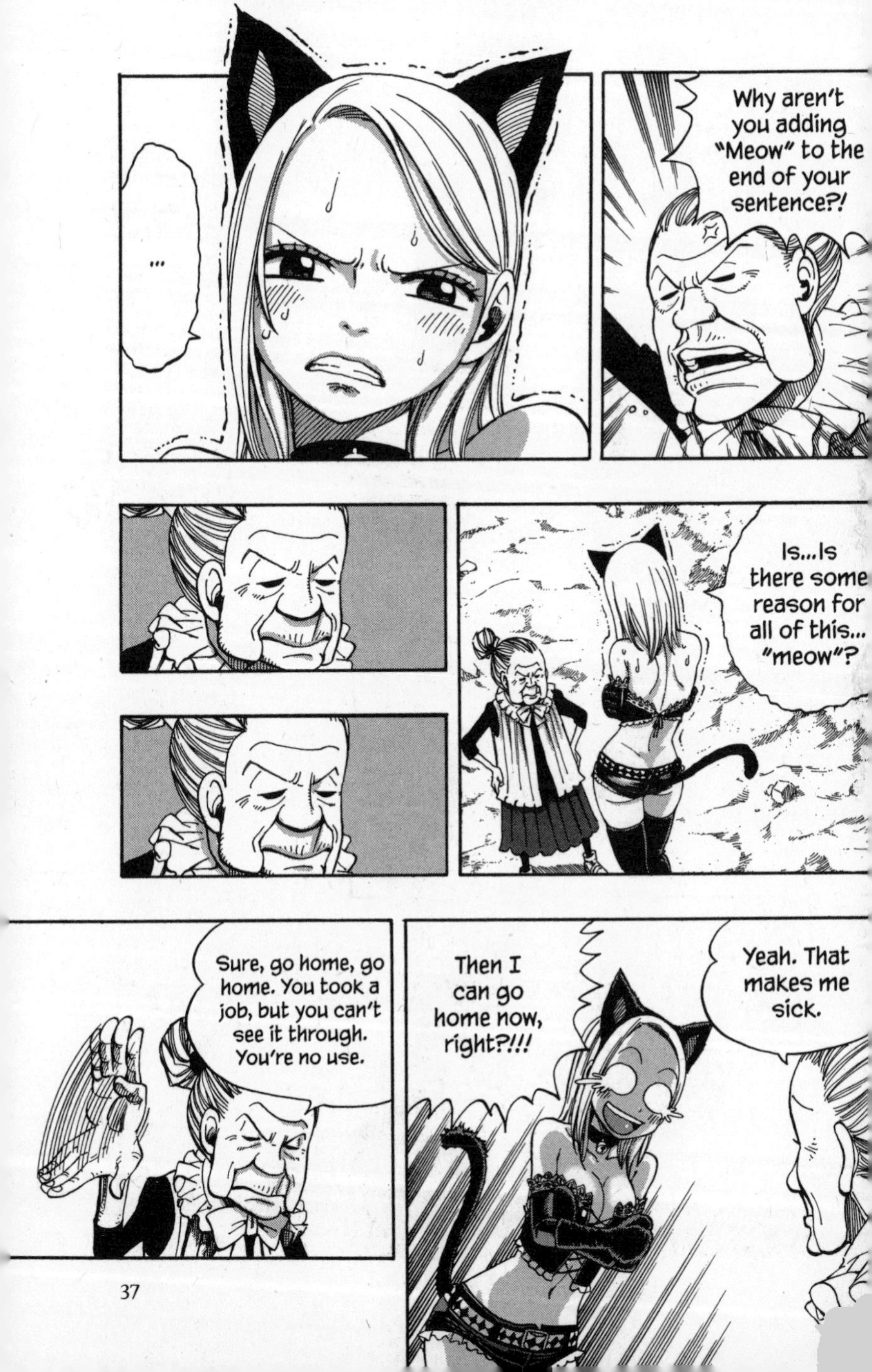
Why aren't you adding "Meow" to the end of your sentence?!
...
Is...Is there some reason for all of this... "meow"?
Yeah. That makes me sick.
Then I can go home now, right?!!!
Sure, go home, go home. You took a job, but you can't see it through. You're no use.

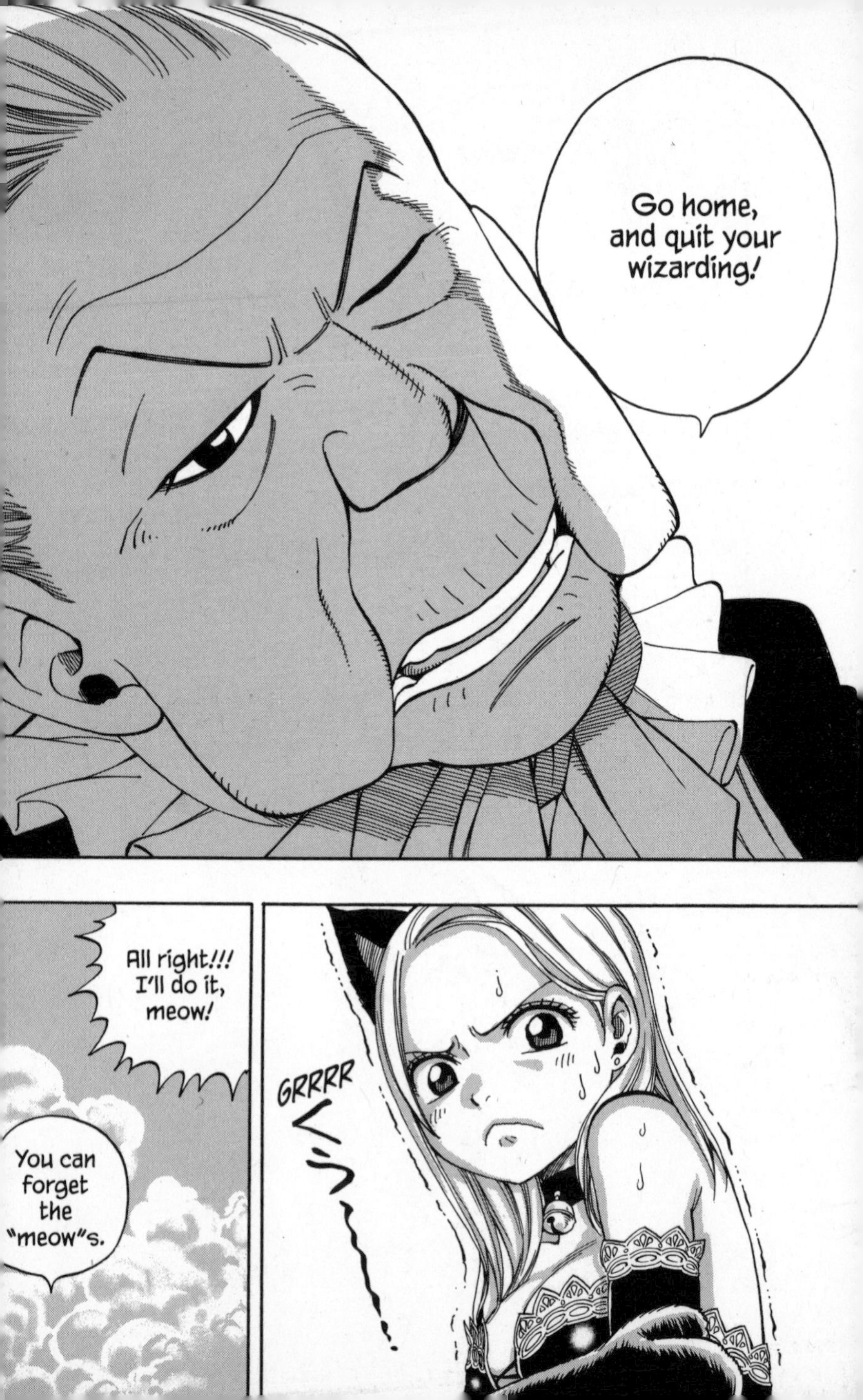
Go home, and quit your wizarding!
GRRRR
All right!!! I'll do it, meow!
You can forget the "meow"s.

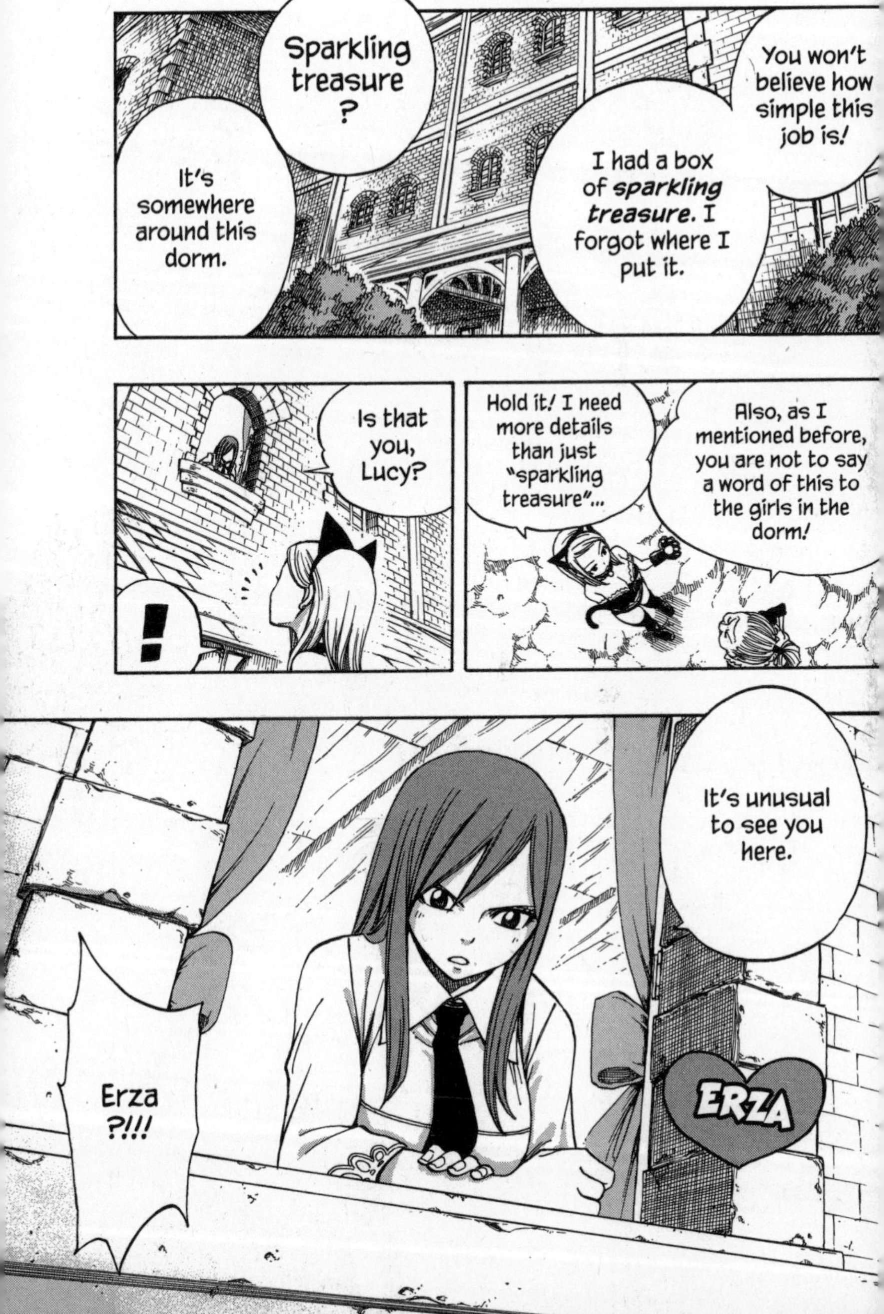
You won't believe how simple this job is!
I had a box of *sparkling treasure*. I forgot where I put it.
Sparkling treasure?
It's somewhere around this dorm.
Also, as I mentioned before, you are not to say a word of this to the girls in the dorm!
Hold it! I need more details than just "sparkling treasure"...
Is that you, Lucy?
!
It's unusual to see you here.
ERZA
Erza?!!!

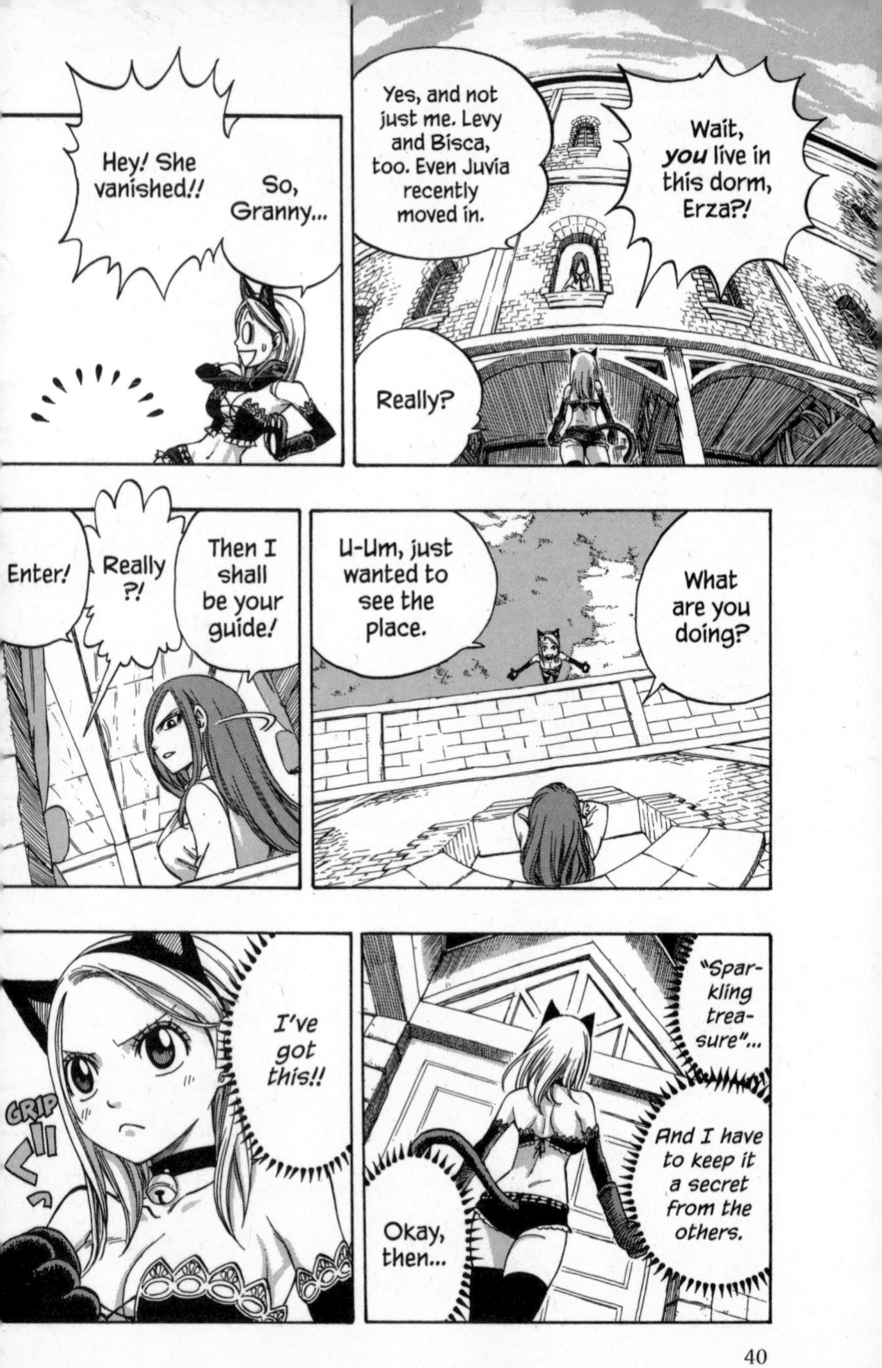
Wait, you live in this dorm, Erza?!
Yes, and not just me. Levy and Bisca, too. Even Juvia recently moved in.
Really?
Hey! She vanished!!
So, Granny...
What are you doing?
U-Um, just wanted to see the place.
Then I shall be your guide!
Really ?!
Enter!
"Spar-kling trea-sure"...
And I have to keep it a secret from the others.
Okay, then...
I've got this!!
GRIP

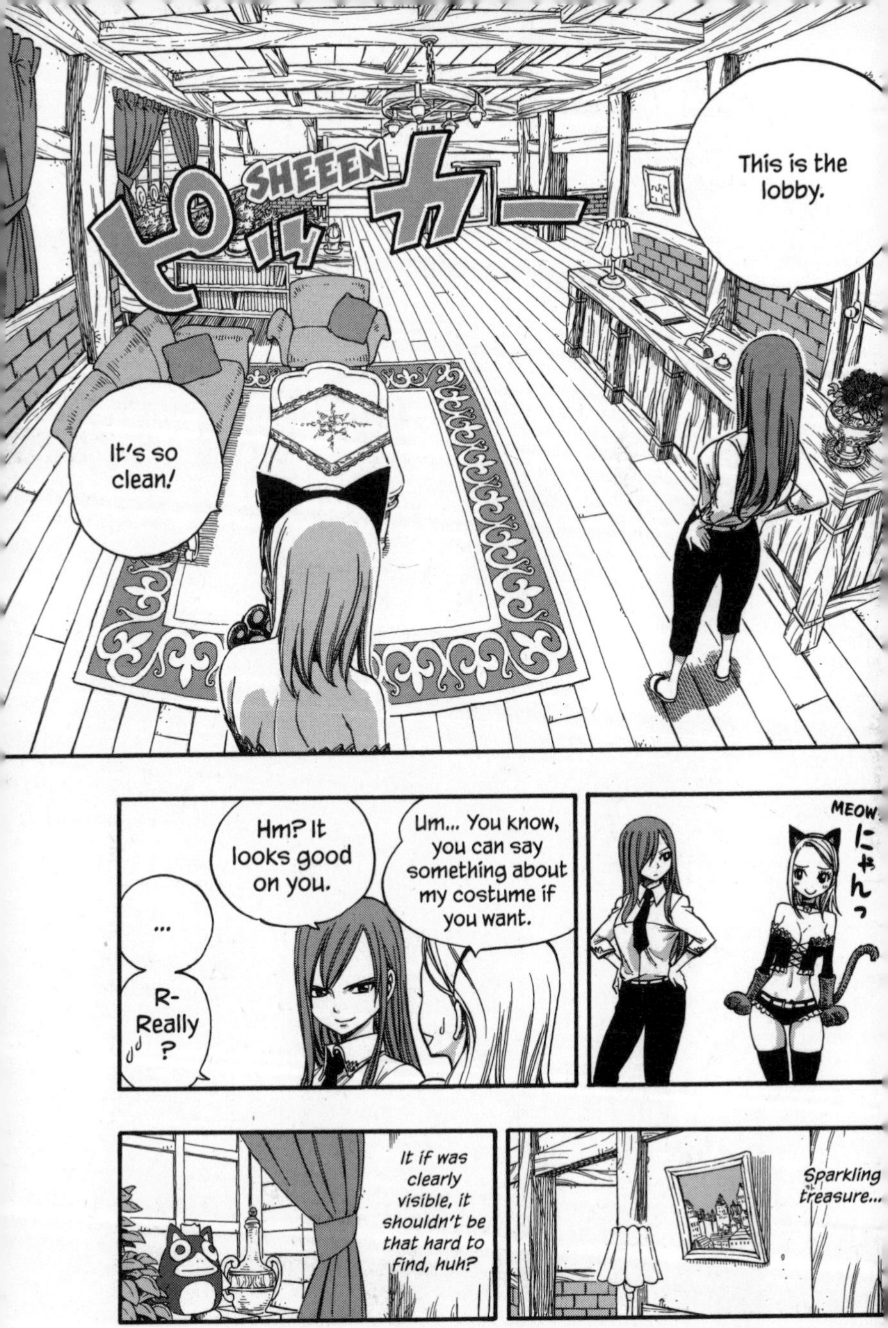
This is the lobby.
SHEEEN
ピッカー
It's so clean!
MEOW
にゃんっ
Um... You know, you can say something about my costume if you want.
Hm? It looks good on you.
...
R-Really?
Sparkling treasure...
It if was clearly visible, it shouldn't be that hard to find, huh?

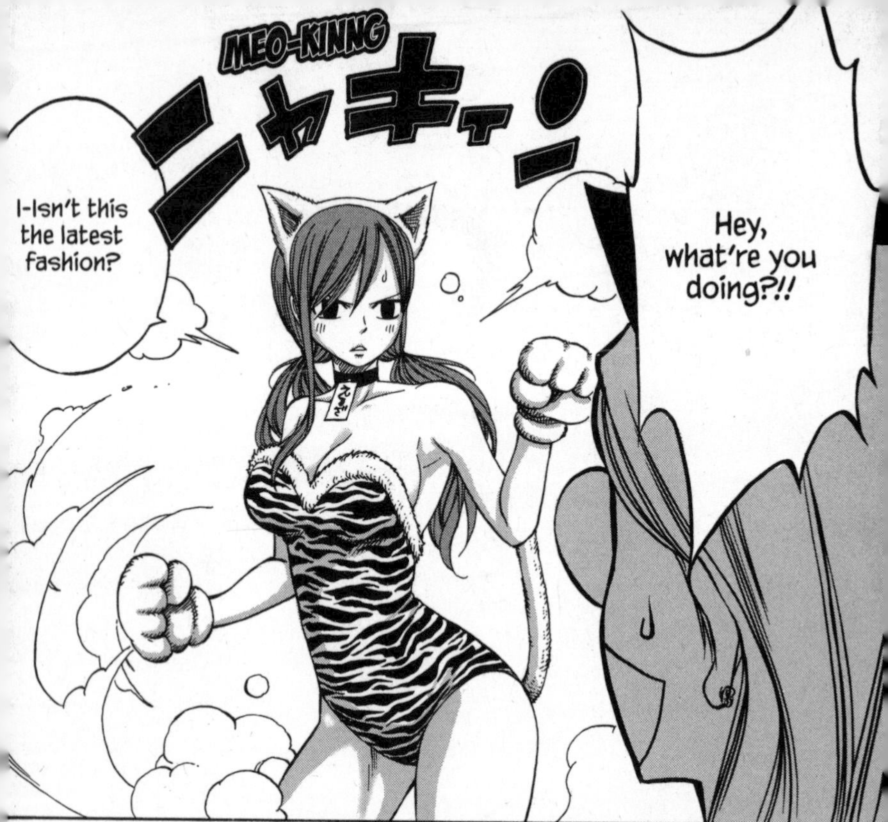
MEO-KINNG
Hey, what're you doing?!!
I-Isn't this the latest fashion?

Cat tag: Erza

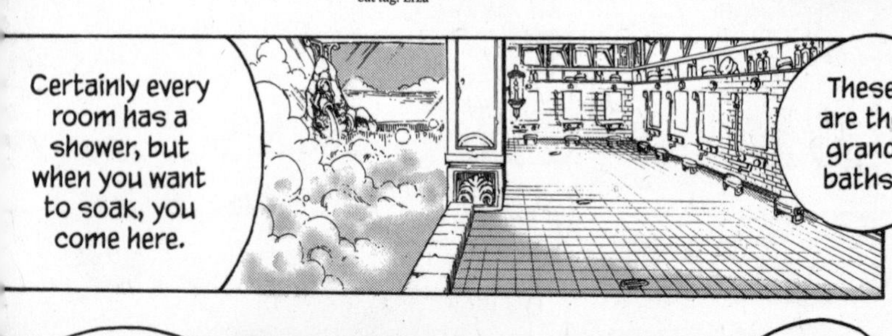
These are the grand baths.
Certainly every room has a shower, but when you want to soak, you come here.

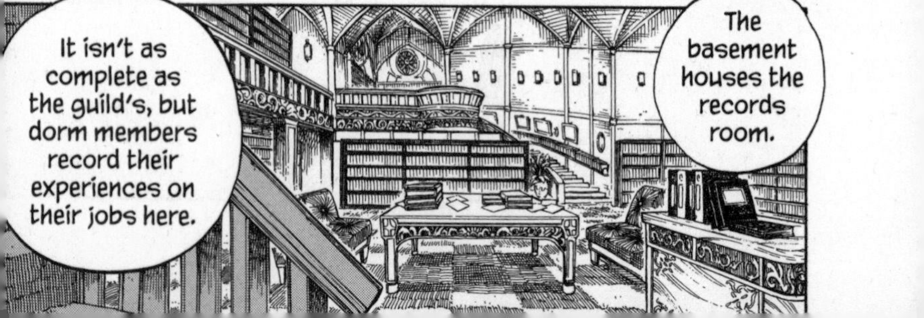
The basement houses the records room.
It isn't as complete as the guild's, but dorm members record their experiences on their jobs here.

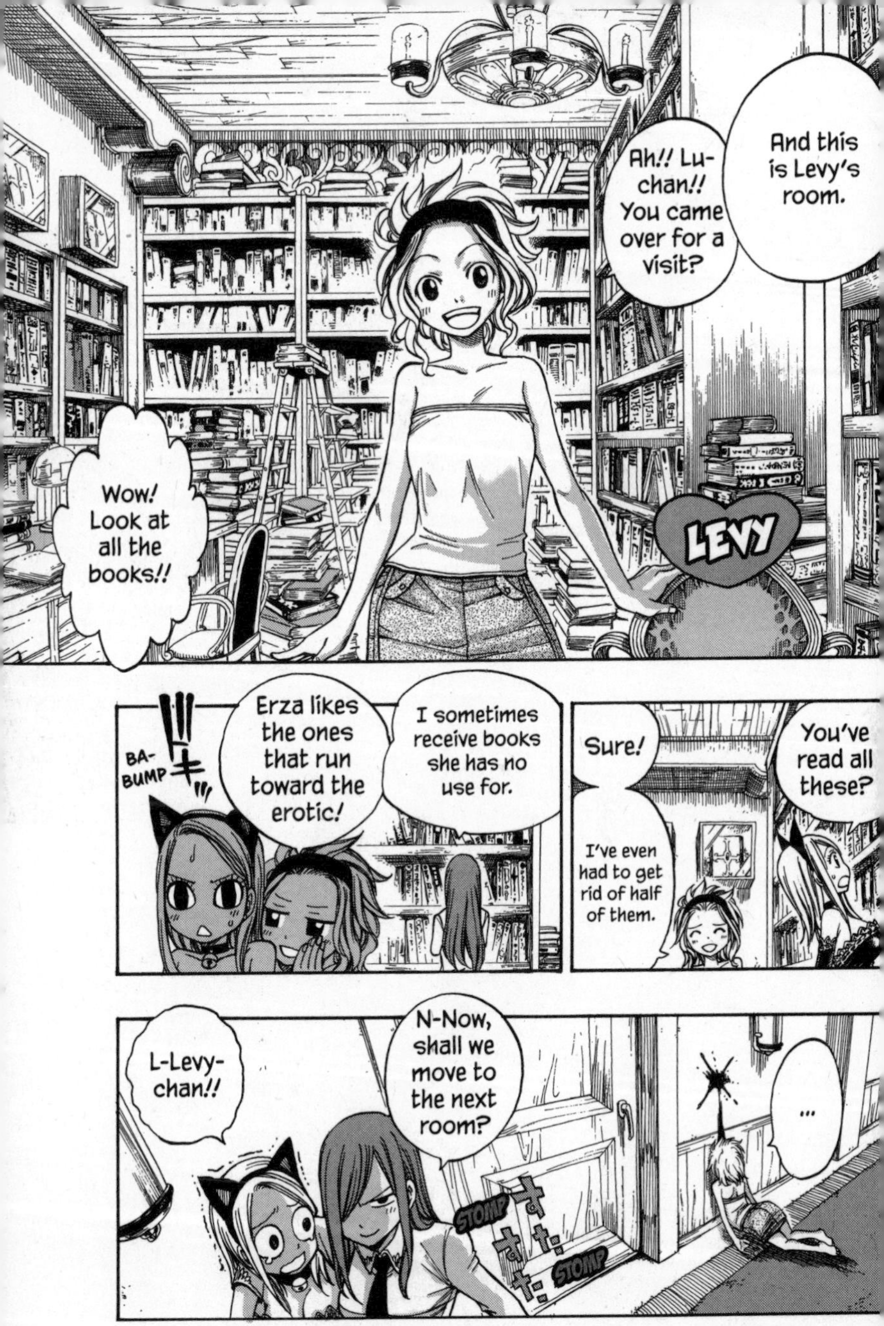
And this is Levy's room.
Ah!! Lu-chan!! You came over for a visit?
LEVY
Wow! Look at all the books!!
You've read all these?
Sure!
I've even had to get rid of half of them.
I sometimes receive books she has no use for.
Erza likes the ones that run toward the erotic!
BA-BUMP
...
N-Now, shall we move to the next room?
STOMP
STOMP
L-Levy-chan!!

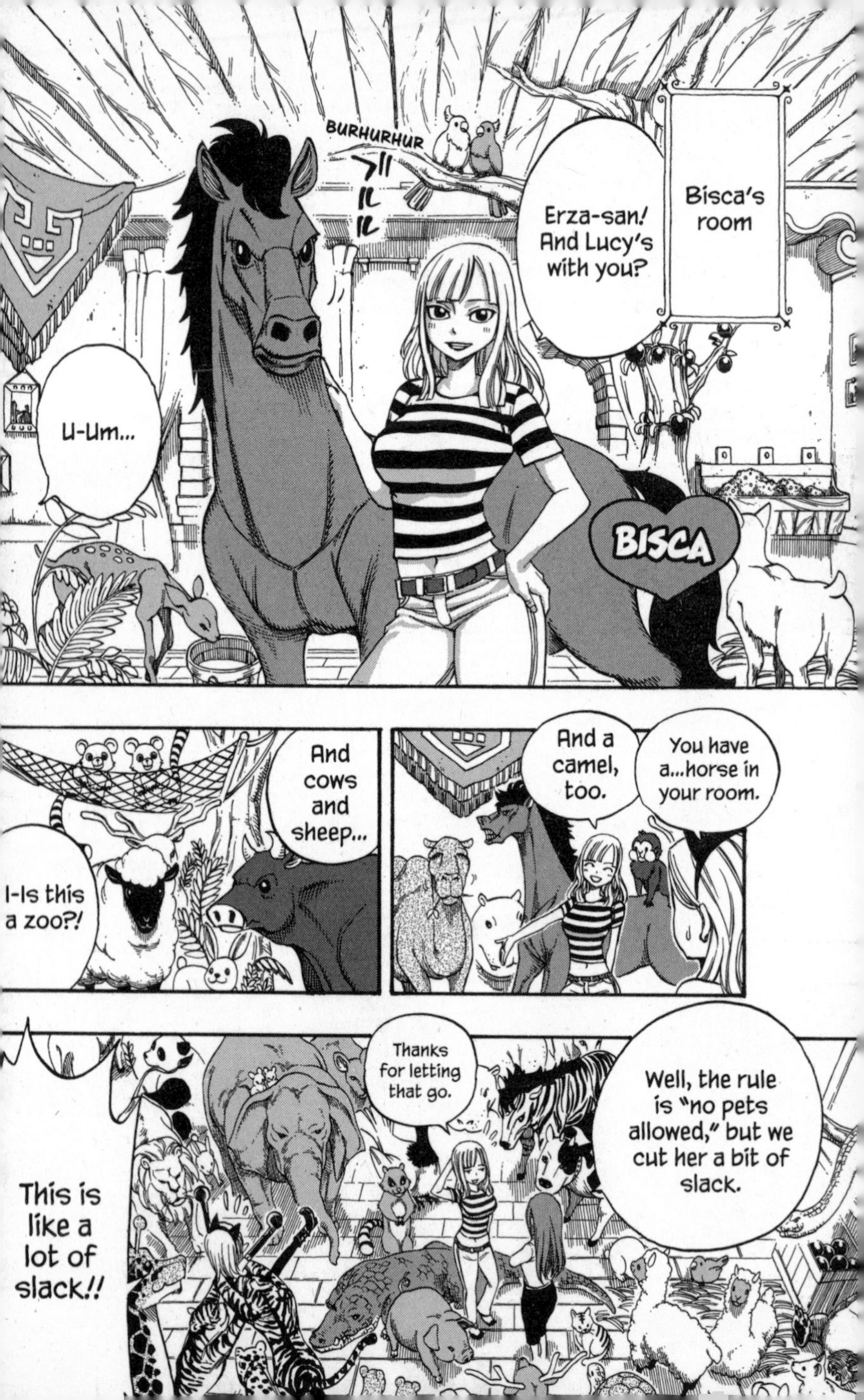
Bisca's room
Erza-san! And Lucy's with you?
BURHURHUR
BISCA
U-Um...
You have a...horse in your room.
And a camel, too.
And cows and sheep...
I-Is this a zoo?!
Well, the rule is "no pets allowed," but we cut her a bit of slack.
Thanks for letting that go.
This is like a lot of slack!!

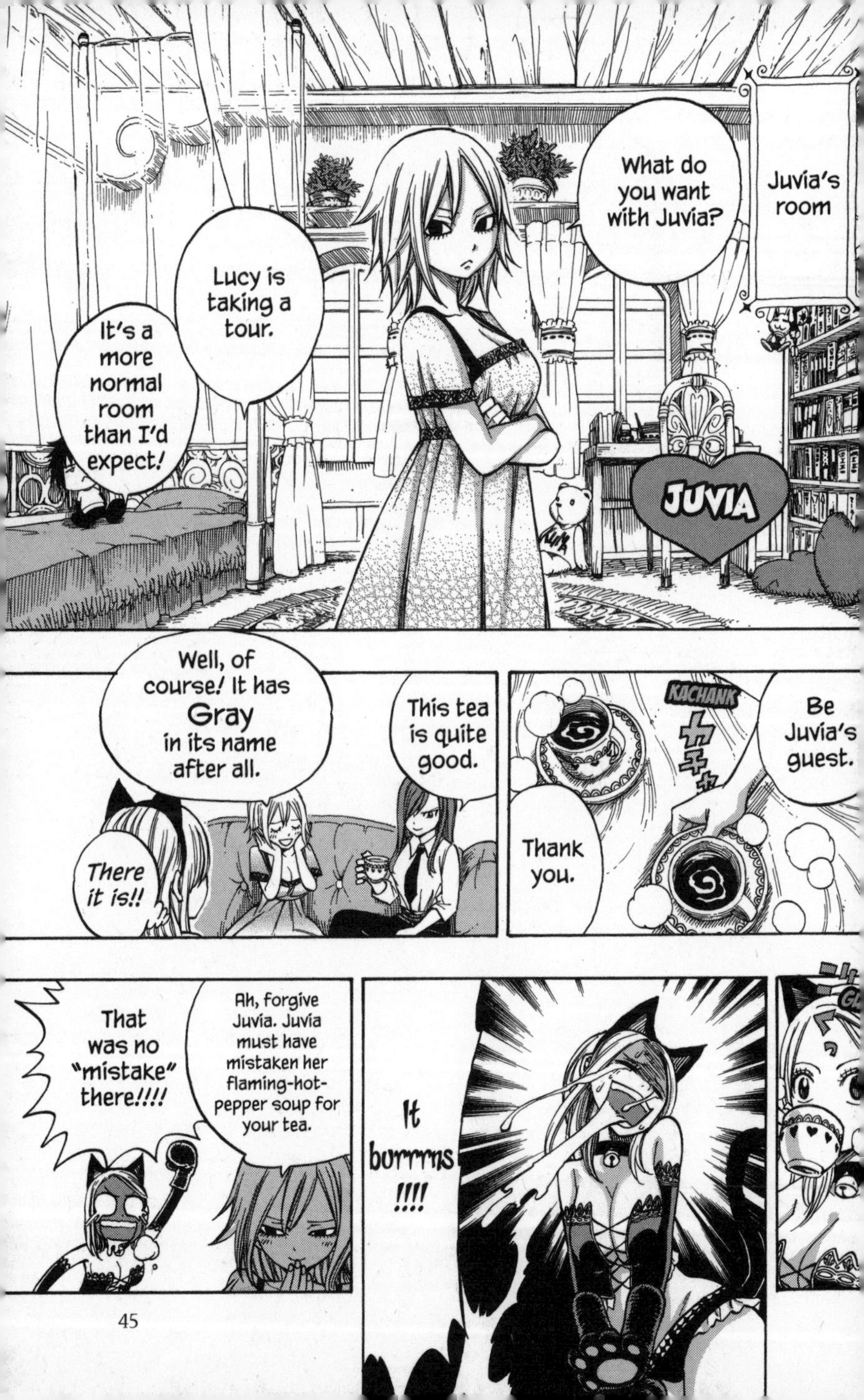
Juvia's room
What do you want with Juvia?
Lucy is taking a tour.
It's a more normal room than I'd expect!
JUVIA
KACHANK
Be Juvia's guest.
Thank you.
This tea is quite good.
Well, of course! It has Gray in its name after all.
There it is!!
It burrrns!!!!
Ah, forgive Juvia. Juvia must have mistaken her flaming-hot-pepper soup for your tea.
That was no "mistake" there!!!!

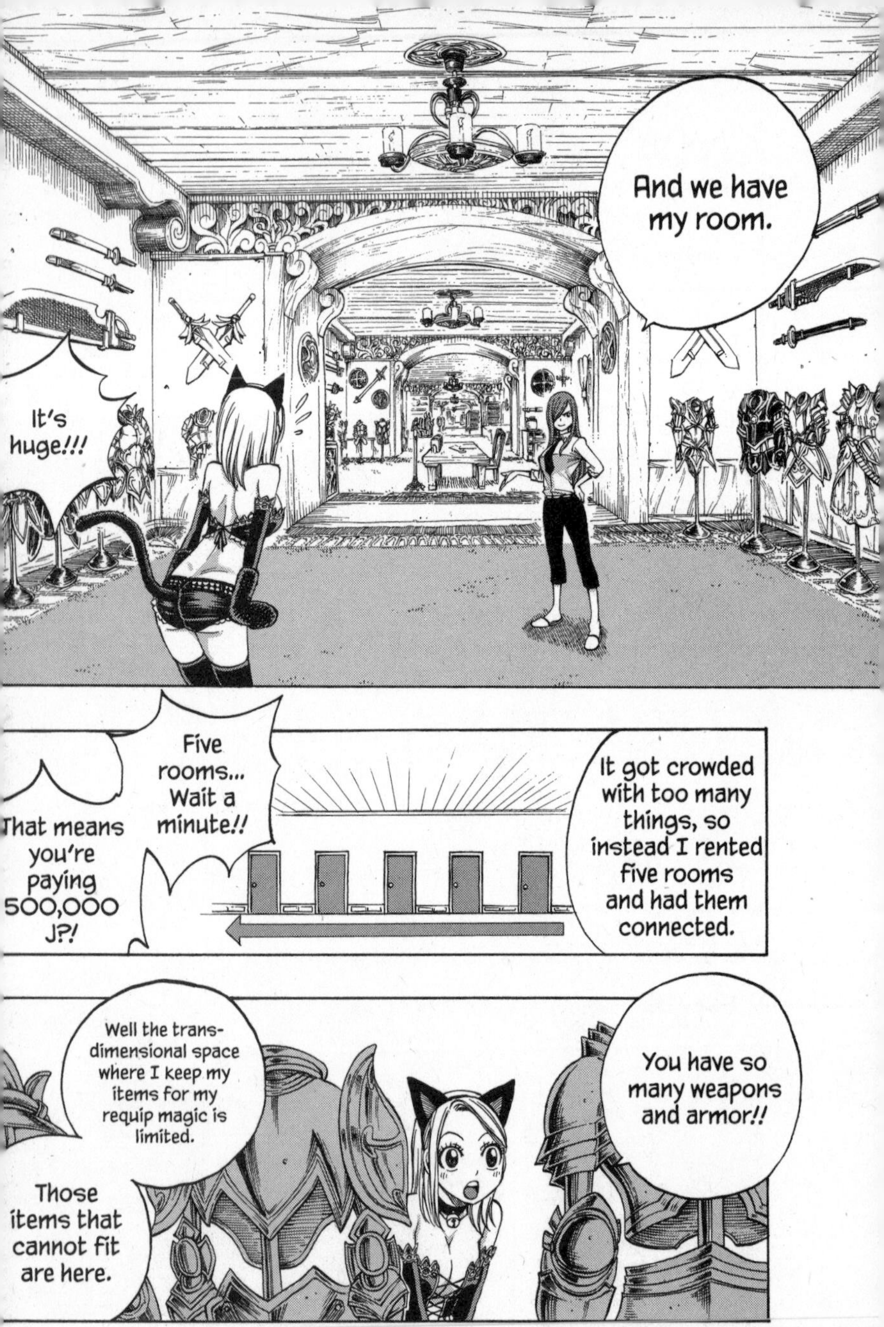
And we have my room.
It's huge!!!
It got crowded with too many things, so instead I rented five rooms and had them connected.
Five rooms... Wait a minute!!
That means you're paying 500,000 J?!
You have so many weapons and armor!!
Well the trans-dimensional space where I keep my items for my requip magic is limited.
Those items that cannot fit are here.

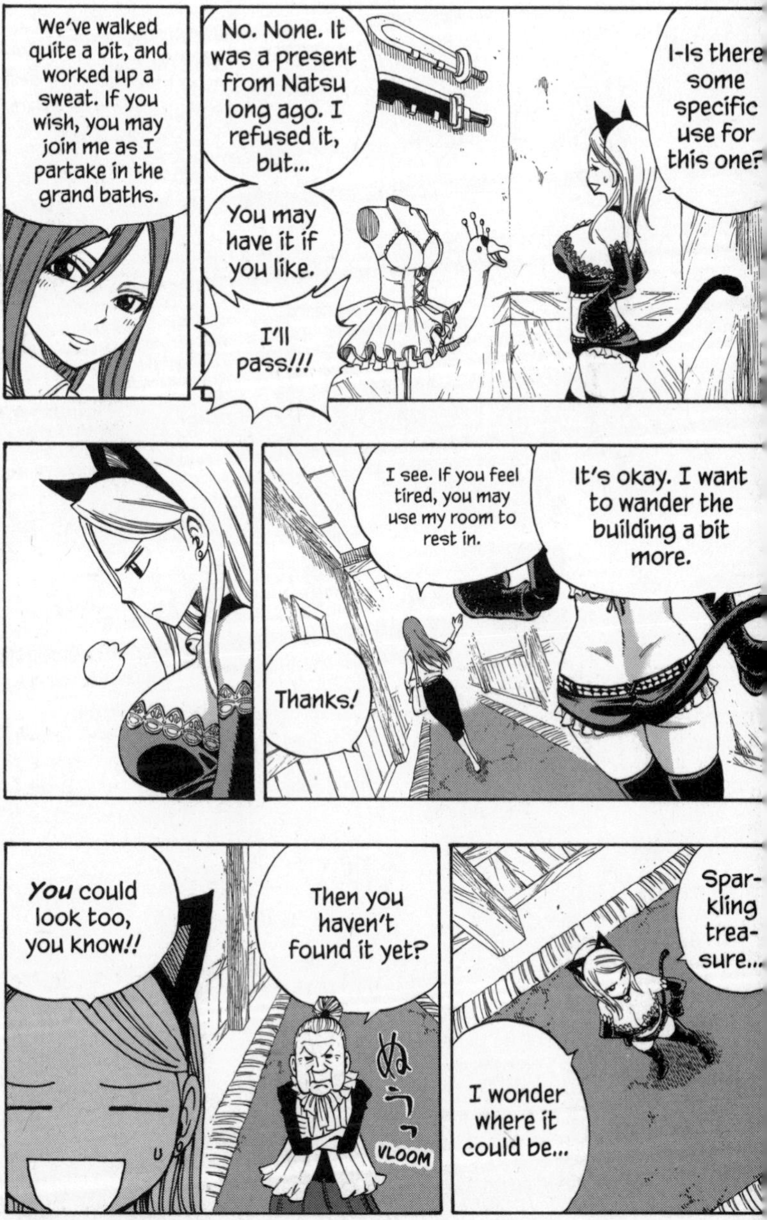
I-Is there some specific use for this one?
No. None. It was a present from Natsu long ago. I refused it, but...
You may have it if you like.
I'll pass!!!
We've walked quite a bit, and worked up a sweat. If you wish, you may join me as I partake in the grand baths.
It's okay. I want to wander the building a bit more.
I see. If you feel tired, you may use my room to rest in.
Thanks!
Spar-kling trea-sure...
I wonder where it could be...
Then you haven't found it yet?
ぬっ
VLOOM
You could look too, you know!!

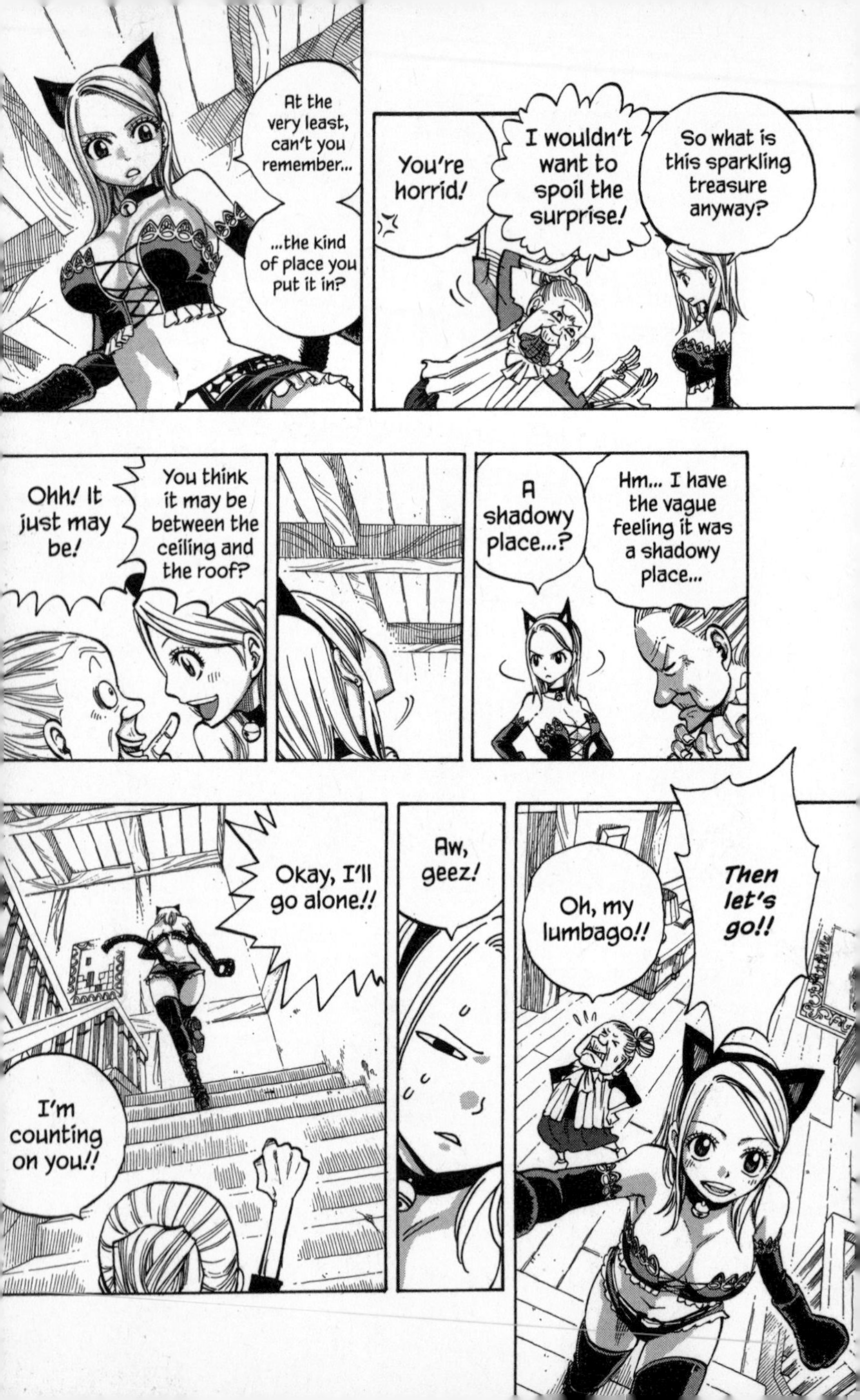
So what is this sparkling treasure anyway?
I wouldn't want to spoil the surprise!
You're horrid!
At the very least, can't you remember...
...the kind of place you put it in?
Hm... I have the vague feeling it was a shadowy place...
A shadowy place...?
You think it may be between the ceiling and the roof?
Ohh! It just may be!
Then let's go!!
Oh, my lumbago!!
Aw, geez!
Okay, I'll go alone!!
I'm counting on you!!

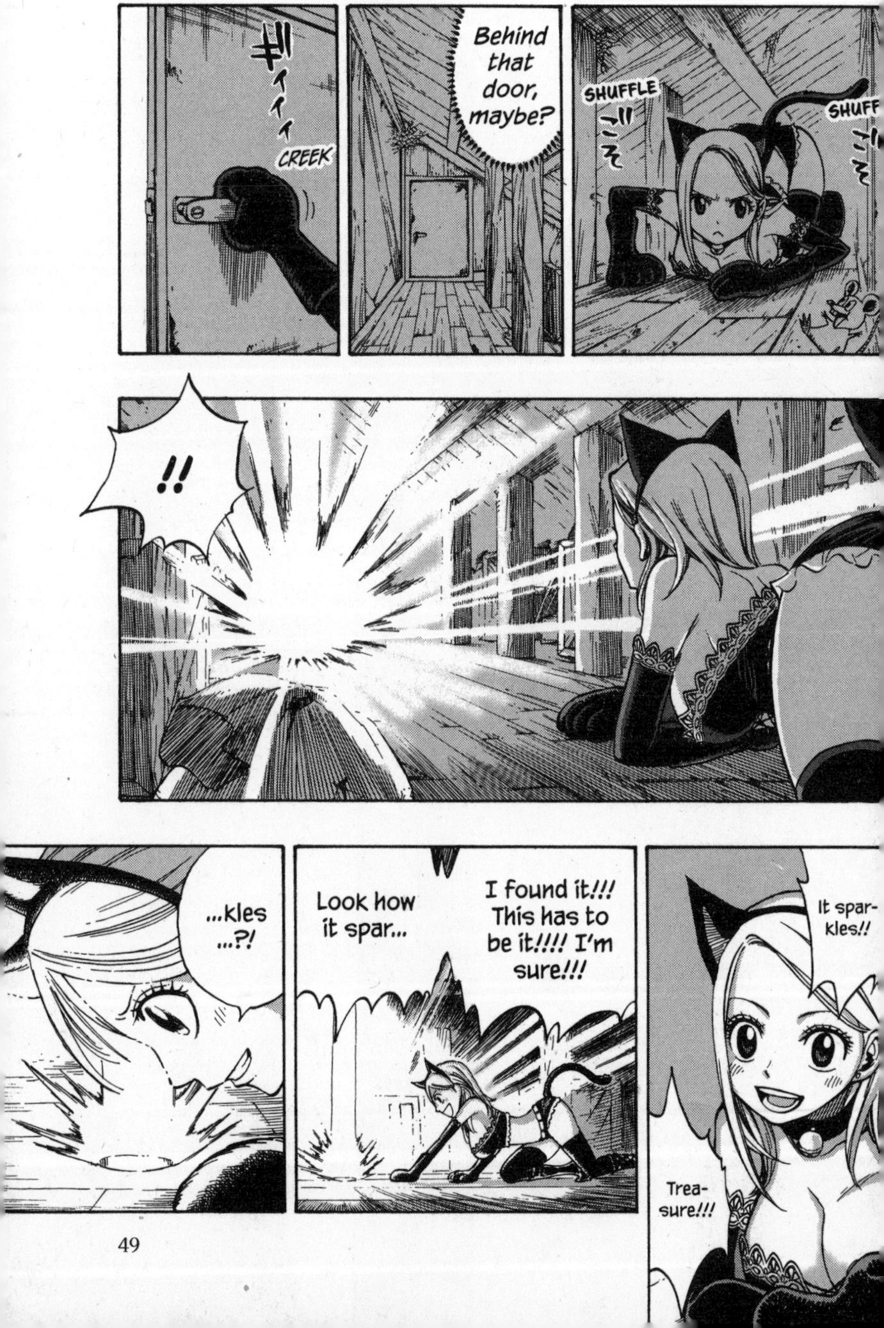
SHUFFLE
SHUFF
Behind that door, maybe?
CREEK
!!
It sparkles!!
Treasure!!!
I found it!!! This has to be it!!!! I'm sure!!!
Look how it spar...
...kles ...?!

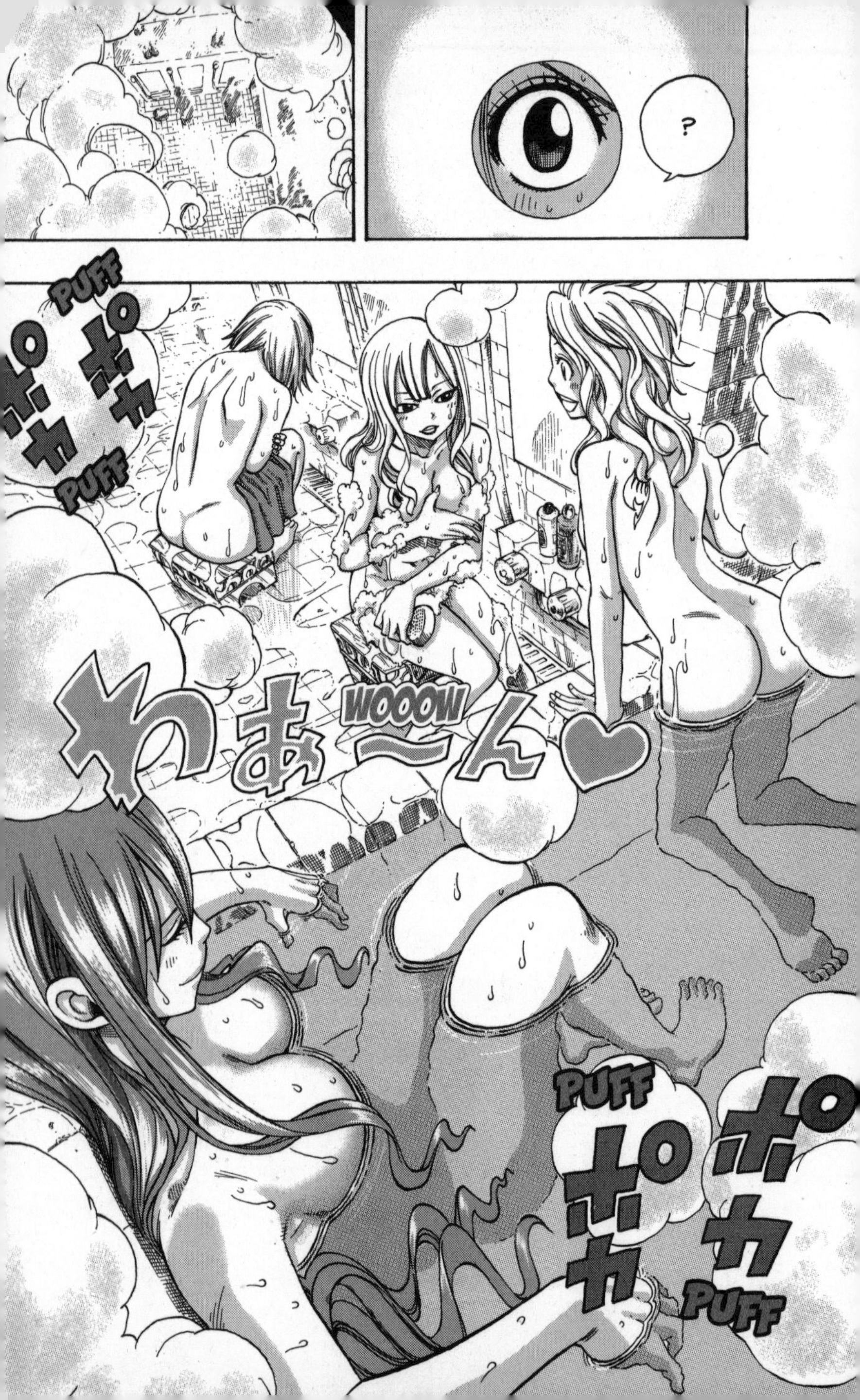
?
PUFF
ポカポカ
PUFF
わぁ～ん♥
WOOOW
PUFF
ポカポカ
PUFF

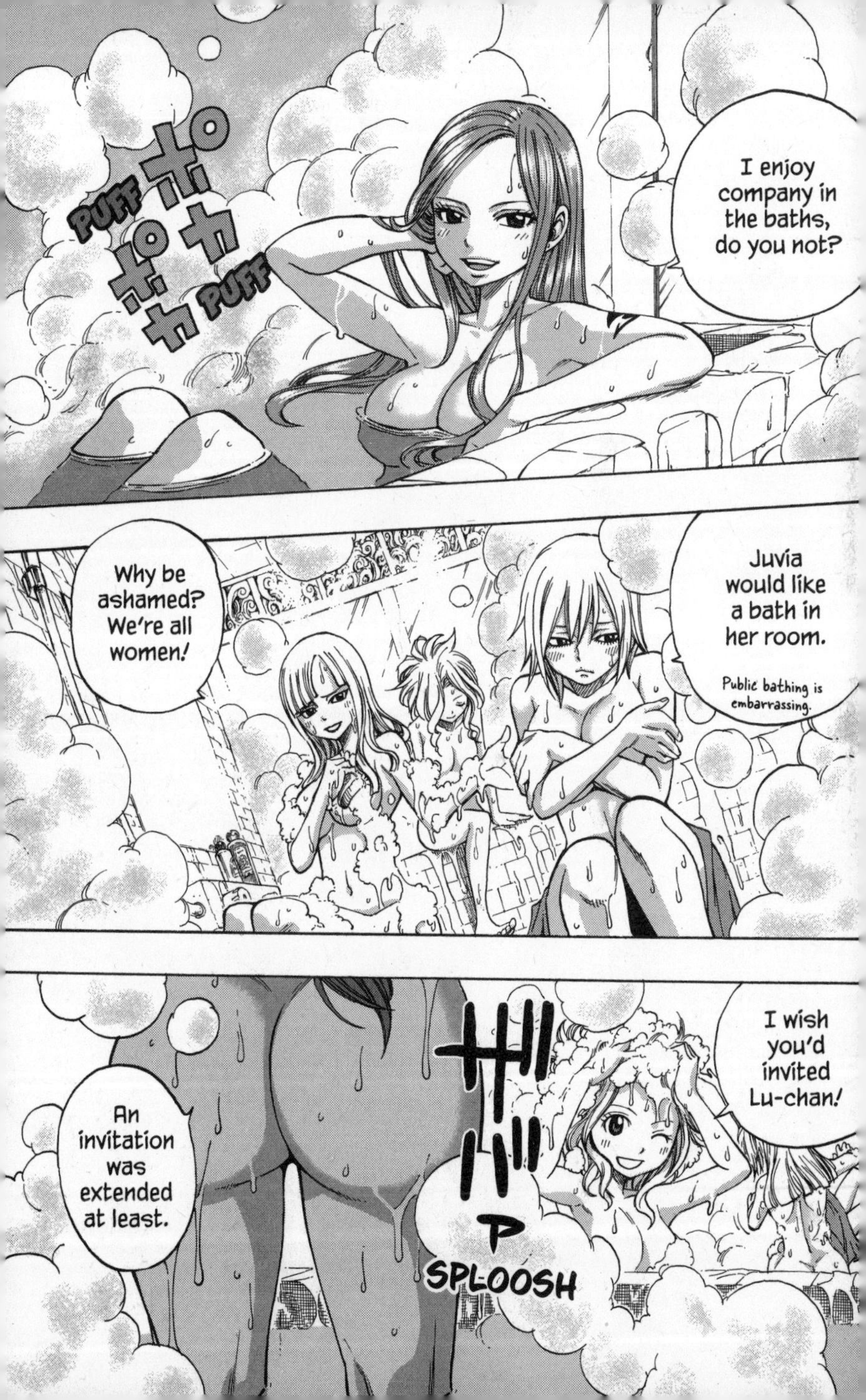
I enjoy company in the baths, do you not?
PUFF
PUFF
Juvia would like a bath in her room.
Public bathing is embarrassing.
Why be ashamed? We're all women!
I wish you'd invited Lu-chan!
SPLOOSH
An invitation was extended at least.

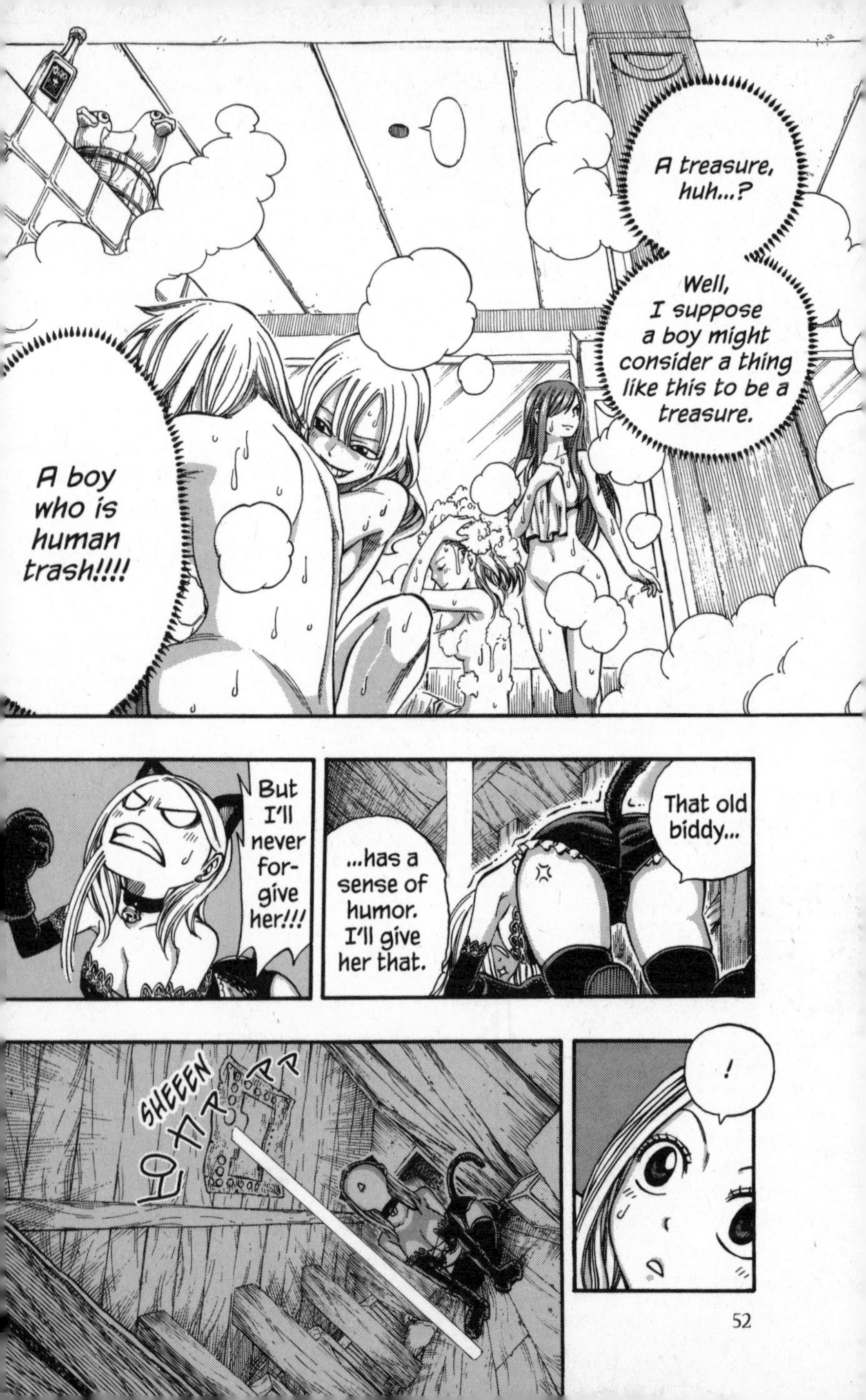
A treasure, huh...?
Well, I suppose a boy might consider a thing like this to be a treasure.
...
A boy who is human trash!!!!
That old biddy...
...has a sense of humor. I'll give her that.
But I'll never for-give her!!!
!
SHEEEN

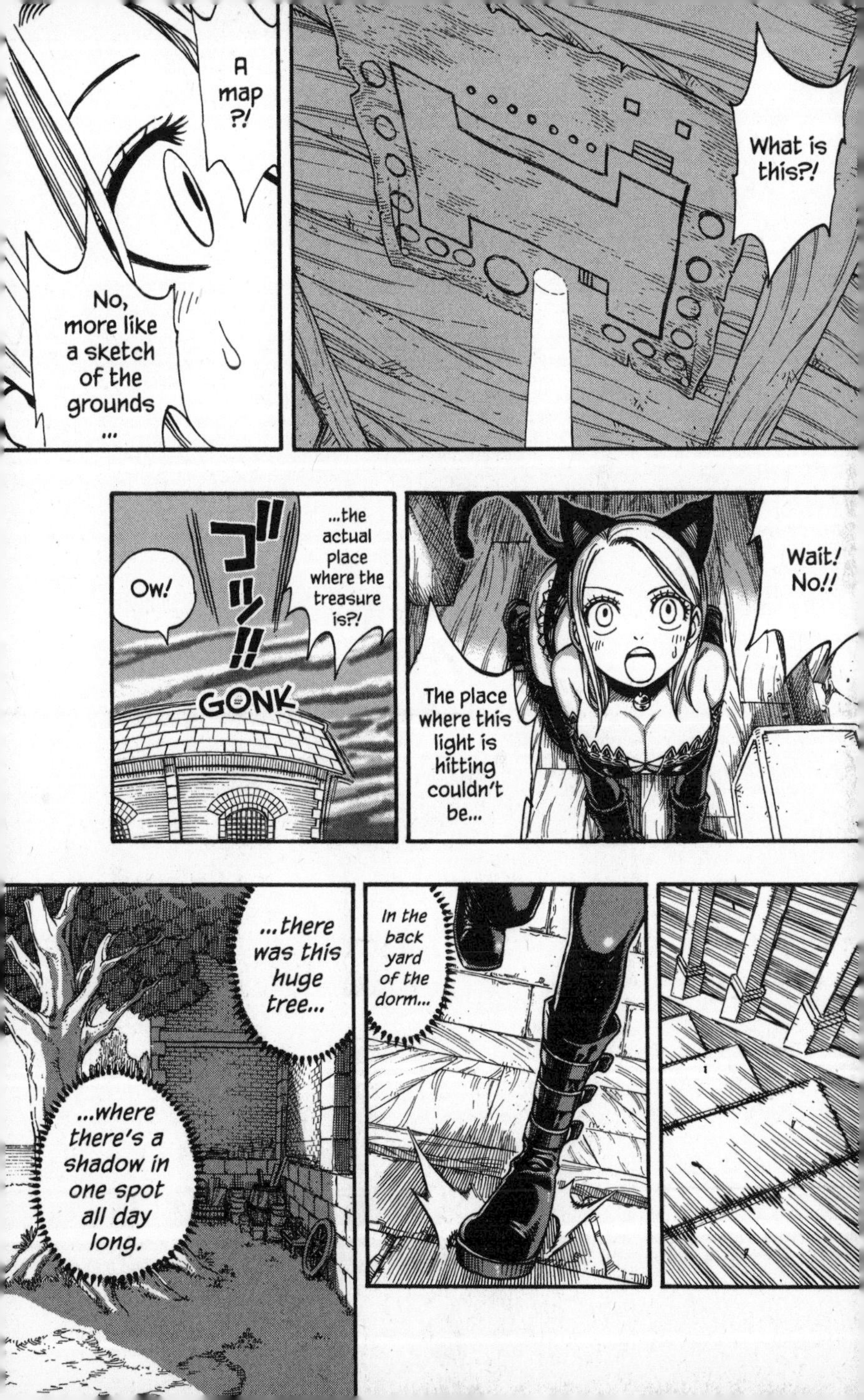
What is this?!
A map?!
No, more like a sketch of the grounds...
Wait! No!!
The place where this light is hitting couldn't be...
...the actual place where the treasure is?!
Ow!
GONK
In the back yard of the dorm...
...there was this huge tree...
...where there's a shadow in one spot all day long.

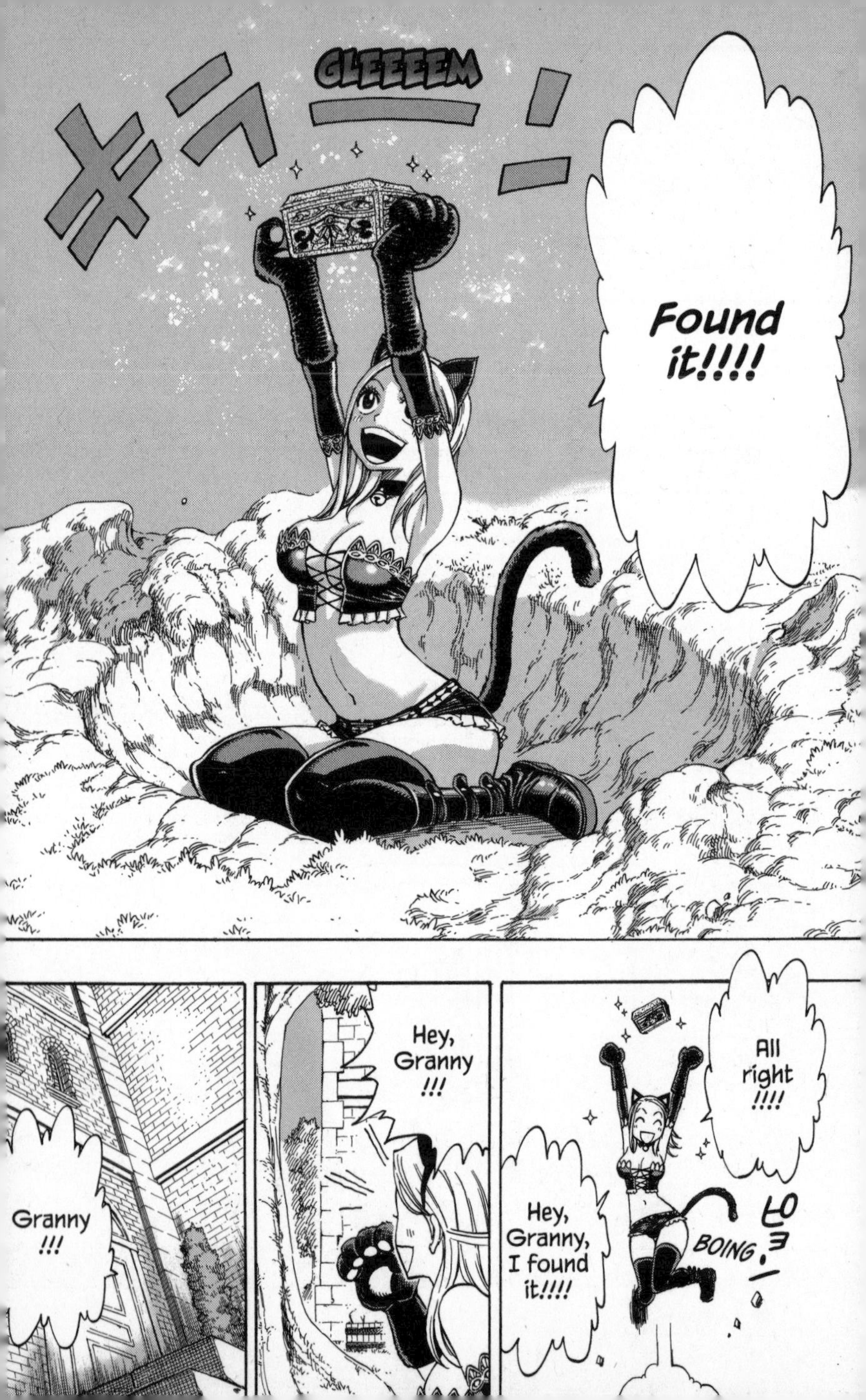
GLEEEEM
Found it!!!!
All right!!!!
Hey, Granny, I found it!!!!
BOING
Hey, Granny!!!
Granny!!!

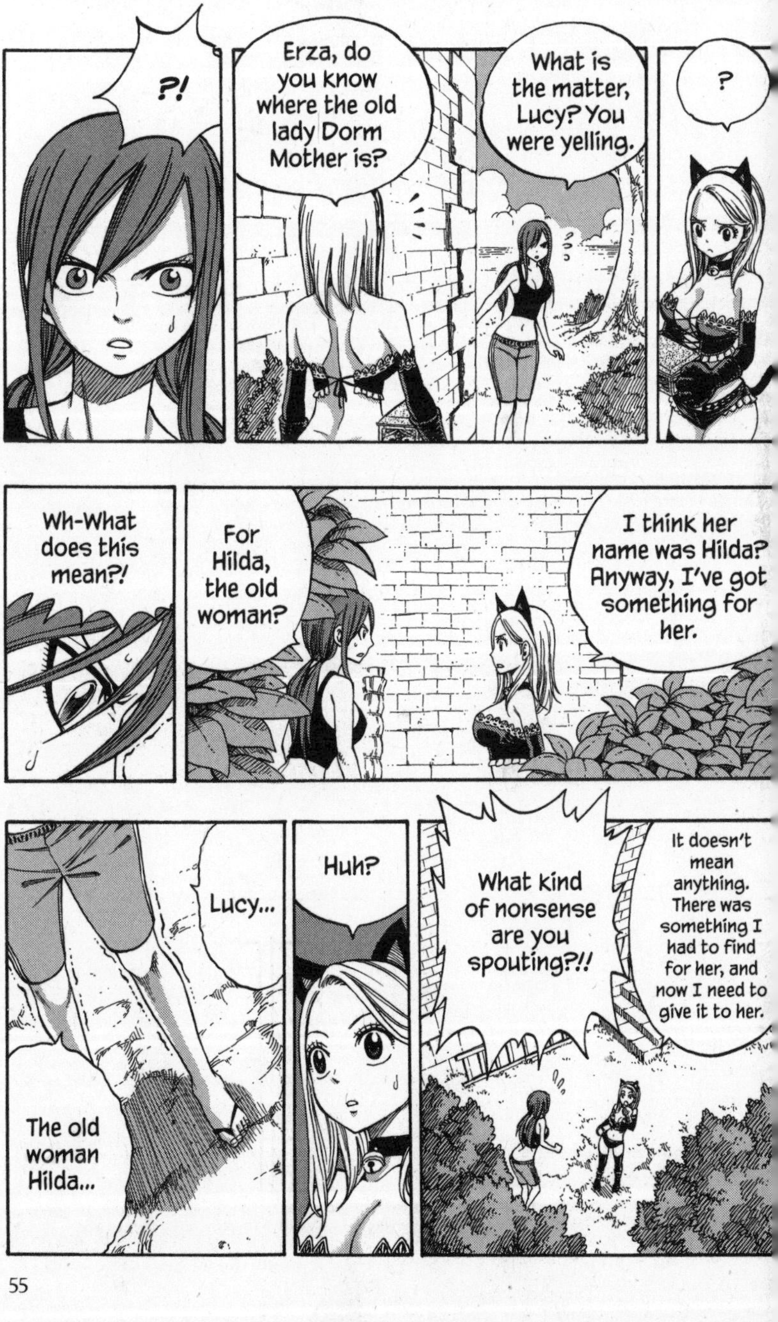
?
What is the matter, Lucy? You were yelling.
Erza, do you know where the old lady Dorm Mother is?
?!
I think her name was Hilda? Anyway, I've got something for her.
For Hilda, the old woman?
Wh-What does this mean?!
It doesn't mean anything. There was something I had to find for her, and now I need to give it to her.
What kind of nonsense are you spouting?!!
Huh?
Lucy...
The old woman Hilda...

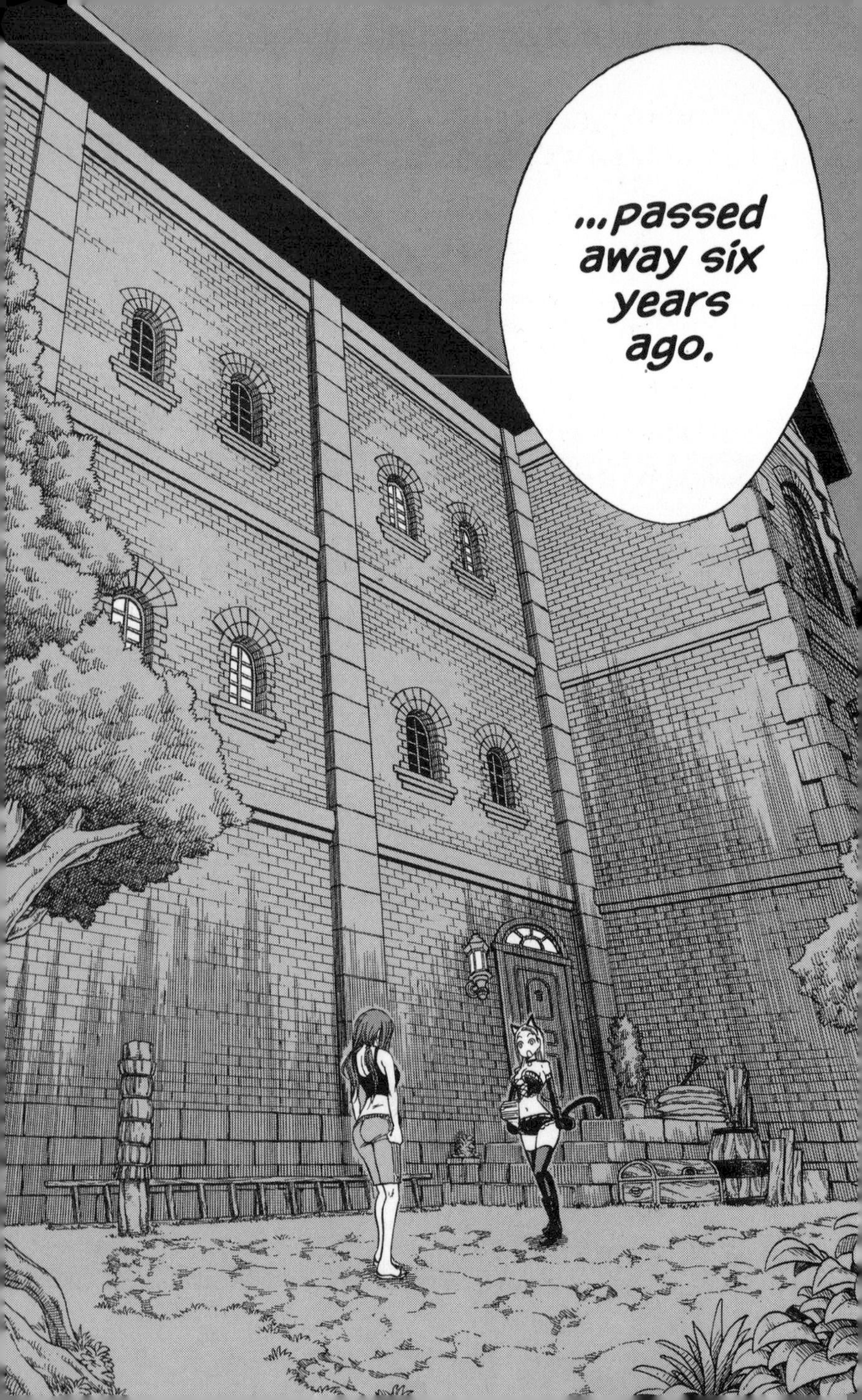
...passed away six years ago.

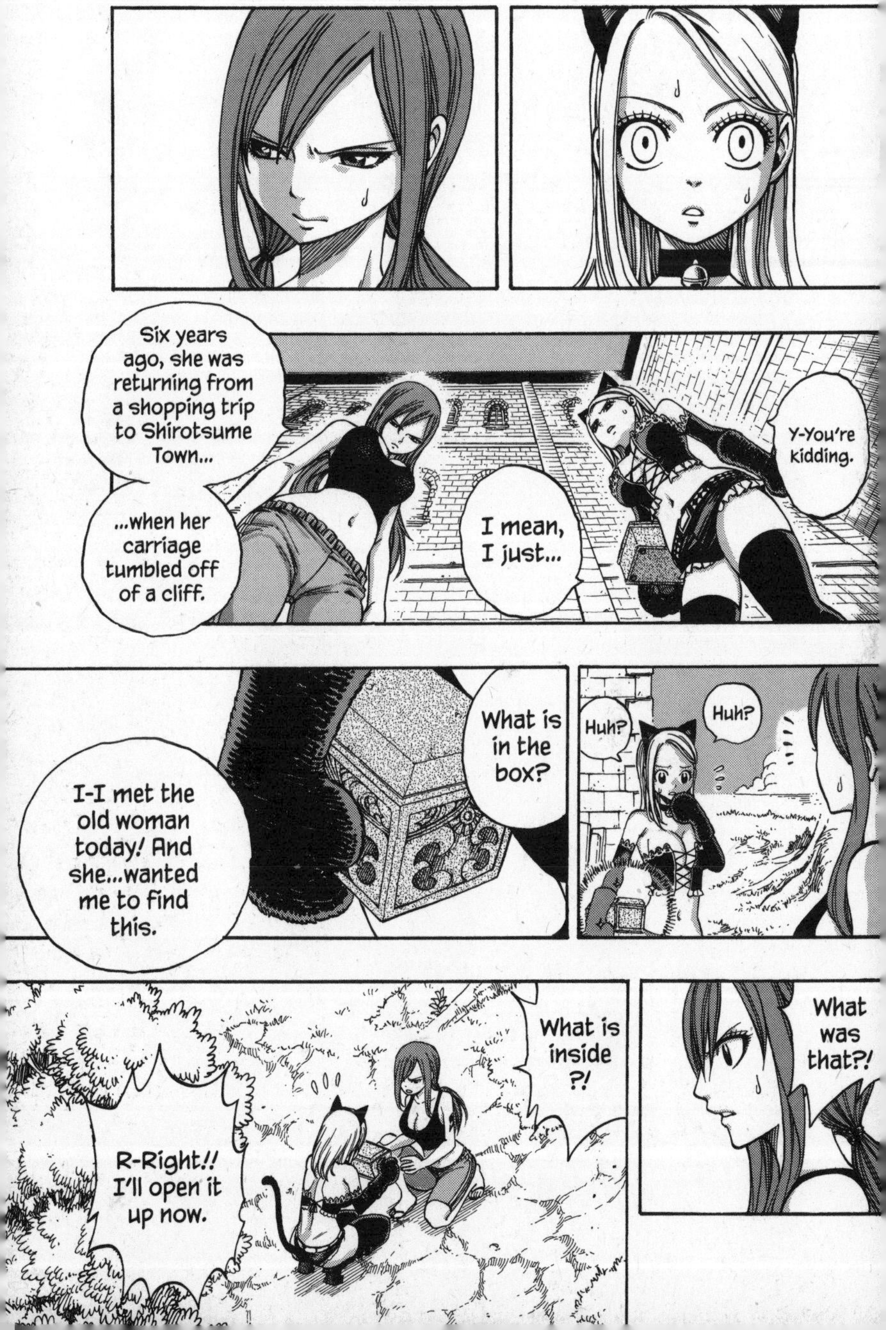
Y-You're kidding.
I mean, I just...
Six years ago, she was returning from a shopping trip to Shirotsume Town...
...when her carriage tumbled off of a cliff.
Huh?
Huh?
What is in the box?
I-I met the old woman today! And she...wanted me to find this.
What was that?!
What is inside ?!
R-Right!! I'll open it up now.

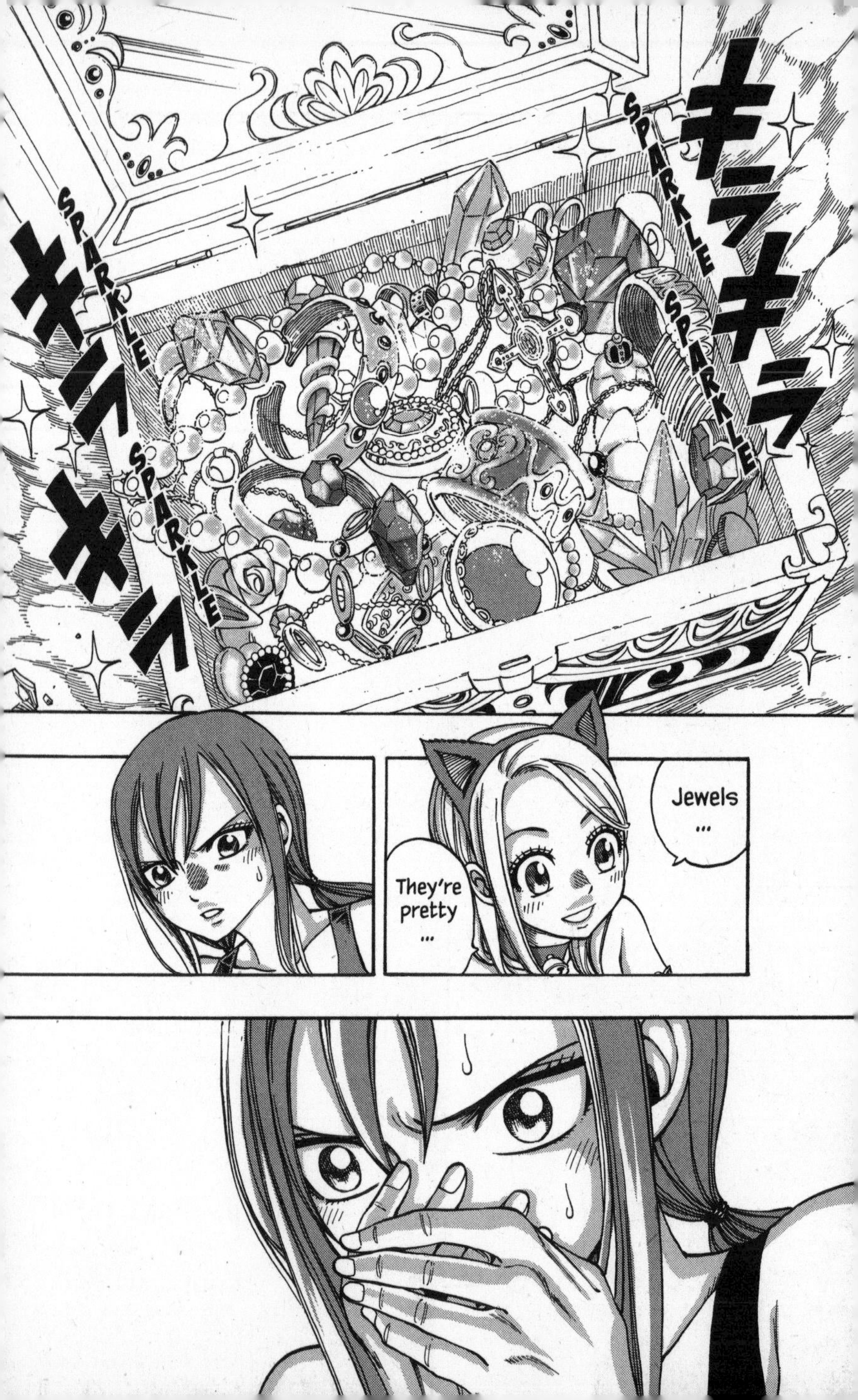
キラキラ
SPARKLE SPARKLE
キランキラン
SPARKLE SPARKLE
Jewels ...
They're pretty ...

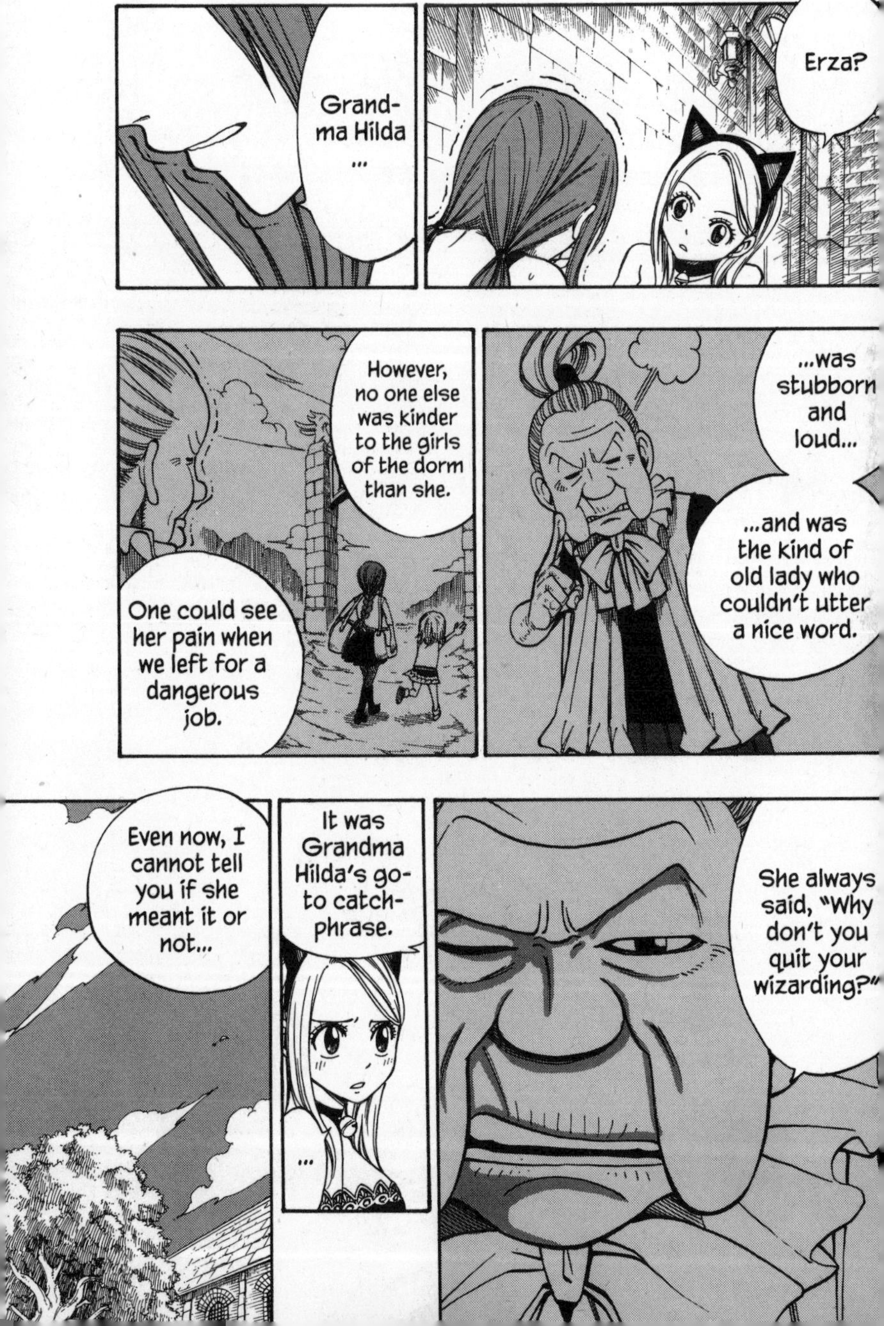
Erza?
Grandma Hilda ...
...was stubborn and loud...
...and was the kind of old lady who couldn't utter a nice word.
However, no one else was kinder to the girls of the dorm than she.
One could see her pain when we left for a dangerous job.
She always said, "Why don't you quit your wizarding?"
It was Grandma Hilda's go-to catch-phrase.
...
Even now, I cannot tell you if she meant it or not...

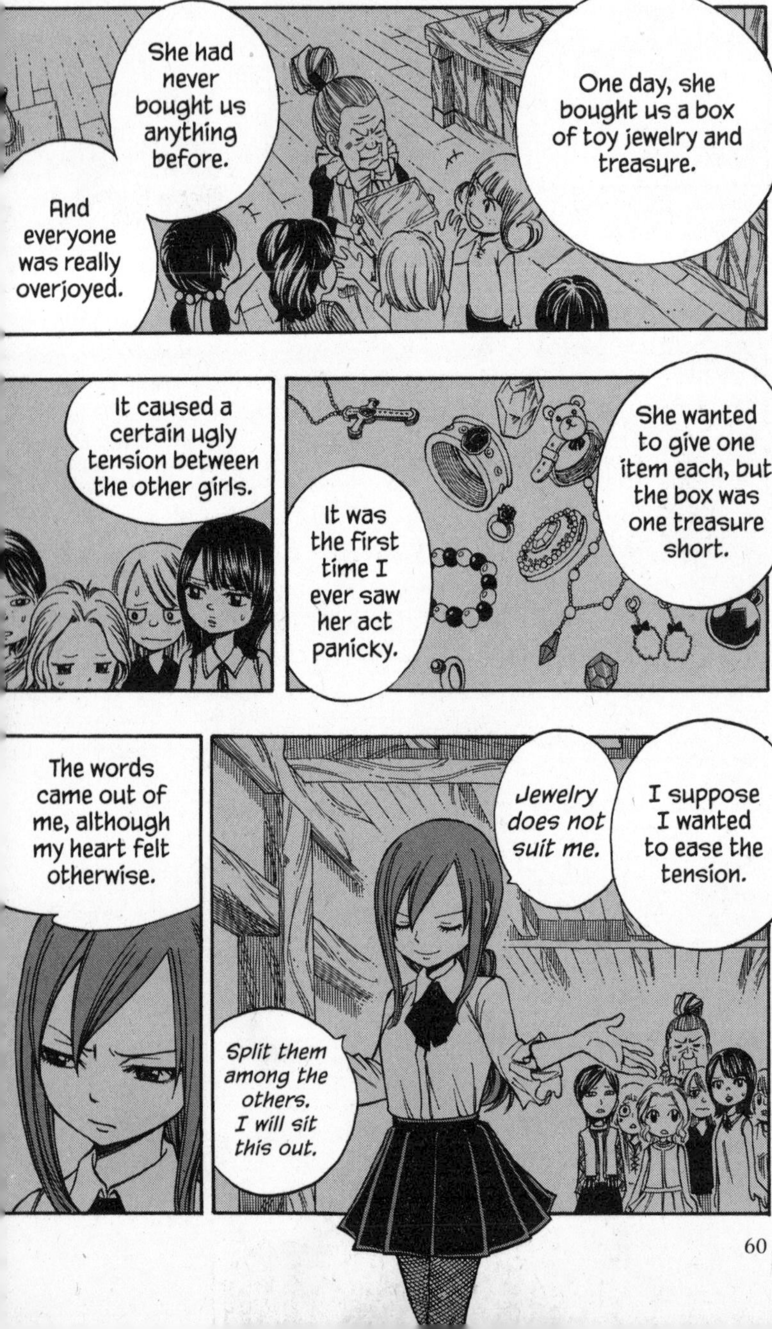
One day, she bought us a box of toy jewelry and treasure.
She had never bought us anything before.
And everyone was really overjoyed.
She wanted to give one item each, but the box was one treasure short.
It was the first time I ever saw her act panicky.
It caused a certain ugly tension between the other girls.
I suppose I wanted to ease the tension.
Jewelry does not suit me.
Split them among the others. I will sit this out.
The words came out of me, although my heart felt otherwise.

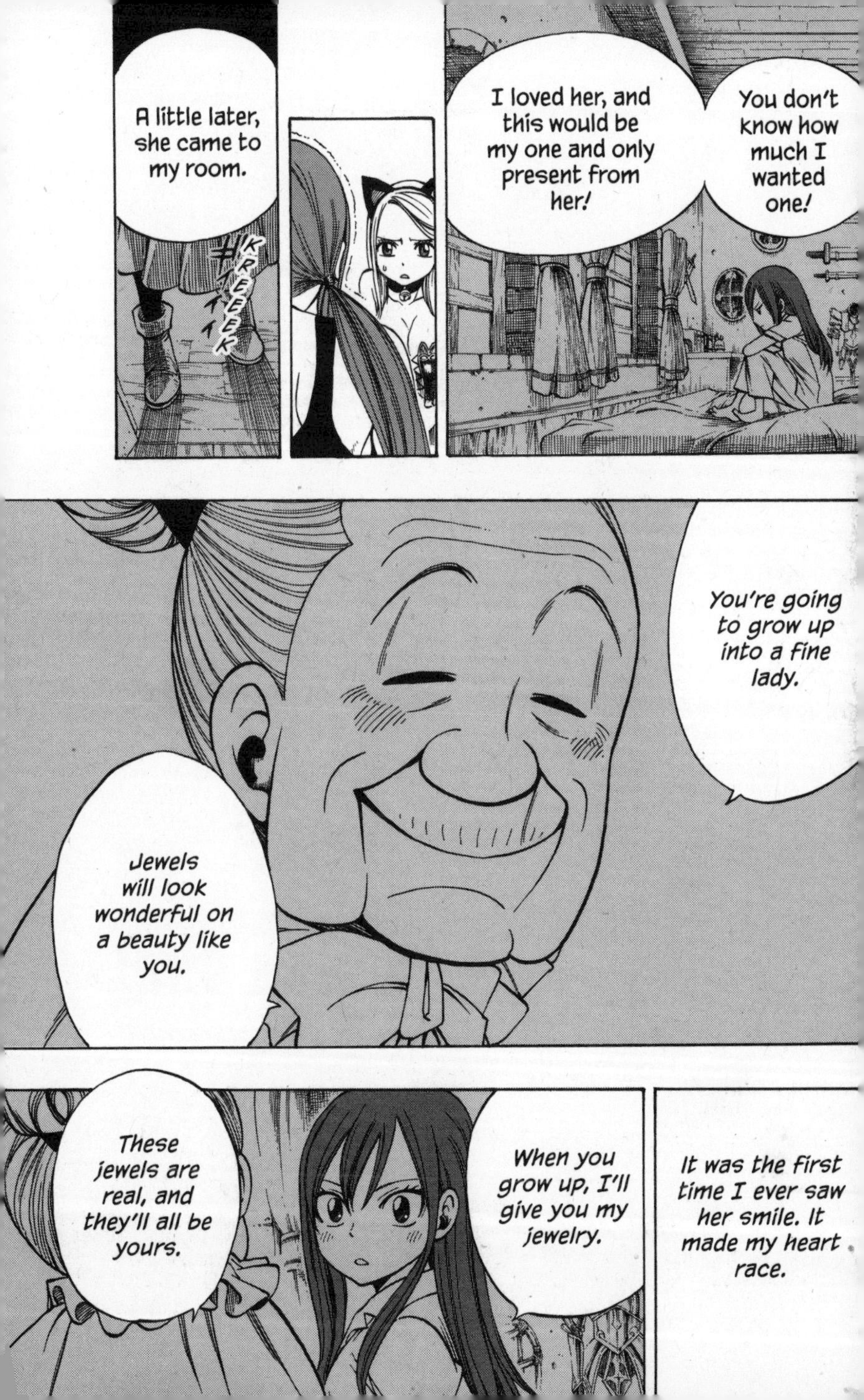
You don't know how much I wanted one!
I loved her, and this would be my one and only present from her!
A little later, she came to my room.
KREEEK
You're going to grow up into a fine lady.
Jewels will look wonderful on a beauty like you.
It was the first time I ever saw her smile. It made my heart race.
When you grow up, I'll give you my jewelry.
These jewels are real, and they'll all be yours.

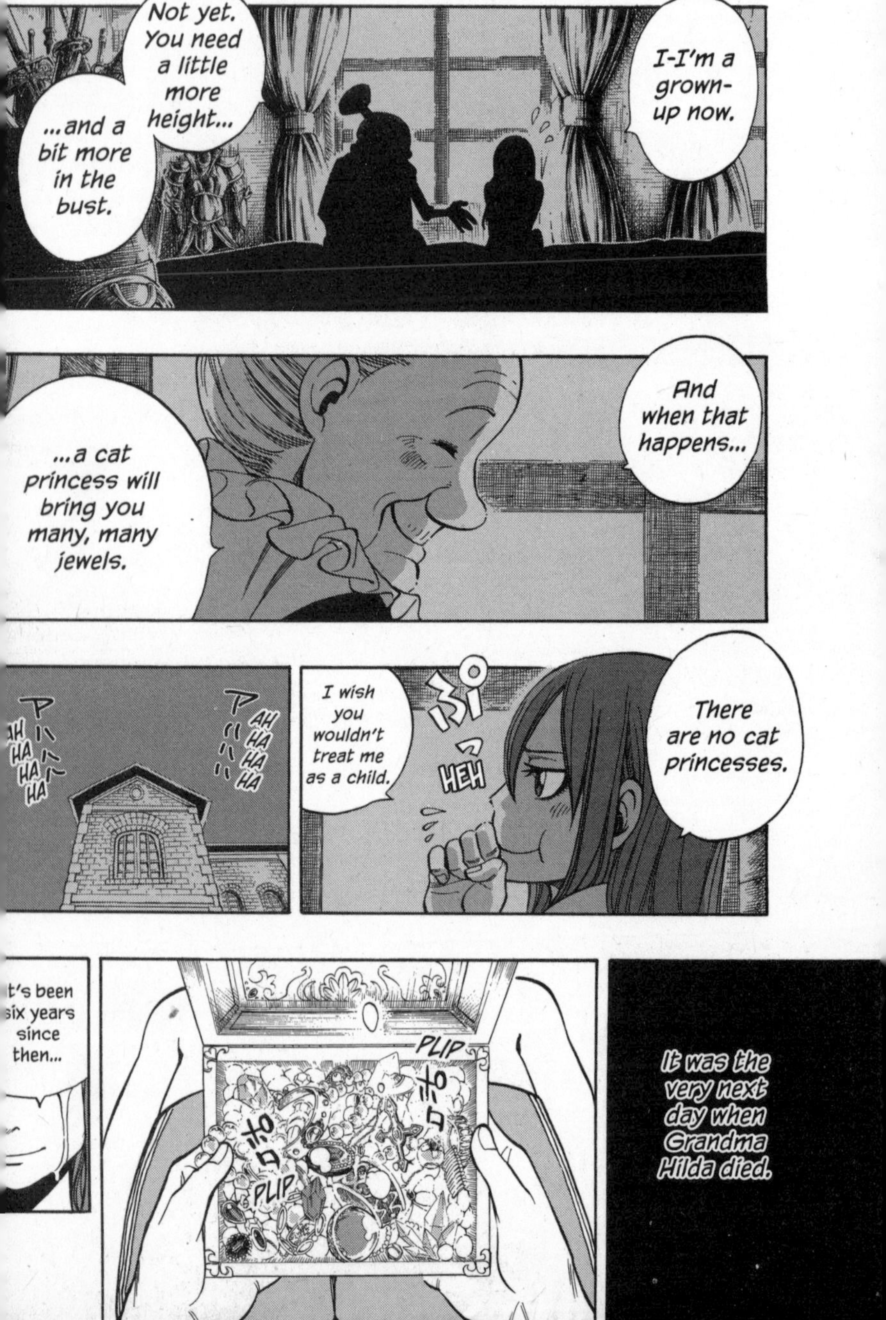
I-I'm a grown-up now.
Not yet. You need a little more height...
...and a bit more in the bust.
And when that happens...
...a cat princess will bring you many, many jewels.
There are no cat princesses.
ぷっ HEH
I wish you wouldn't treat me as a child.
アハハハ AH HA HA HA
アハハハ AH HA HA HA
It was the very next day when Grandma Hilda died.
PLIP
ポロ
ポロ
PLIP
t's been six years since then...

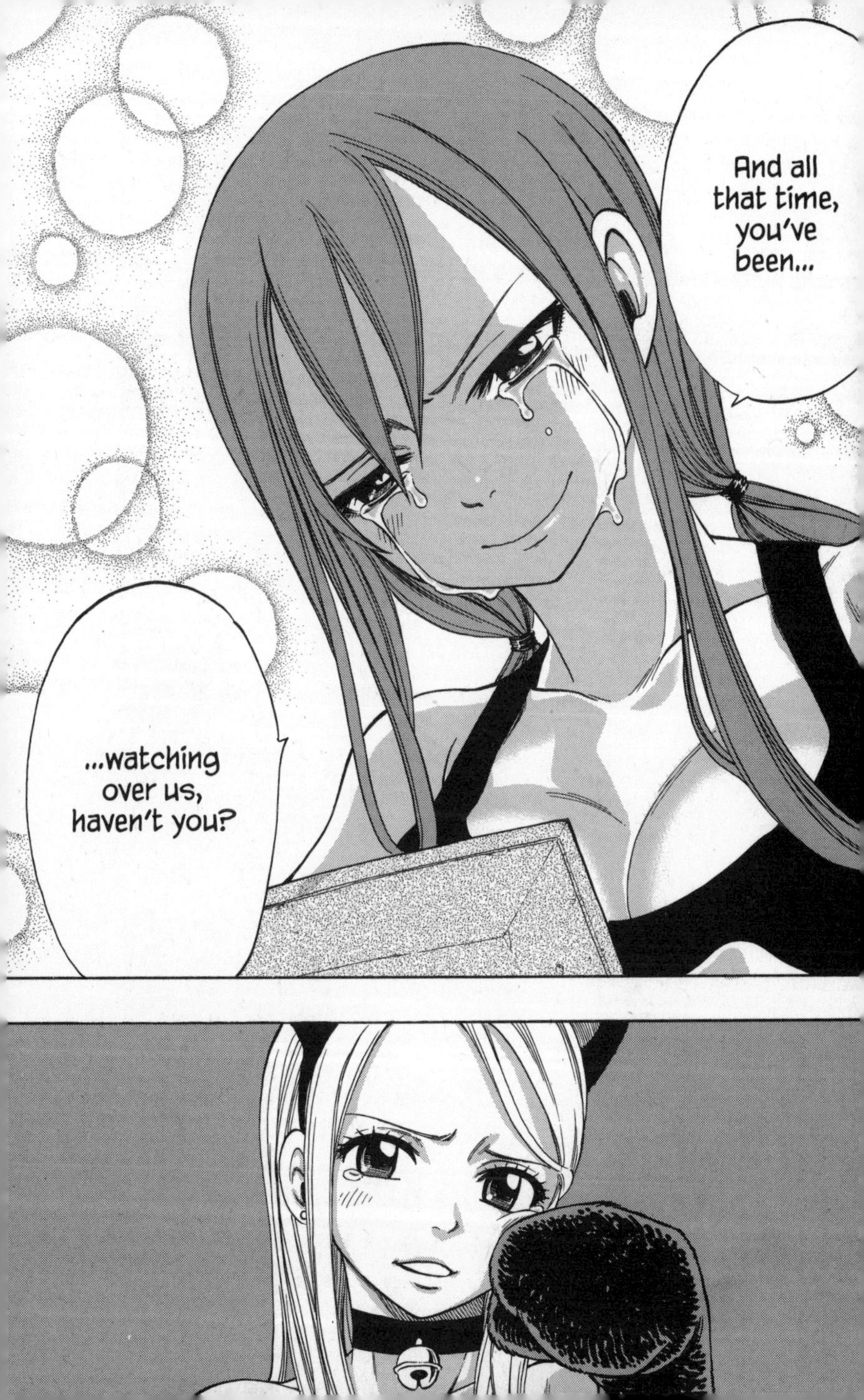

And all that time, you've been...
...watching over us, haven't you?

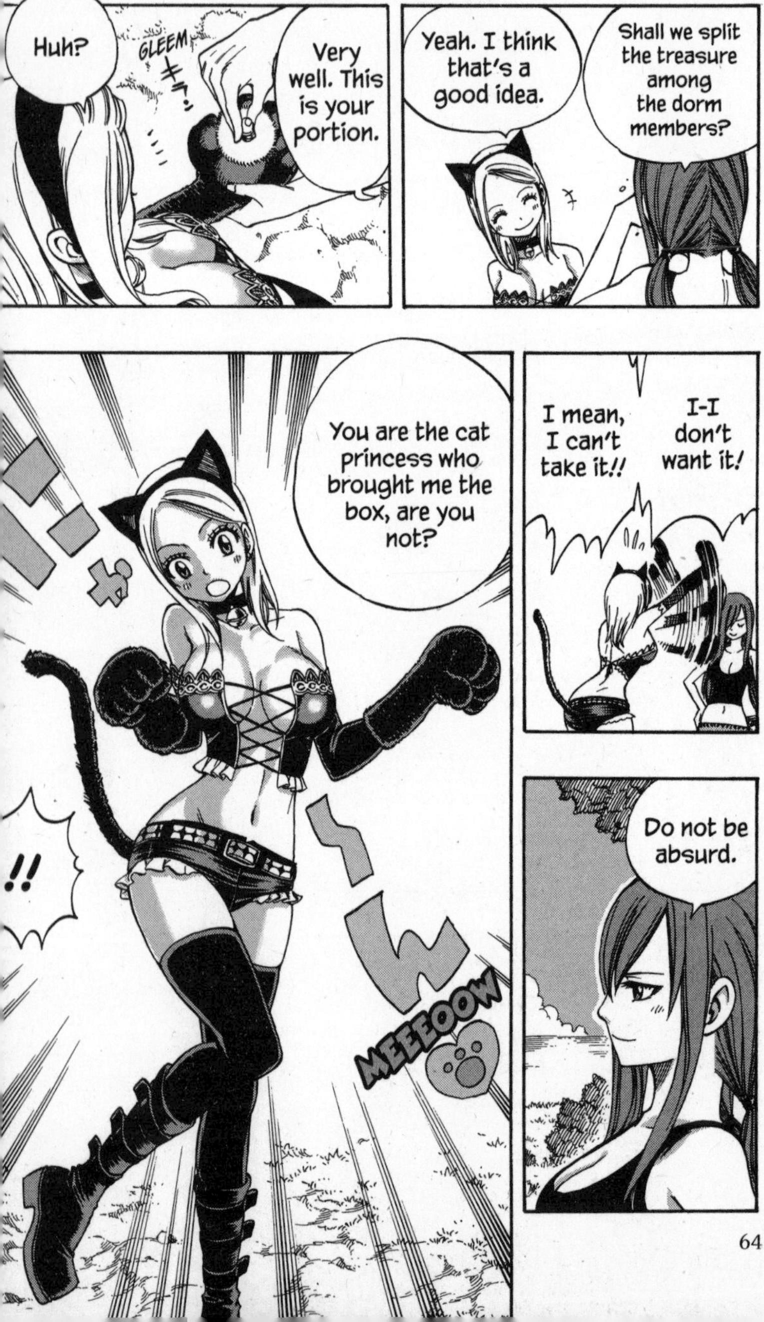
Shall we split the treasure among the dorm members?
Yeah. I think that's a good idea.
Very well. This is your portion.
GLEEM
Huh?
I-I don't want it!
I mean, I can't take it!!
Do not be absurd.
You are the cat princess who brought me the box, are you not?
MEEEOOW
!!

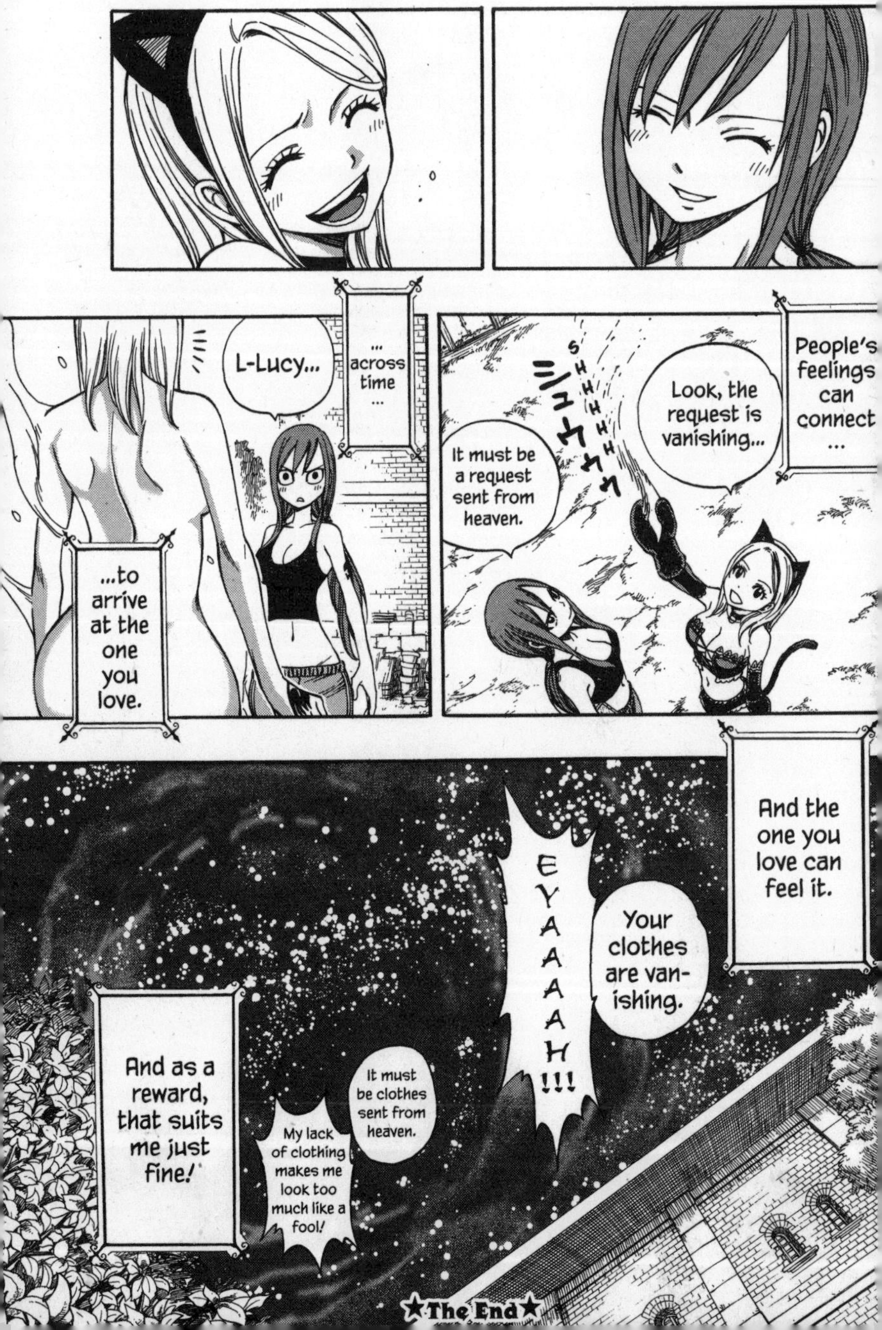
People's feelings can connect ...
Look, the request is vanishing...
シュウウウ
SHHHHHH
It must be a request sent from heaven.
... across time ...
L-Lucy...
...to arrive at the one you love.
And the one you love can feel it.
Your clothes are van-ishing.
EYAAAAAH!!!
It must be clothes sent from heaven.
My lack of clothing makes me look too much like a fool!
And as a reward, that suits me just fine!
★The End★

FT☆S

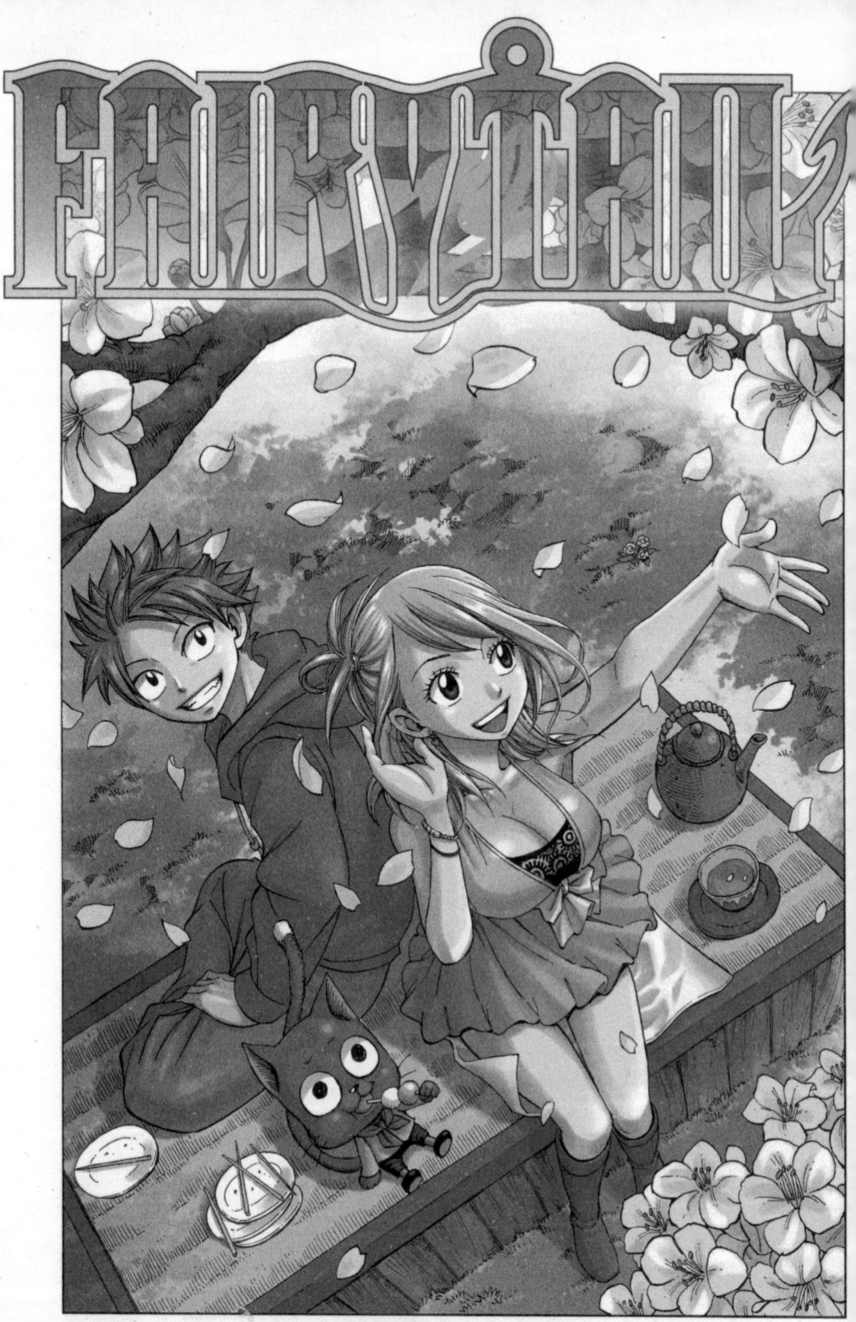
FAIRY TAIL

Rainbow Cherry Blossoms

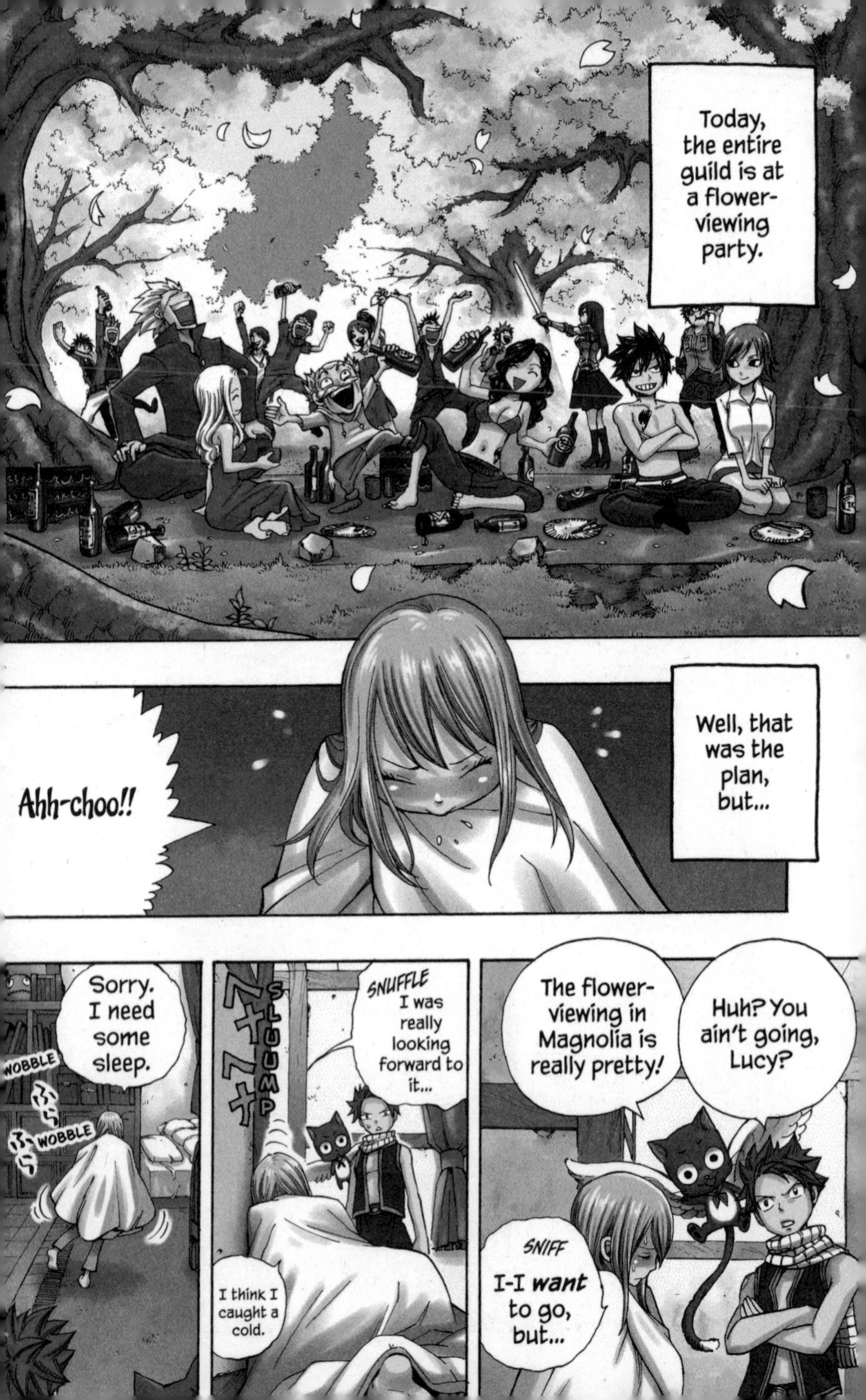

Today, the entire guild is at a flower-viewing party.
Well, that was the plan, but...
Ahh-choo!!
Huh? You ain't going, Lucy?
The flower-viewing in Magnolia is really pretty!
SNIFF
I-I *want* to go, but...
SNUFFLE
I was really looking forward to it...
SLUUMP
I think I caught a cold.
Sorry. I need some sleep.
WOBBLE
WOBBLE

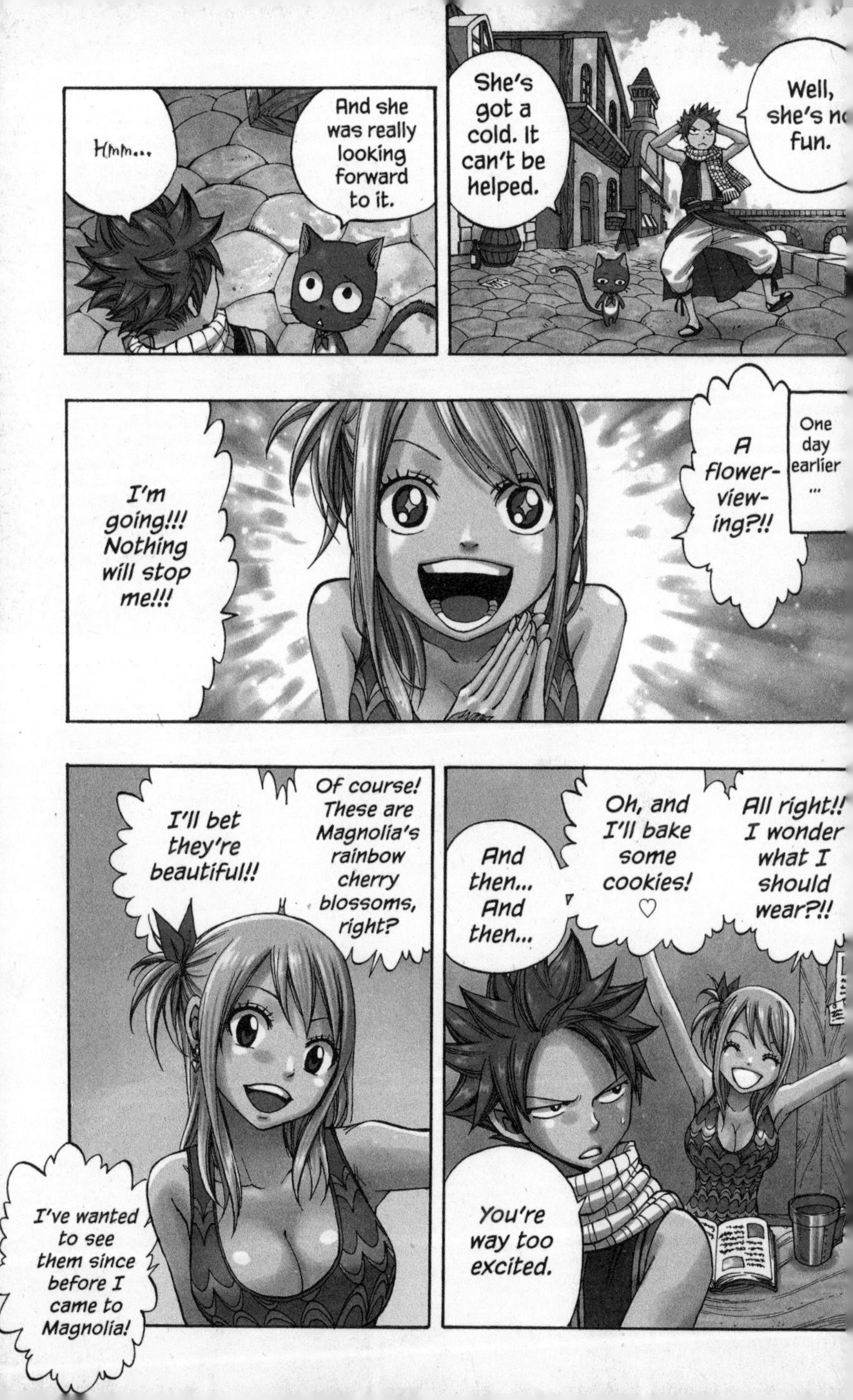

Well, she's no fun.
She's got a cold. It can't be helped.
And she was really looking forward to it.
Hmm...
One day earlier...
A flower-viewing?!!
I'm going!!! Nothing will stop me!!!
All right!! I wonder what I should wear?!!
Oh, and I'll bake some cookies! ♡
And then... And then...
You're way too excited.
Of course! These are Magnolia's rainbow cherry blossoms, right?
I'll bet they're beautiful!!
I've wanted to see them since before I came to Magnolia!

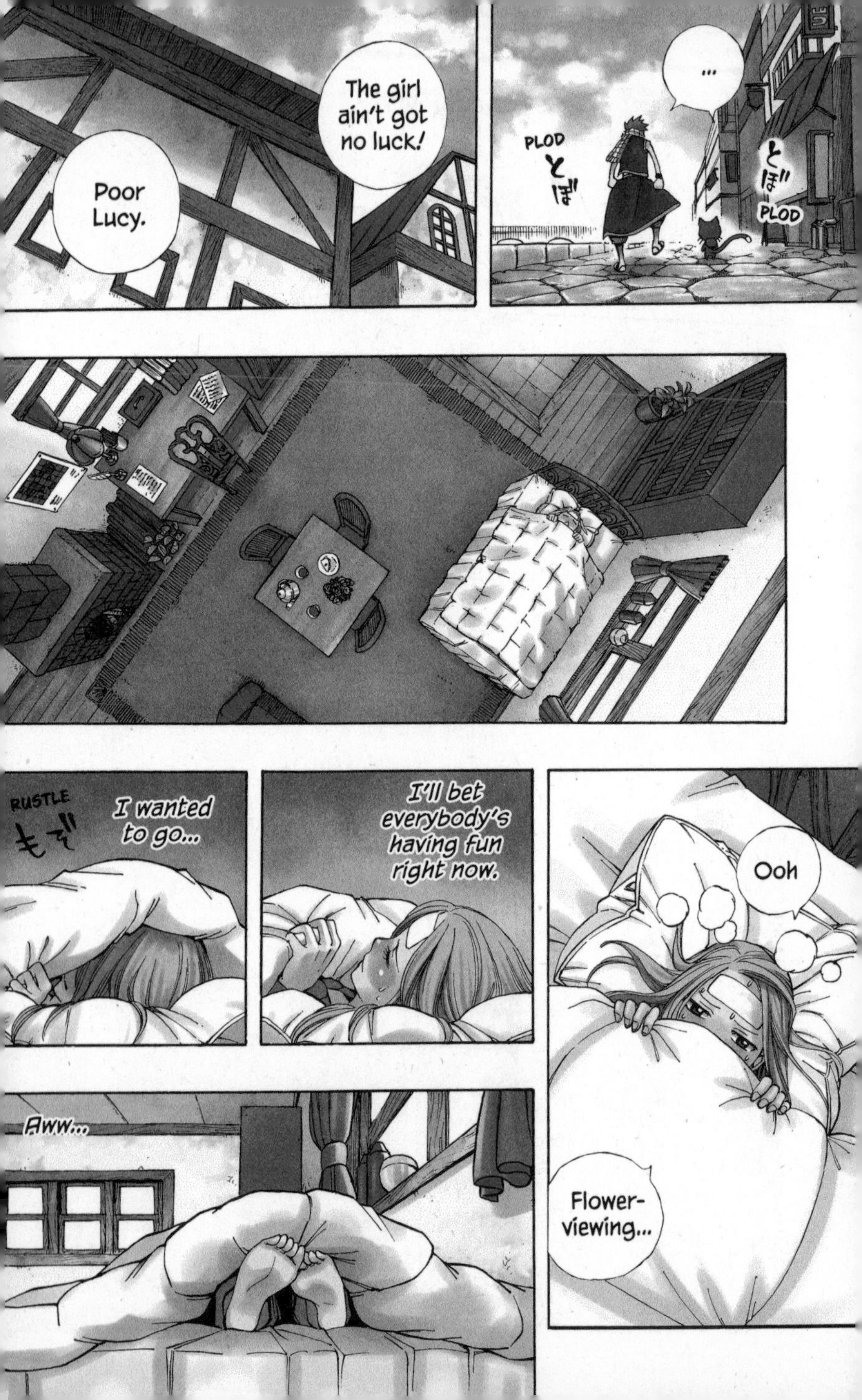
...
PLOD
とぼ
とぼ
PLOD
The girl ain't got no luck!
Poor Lucy.
Ooh
Flower-viewing...
I'll bet everybody's having fun right now.
RUSTLE
もぞ
I wanted to go...
Aww...

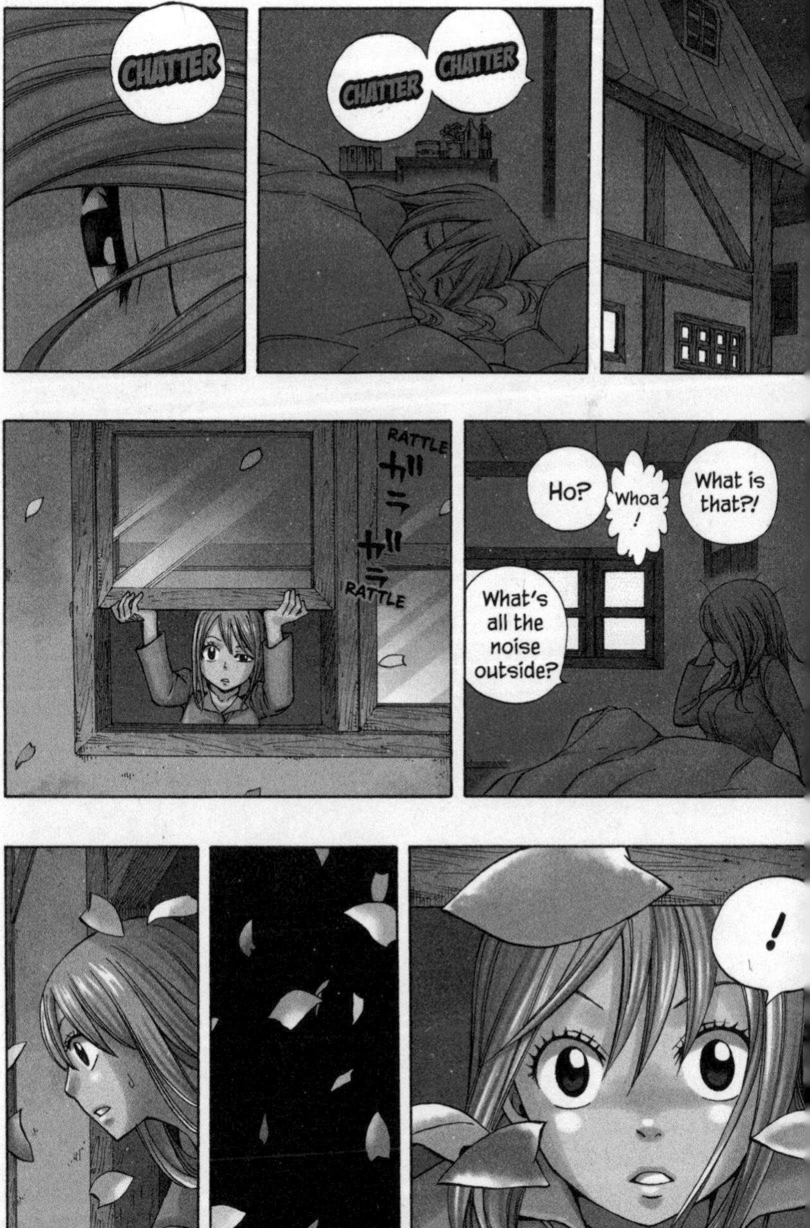
CHATTER
CHATTER
CHATTER
What is that?!
Whoa!
Ho?
What's all the noise outside?
RATTLE
ガラ
ガラ
RATTLE
!

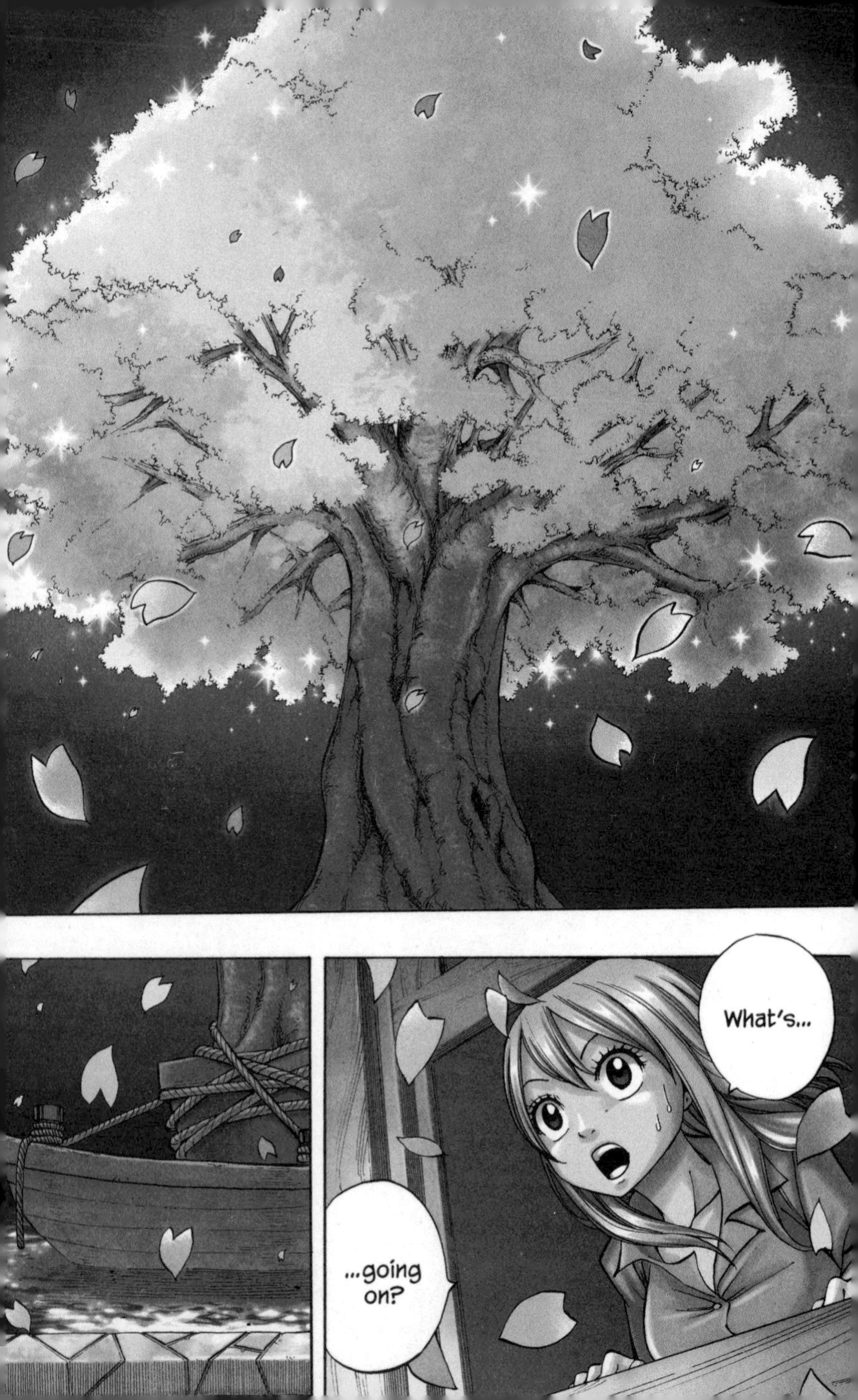
What's...
...going on?

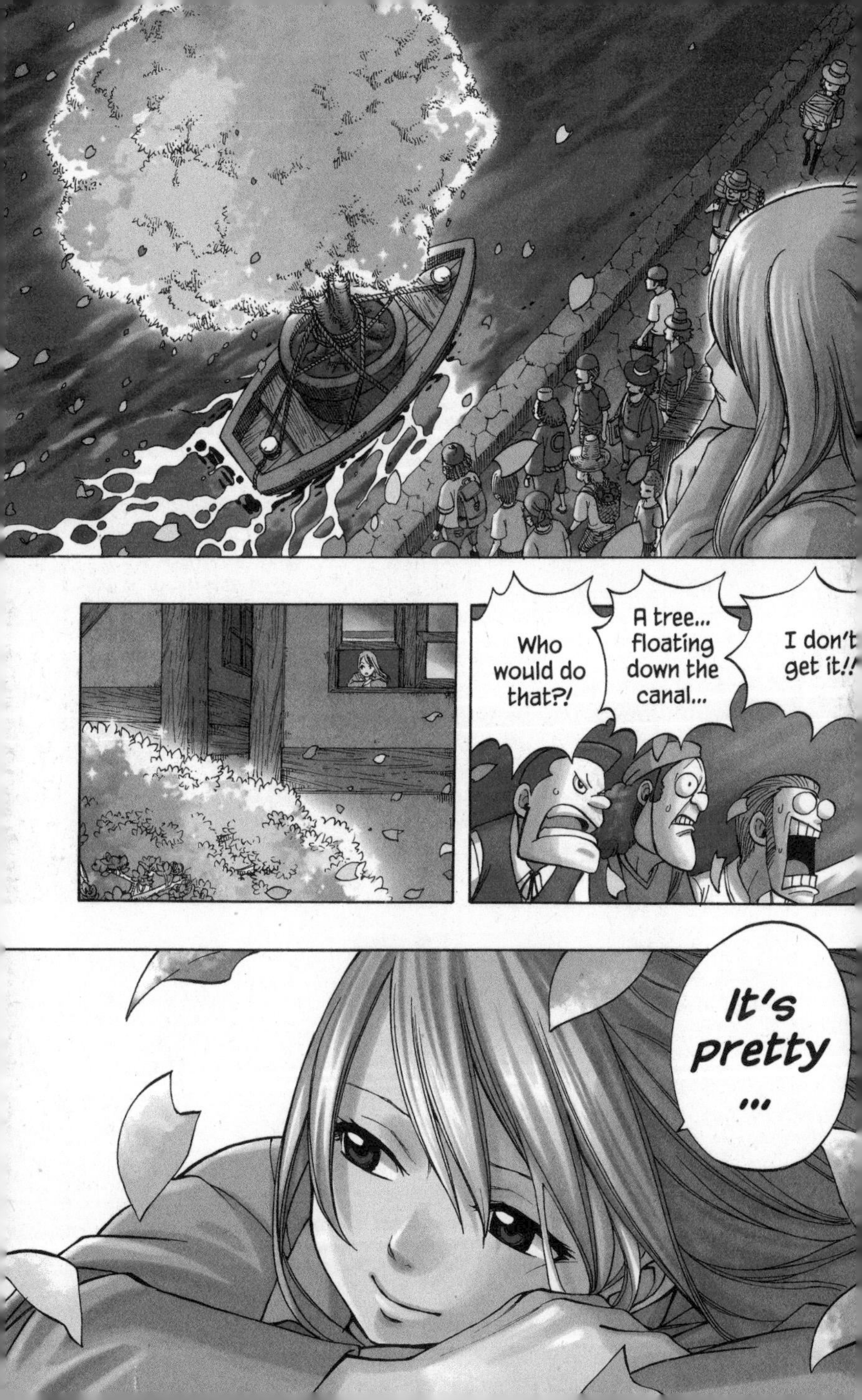
I don't get it!!
A tree... floating down the canal...
Who would do that?!
It's pretty ...

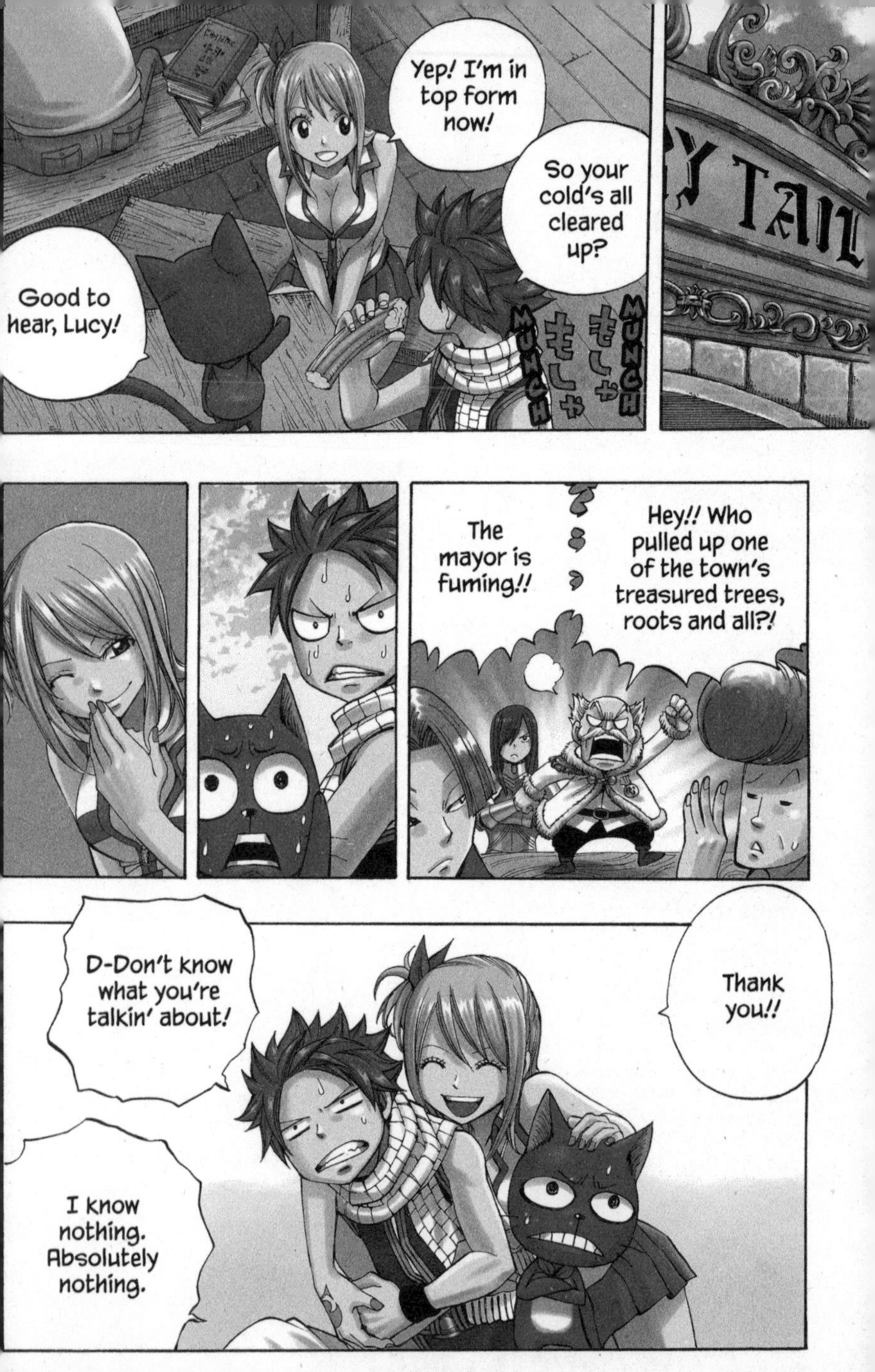
So your cold's all cleared up?
Yep! I'm in top form now!
MUNCH
MUNCH
Good to hear, Lucy!
Hey!! Who pulled up one of the town's treasured trees, roots and all?!
The mayor is fuming!!
Thank you!!
D-Don't know what you're talkin' about!
I know nothing. Absolutely nothing.

★The End★

FT☆S

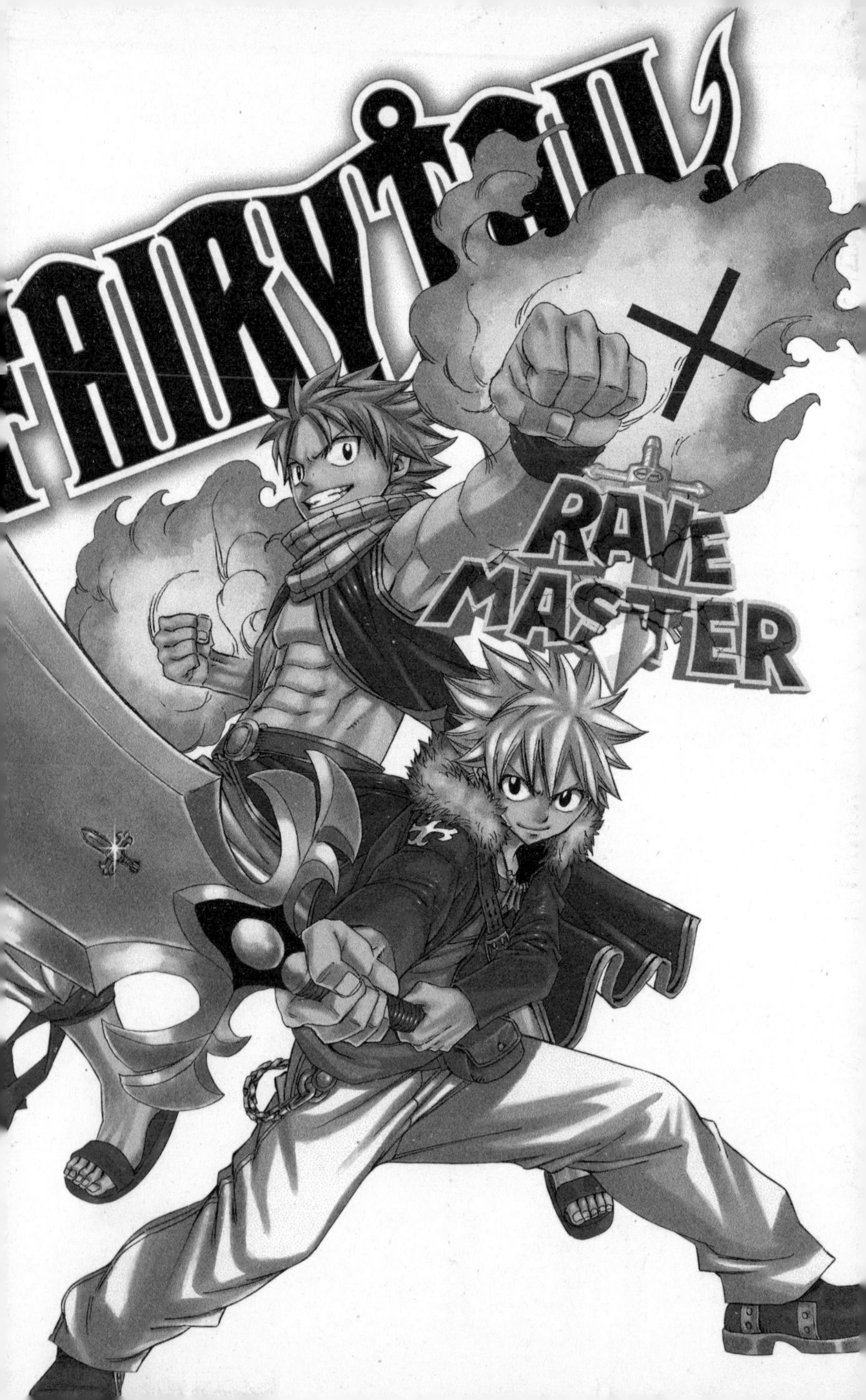
FAIRY TAIL ×
RAVE MASTER

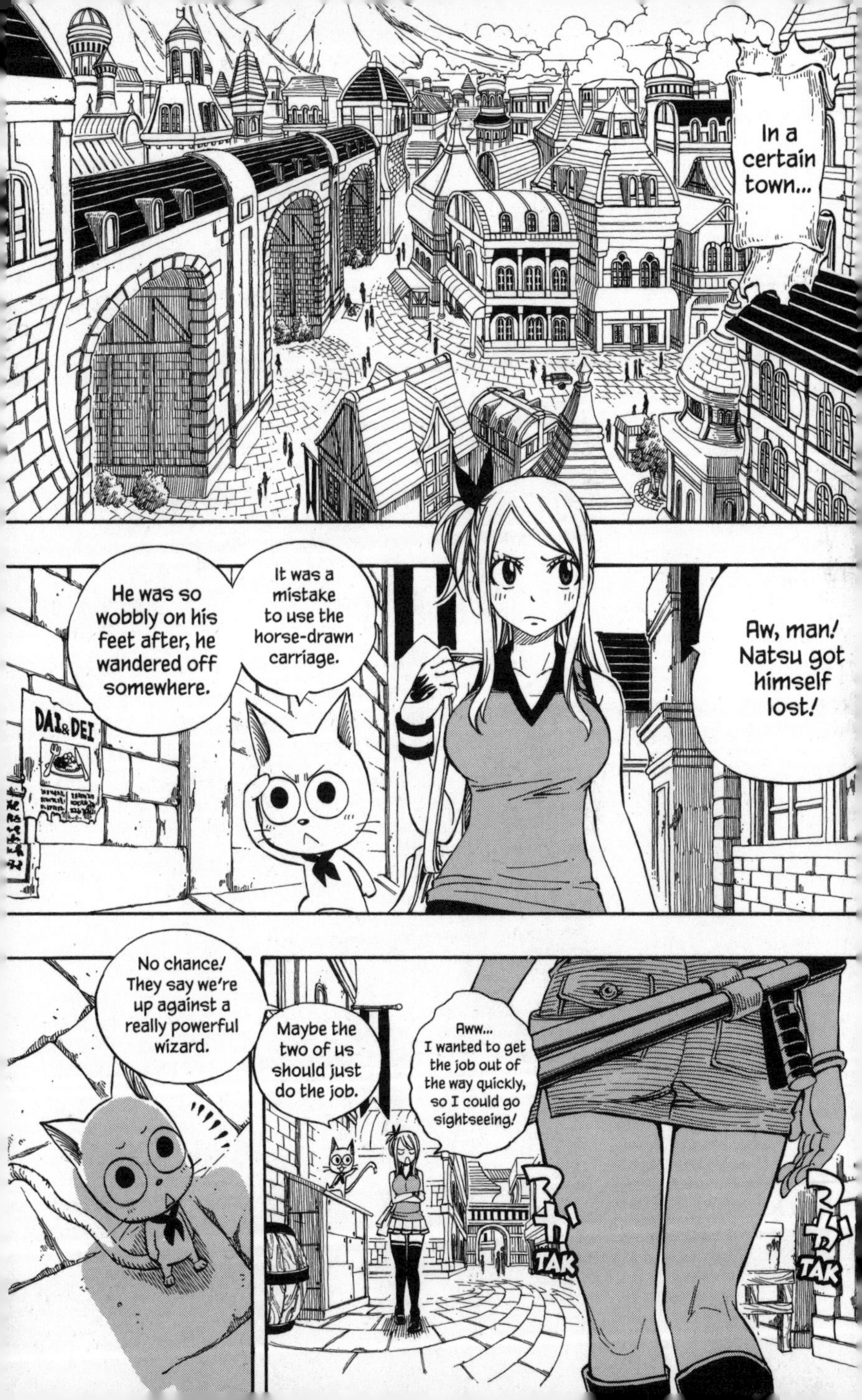
In a certain town...
Aw, man! Natsu got himself lost!
It was a mistake to use the horse-drawn carriage.
He was so wobbly on his feet after, he wandered off somewhere.
DAI&DEI
Aww... I wanted to get the job out of the way quickly, so I could go sightseeing!
Maybe the two of us should just do the job.
TAK
TAK
No chance! They say we're up against a really powerful wizard.

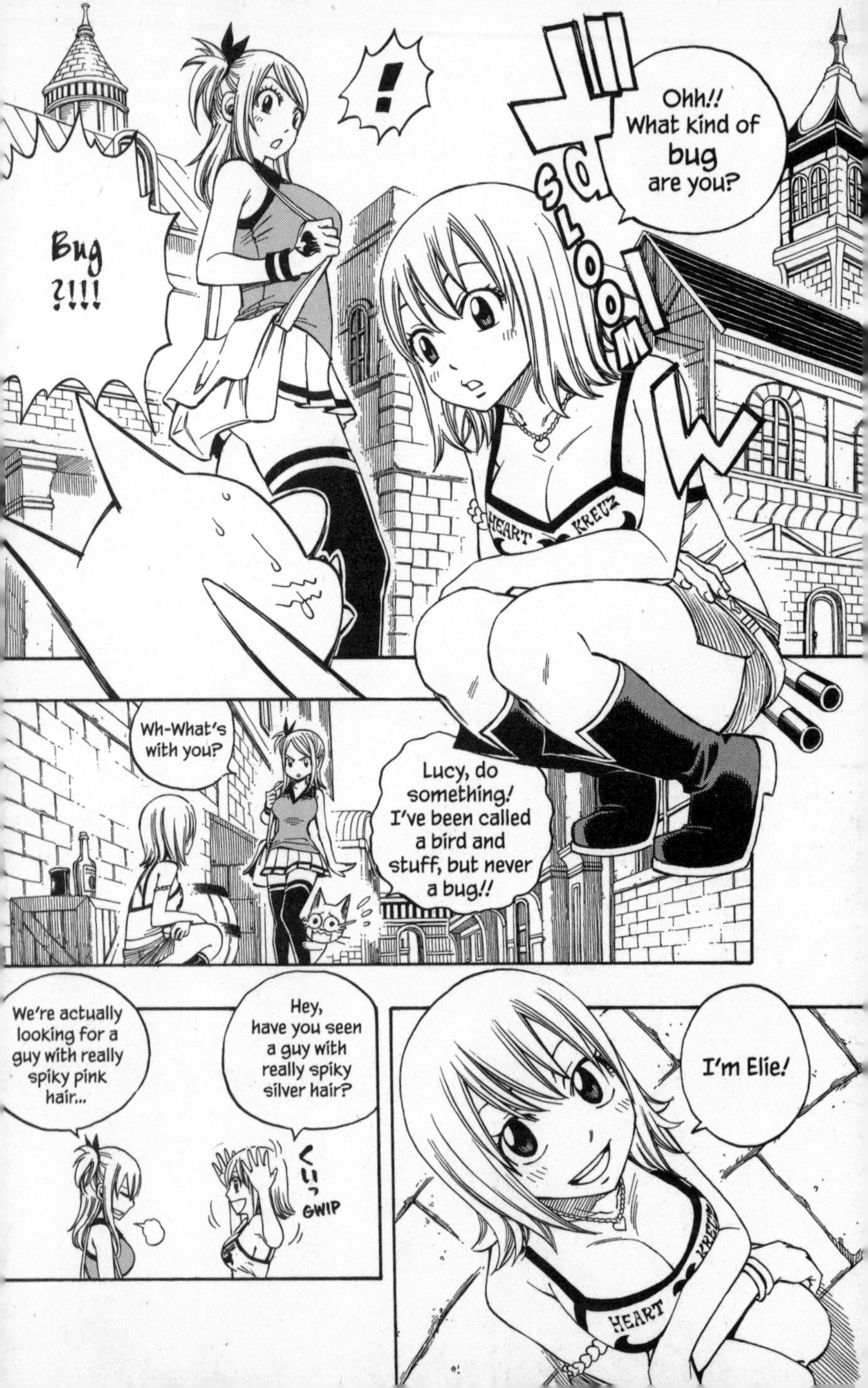
Ohh!! What kind of bug are you?
SLOOOM
!
Bug ?!!!
Wh-What's with you?
Lucy, do something! I've been called a bird and stuff, but never a bug!!
I'm Elie!
Hey, have you seen a guy with really spiky silver hair?
くいっ GWIP
We're actually looking for a guy with really spiky pink hair...

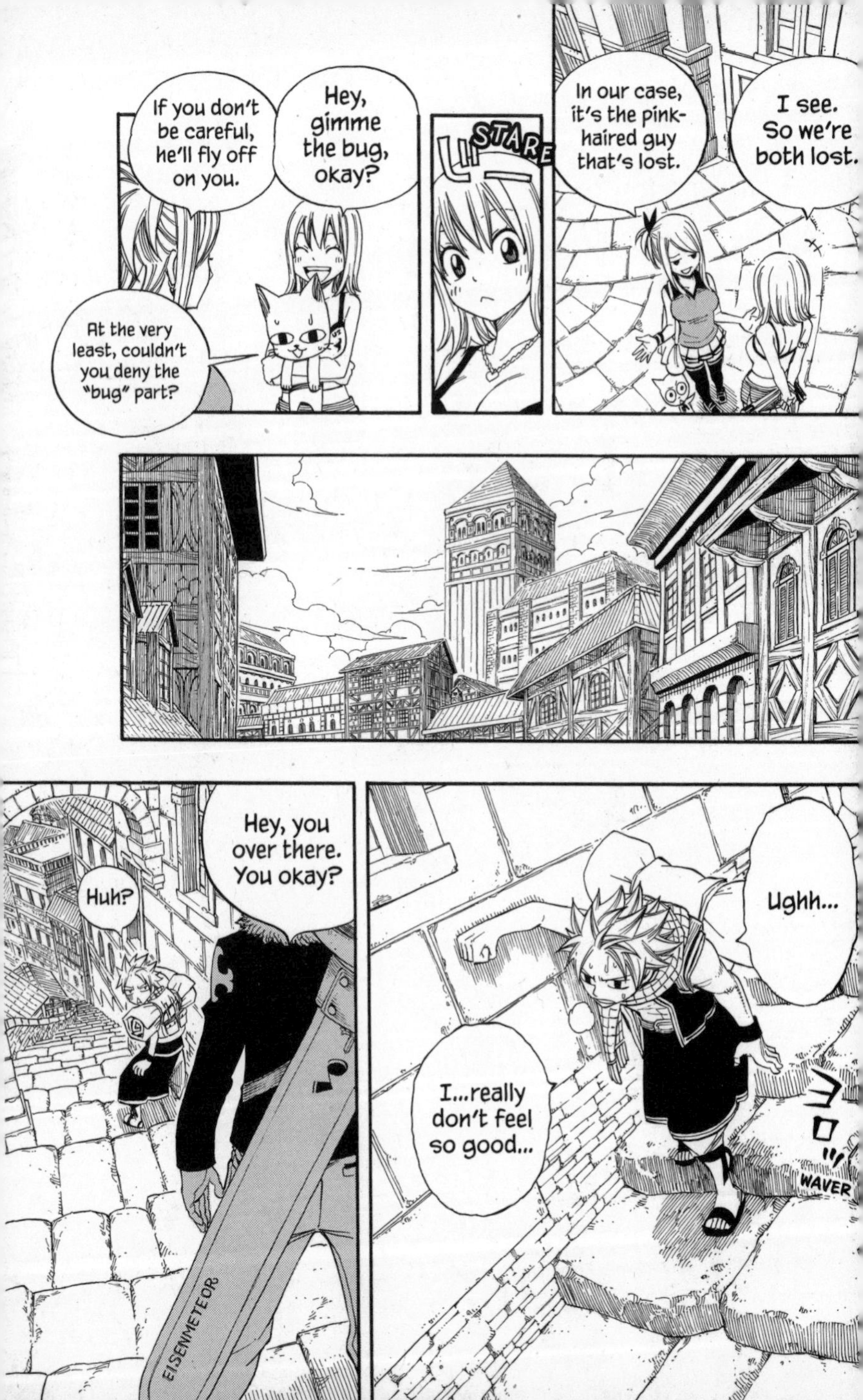
I see. So we're both lost.
In our case, it's the pink-haired guy that's lost.
STARE
Hey, gimme the bug, okay?
If you don't be careful, he'll fly off on you.
At the very least, couldn't you deny the "bug" part?
Ughh...
I...really don't feel so good...
WAVER
Hey, you over there. You okay?
Huh?
EISENMETEOR

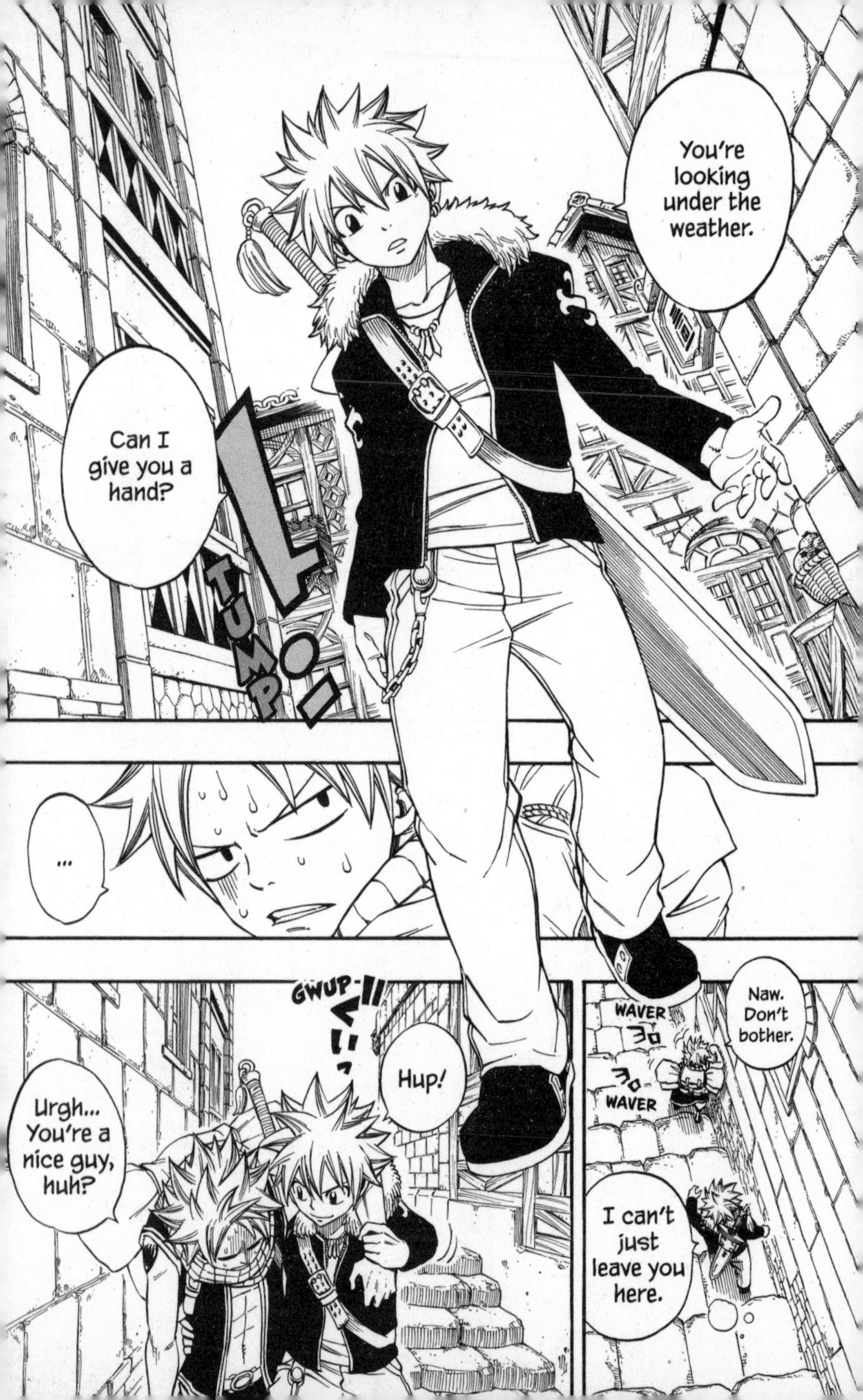
You're looking under the weather.
Can I give you a hand?
TUMP
...
Naw. Don't bother.
WAVER
WAVER
I can't just leave you here.
GWUP-!!
Hup!
Urgh... You're a nice guy, huh?

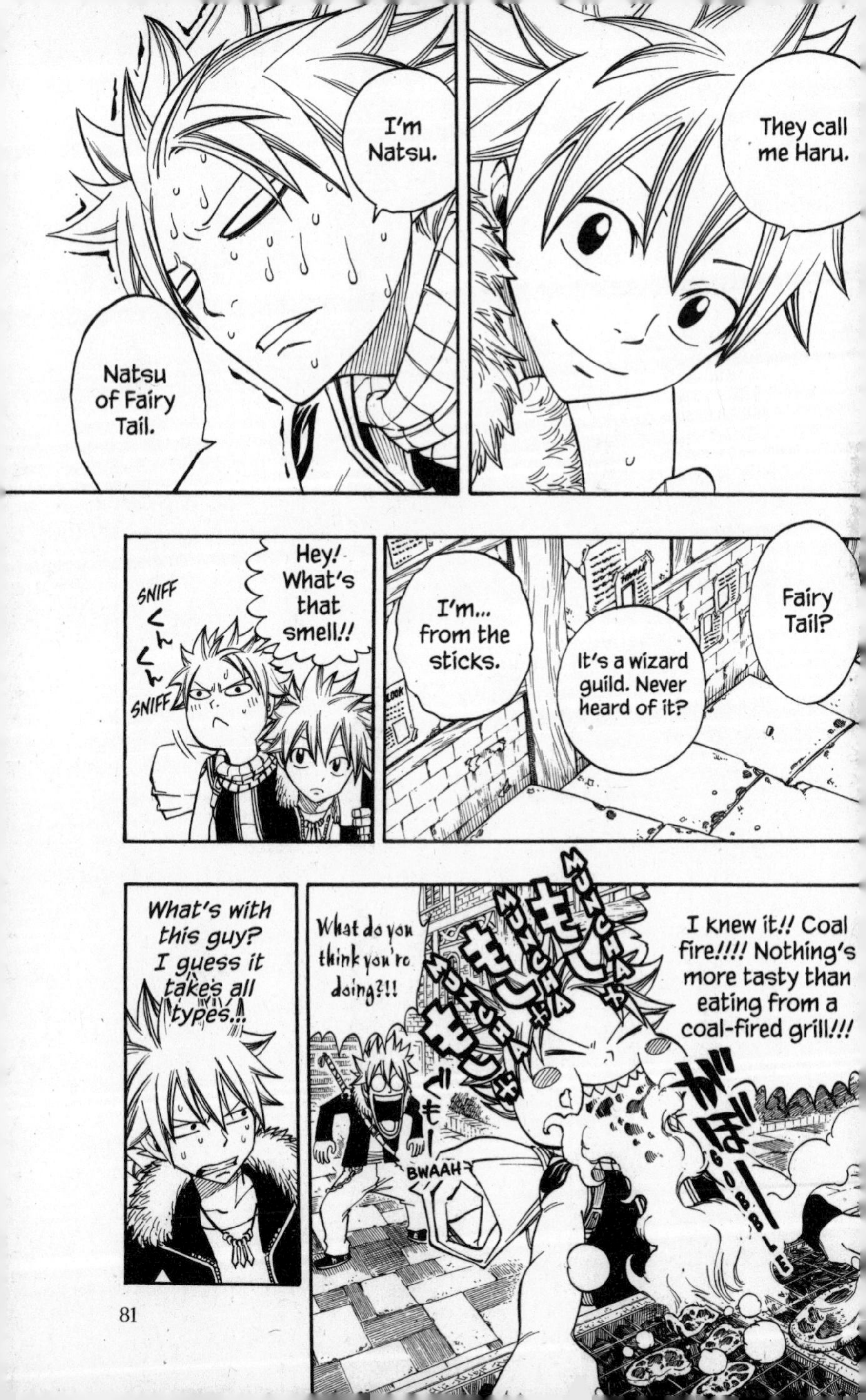
They call me Haru.
I'm Natsu.
Natsu of Fairy Tail.
Fairy Tail?
It's a wizard guild. Never heard of it?
I'm... from the sticks.
Hey! What's that smell!!
SNIFF
SNIFF
I knew it!! Coal fire!!!! Nothing's more tasty than eating from a coal-fired grill!!!
MUNCHA
MUNCHA
MUNCHA
GOBBLE
What do you think you're doing?!!
BWAAH
What's with this guy? I guess it takes all types...

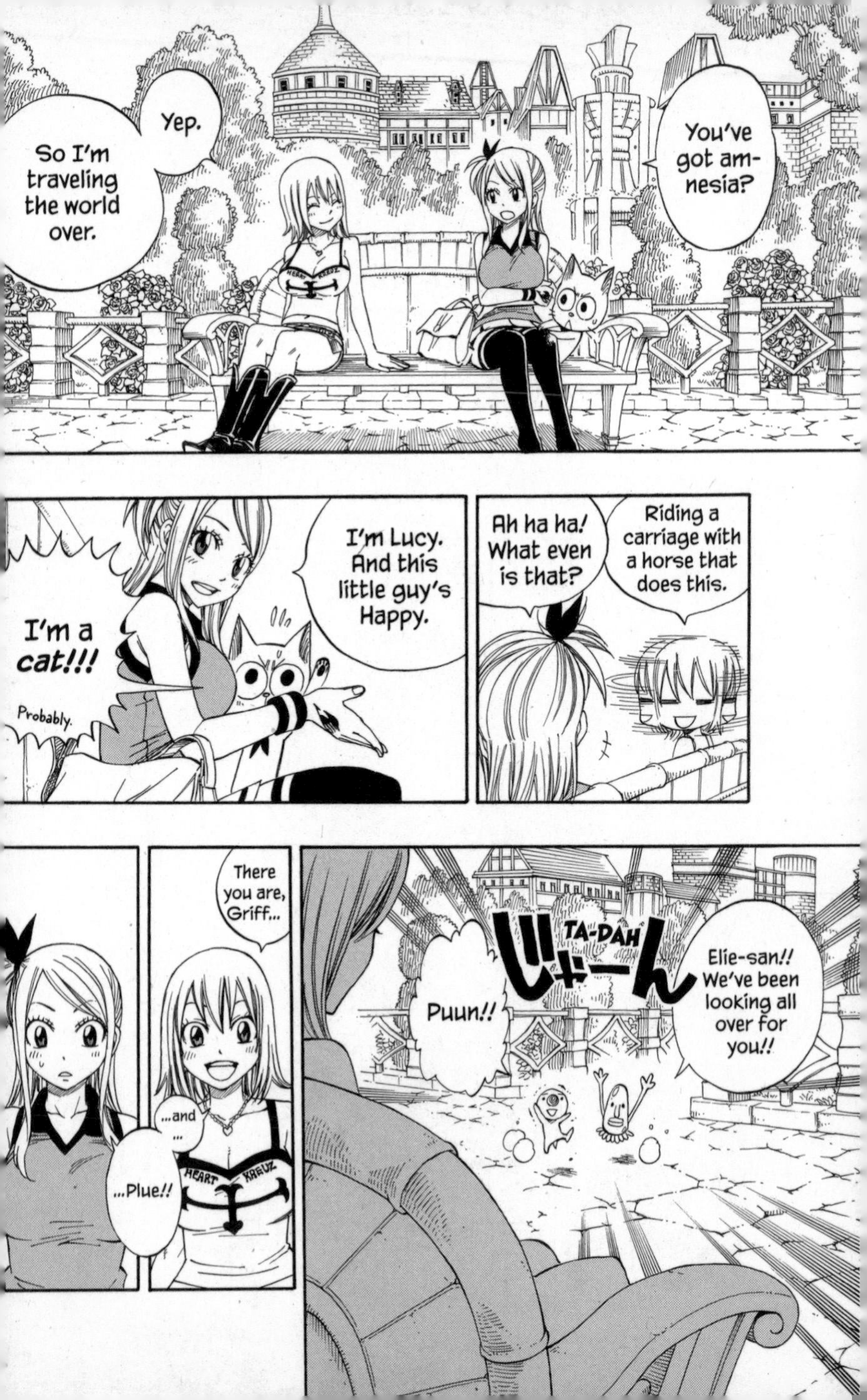
You've got am- nesia?
Yep.
So I'm traveling the world over.
Riding a carriage with a horse that does this.
Ah ha ha! What even is that?
I'm Lucy. And this little guy's Happy.
I'm a cat!!!
Probably.
Elie-san!! We've been looking all over for you!!
TA-DAH
Puun!!
There you are, Griff...
...and ...
...Plue!!

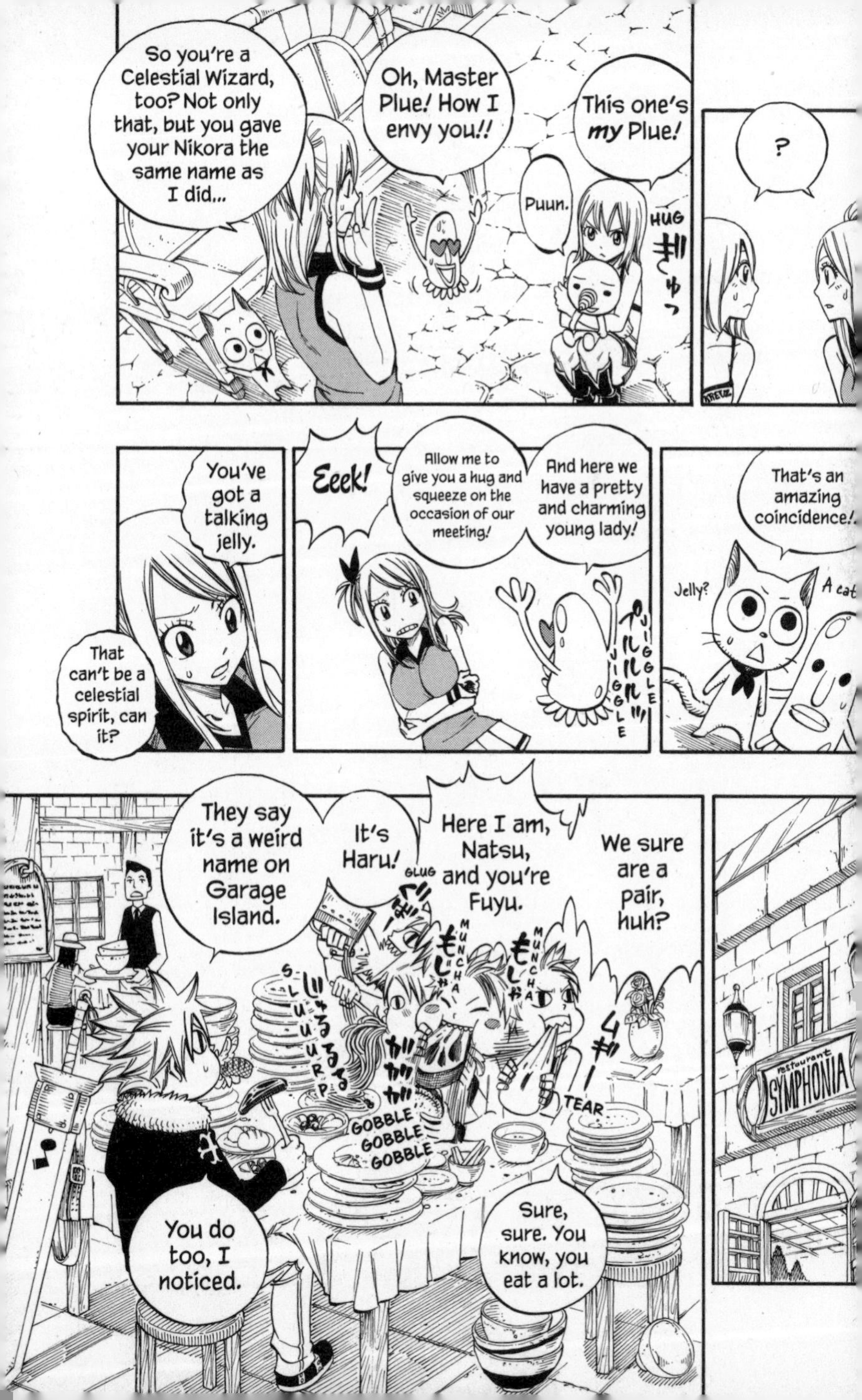
?
This one's *my* Plue!
Oh, Master Plue! How I envy you!!
So you're a Celestial Wizard, too? Not only that, but you gave your Nikora the same name as I did...
Puun.
HUG
That's an amazing coincidence!!
Jelly?
A cat
And here we have a pretty and charming young lady!
Allow me to give you a hug and squeeze on the occasion of our meeting!
Eeek!
JIGGLE
JIGGLE
You've got a talking jelly.
That can't be a celestial spirit, can it?
Restaurant SYMPHONIA
We sure are a pair, huh?
Here I am, Natsu, and you're Fuyu.
It's Haru!
They say it's a weird name on Garage Island.
GLUG
MUNCHA
MUNCHA
SLUUUURP
GOBBLE GOBBLE GOBBLE
TEAR
Sure, sure. You know, you eat a lot.
You do too, I noticed.

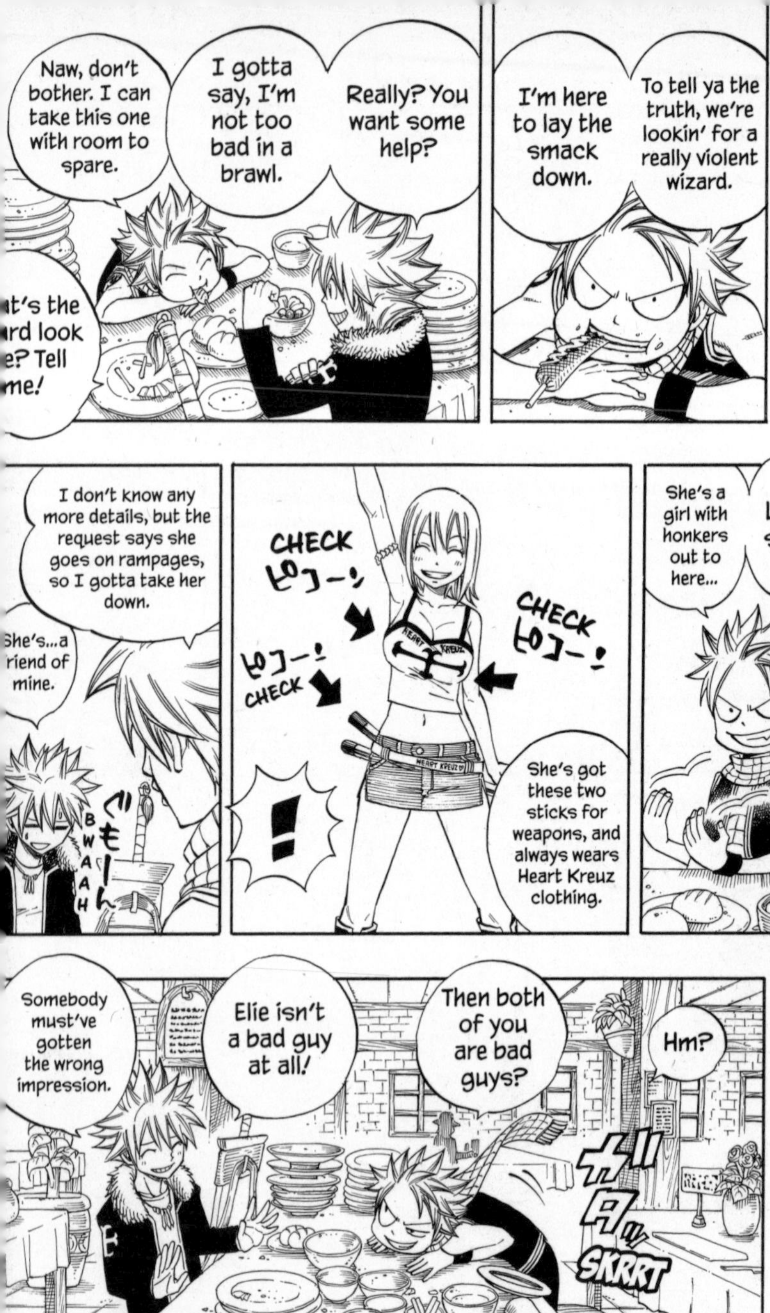
To tell ya the truth, we're lookin' for a really violent wizard.
I'm here to lay the smack down.
Really? You want some help?
I gotta say, I'm not too bad in a brawl.
Naw, don't bother. I can take this one with room to spare.
t's the rd look e? Tell me!
Let's see...
She's a girl with honkers out to here...
CHECK ピコーン
CHECK ピコーン!
ピコーン! CHECK
HEART KREUZ
!
She's got these two sticks for weapons, and always wears Heart Kreuz clothing.
I don't know any more details, but the request says she goes on rampages, so I gotta take her down.
She's...a riend of mine.
BWAAH
Hm?
Then both of you are bad guys?
Elie isn't a bad guy at all!
Somebody must've gotten the wrong impression.
SKRRT

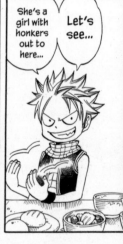

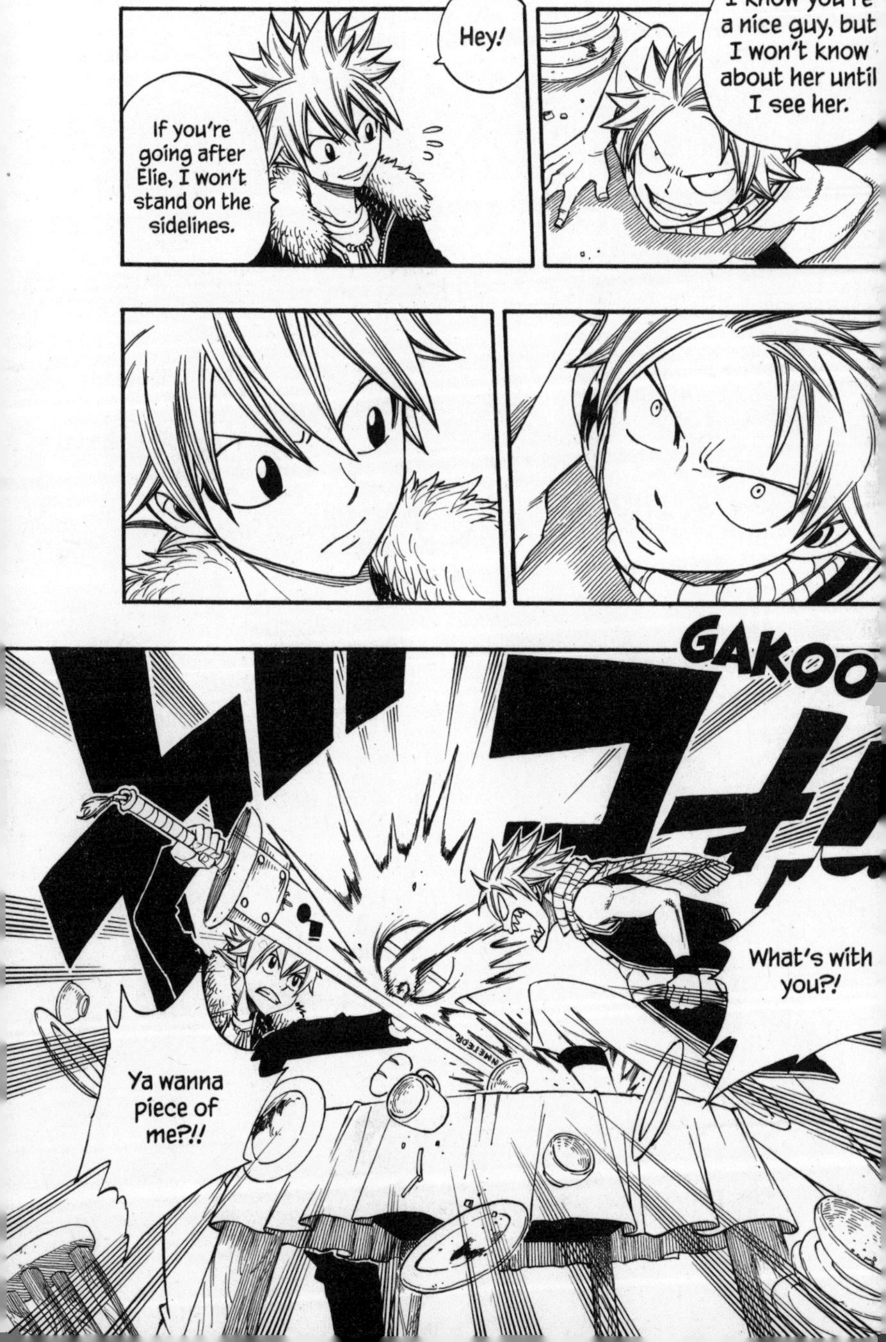
I know you're a nice guy, but I won't know about her until I see her.
Hey!
If you're going after Elie, I won't stand on the sidelines.
GAKOO
What's with you?!
Ya wanna piece of me?!!

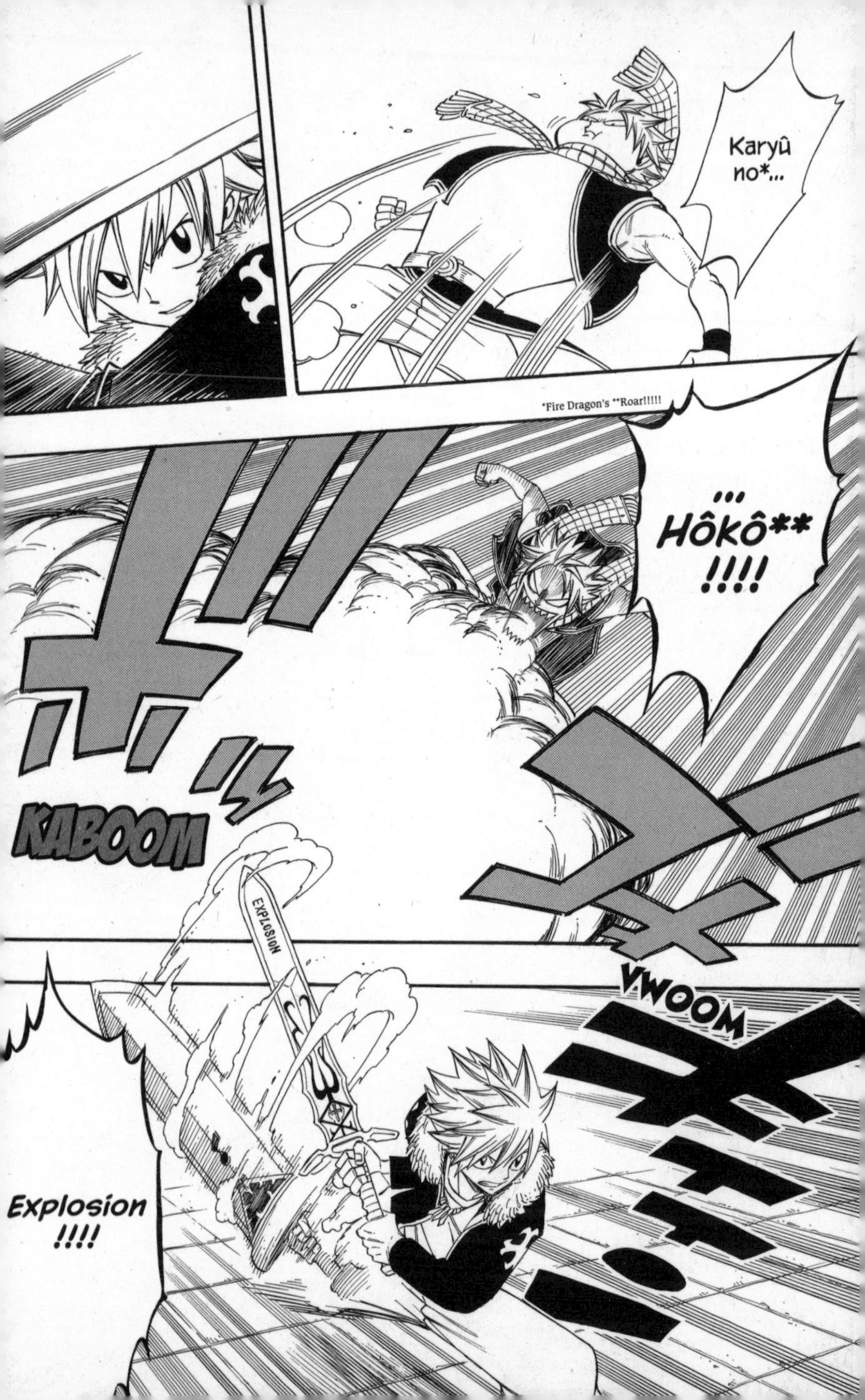
Karyû no*...
*Fire Dragon's **Roar!!!!!
... Hôkô** !!!!
KABOOM
VWOOM
EXPLOSION
Explosion !!!!

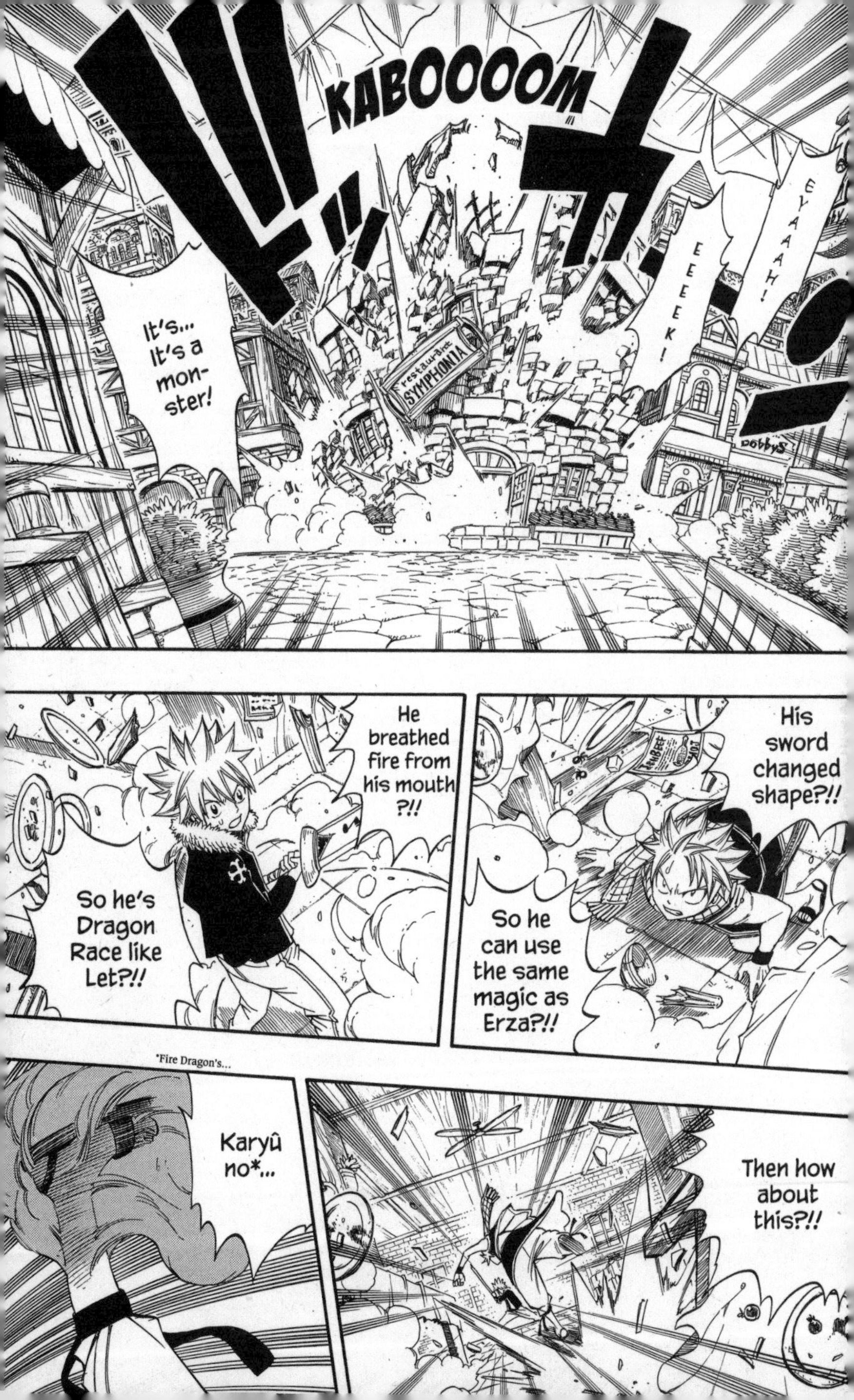
EYAAAAH!
EEEEEK!
KABOOOOM
SYMPHONIA
Dobbys
It's... It's a monster!
His sword changed shape?!!
So he can use the same magic as Erza?!!
He breathed fire from his mouth?!!
So he's Dragon Race like Let?!!
Then how about this?!!
Karyû no*...
*Fire Dragon's...

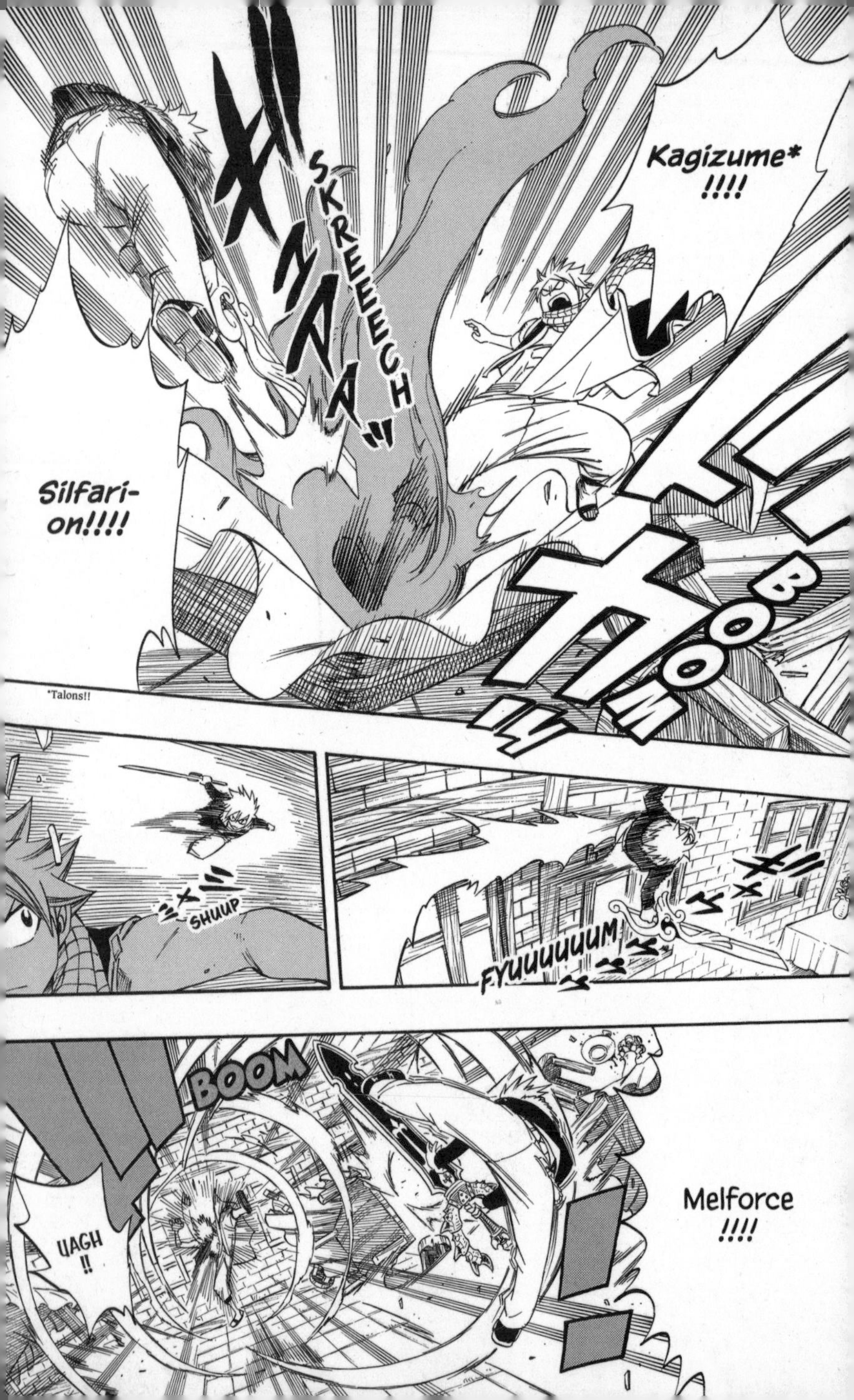
Kagizume* !!!!
SKREEEECH
Silfari-on!!!!
BOOOM
FYUUUUUUM
SHUUP
Melforce !!!!
BOOM
UAGH !!

*Talons!!

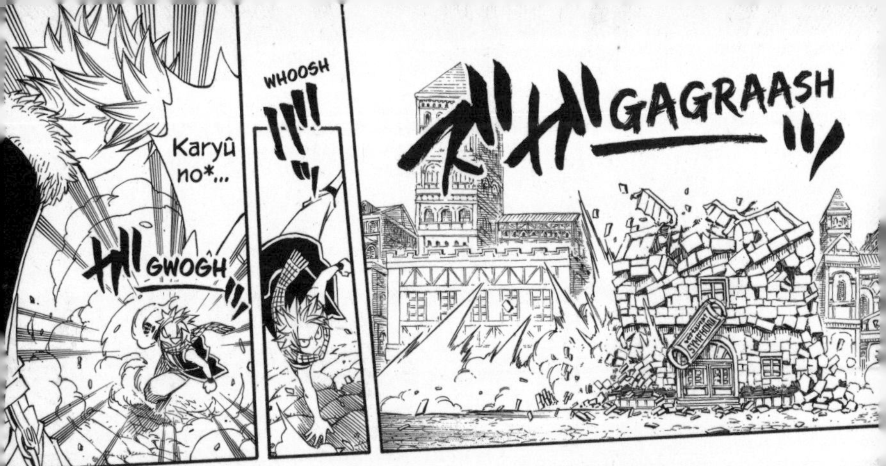
GAGRAASH
WHOOSH
Karyû no*...
GWOGH

*Fire Dragon's **Iron Fist!

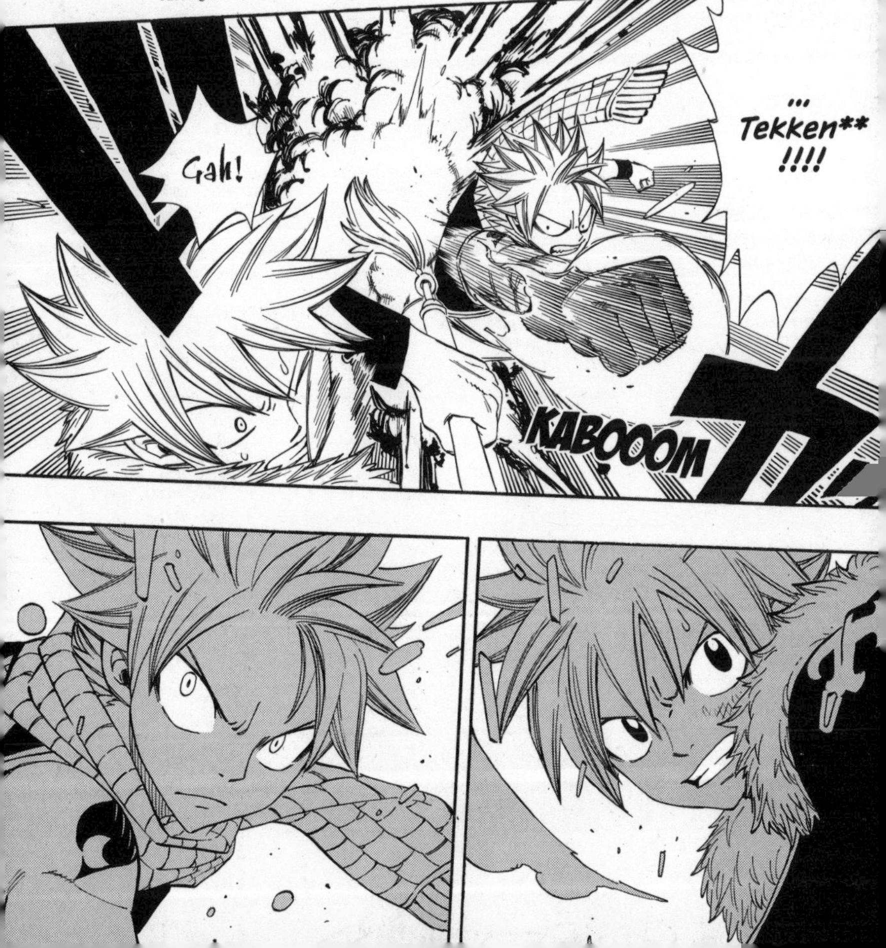
... Tekken** !!!!
Gah!
KABOOOM

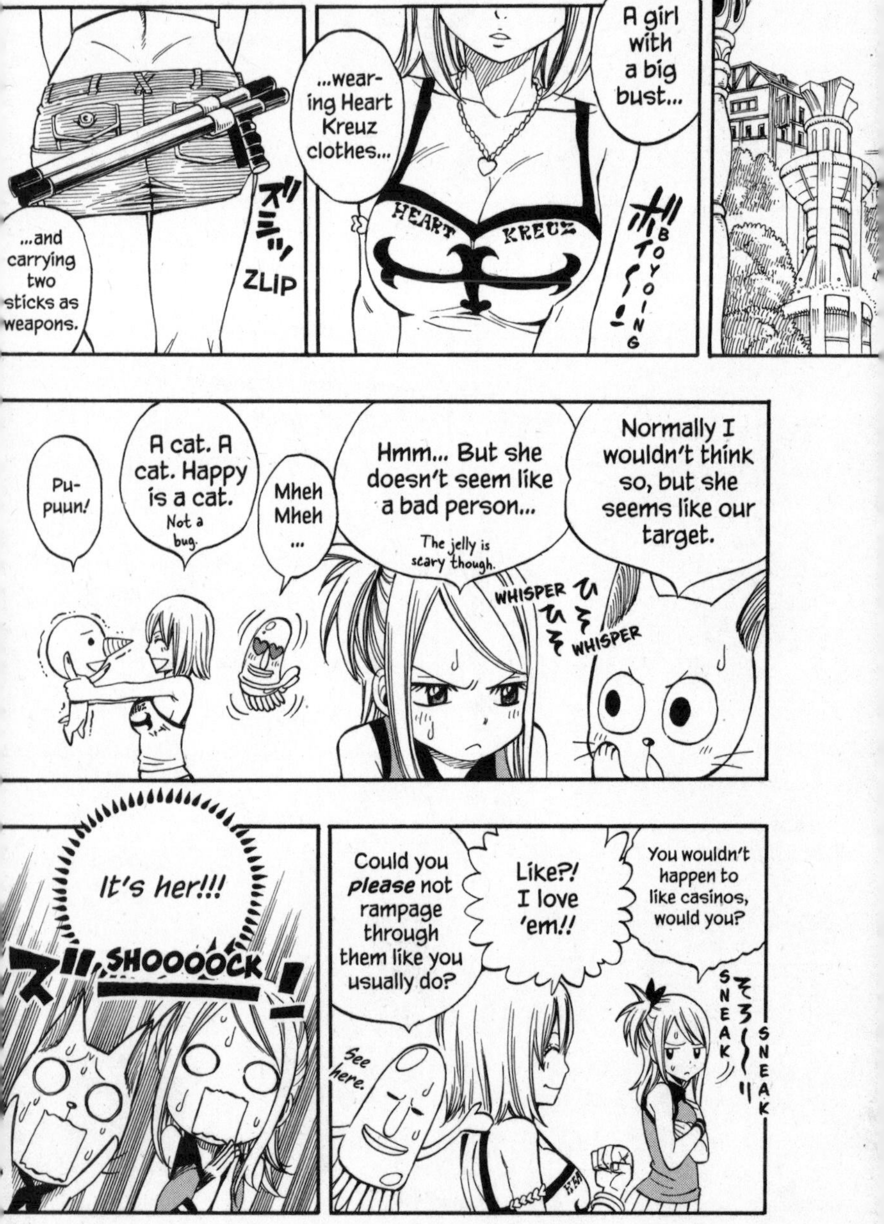
A girl with a big bust...
...wear-ing Heart Kreuz clothes...
HEART KREUZ
BOYOING
...and carrying two sticks as weapons.
ZLIP
Normally I wouldn't think so, but she seems like our target.
WHISPER
WHISPER
Hmm... But she doesn't seem like a bad person...
The jelly is scary though.
Mheh Mheh ...
A cat. A cat. Happy is a cat.
Not a bug.
Pu-puun!
You wouldn't happen to like casinos, would you?
SNEAK
SNEAK
Like?! I love 'em!!
Could you *please* not rampage through them like you usually do?
See here.
It's her!!!
SHOOOOCK

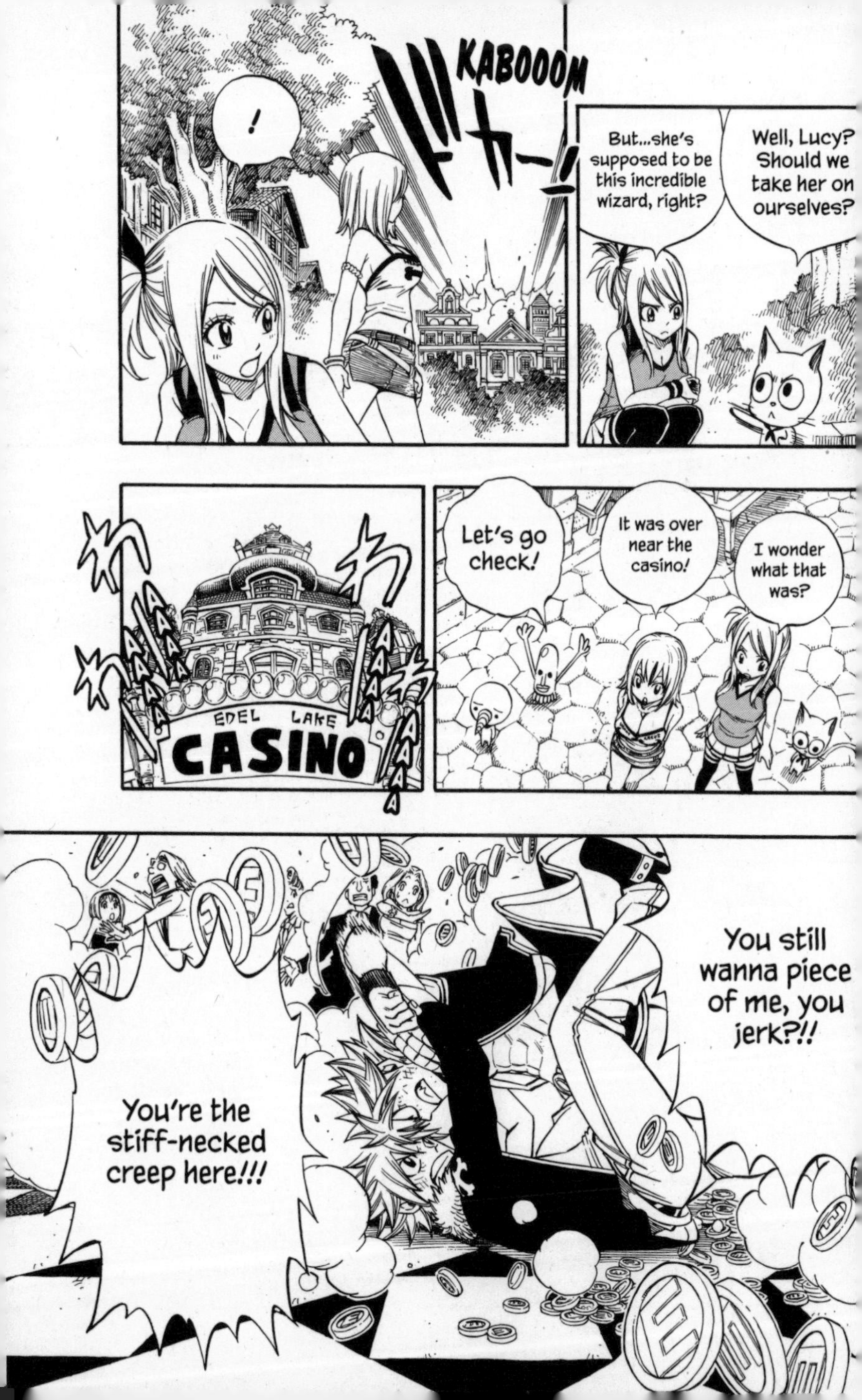
Well, Lucy? Should we take her on ourselves?
But...she's supposed to be this incredible wizard, right?
KABOOOM
!
I wonder what that was?
It was over near the casino!
Let's go check!
EDEL LAKE
CASINO
You still wanna piece of me, you jerk?!!
You're the stiff-necked creep here!!!

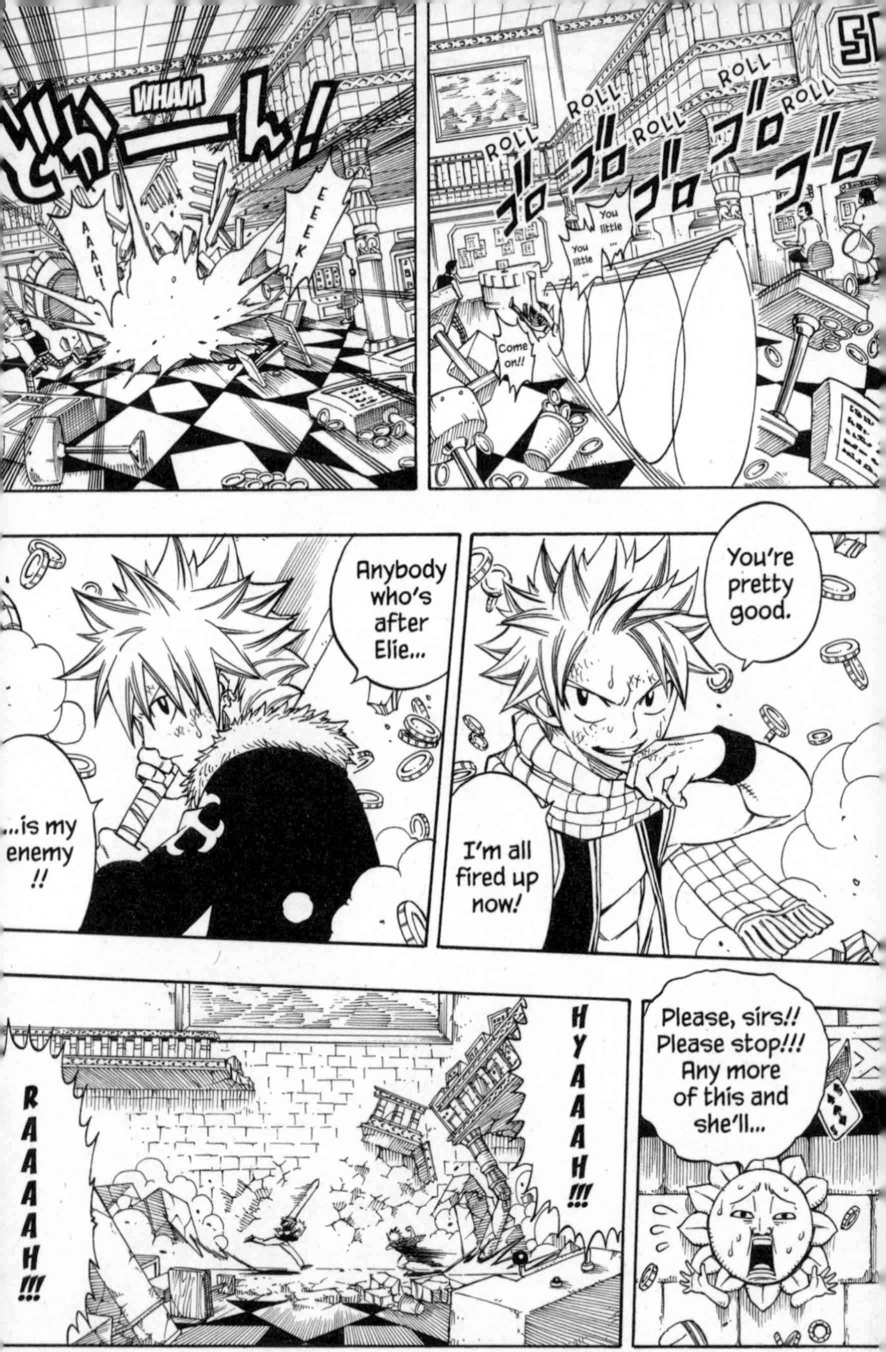
ROLL ROLL ROLL ROLL ROLL ROLL
ゴロゴロゴロゴロ
You little...
You little...
Come on!!
WHAM
どかーん!
AAAH!
EEEEK!
You're pretty good.
I'm all fired up now!
Anybody who's after Elie...
...is my enemy!!
Please, sirs!! Please stop!!! Any more of this and she'll...
HYAAAAH!!!
RAAAAAAH!!!

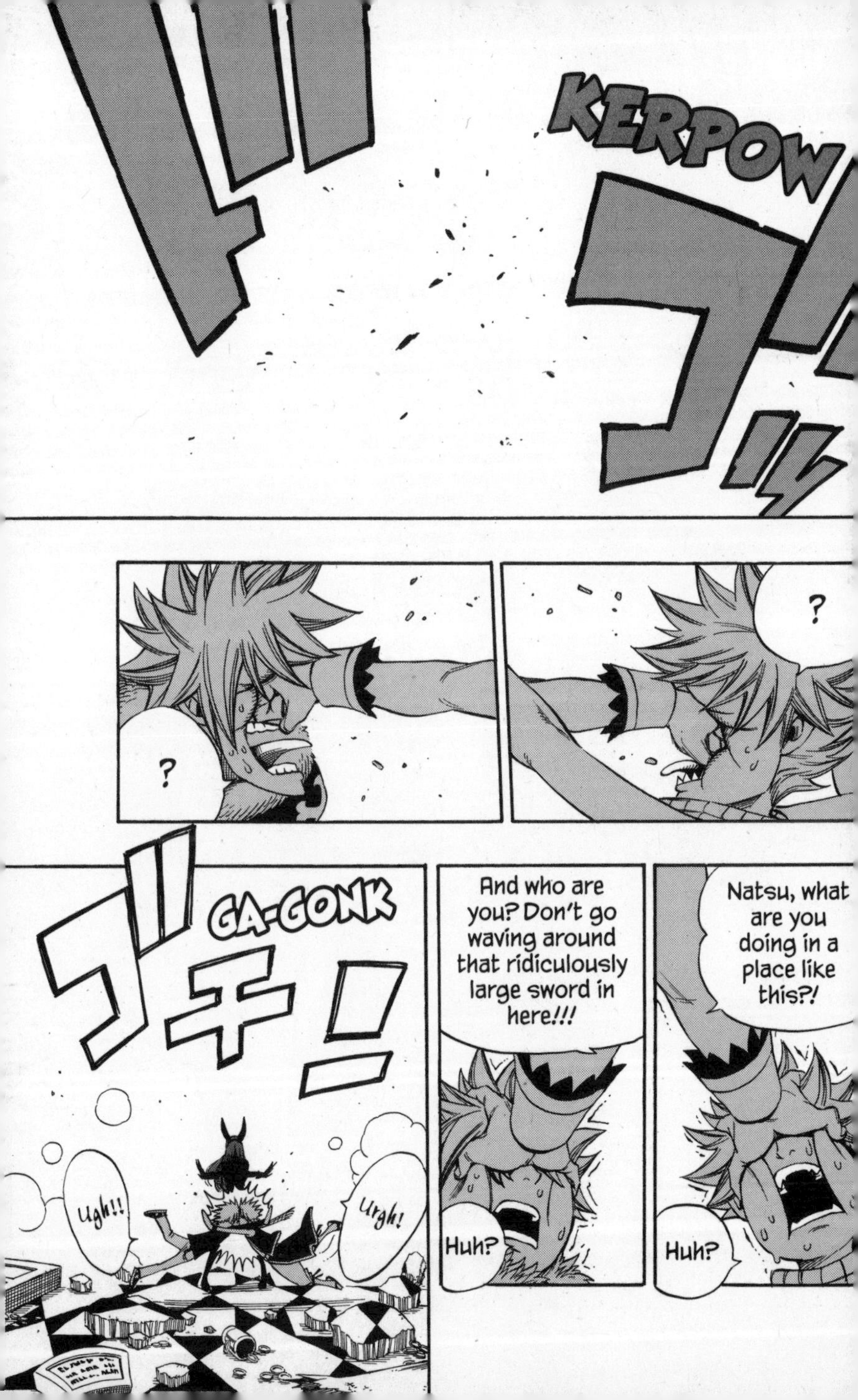
KERPOW
?
?
Natsu, what are you doing in a place like this?!
Huh?
And who are you? Don't go waving around that ridiculously large sword in here!!!
Huh?
GA-GONK
Urgh!
Ugh!!

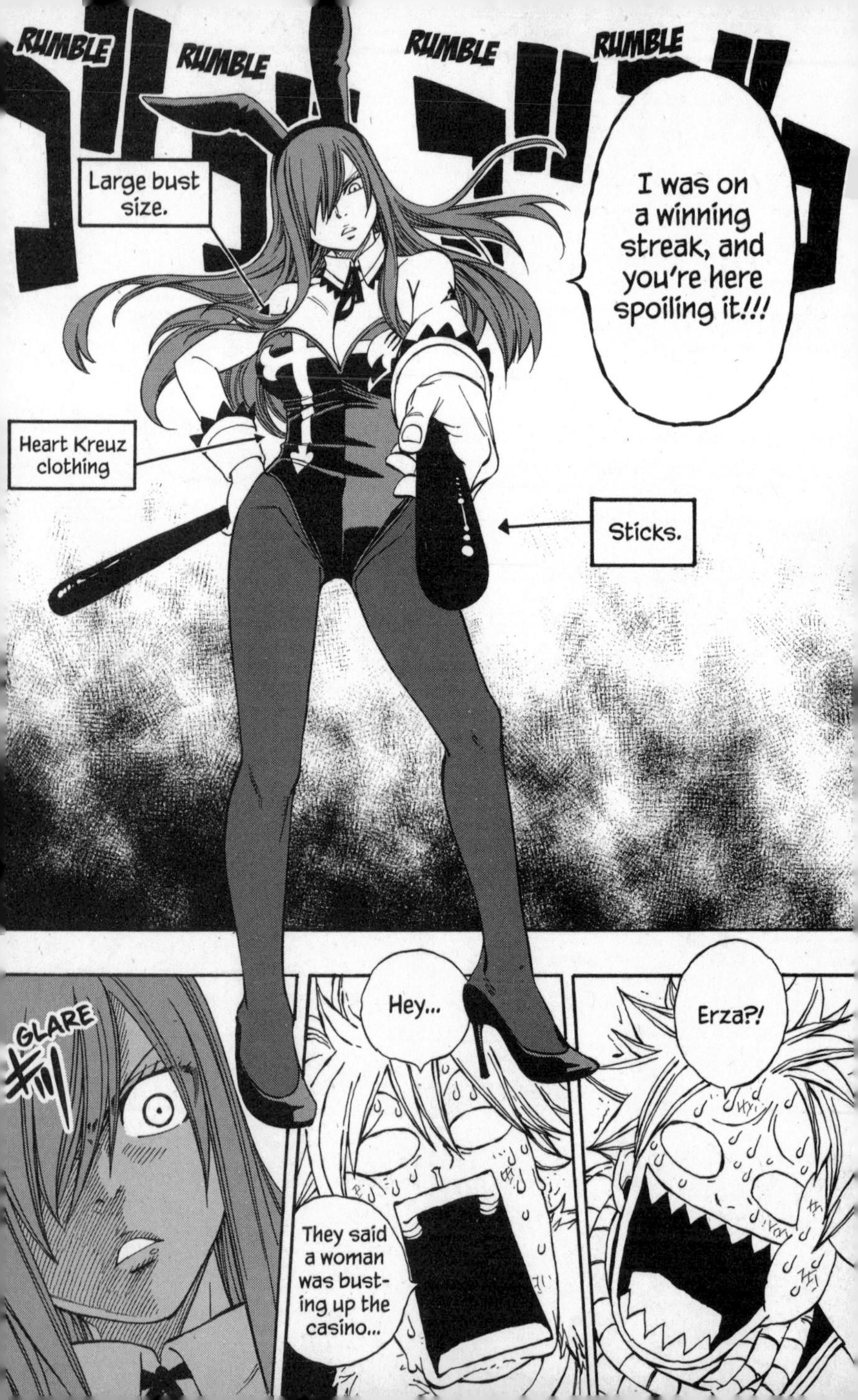
RUMBLE
RUMBLE
RUMBLE
RUMBLE
I was on a winning streak, and you're here spoiling it!!!
Large bust size.
Sticks.
Heart Kreuz clothing
Erza?!
Hey...
They said a woman was bust-ing up the casino...
GLARE

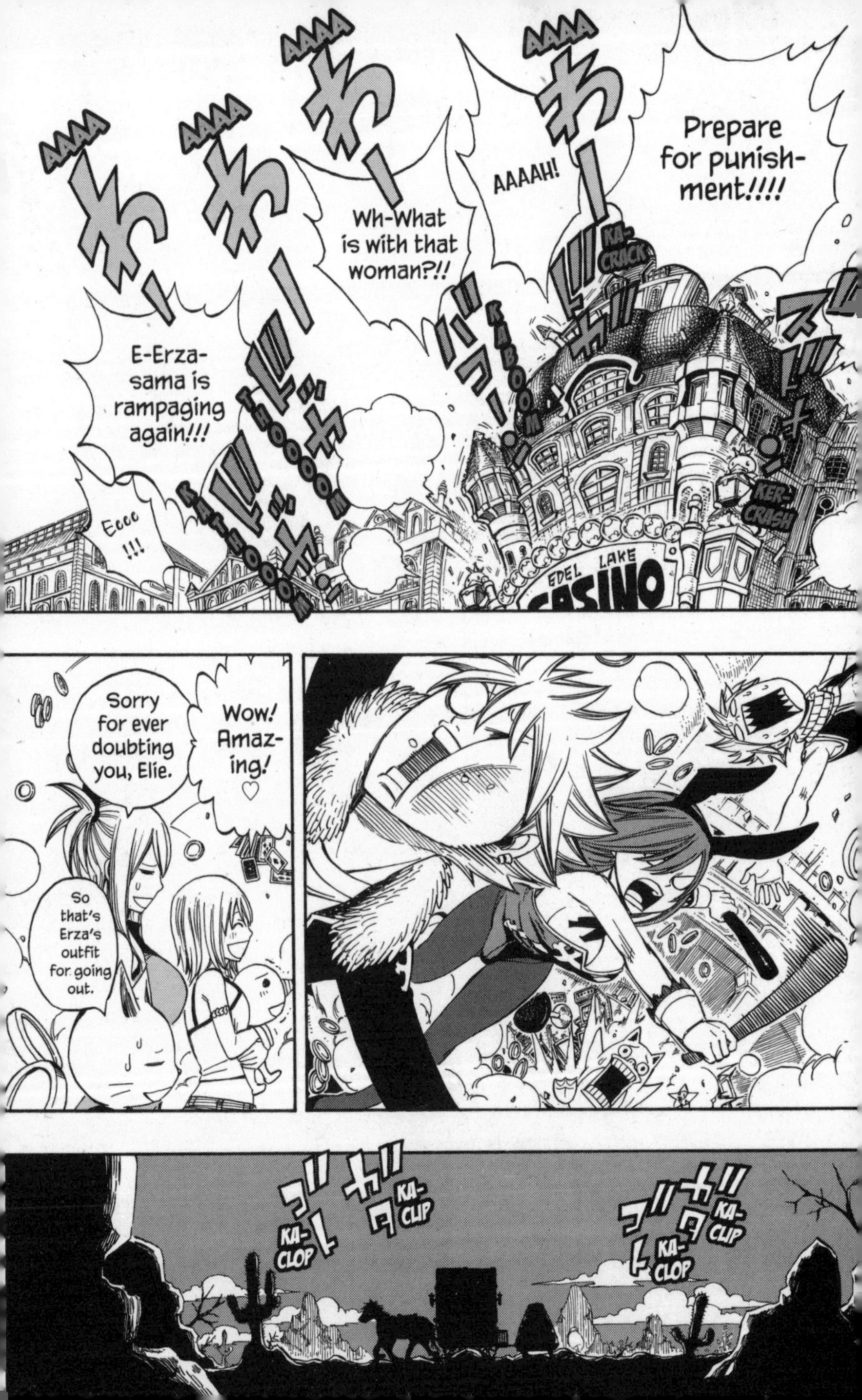
Prepare for punish-ment!!!!
AAAA
AAAAH!
KA-CRACK
KER-CRASH
Wh-What is with that woman?!!
AAAA
KABOOOM
AAAA
AAAA
E-Erza-sama is rampaging again!!!
KA-THOOOOOM
KA-THOOOOOM
Eeee !!!
EDEL LAKE CASINO
Wow! Amaz-ing! ♡
Sorry for ever doubting you, Elie.
So that's Erza's outfit for going out.
KA-CLIP
KA-CLOP
KA-CLIP
KA-CLOP

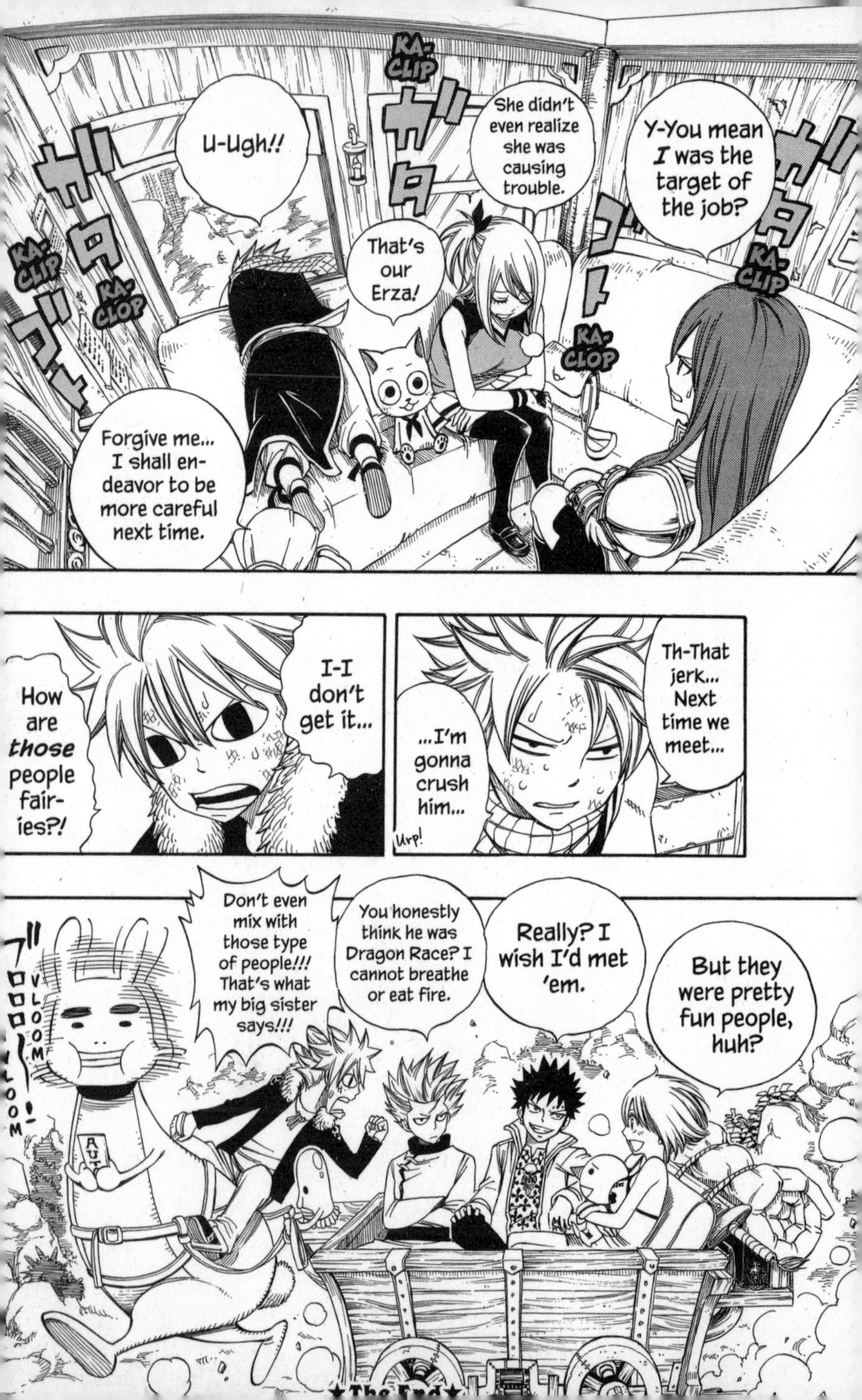
KA-CLIP
Y-You mean *I* was the target of the job?
KA-CLIP
She didn't even realize she was causing trouble.
KA-CLIP
That's our Erza!
KA-CLOP
U-Ugh!!
KA-CLIP
KA-CLOP
Forgive me... I shall endeavor to be more careful next time.
Th-That jerk... Next time we meet...
...I'm gonna crush him...
Urp!
I-I don't get it...
How are *those* people fairies?!
But they were pretty fun people, huh?
Really? I wish I'd met 'em.
You honestly think he was Dragon Race? I cannot breathe or eat fire.
Don't even mix with those type of people!!! That's what my big sister says!!!
VLOOM
VLOOM!
★The End★

Fairy Woman

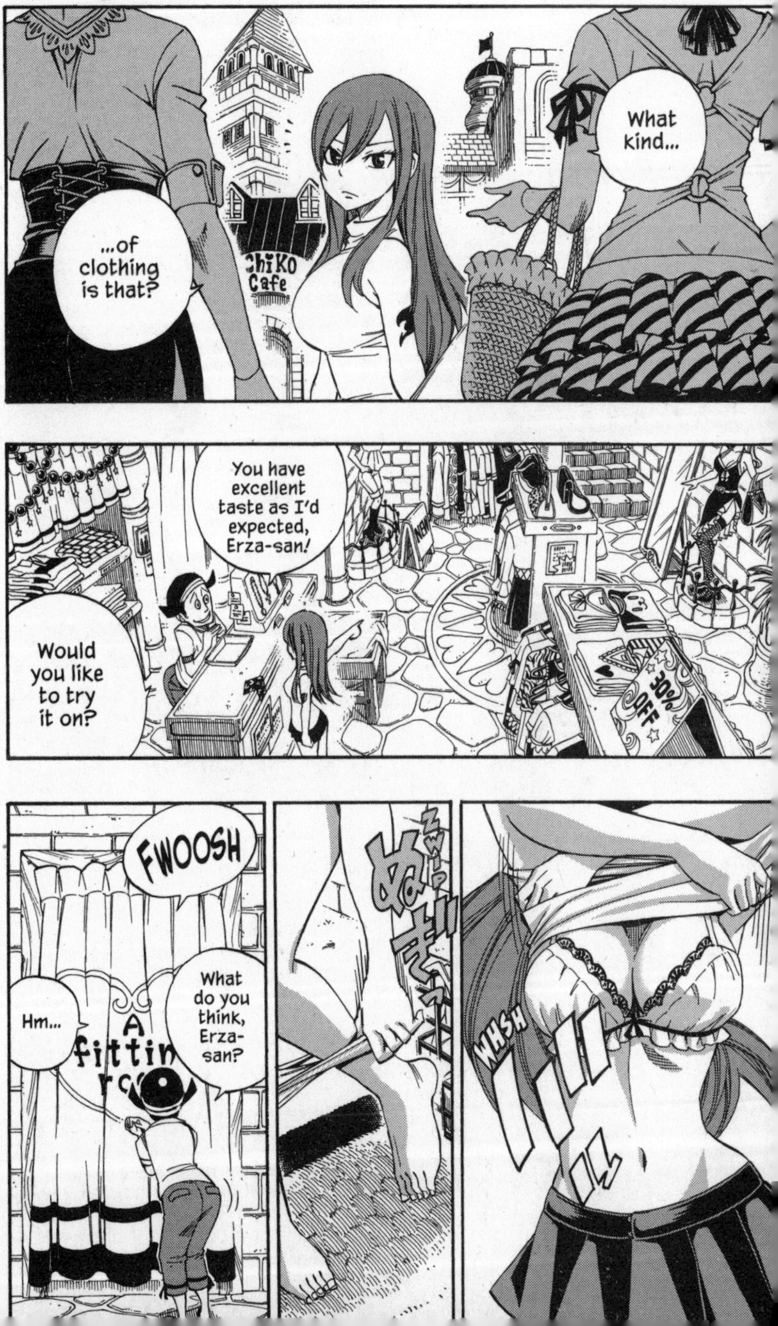
What kind...
...of clothing is that?
You have excellent taste as I'd expected, Erza-san!
Would you like to try it on?
WHSH
FWOOSH
What do you think, Erza-san?
Hm...

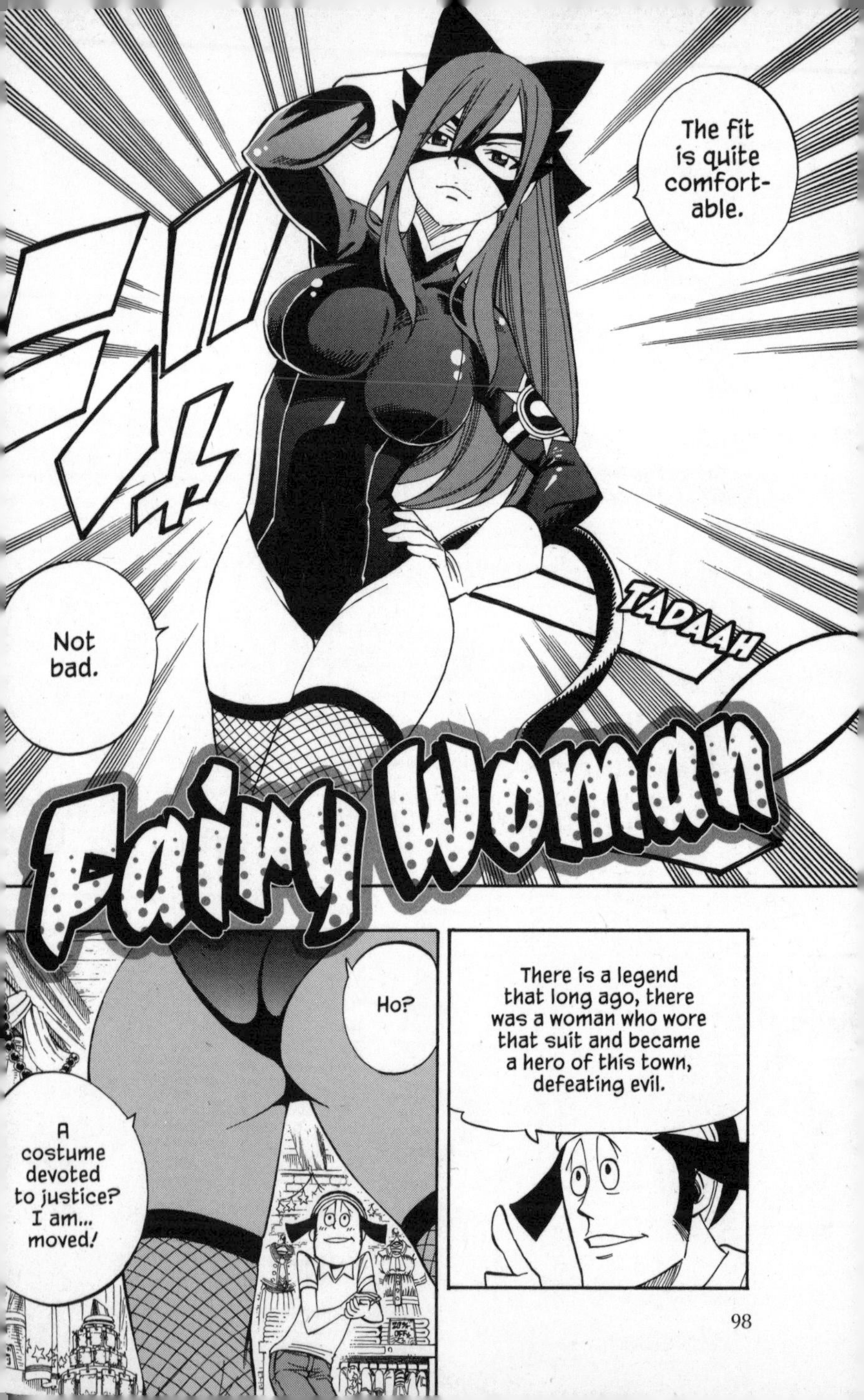
The fit is quite comfortable.
TADAAH
Not bad.
Fairy Woman
There is a legend that long ago, there was a woman who wore that suit and became a hero of this town, defeating evil.
Ho?
A costume devoted to justice? I am... moved!
20% OFF

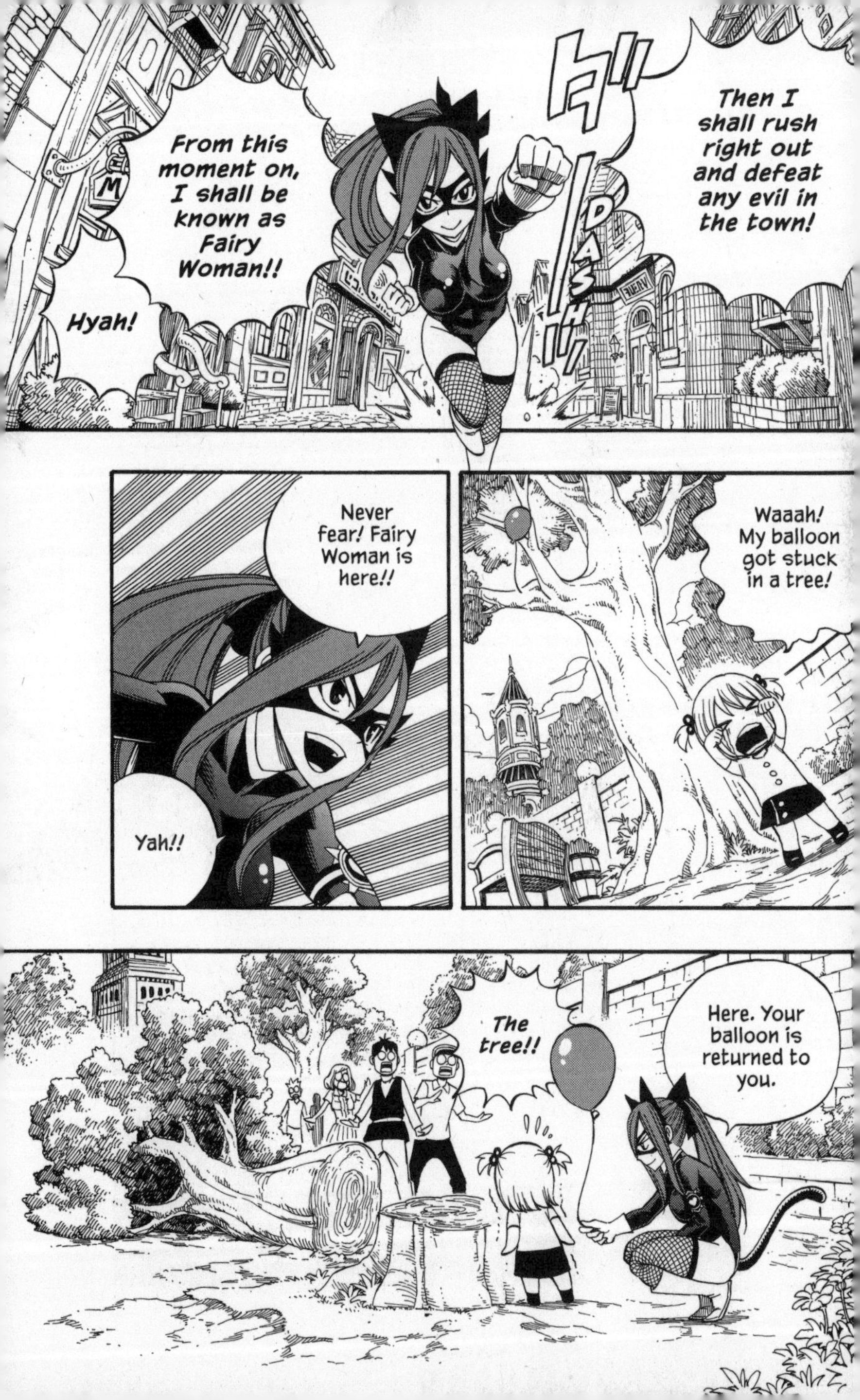
Then I shall rush right out and defeat any evil in the town!
DASH!!
From this moment on, I shall be known as Fairy Woman!!
Hyah!
Waaah! My balloon got stuck in a tree!
Never fear! Fairy Woman is here!!
Yah!!
Here. Your balloon is returned to you.
The tree!!

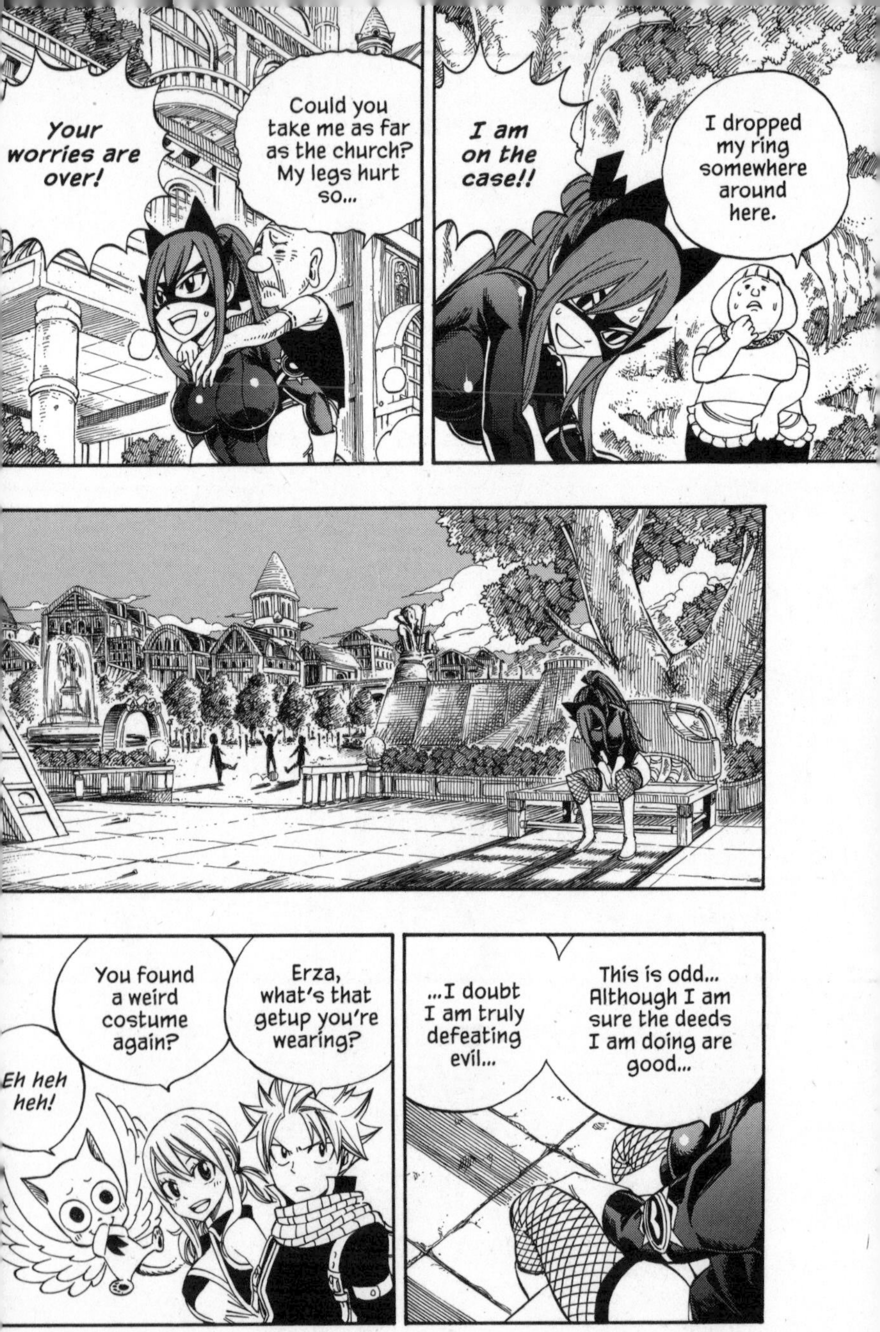
I dropped my ring somewhere around here.
I am on the case!!
Could you take me as far as the church? My legs hurt so...
Your worries are over!
This is odd... Although I am sure the deeds I am doing are good...
...I doubt I am truly defeating evil...
Erza, what's that getup you're wearing?
You found a weird costume again?
Eh heh heh!

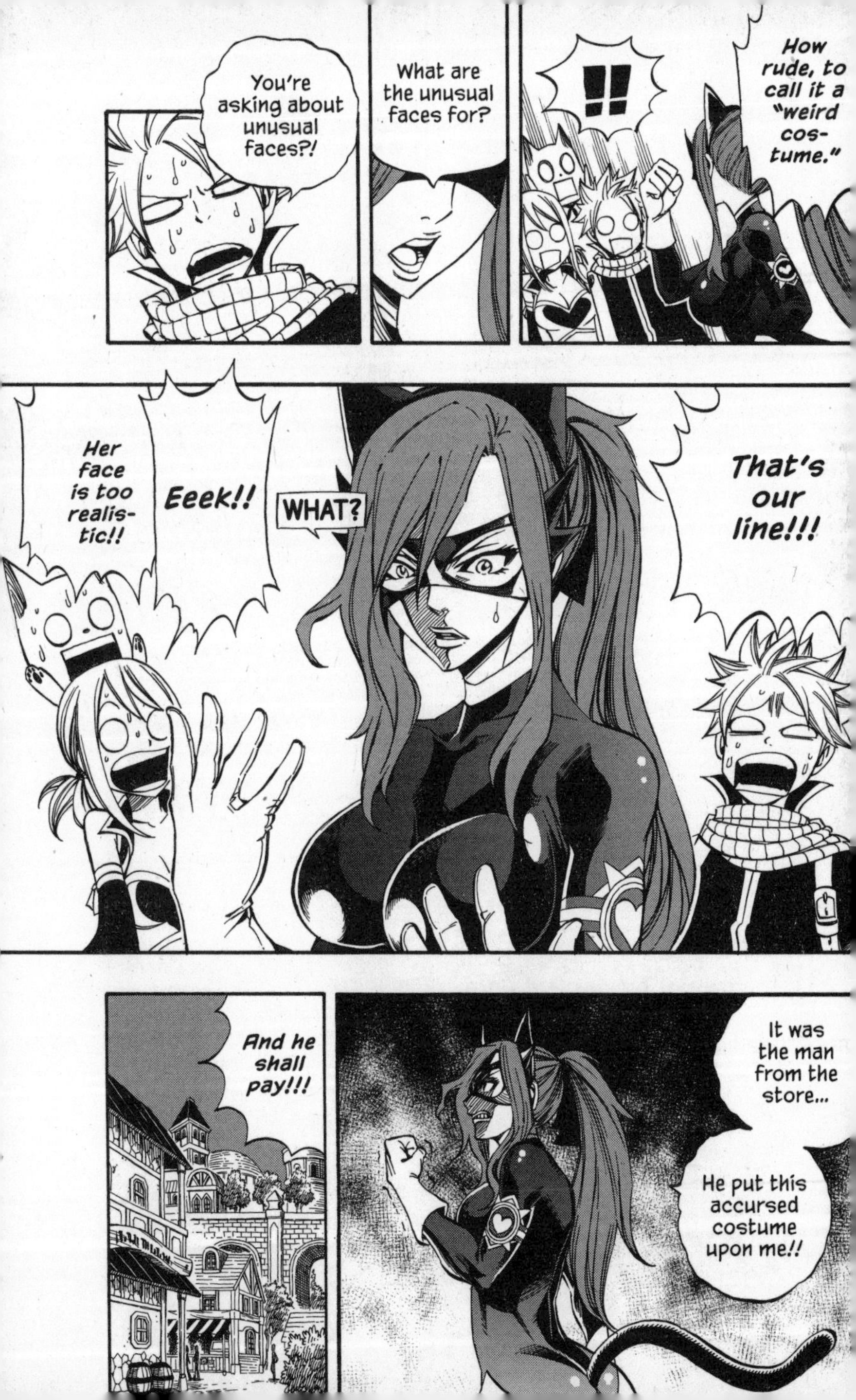
How rude, to call it a "weird costume."
!!
What are the unusual faces for?
You're asking about unusual faces?!
That's our line!!!
WHAT?
Eeek!!
Her face is too realistic!!
It was the man from the store...
He put this accursed costume upon me!!
And he shall pay!!!

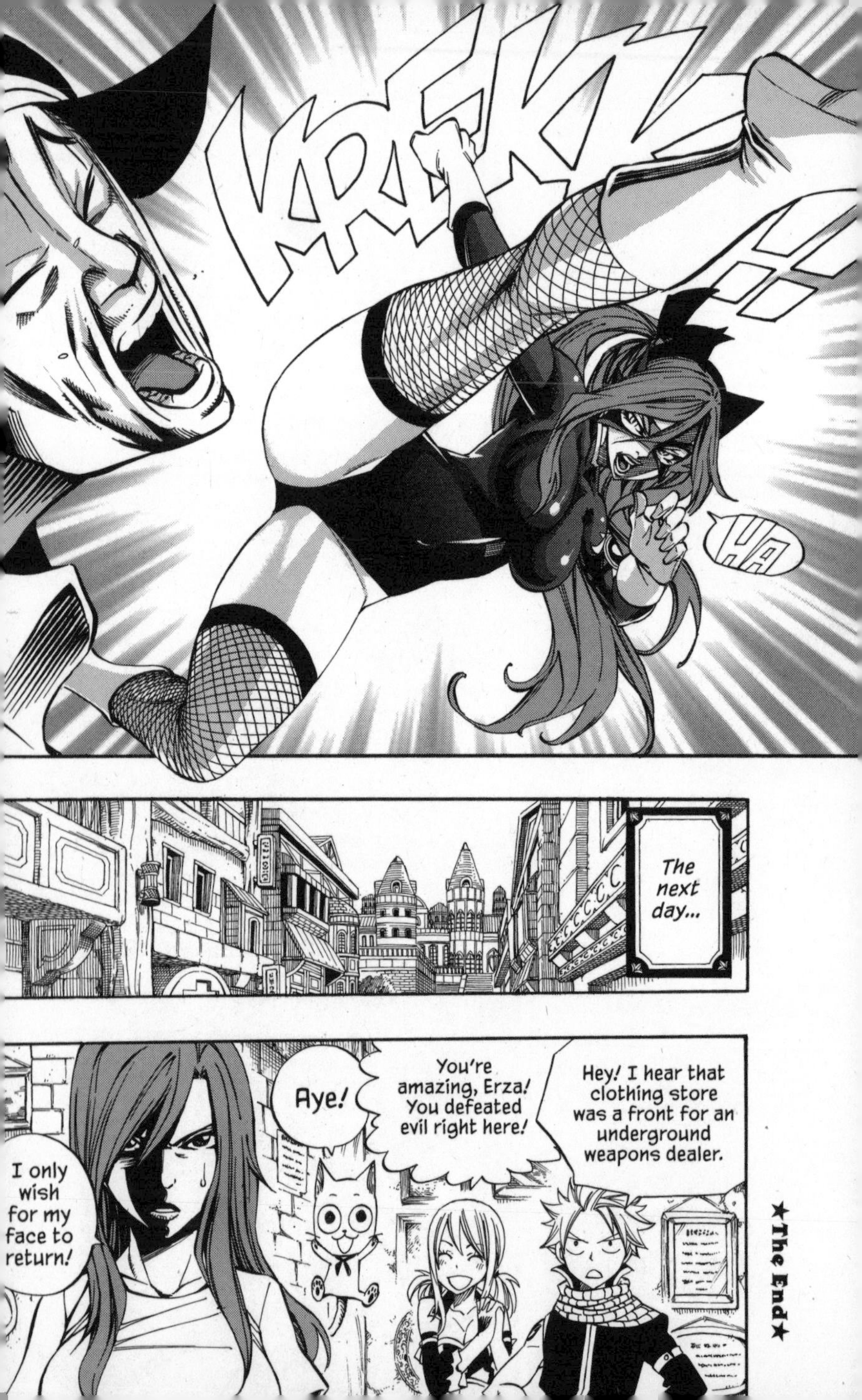
HA
The next day...
Hey! I hear that clothing store was a front for an underground weapons dealer.
You're amazing, Erza! You defeated evil right here!
Aye!
I only wish for my face to return!
★The End★

FT★S

FAIRY TAIL

フェアリーテイル

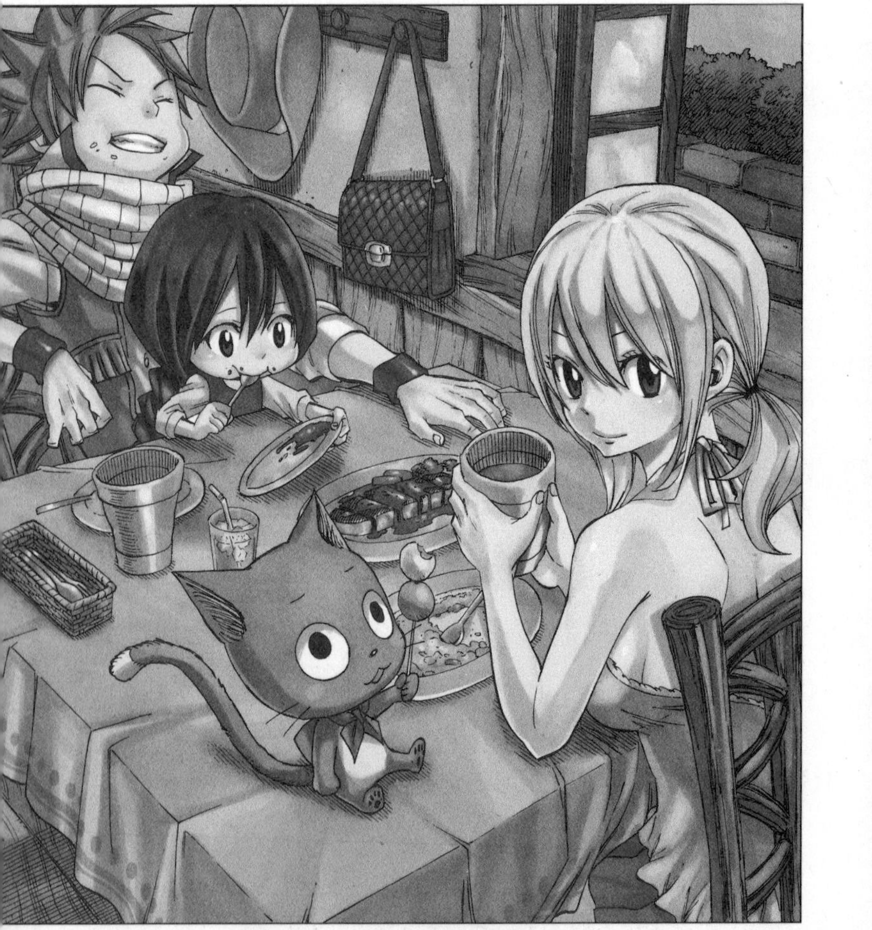

Natsu and Asuka

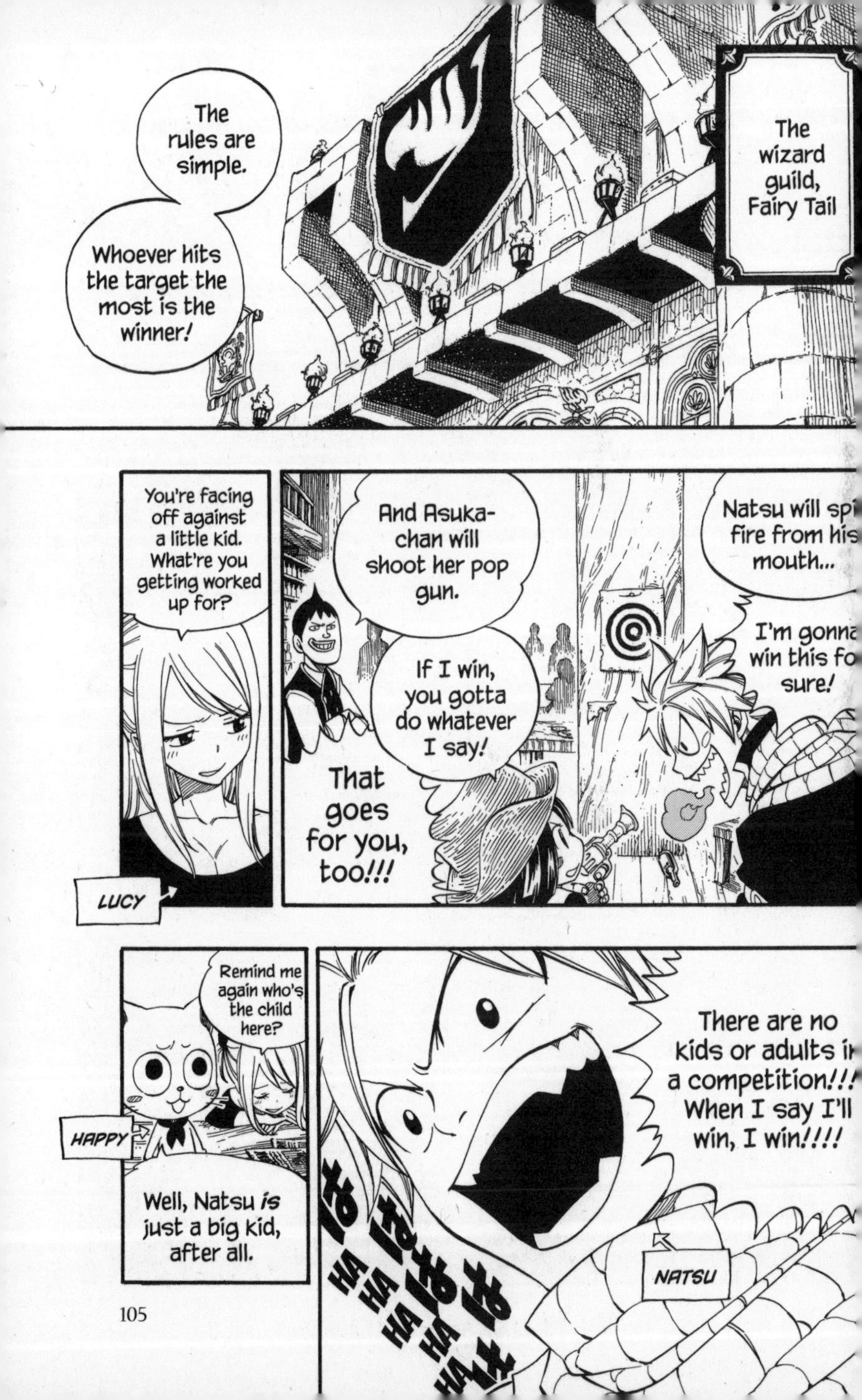

The wizard guild, Fairy Tail
The rules are simple.
Whoever hits the target the most is the winner!
Natsu will spi fire from his mouth...
And Asuka-chan will shoot her pop gun.
I'm gonna win this fo sure!
If I win, you gotta do whatever I say!
That goes for you, too!!!
You're facing off against a little kid. What're you getting worked up for?
LUCY
There are no kids or adults i a competition!!! When I say I'll win, I win!!!!
NATSU
HA HA HA HA HA
Remind me again who's the child here?
HAPPY
Well, Natsu *is* just a big kid, after all.

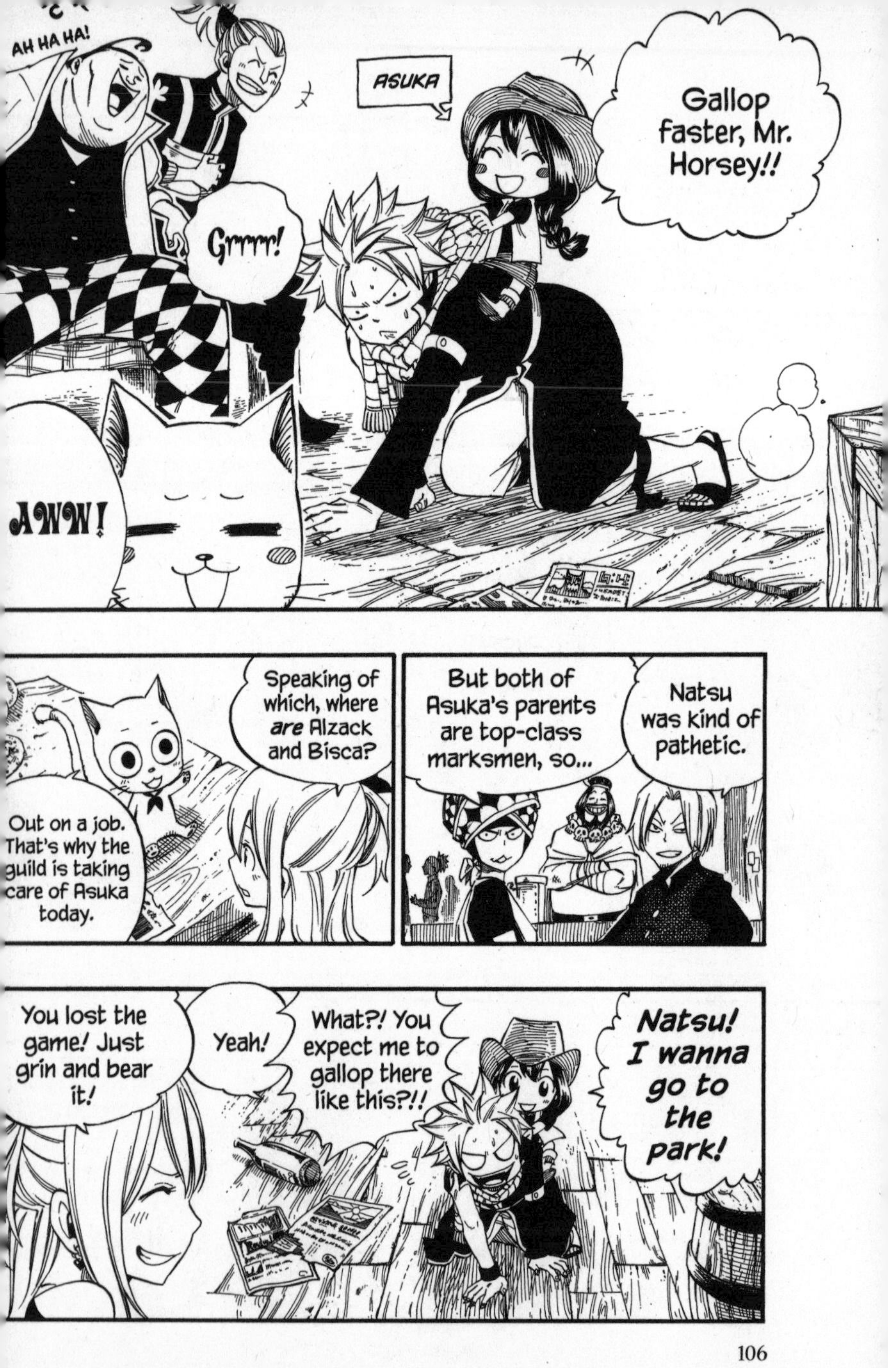
Gallop faster, Mr. Horsey!!
ASUKA
AH HA HA!
Grrrr!
AWW!
Natsu was kind of pathetic.
But both of Asuka's parents are top-class marksmen, so...
Speaking of which, where *are* Alzack and Bisca?
Out on a job. That's why the guild is taking care of Asuka today.
Natsu! I wanna go to the park!
What?! You expect me to gallop there like this?!!
Yeah!
You lost the game! Just grin and bear it!

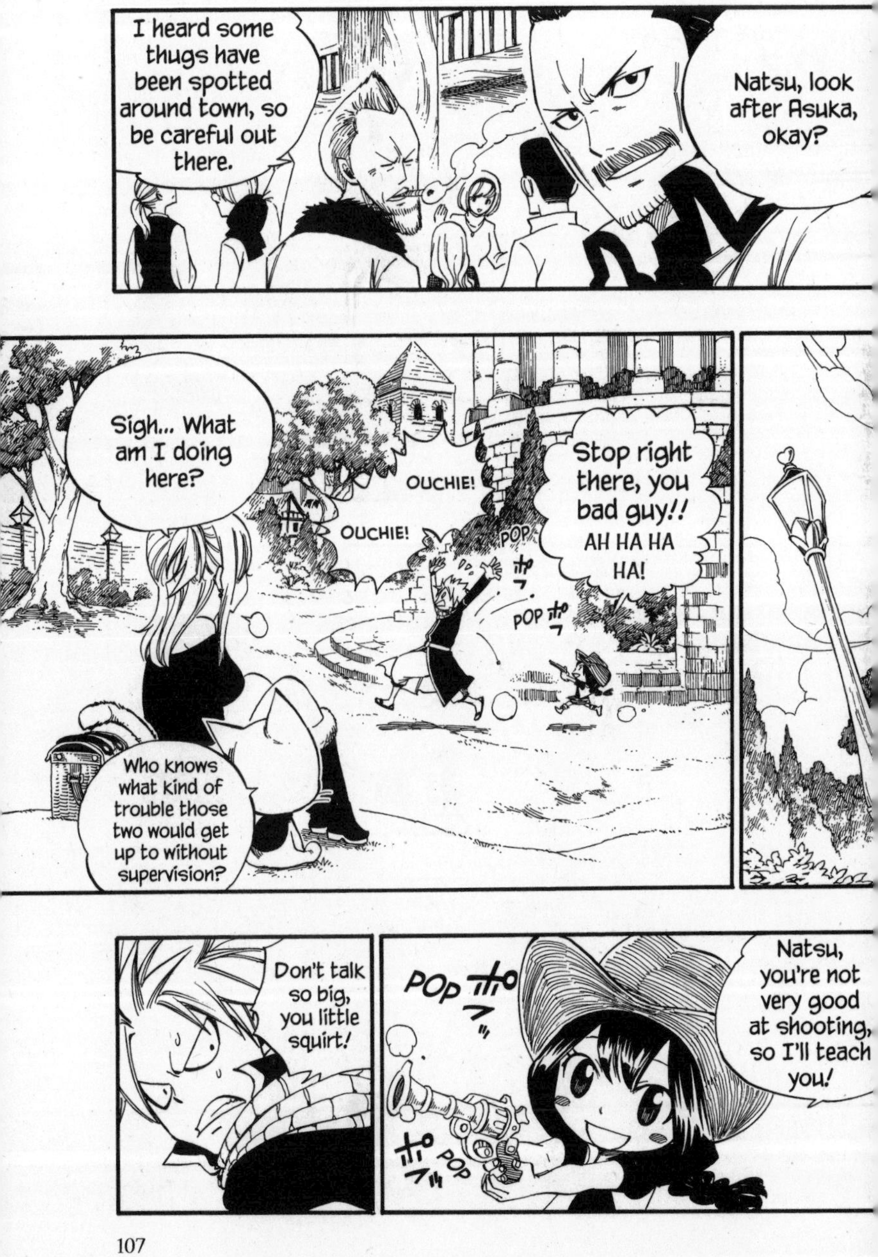

Natsu, look after Asuka, okay?
I heard some thugs have been spotted around town, so be careful out there.
Stop right there, you bad guy!! AH HA HA HA!
OUCHIE!
OUCHIE!
POP
POP
Sigh... What am I doing here?
Who knows what kind of trouble those two would get up to without supervision?
Natsu, you're not very good at shooting, so I'll teach you!
POP
POP
Don't talk so big, you little squirt!

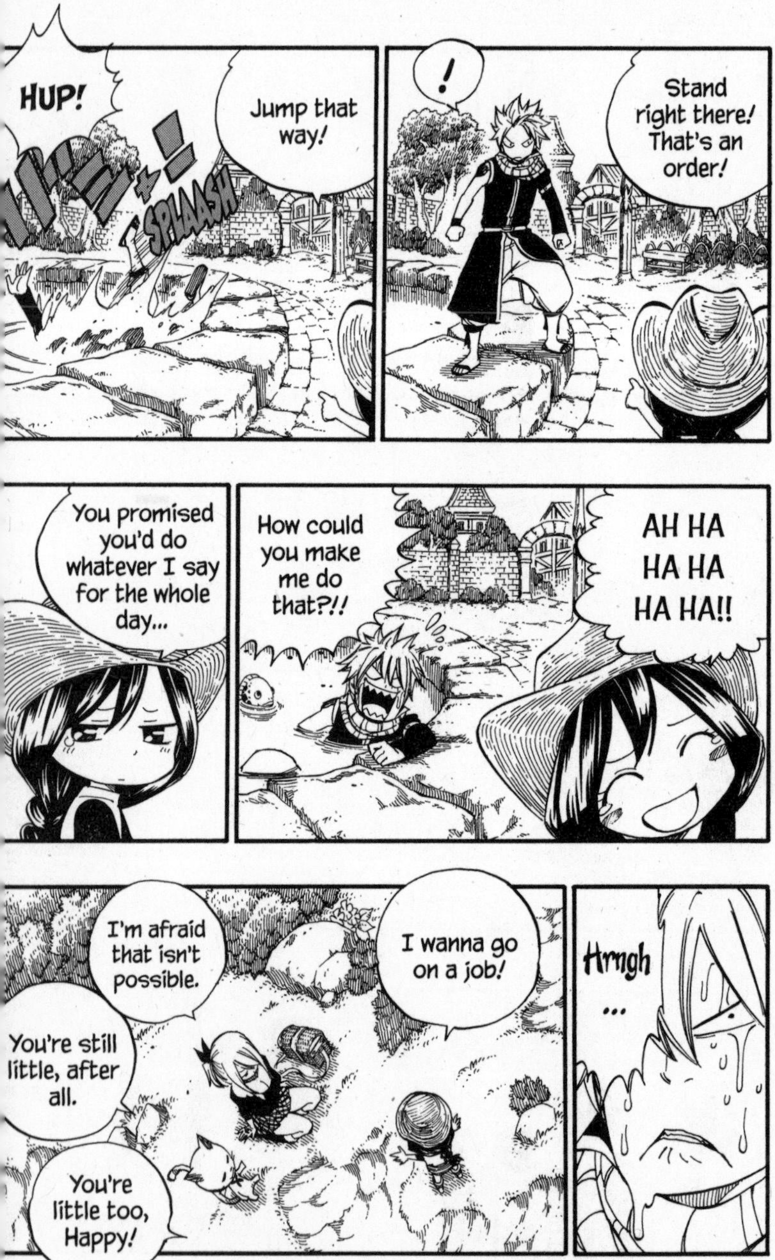
!
Stand right there! That's an order!
Jump that way!
HUP!
SPLAASH
AH HA HA HA HA HA!!
How could you make me do that?!!
You promised you'd do whatever I say for the whole day...
Hrngh ...
I wanna go on a job!
I'm afraid that isn't possible.
You're still little, after all.
You're little too, Happy!

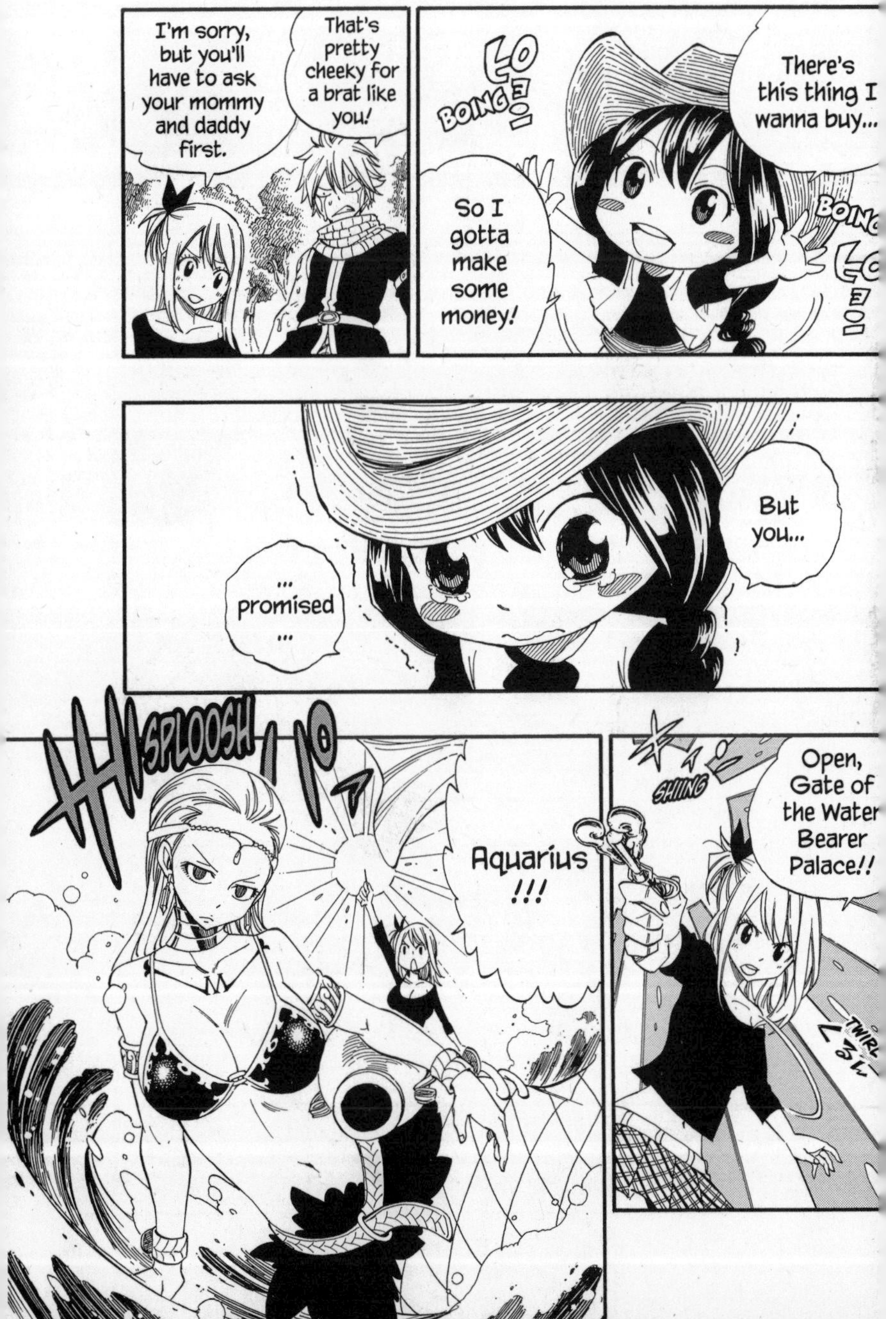

BOING
There's this thing I wanna buy...
BOING
So I gotta make some money!
That's pretty cheeky for a brat like you!
I'm sorry, but you'll have to ask your mommy and daddy first.
But you...
... promised ...
SHIING
Open, Gate of the Water Bearer Palace!!
TWIRL
SPLOOSH
Aquarius !!!

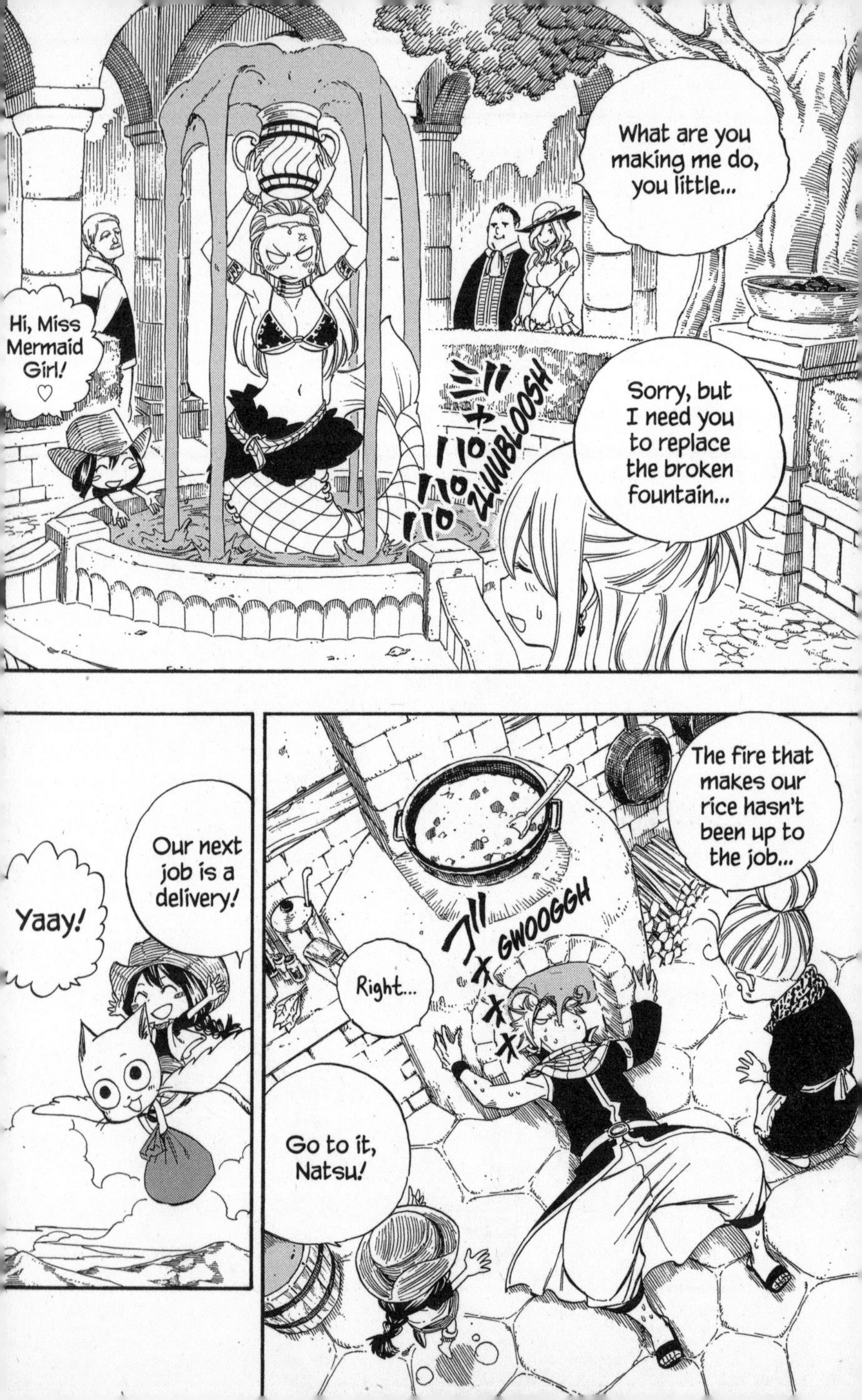
What are you making me do, you little...
Sorry, but I need you to replace the broken fountain...
ZUUUBLOOSH
Hi, Miss Mermaid Girl! ♡
The fire that makes our rice hasn't been up to the job...
GWOOGGH
Right...
Go to it, Natsu!
Our next job is a delivery!
Yaay!

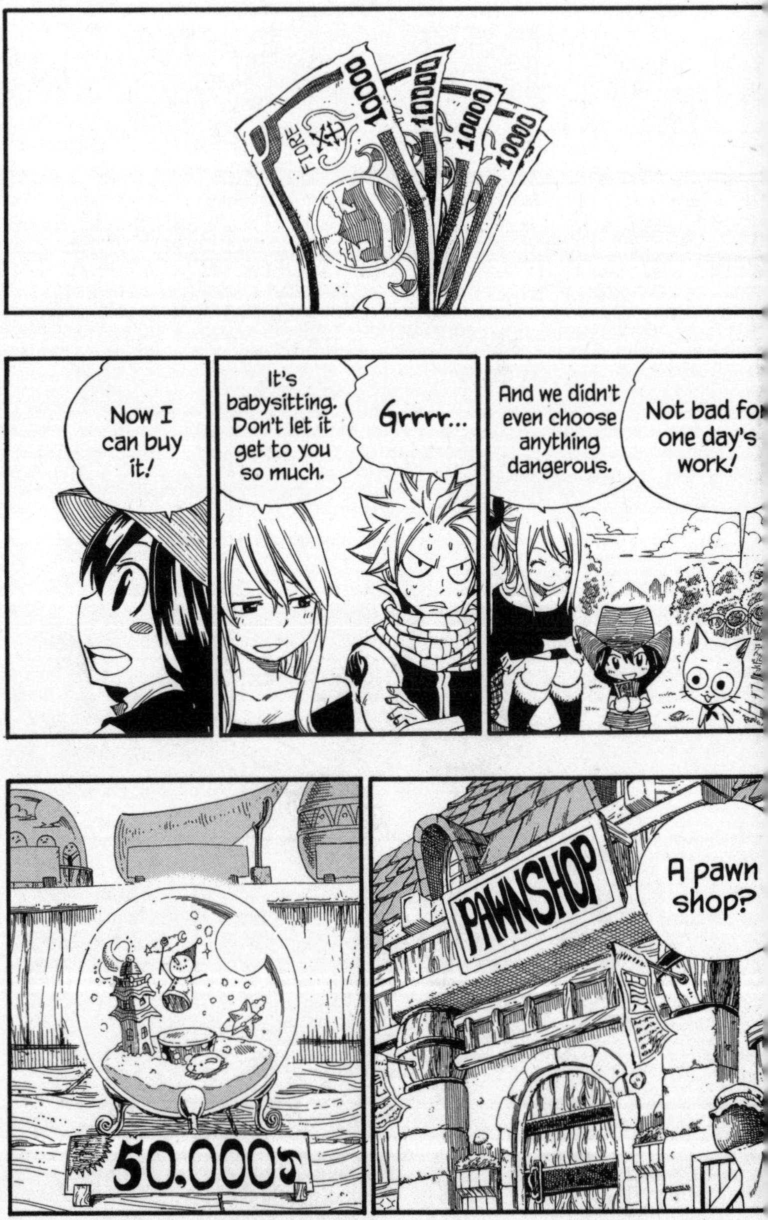
10000
FIORE
Not bad for one day's work!
And we didn't even choose anything dangerous.
Grrrr...
It's babysitting. Don't let it get to you so much.
Now I can buy it!
PAWNSHOP
A pawn shop?
50,000J

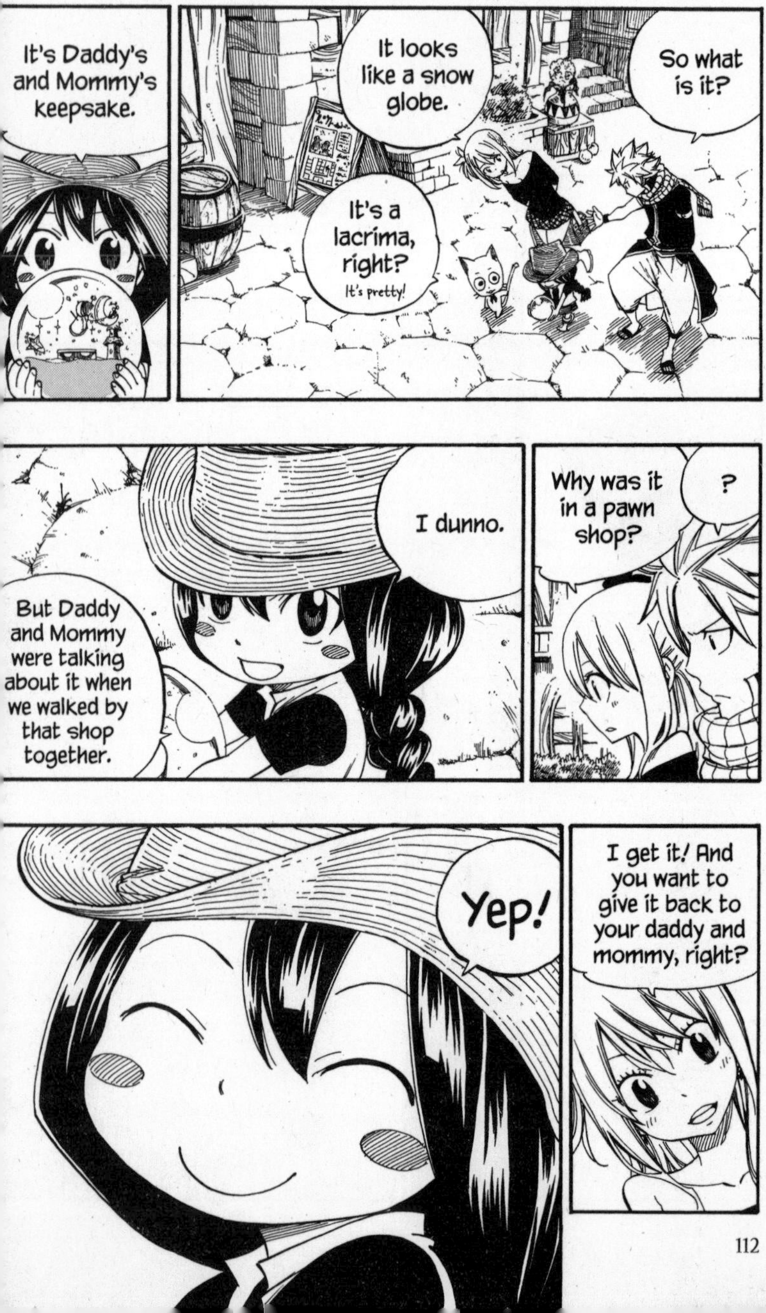
So what is it?
It looks like a snow globe.
It's a lacrima, right?
It's pretty!
It's Daddy's and Mommy's keepsake.
?
Why was it in a pawn shop?
I dunno.
But Daddy and Mommy were talking about it when we walked by that shop together.
I get it! And you want to give it back to your daddy and mommy, right?
Yep!

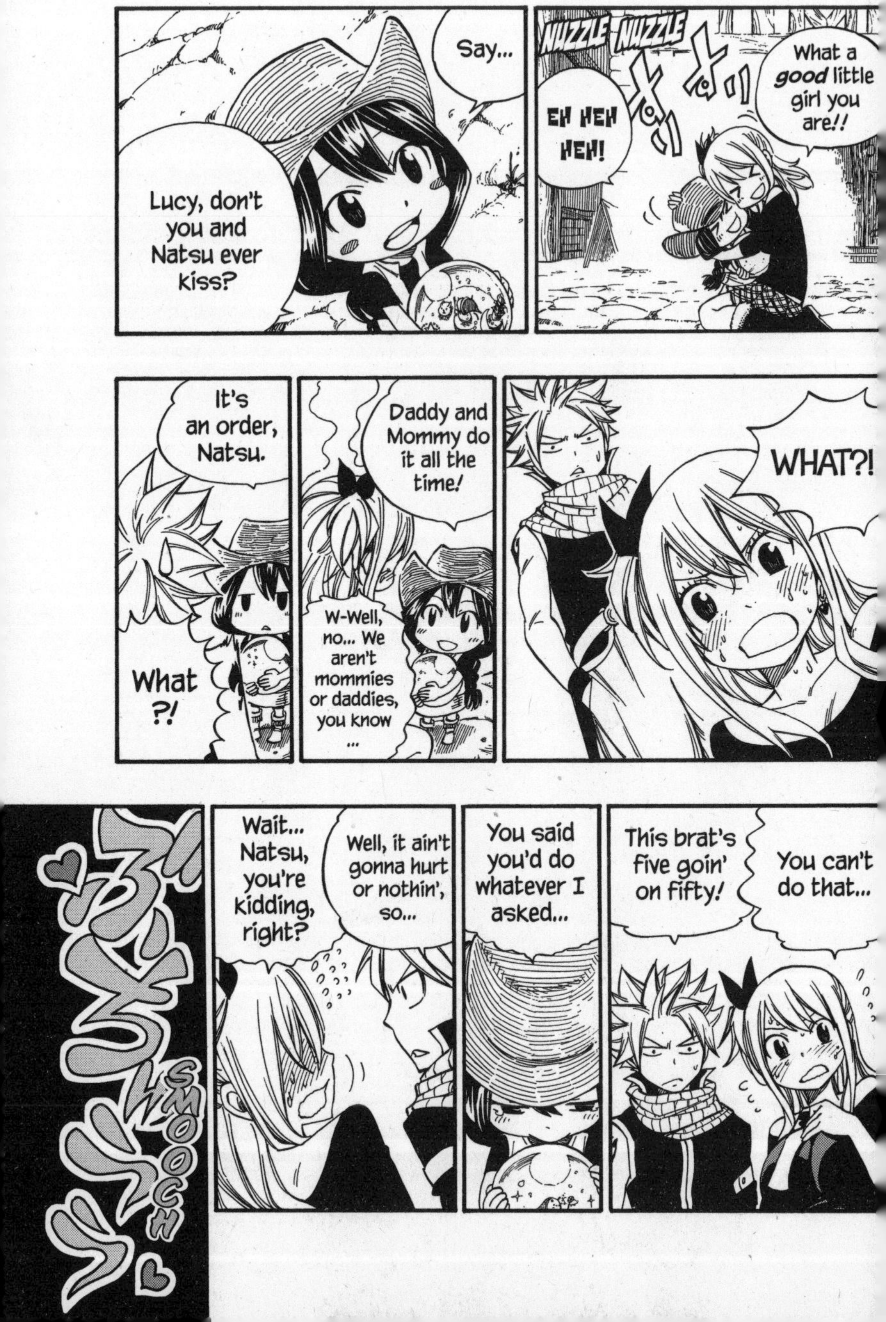
NUZZLE NUZZLE
What a good little girl you are!!
EH HEH HEH!
Say...
Lucy, don't you and Natsu ever kiss?
WHAT?!
Daddy and Mommy do it all the time!
W-Well, no... We aren't mommies or daddies, you know ...
It's an order, Natsu.
What ?!
You can't do that...
This brat's five goin' on fifty!
You said you'd do whatever I asked...
Well, it ain't gonna hurt or nothin', so...
Wait... Natsu, you're kidding, right?
SMOOCH

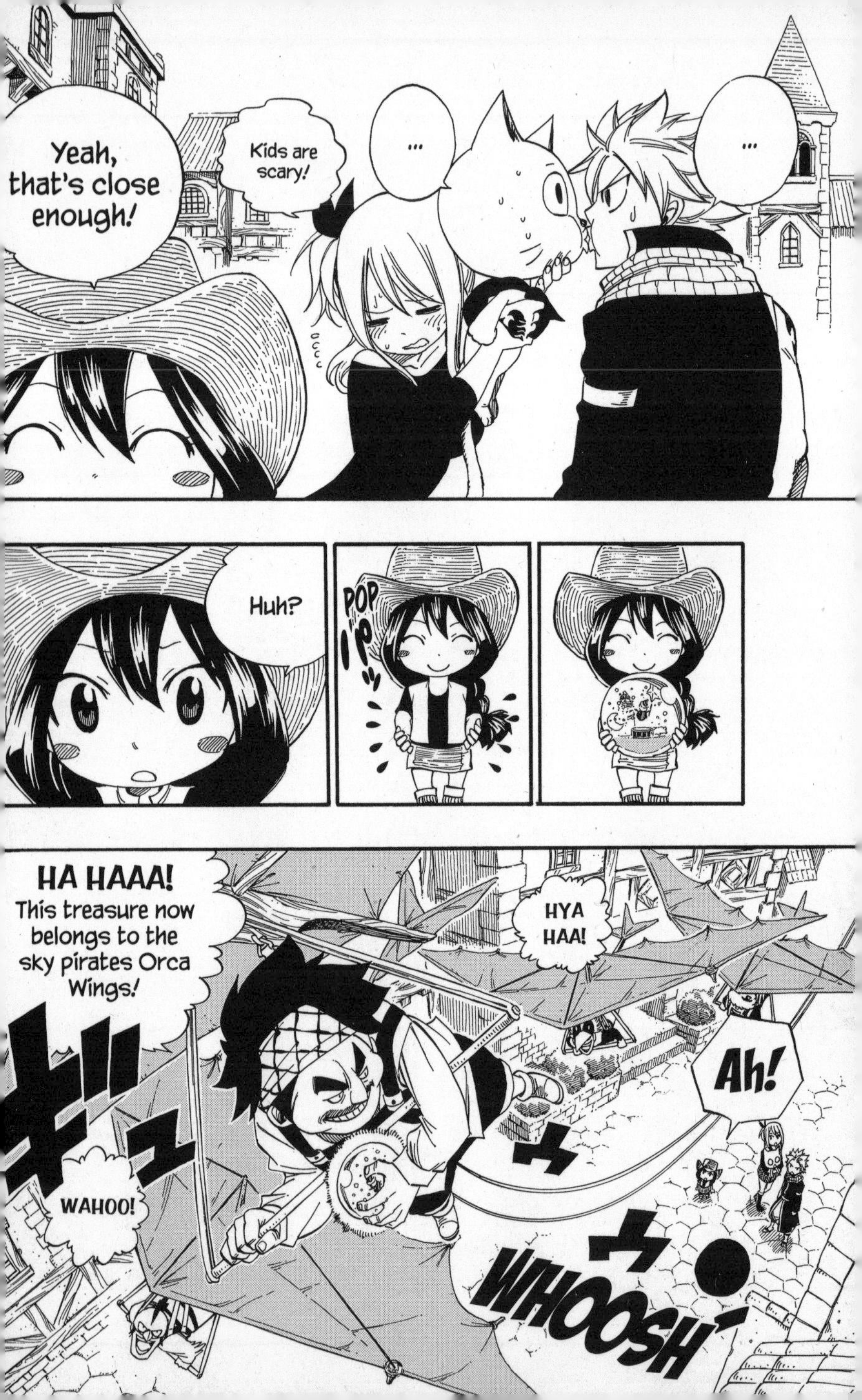
...
...
Kids are scary!
Yeah, that's close enough!
POP POP
Huh?
HYA HAA!
HA HAAA! This treasure now belongs to the sky pirates Orca Wings!
Ah!
WHOOSH
WAHOO!

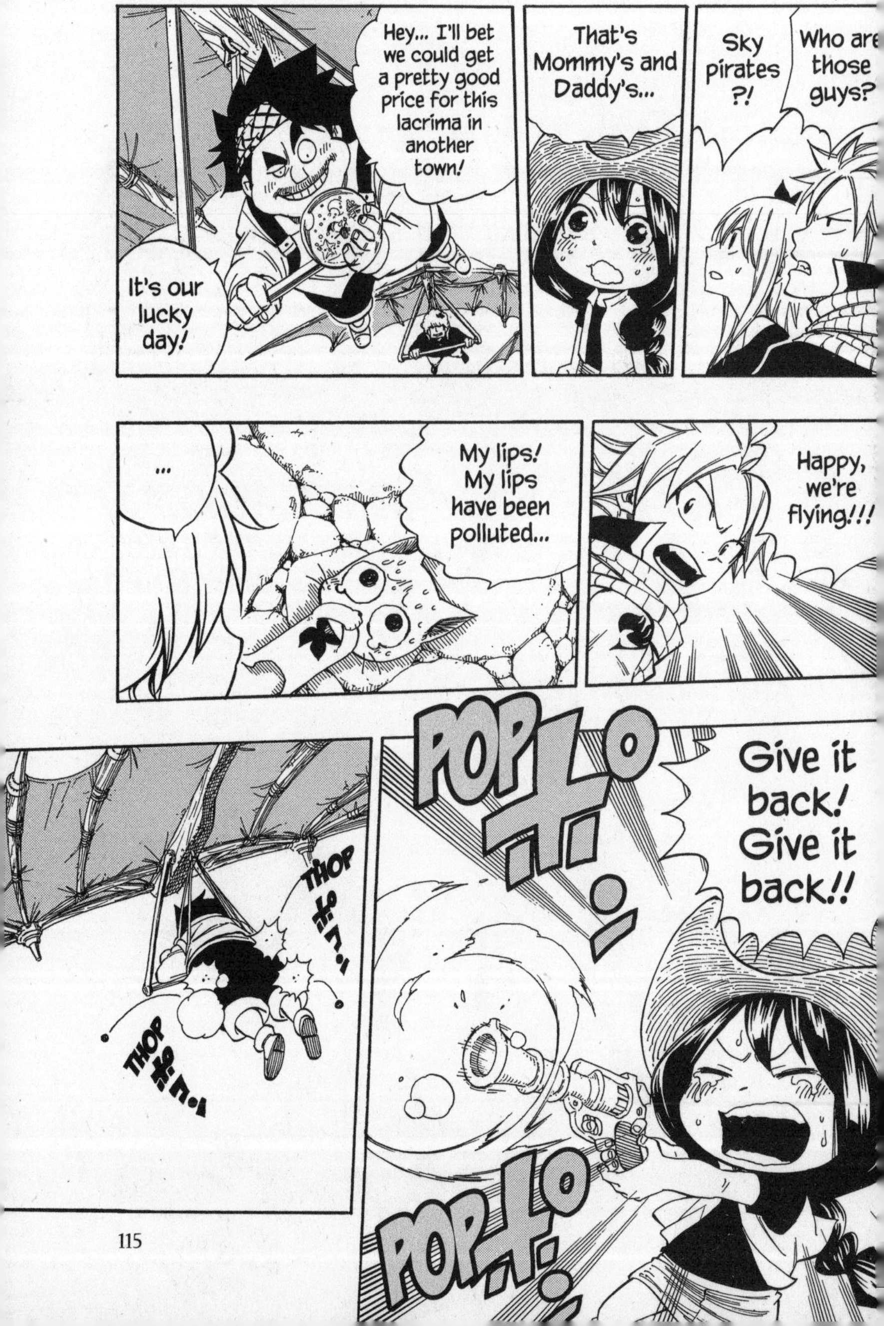

Who are those guys?
Sky pirates ?!
That's Mommy's and Daddy's...
Hey... I'll bet we could get a pretty good price for this lacrima in another town!
It's our lucky day!
Happy, we're flying!!!
My lips! My lips have been polluted...
...
POP
Give it back! Give it back!!
POP
THOP
THOP

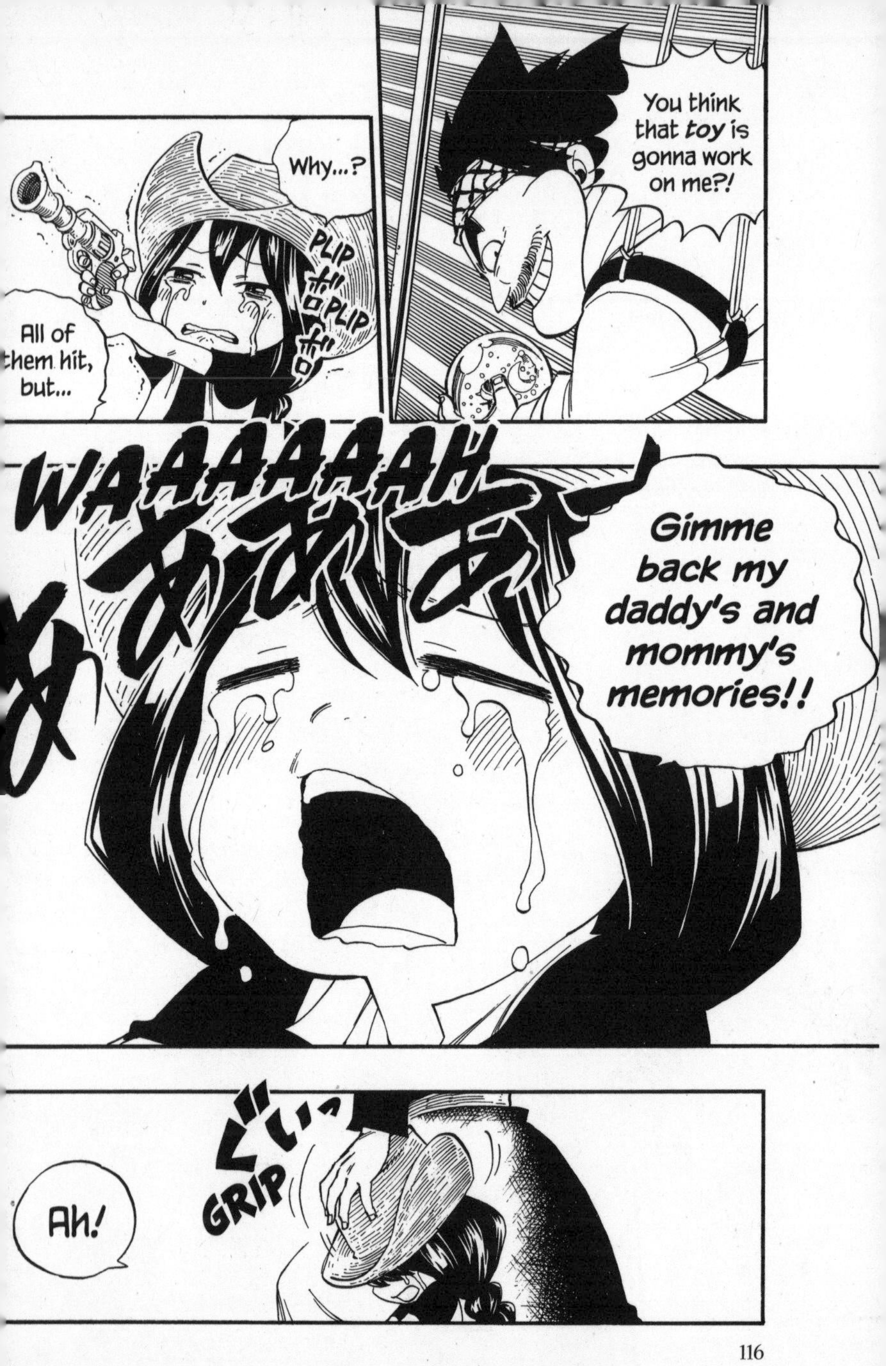
You think that *toy* is gonna work on me?!
Why...?
PLIP PLIP
All of them hit, but...
WAAAAAAH
Gimme back my daddy's and mommy's memories!!
GRIP
Ah!

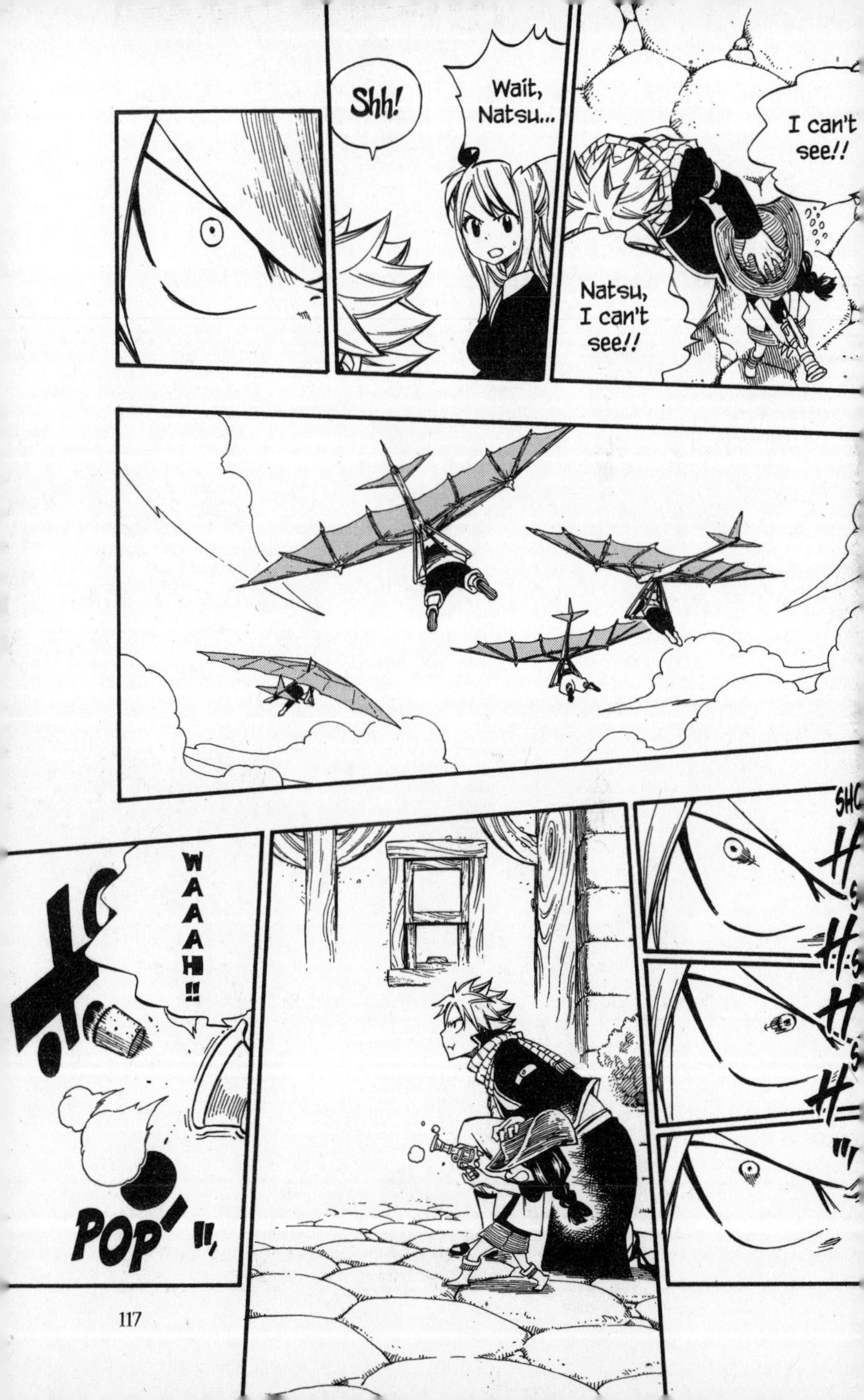
I can't see!!
Natsu, I can't see!!
Wait, Natsu...
Shh!
WAAAAH!!
POP!!

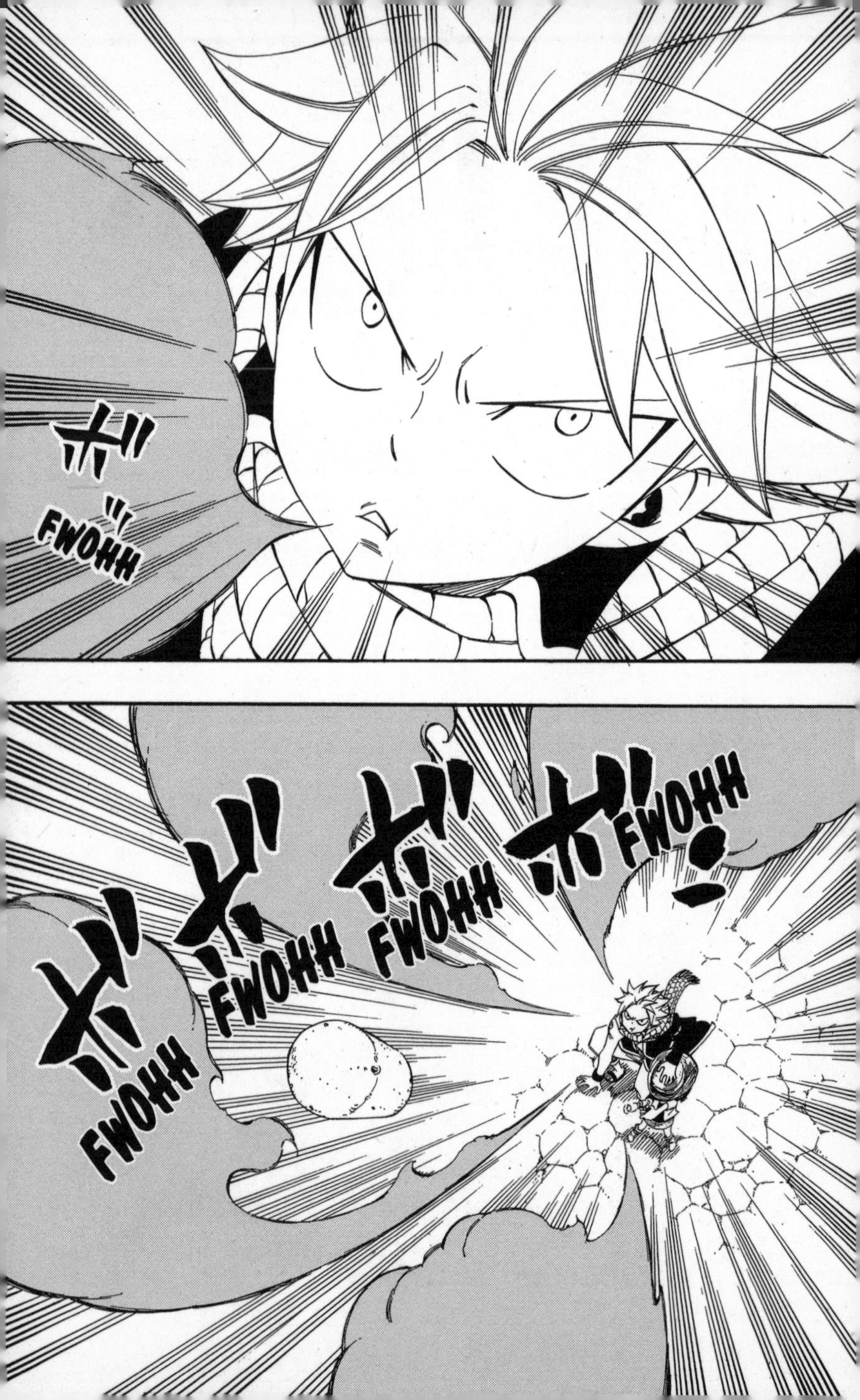
ボ
FWOHH
ボ
FWOHH
ボ
FWOHH
ボ
FWOHH
ボ
FWOHH

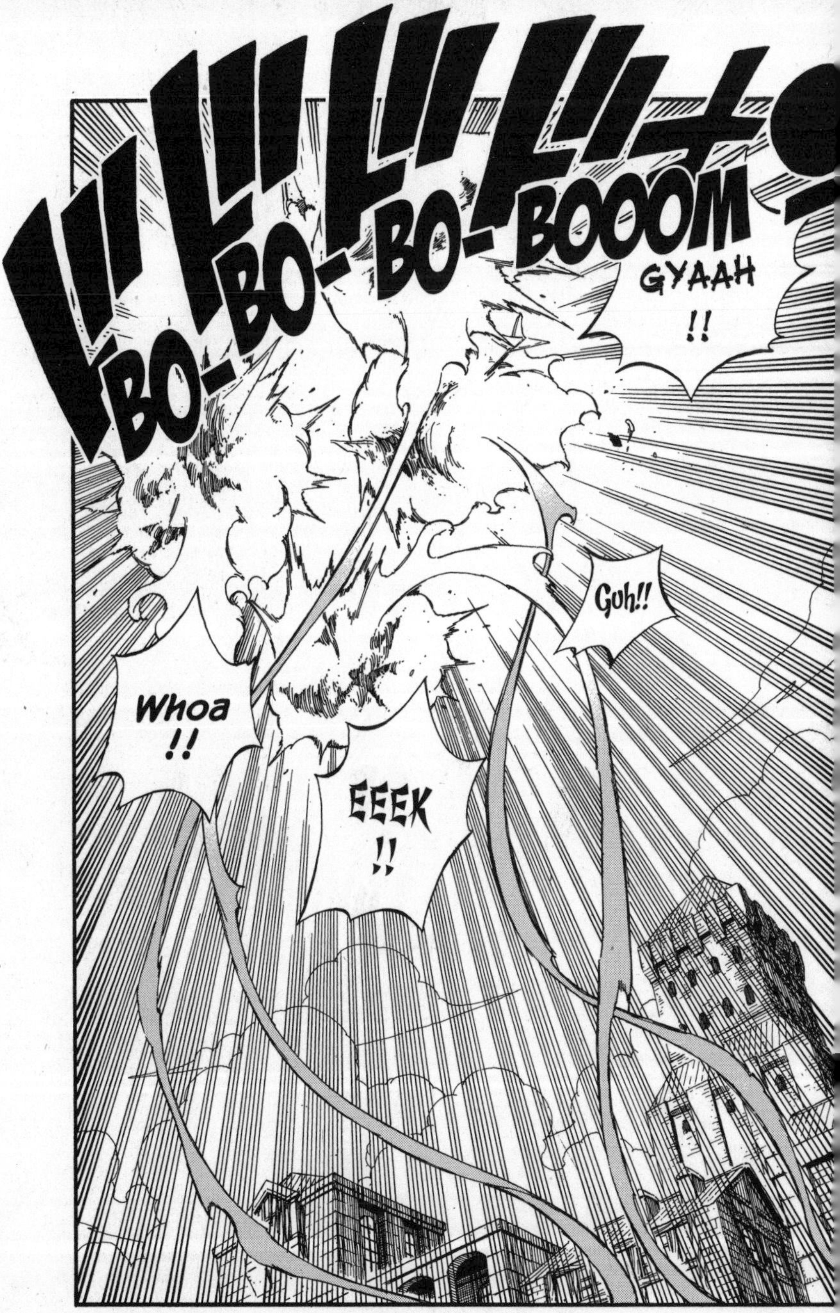
BO-BO-BO-BO-BOOOM
GYAAH !!
Guh!!
EEEK !!
Whoa !!

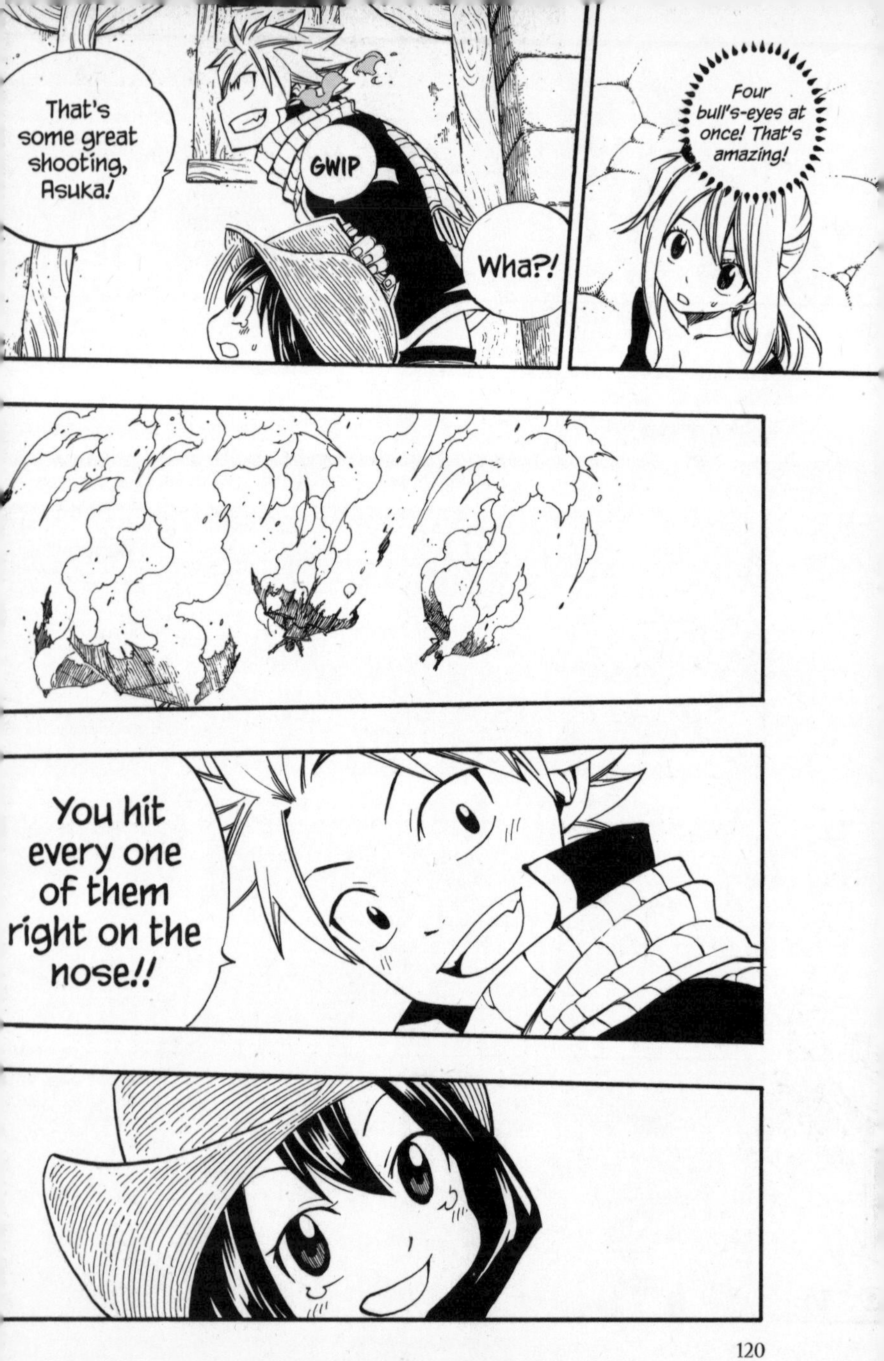

Four bull's-eyes at once! That's amazing!
That's some great shooting, Asuka!
GWIP
Wha?!
You hit every one of them right on the nose!!

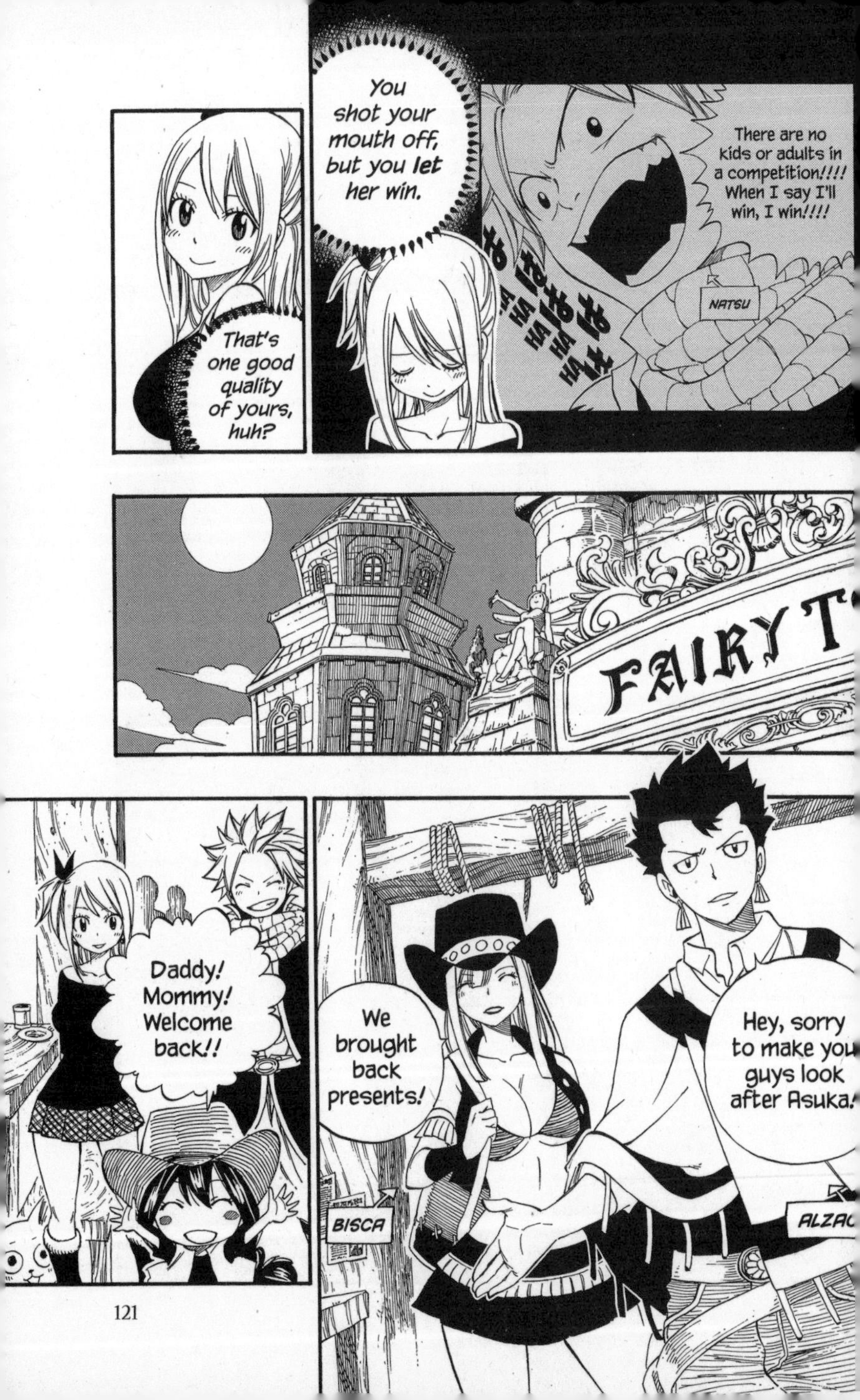

You shot your mouth off, but you let her win.
There are no kids or adults in a competition!!!! When I say I'll win, I win!!!!
NATSU
HA HA HA HA
That's one good quality of yours, huh?
FAIRY T
Hey, sorry to make you guys look after Asuka!
ALZAC
We brought back presents!
BISCA
Daddy! Mommy! Welcome back!!

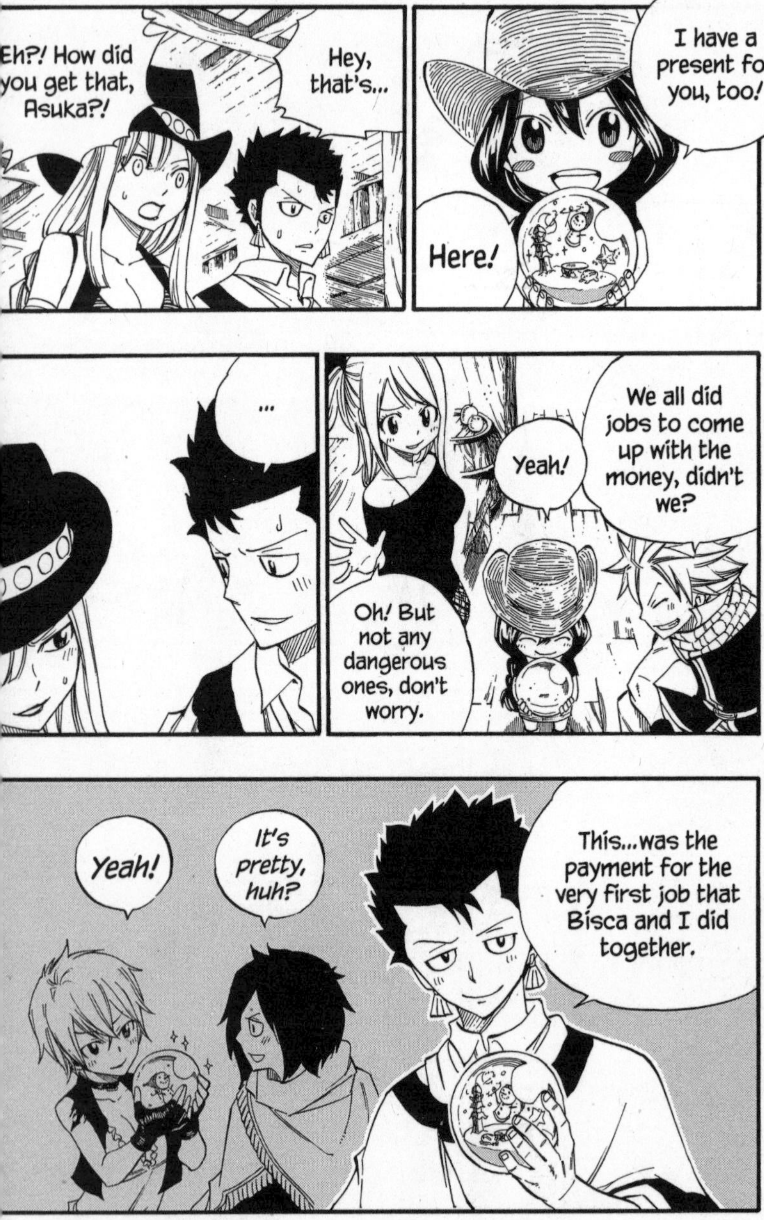
I have a present for you, too!
Here!
Hey, that's...
Eh?! How did you get that, Asuka?!
We all did jobs to come up with the money, didn't we?
Yeah!
Oh! But not any dangerous ones, don't worry.
...
This...was the payment for the very first job that Bisca and I did together.
It's pretty, huh?
Yeah!

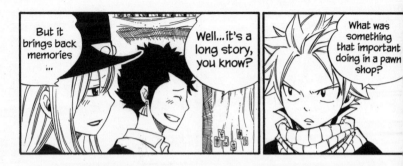

What was something that important doing in a pawn shop?
Well...it's a long story, you know?
But it brings back memories ...
You sold it because you didn't need it anymore?
No. We sold it because we needed to.
HUP
?
Someday, you'll understand.
Now, let's go home.
Yeah!
Hey, listen to this! Natsu *kissed* Happy full on the mouth!
AH HA HA!! Isn't friendship grand?!
HEE HEE HEE!

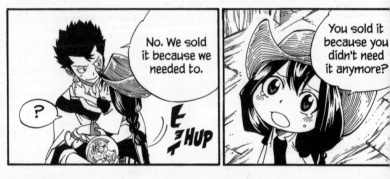

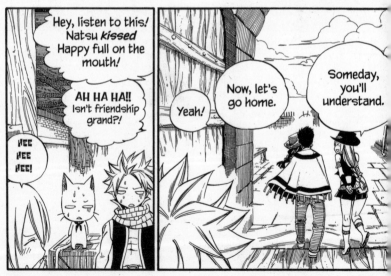

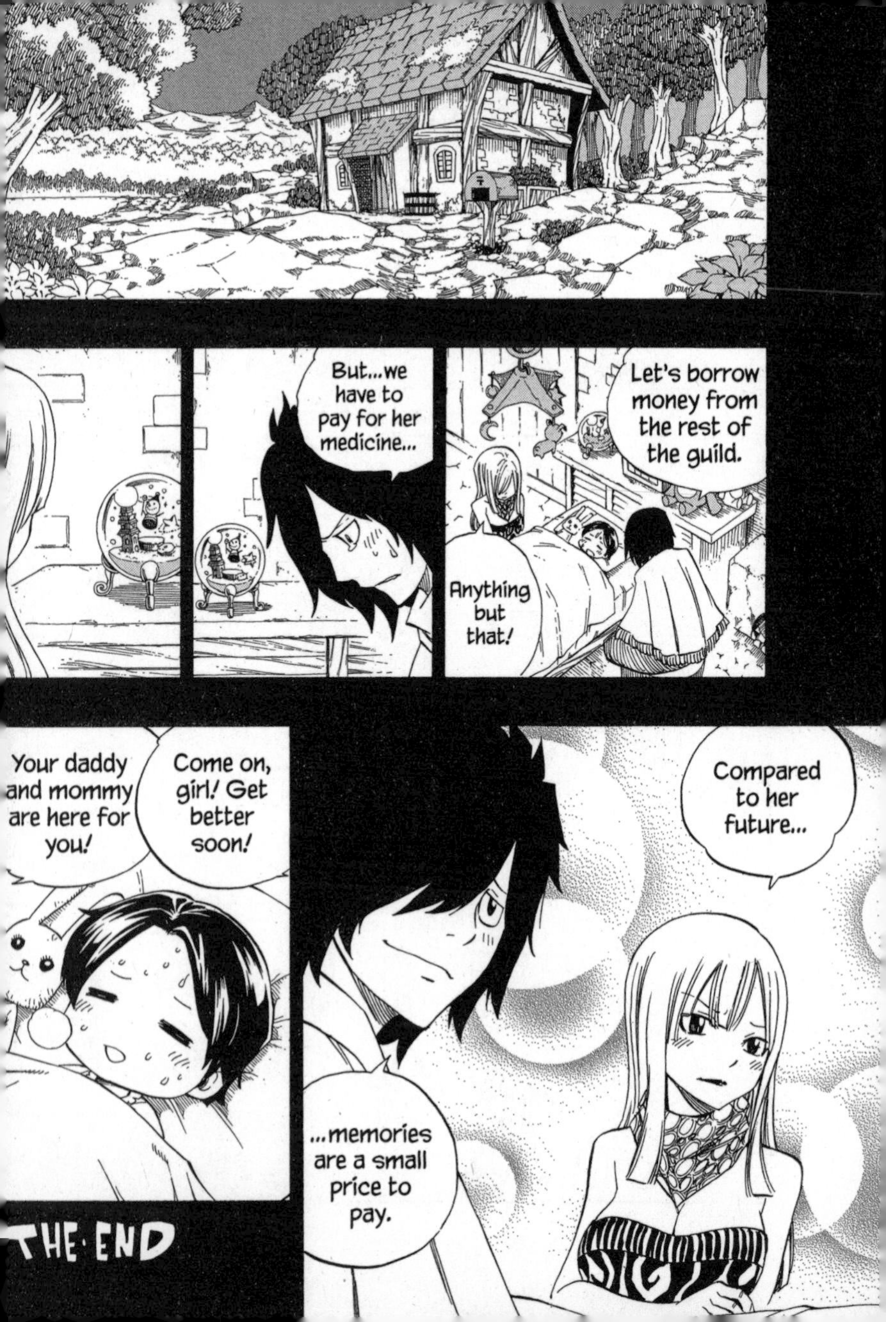
Let's borrow money from the rest of the guild.
Anything but that!
But...we have to pay for her medicine...
Compared to her future...
...memories are a small price to pay.
Come on, girl! Get better soon!
Your daddy and mommy are here for you!
THE END

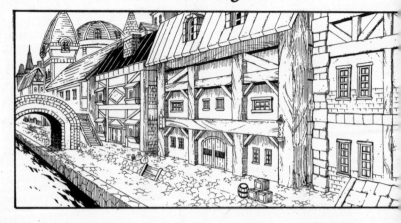

YAAWWN...

I was out like a light!

?!

Good mor...

Good morning.

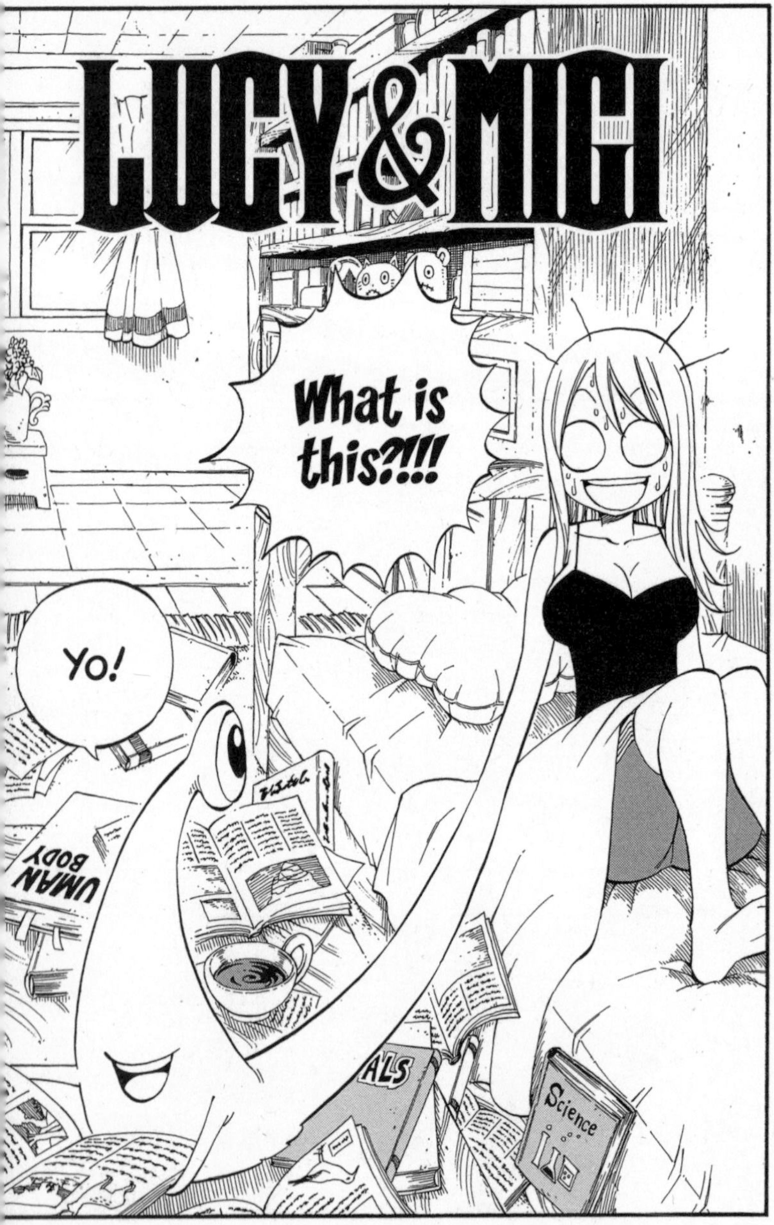

LUCY & MICH
What is this?!!!
Yo!
UMAN BODY
ALS
Science

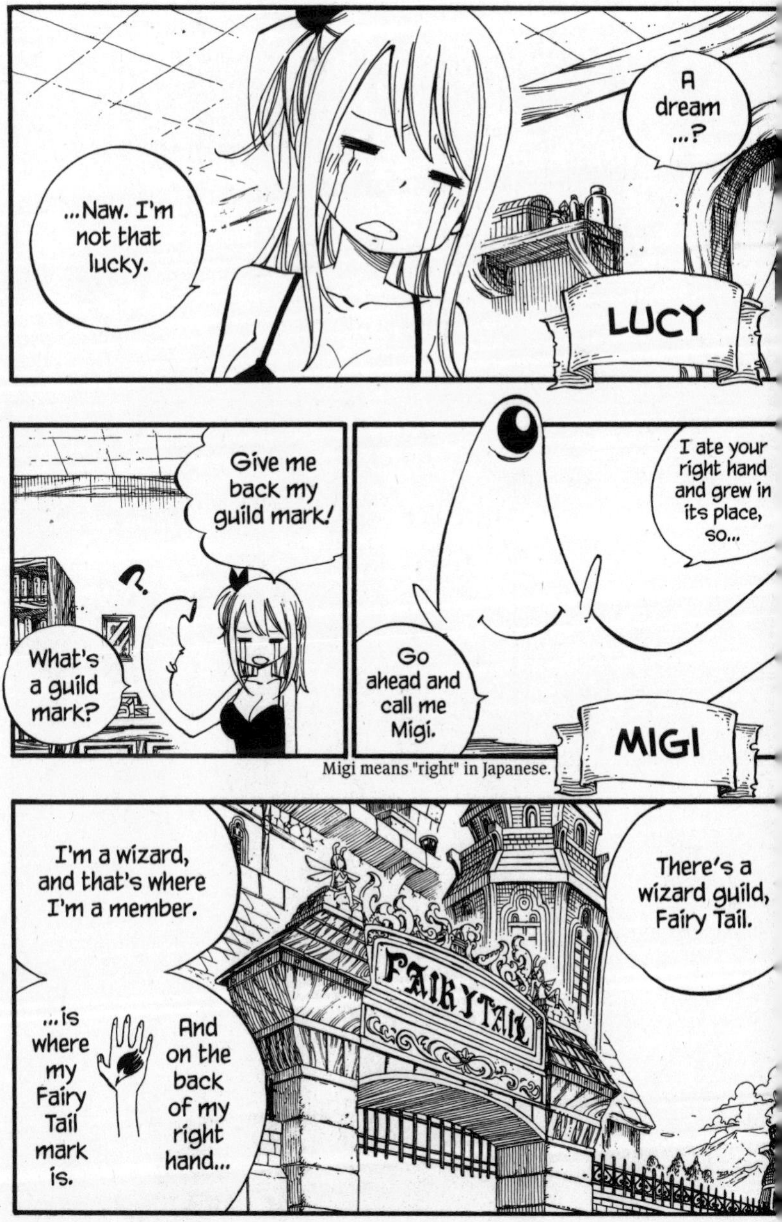
A dream ...?
...Naw. I'm not that lucky.
LUCY
I ate your right hand and grew in its place, so...
Go ahead and call me Migi.
MIGI
Give me back my guild mark!
?
What's a guild mark?
There's a wizard guild, Fairy Tail.
I'm a wizard, and that's where I'm a member.
FAIRY TAIL
And on the back of my right hand...
...is where my Fairy Tail mark is.

Migi means "right" in Japanese.

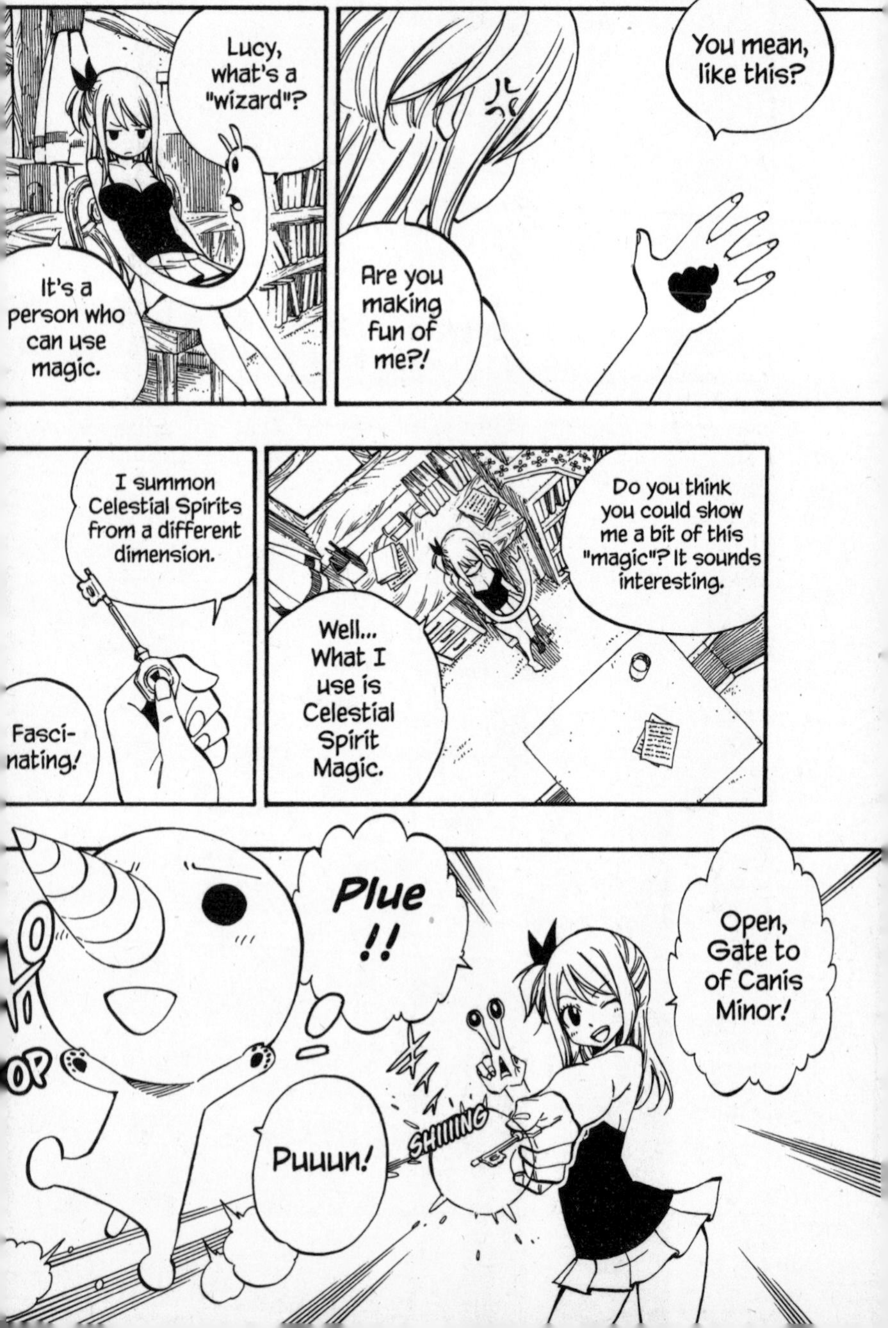

You mean, like this?
Are you making fun of me?!
Lucy, what's a "wizard"?
It's a person who can use magic.
Do you think you could show me a bit of this "magic"? It sounds interesting.
Well... What I use is Celestial Spirit Magic.
I summon Celestial Spirits from a different dimension.
Fasci-nating!
Open, Gate to of Canis Minor!
SHIIIING
Plue !!
Puuun!

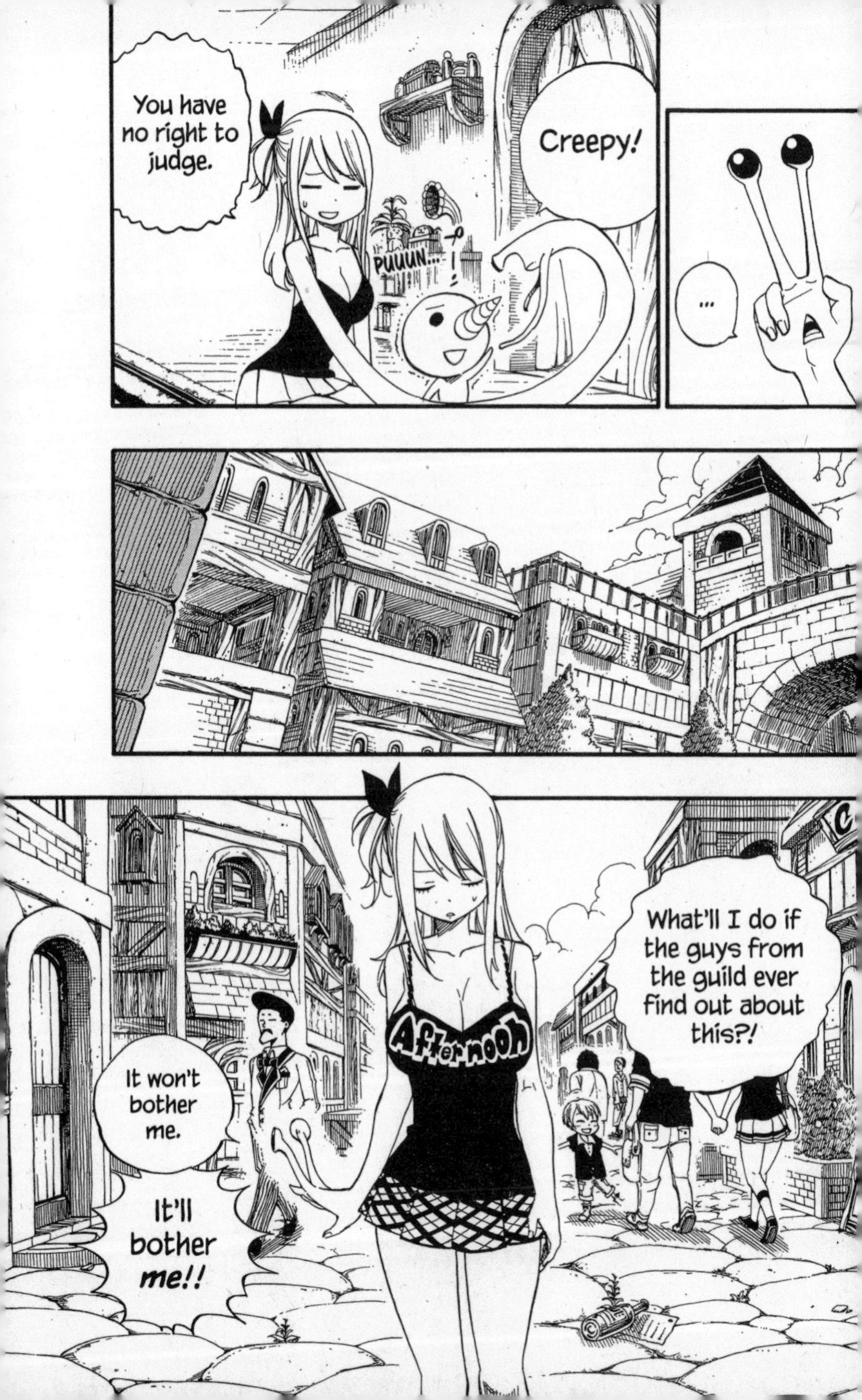
...
Creepy!
You have no right to judge.
PUUUN...
What'll I do if the guys from the guild ever find out about this?!
Afternoon
It won't bother me.
It'll bother *me!!*

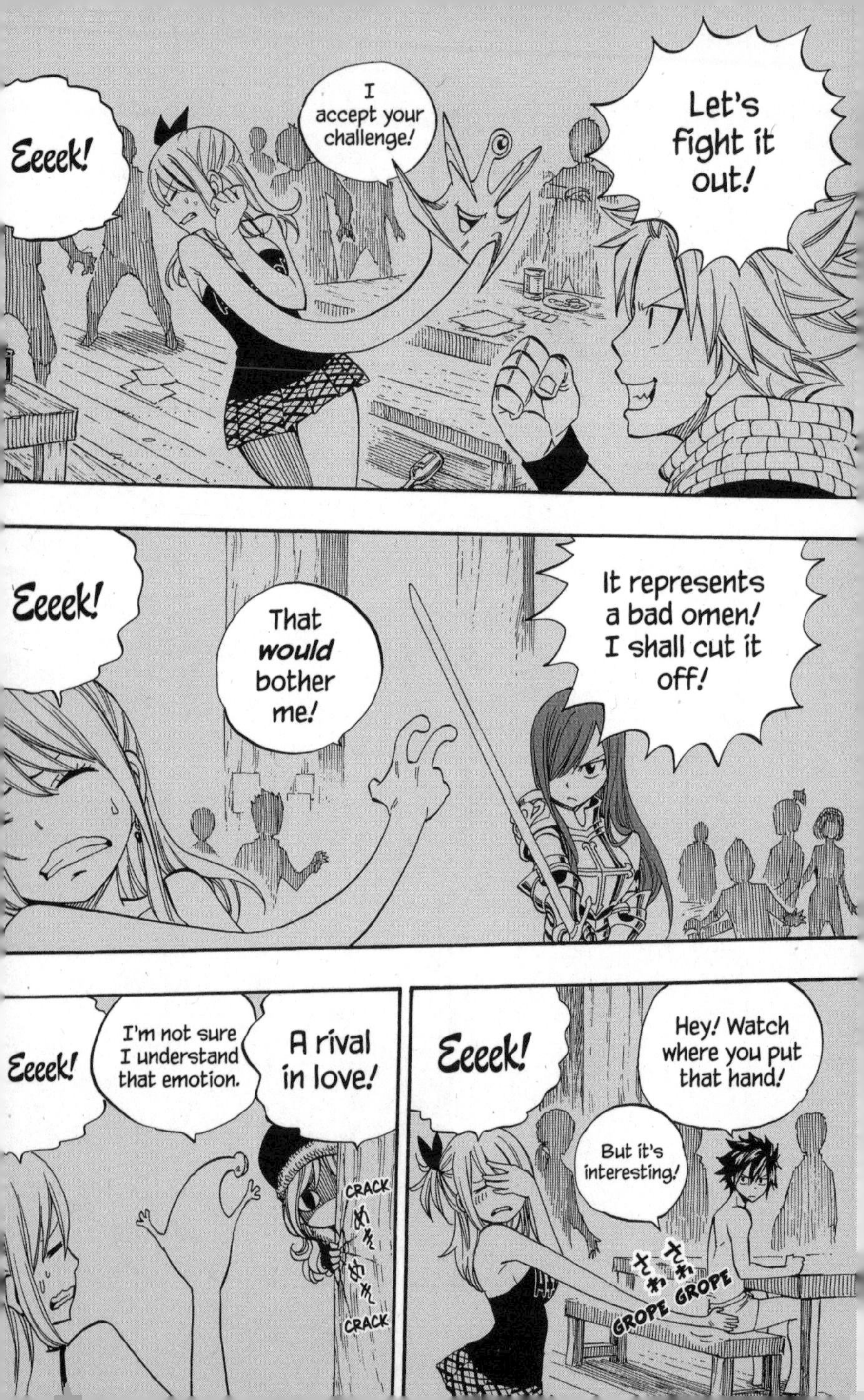
Let's fight it out!
I accept your challenge!
Eeeek!
It represents a bad omen! I shall cut it off!
That *would* bother me!
Eeeek!
Hey! Watch where you put that hand!
Eeeek!
But it's interesting!
GROPE GROPE
A rival in love!
CRACK
CRACK
I'm not sure I understand that emotion.
Eeeek!

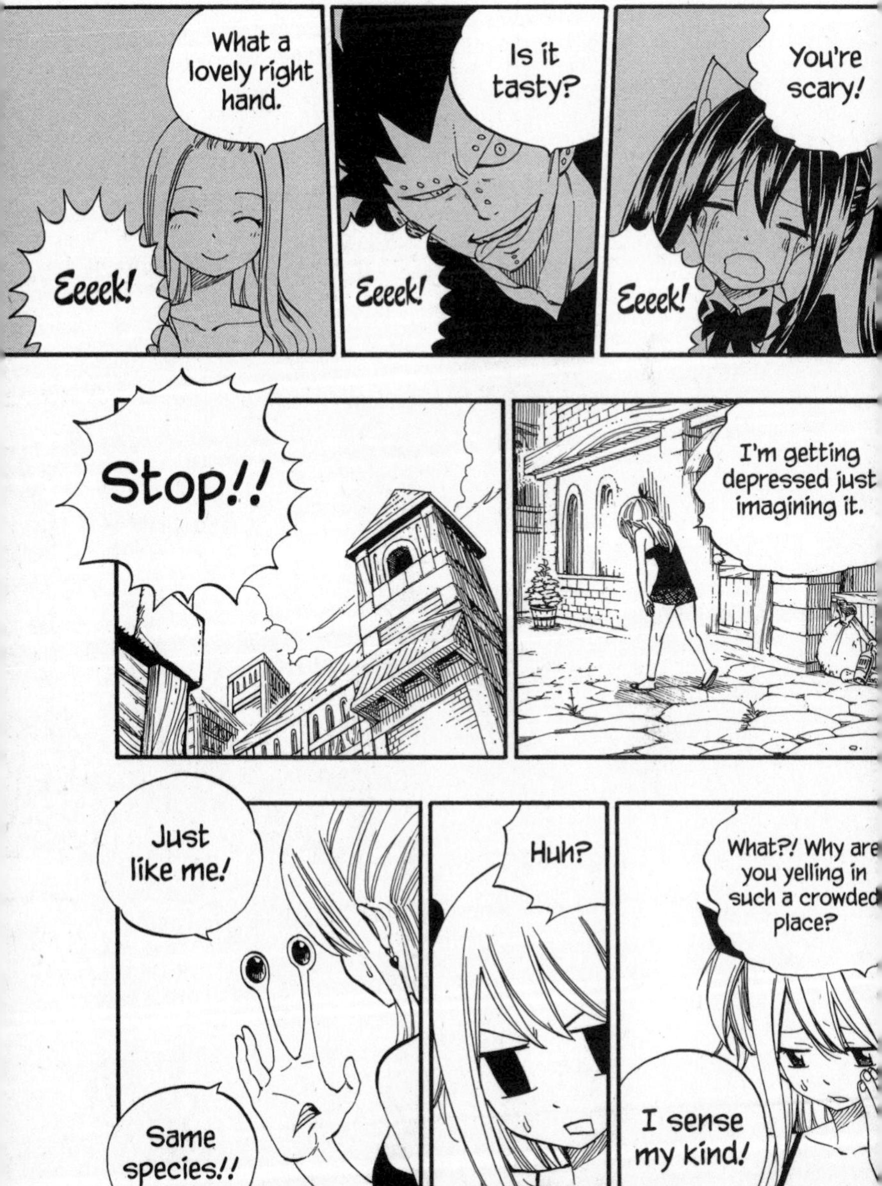
You're scary!
Eeeek!
Is it tasty?
Eeeek!
What a lovely right hand.
Eeeek!
I'm getting depressed just imagining it.
Stop!!
What?! Why are you yelling in such a crowded place?
I sense my kind!
Huh?
Just like me!
Same species!!

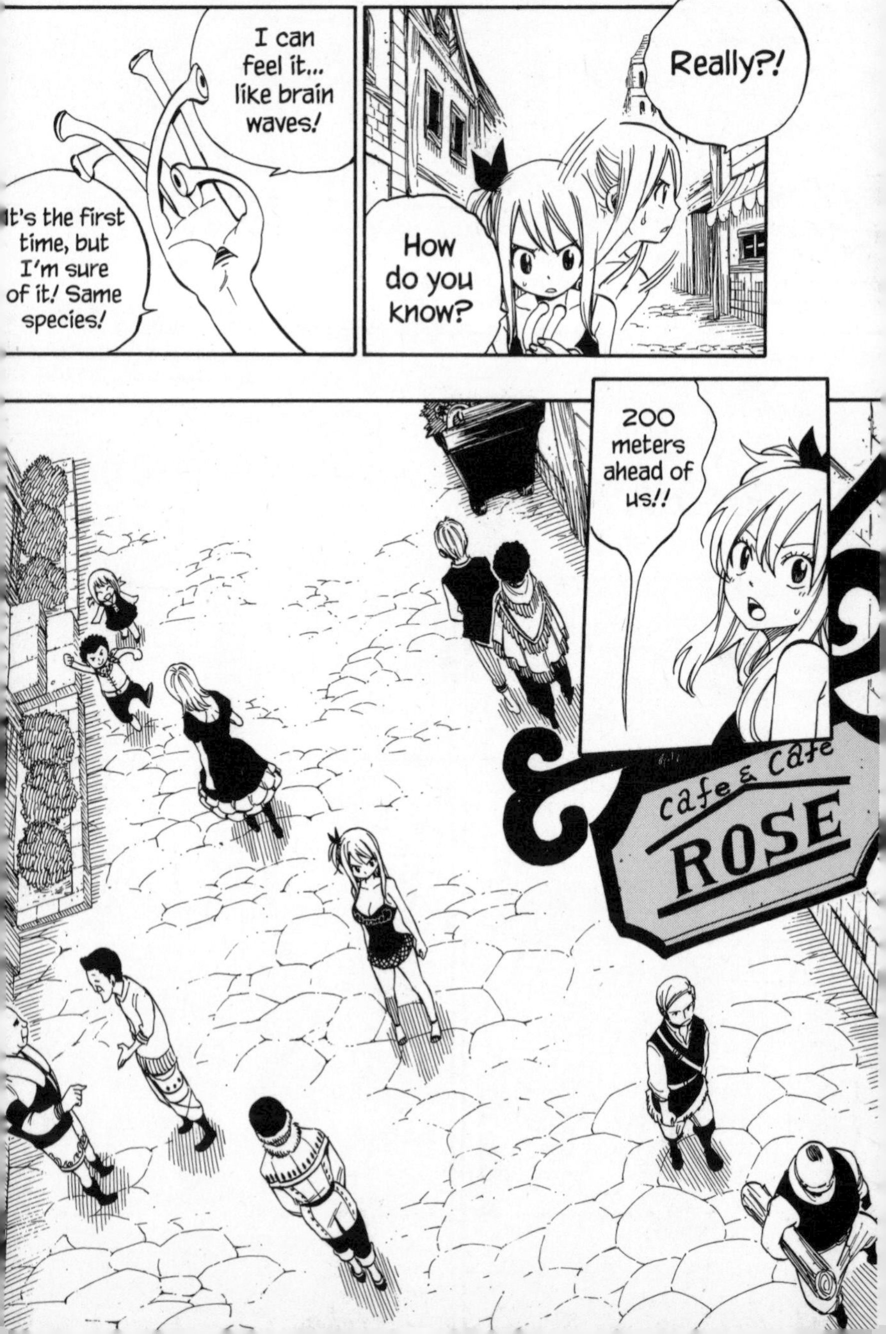
Really?!
How do you know?
I can feel it... like brain waves!
It's the first time, but I'm sure of it! Same species!
200 meters ahead of us!!
cafe & cafe
ROSE

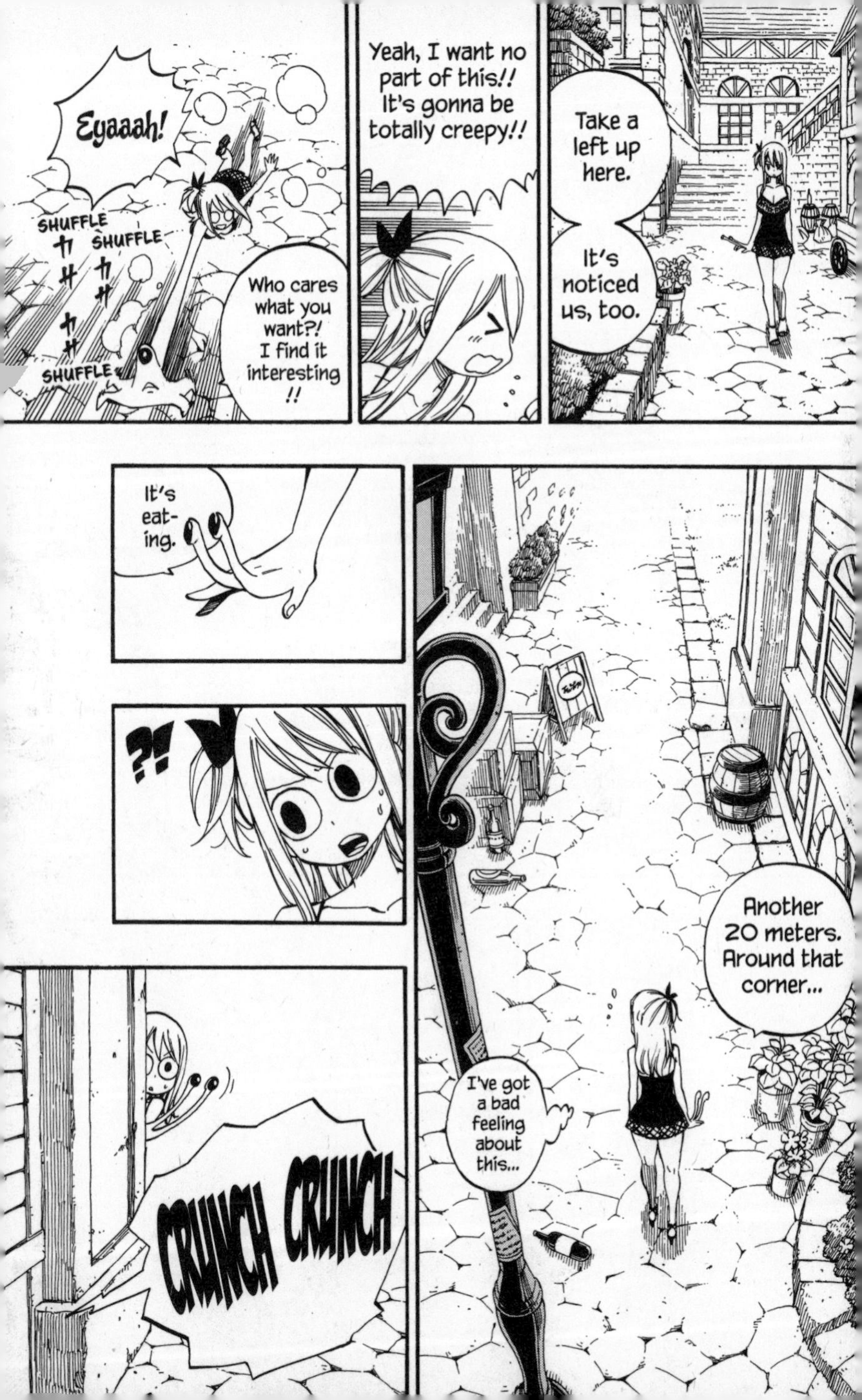
Take a left up here.
It's noticed us, too.
Yeah, I want no part of this!! It's gonna be totally creepy!!
Eyaaah!
Who cares what you want?! I find it interesting!!
SHUFFLE SHUFFLE SHUFFLE
Another 20 meters. Around that corner...
I've got a bad feeling about this...
It's eating.
?!
CRUNCH CRUNCH

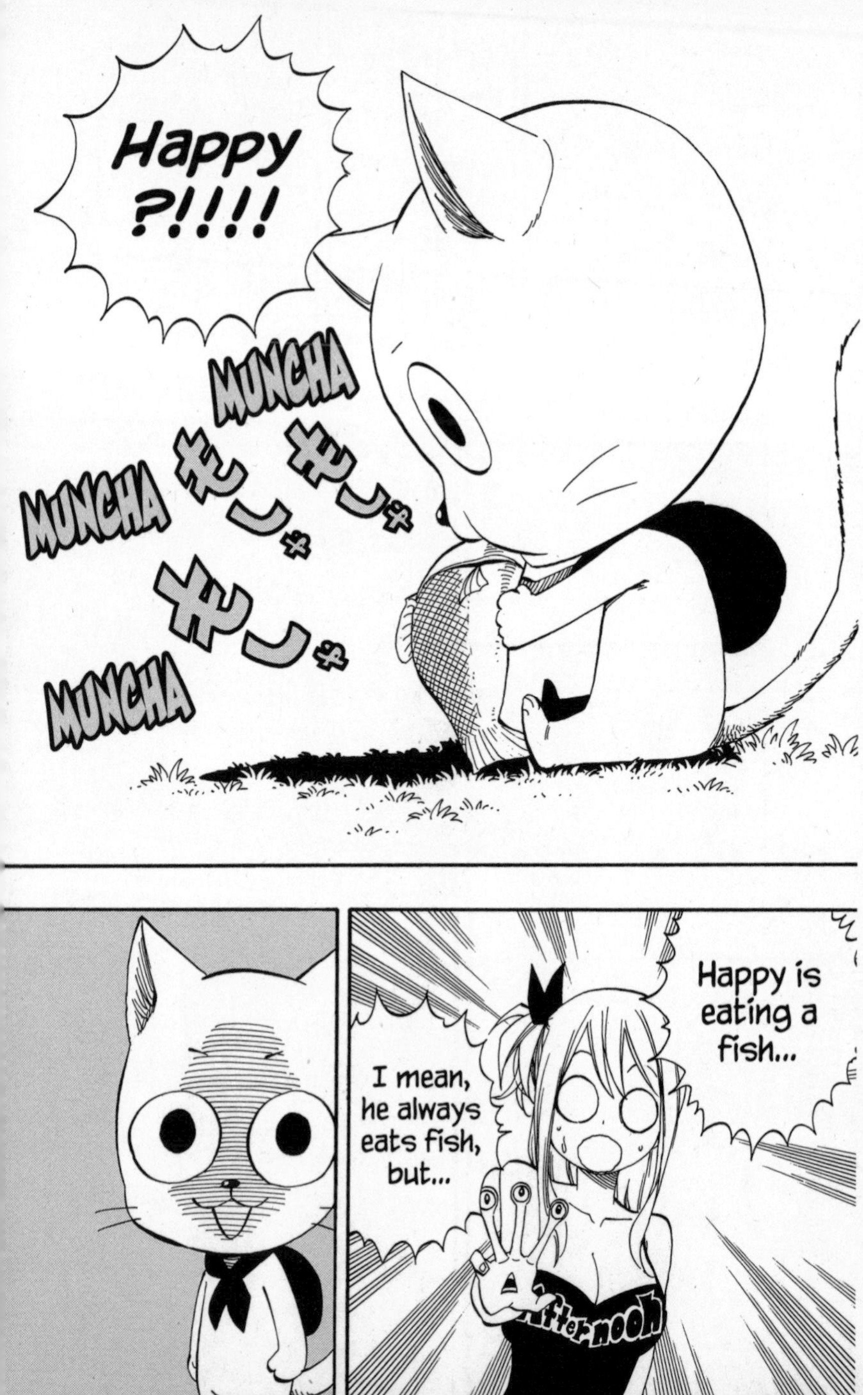
Happy ?!!!!
MUNCHA
もしゃ
MUNCHA
もしゃ
MUNCHA
もしゃ
Happy is eating a fish...
I mean, he always eats fish, but...

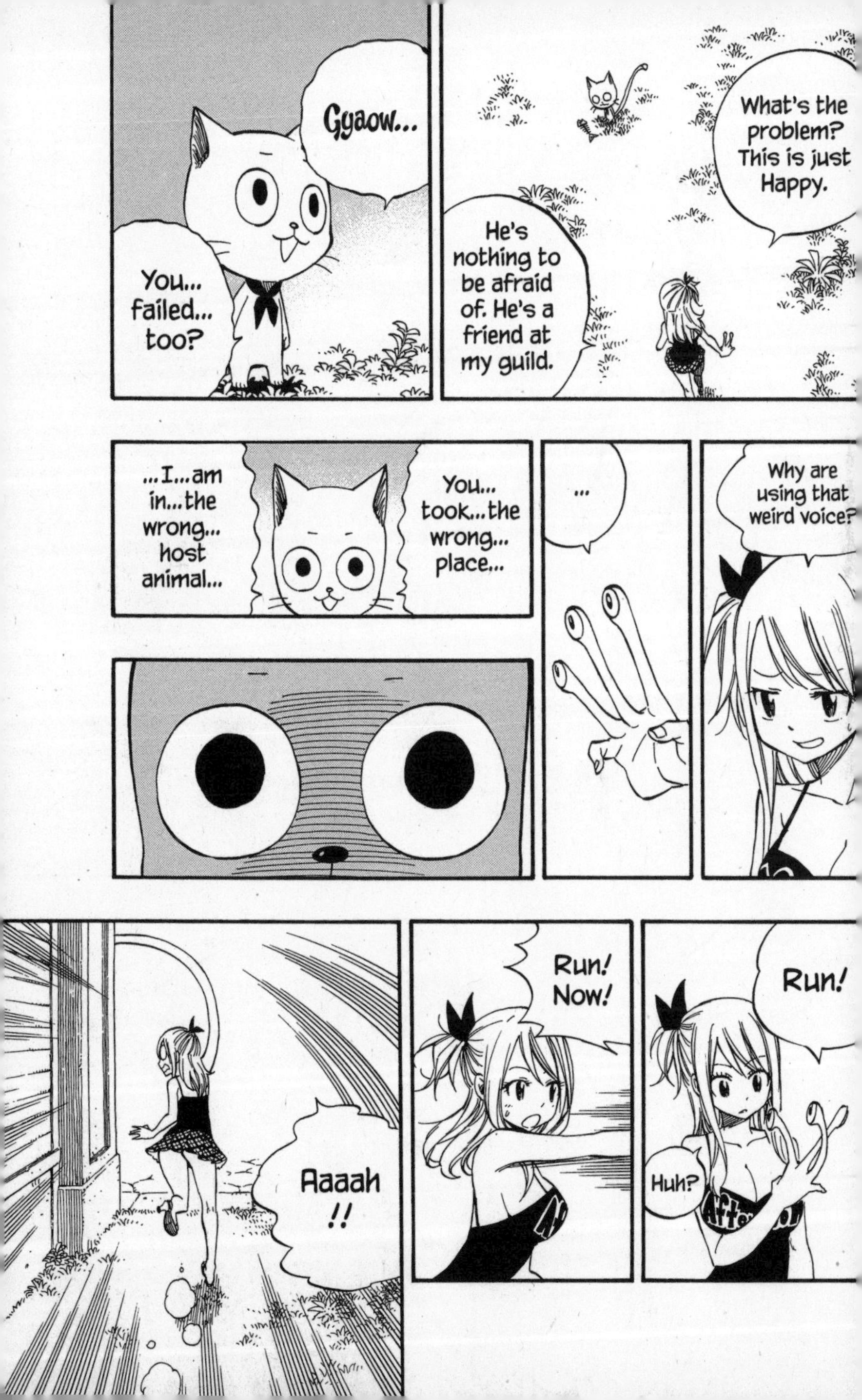
What's the problem? This is just Happy.
He's nothing to be afraid of. He's a friend at my guild.
Gyaow...
You... failed... too?
Why are using that weird voice?
...
You... took...the wrong... place...
...I...am in...the wrong... host animal...
Run!
Huh?
Run! Now!
Aaaah !!

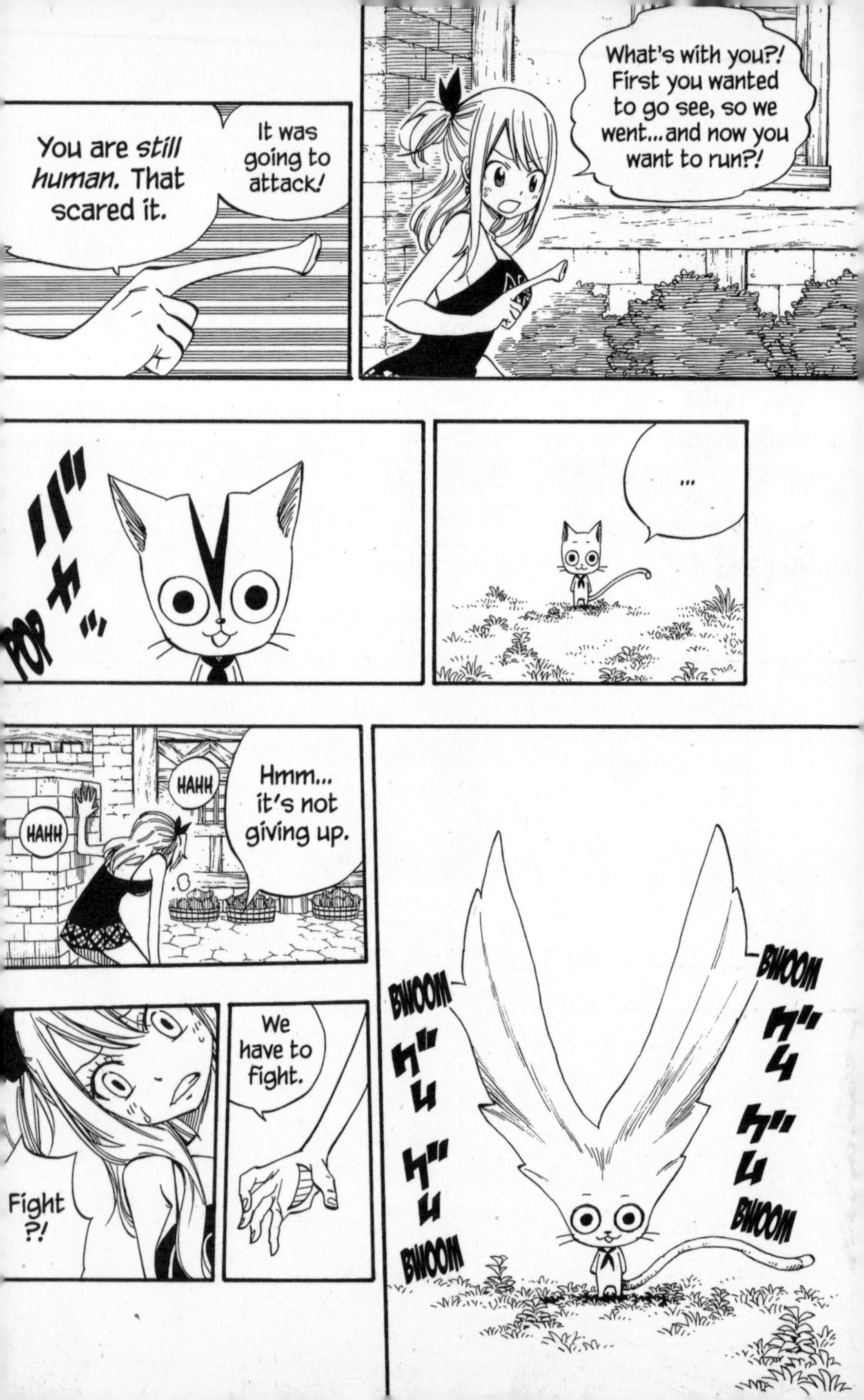

What's with you?! First you wanted to go see, so we went...and now you want to run?!
It was going to attack!
You are *still human.* That scared it.
...
POP
BWOOM
BWOOM
BWOOM
BWOOM
Hmm... it's not giving up.
HAHH
HAHH
We have to fight.
Fight ?!

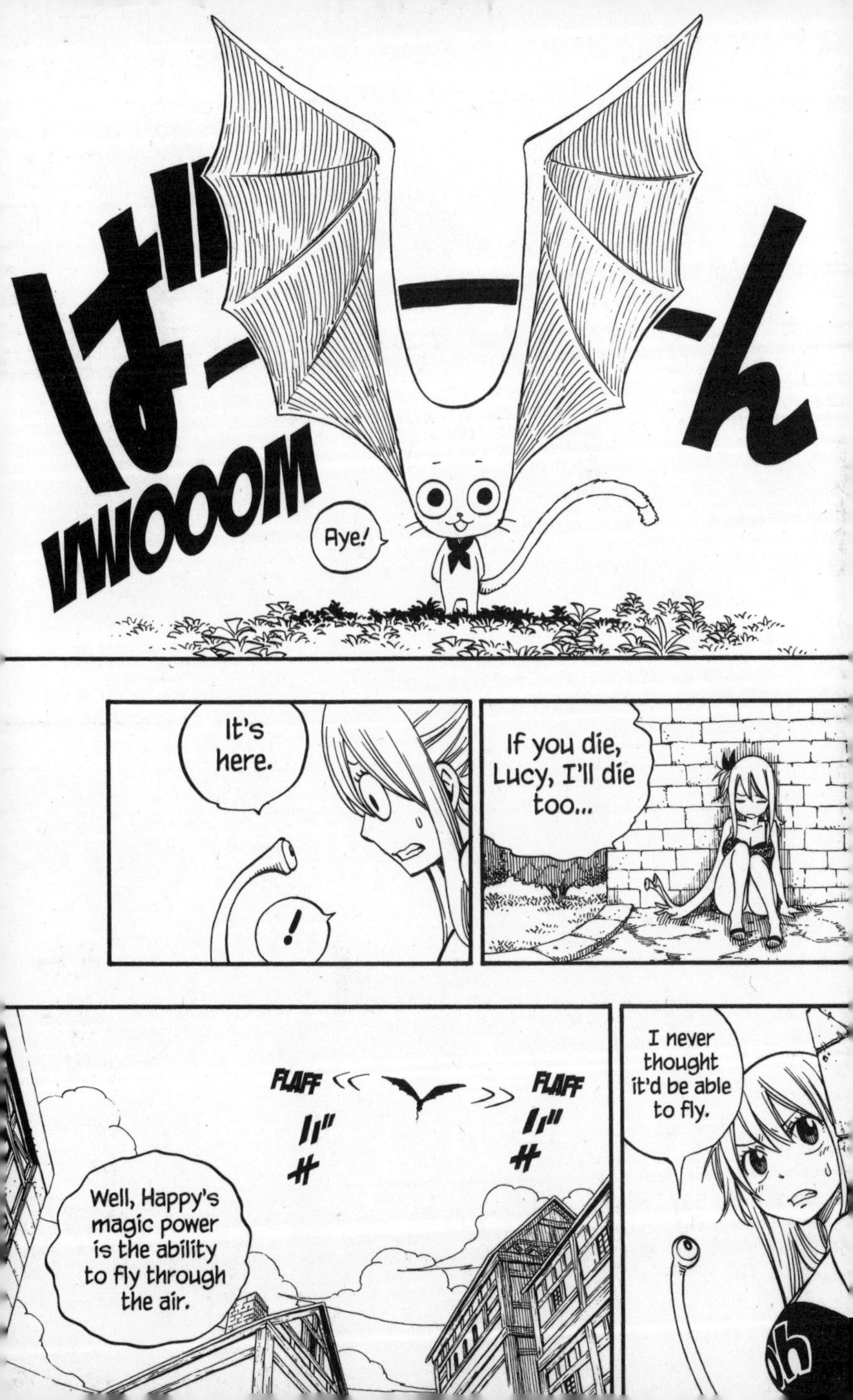
VWOOOM
Aye!
If you die, Lucy, I'll die too...
It's here.
!
I never thought it'd be able to fly.
FLAFF
FLAFF
Well, Happy's magic power is the ability to fly through the air.

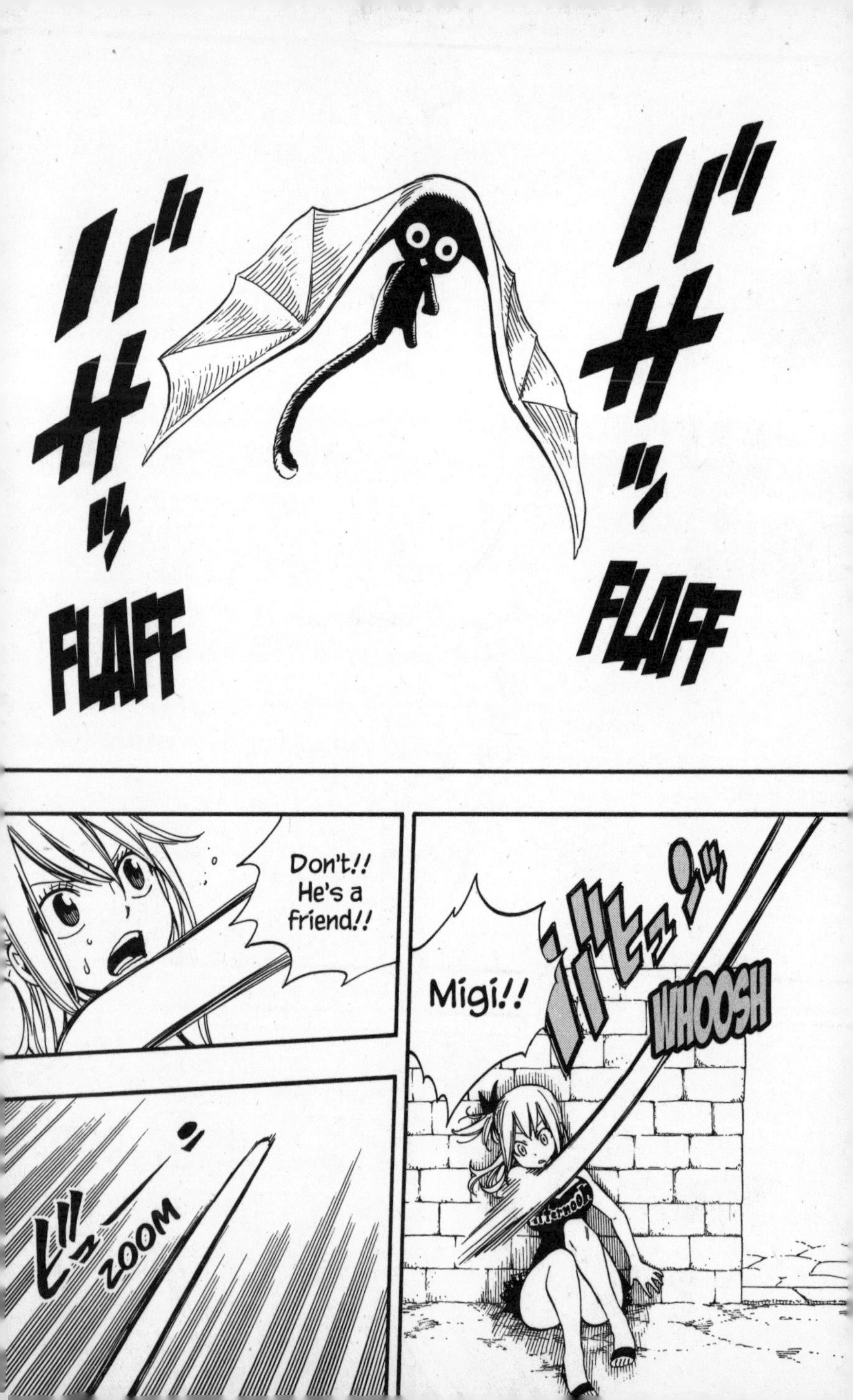
FLAFF
FLAFF
Migi!!
WHOOSH
Don't!! He's a friend!!
ZOOM

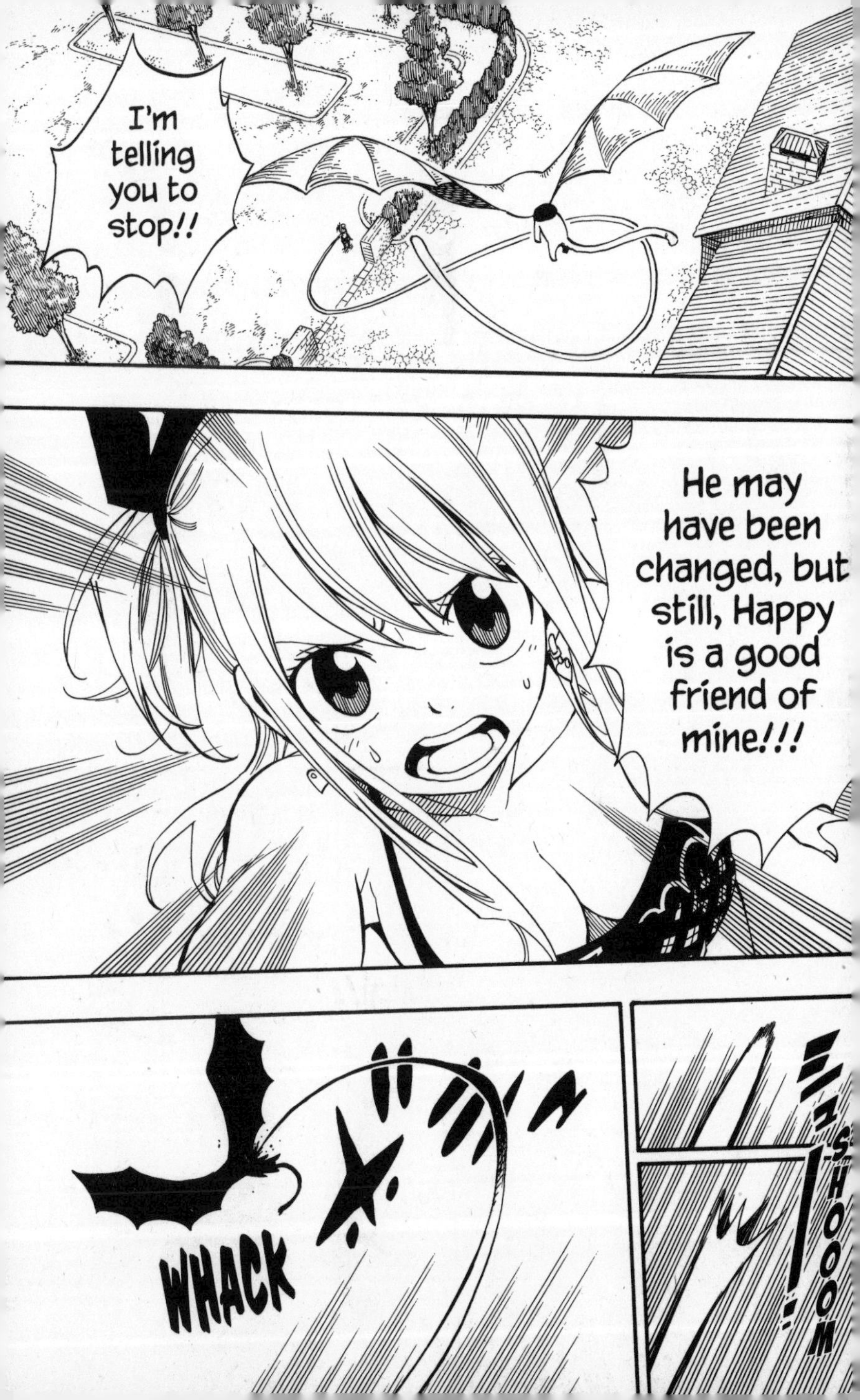
I'm telling you to stop!!
He may have been changed, but still, Happy is a good friend of mine!!!
SHOOOM
WHACK

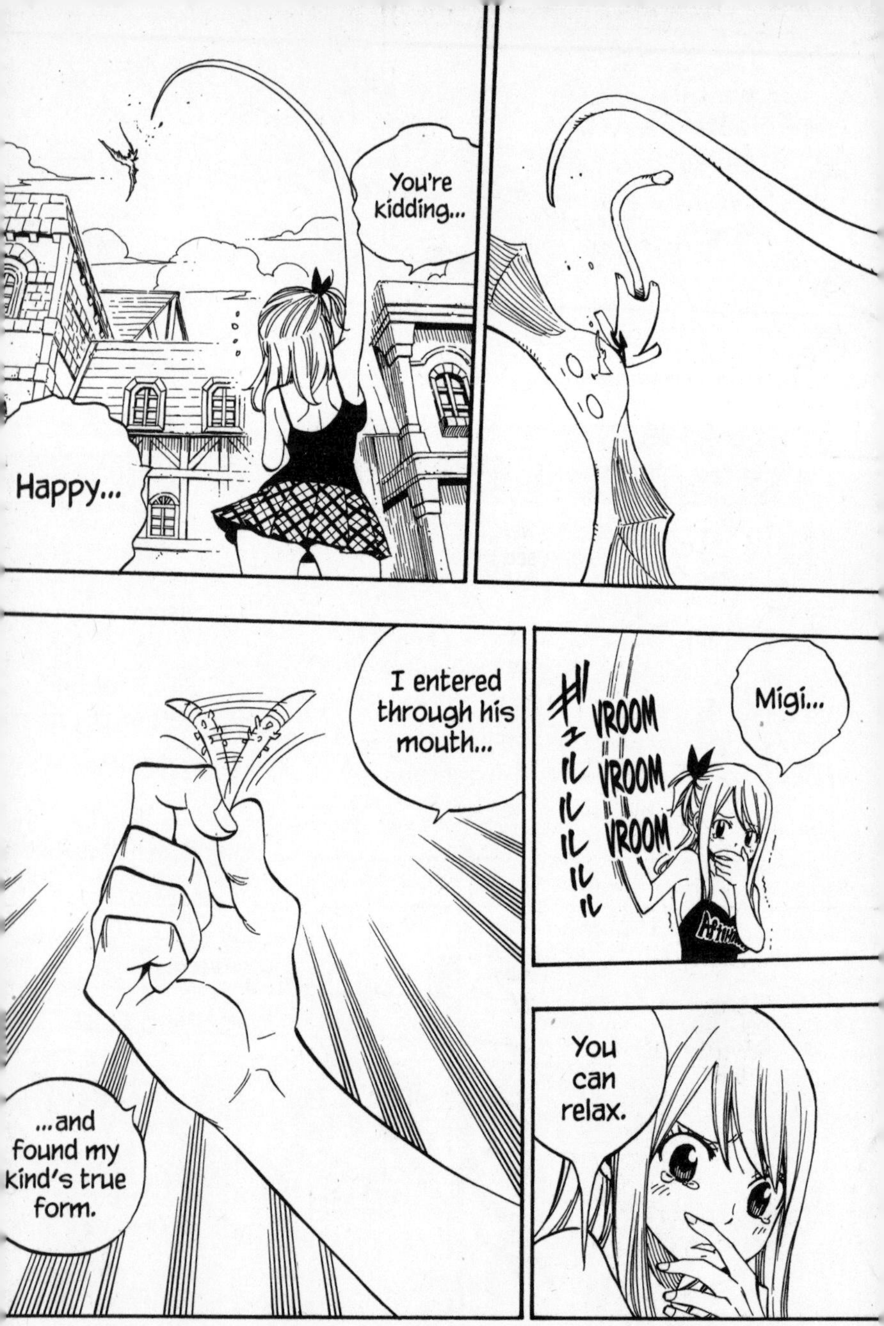

You're kidding...
Happy...
Migi...
ギュルルルルル
VROOM
VROOM
VROOM
You can relax.
I entered through his mouth...
...and found my kind's true form.

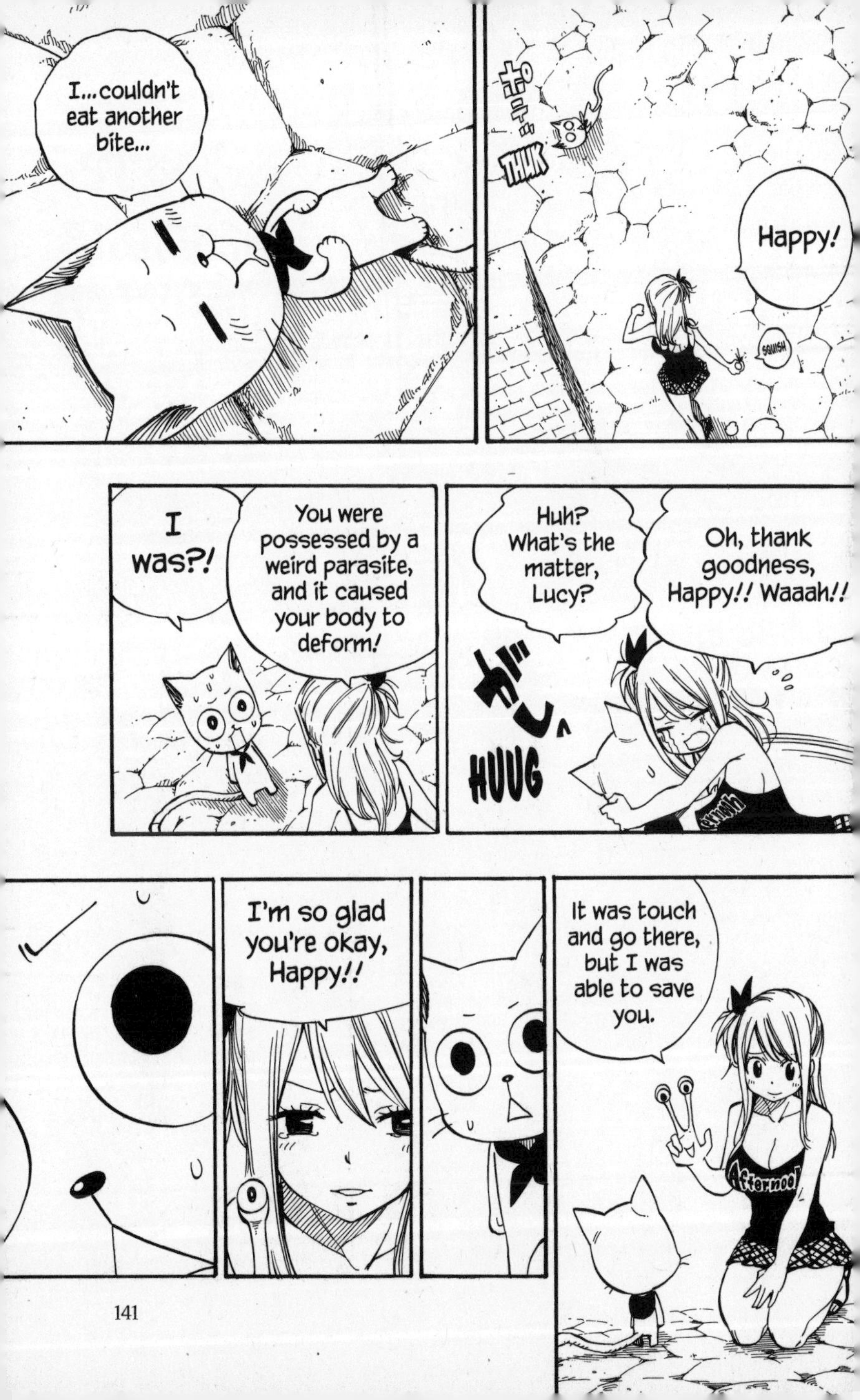
ポテ
THUK
Happy!
SQUISH
I...couldn't eat another bite...
Oh, thank goodness, Happy!! Waaah!!
Huh? What's the matter, Lucy?
がし
HUUG
You were possessed by a weird parasite, and it caused your body to deform!
I was?!
It was touch and go there, but I was able to save you.
I'm so glad you're okay, Happy!!

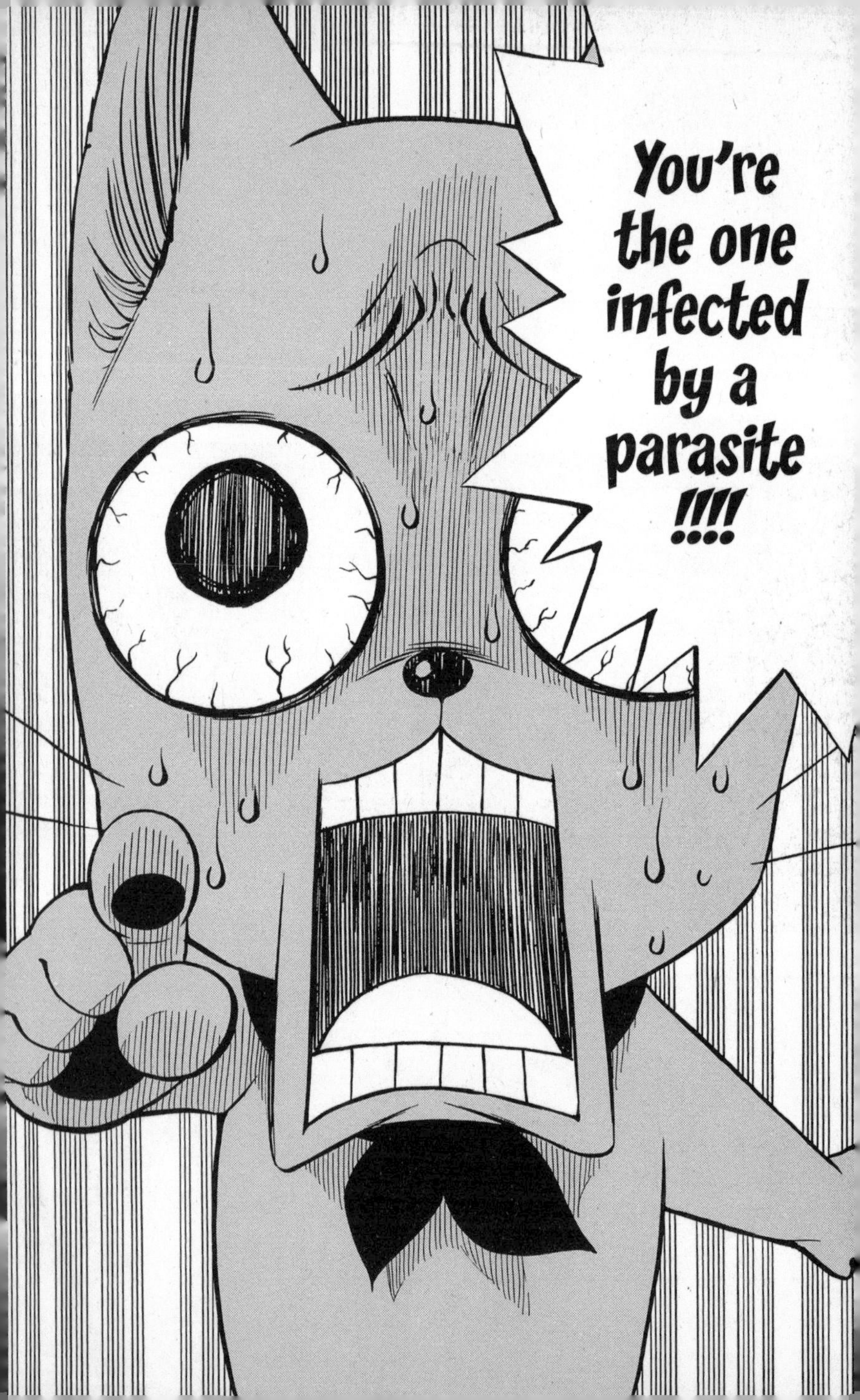
You're the one infected by a parasite!!!!

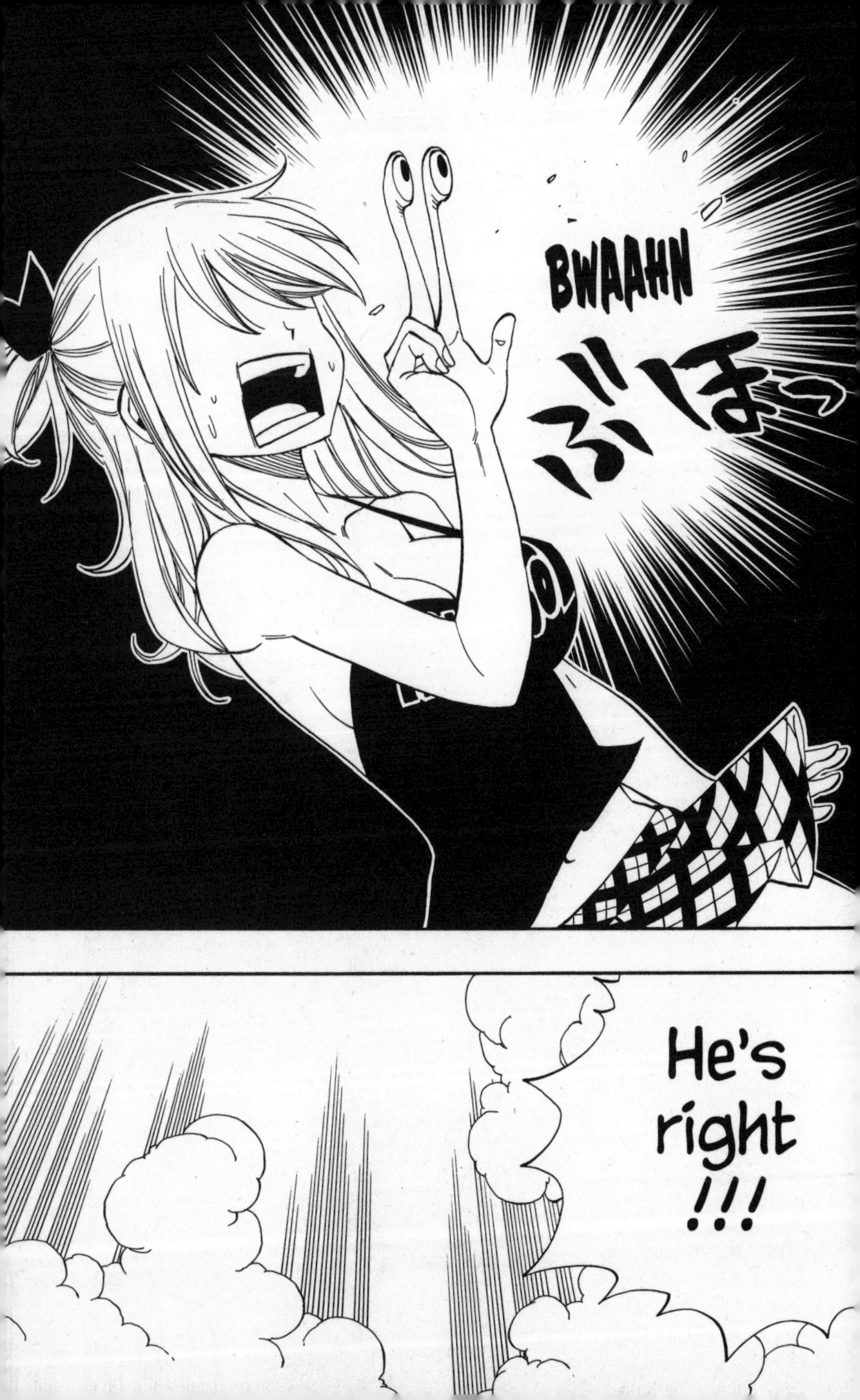
BWAAHN
ぶはっ
He's right !!!

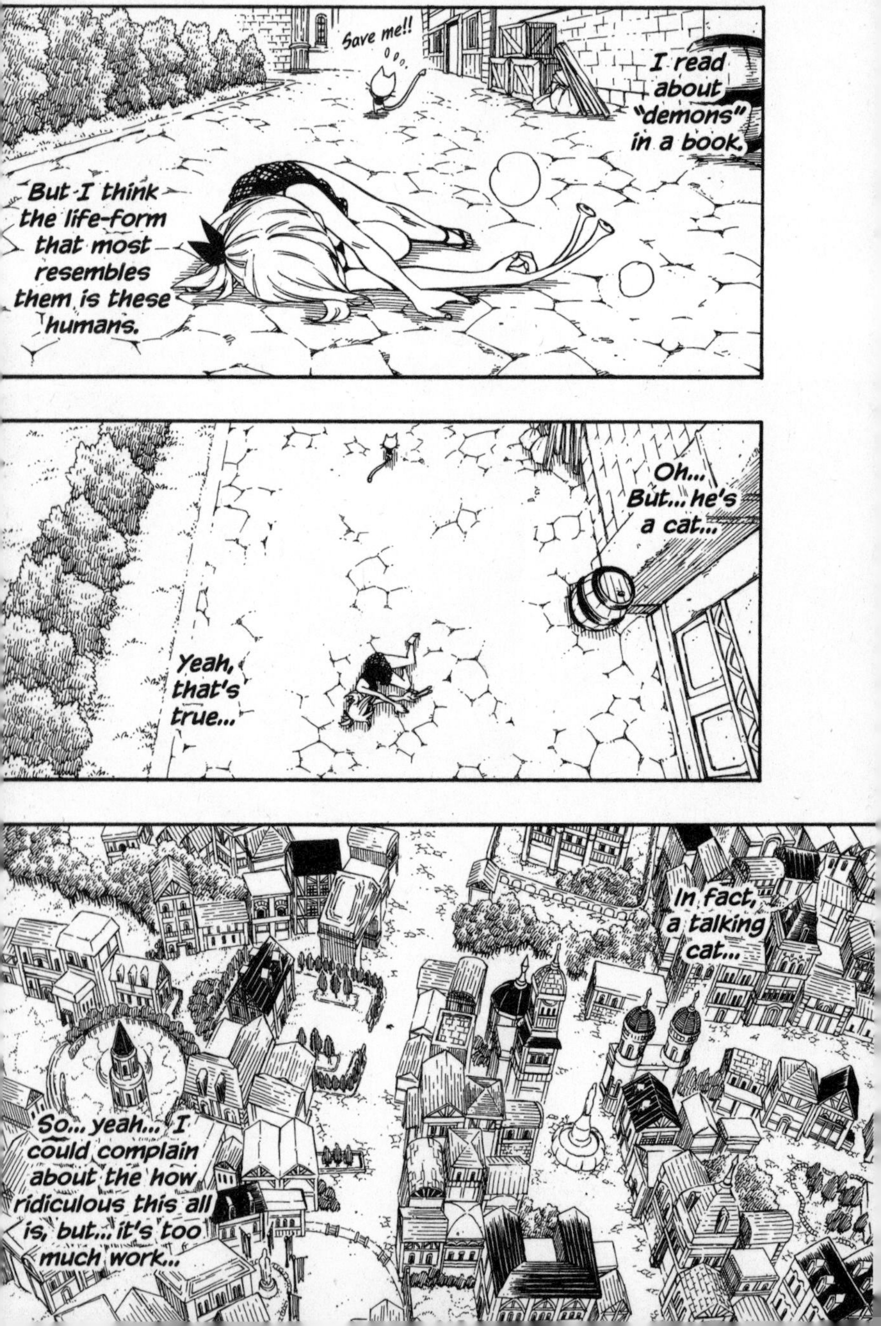
I read about "demons" in a book.
Save me!!
But I think the life-form that most resembles them is these humans.
Oh... But... he's a cat...
Yeah, that's true...
In fact, a talking cat...
So... yeah... I could complain about the how ridiculous this all is, but... it's too much work...

FT★S

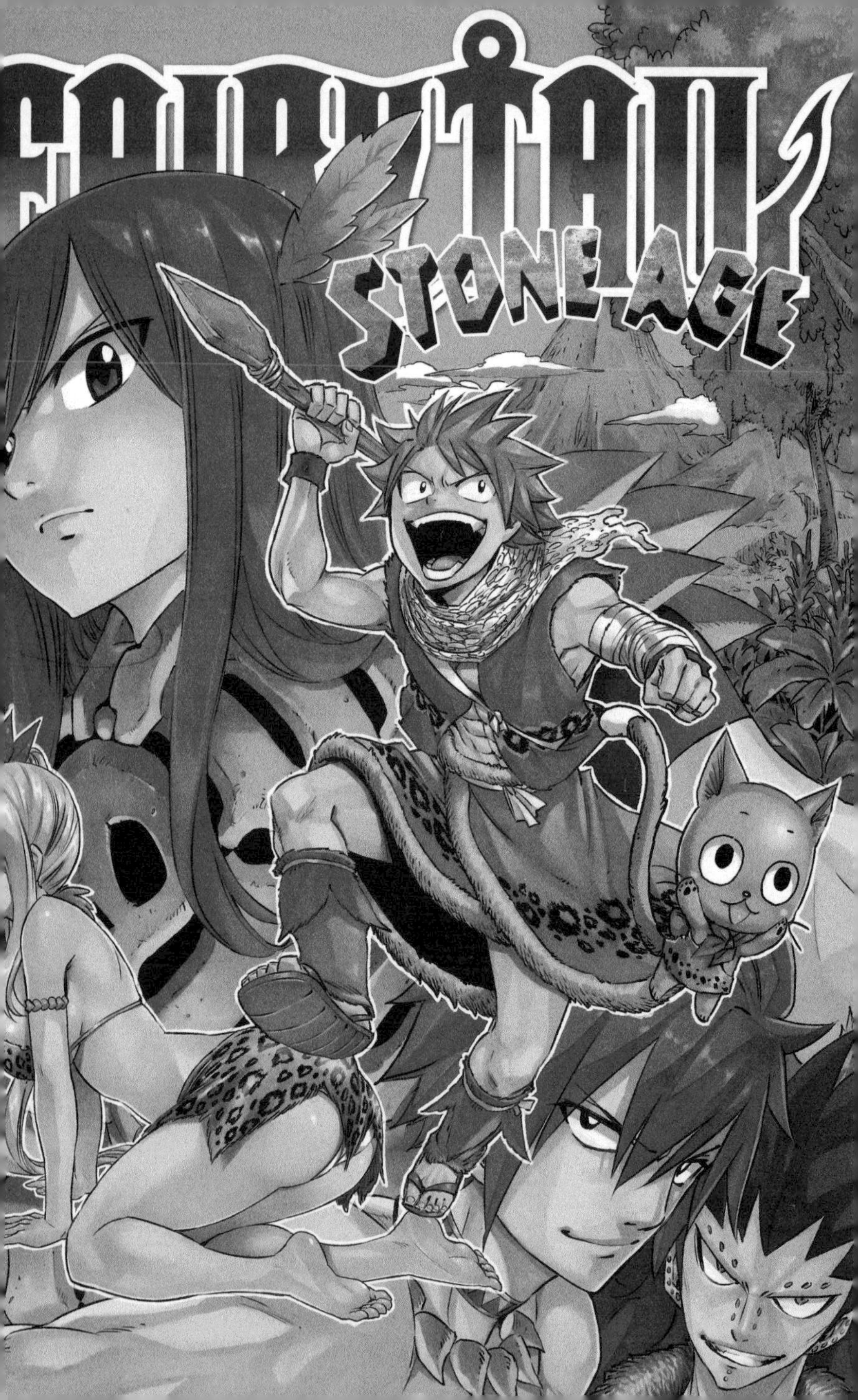
STONE AGE

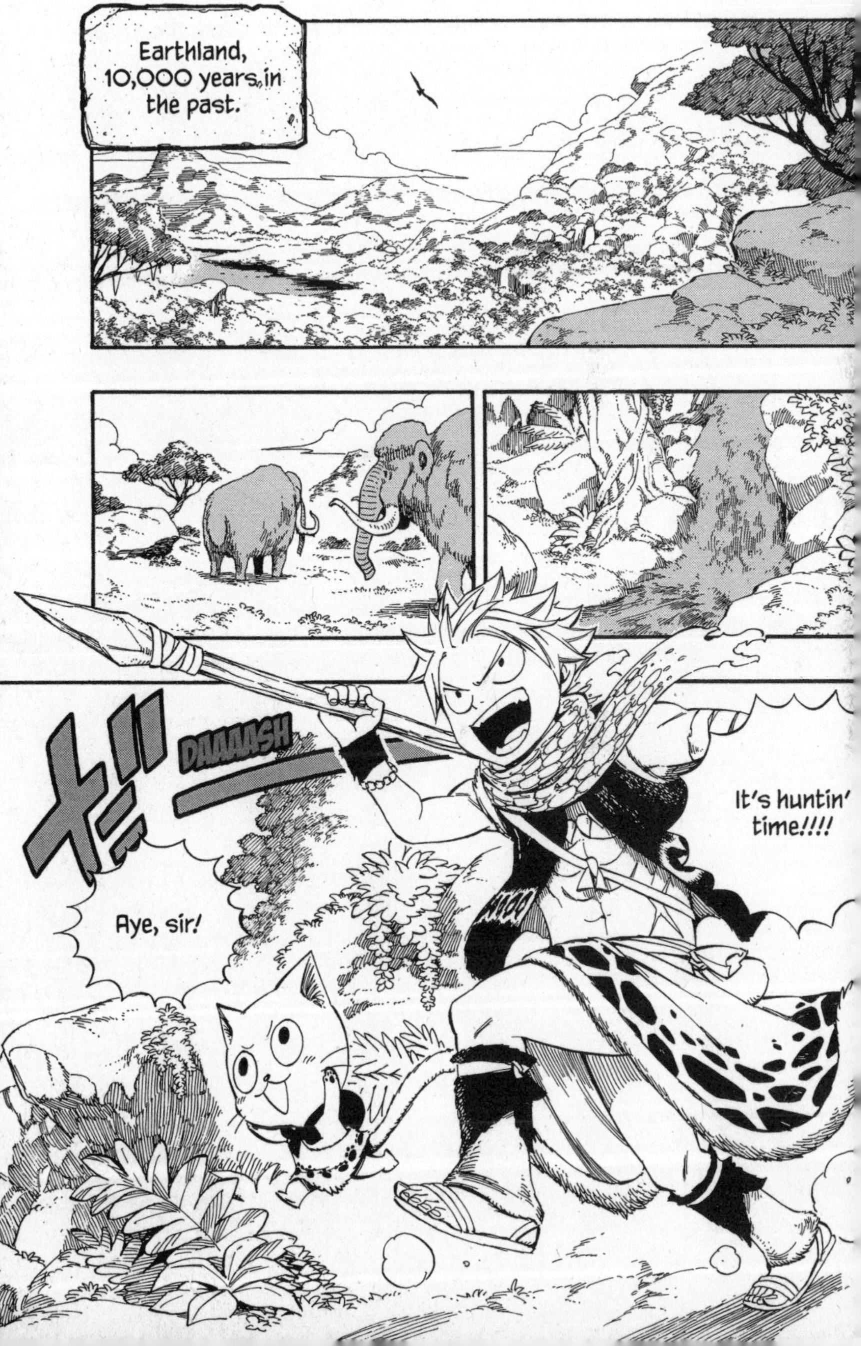
Earthland, 10,000 years in the past.
It's huntin' time!!!!
DAAAASH
Aye, sir!

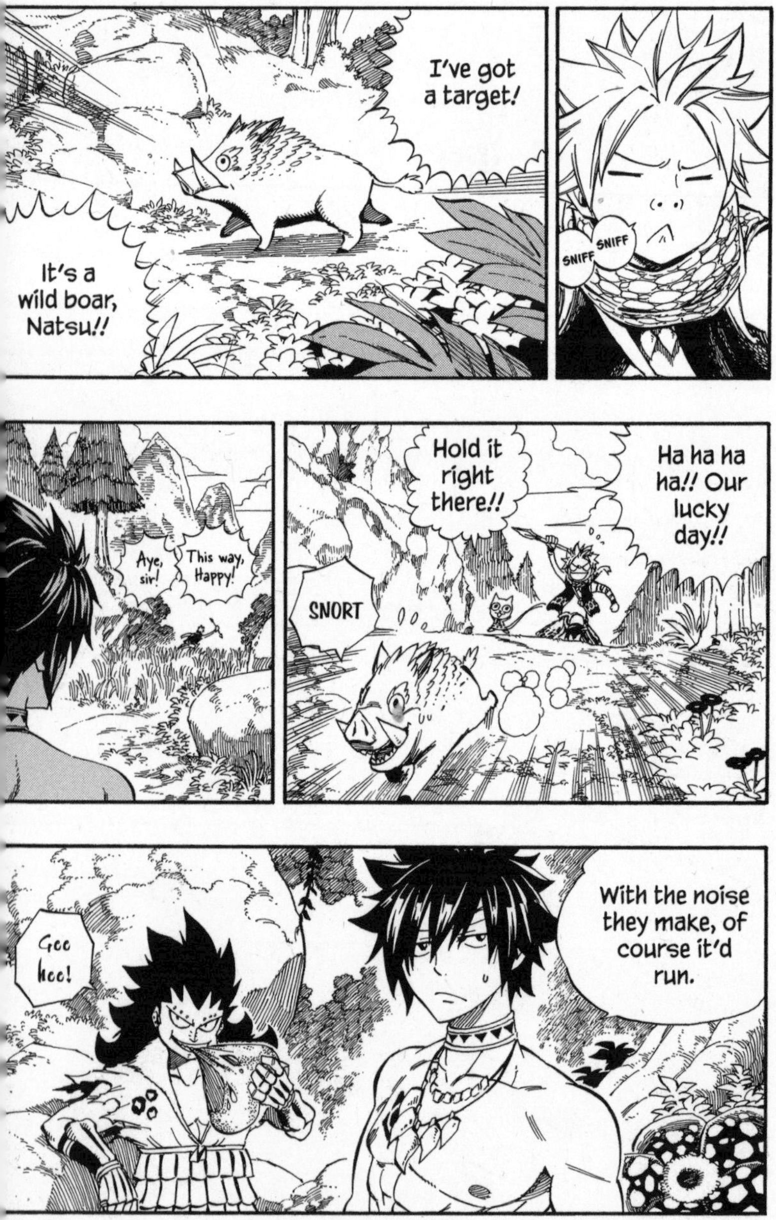
SNIFF
SNIFF
I've got a target!
It's a wild boar, Natsu!!
Ha ha ha!! Our lucky day!!
Hold it right there!!
SNORT
This way, Happy!
Aye, sir!
With the noise they make, of course it'd run.
Gee hee!

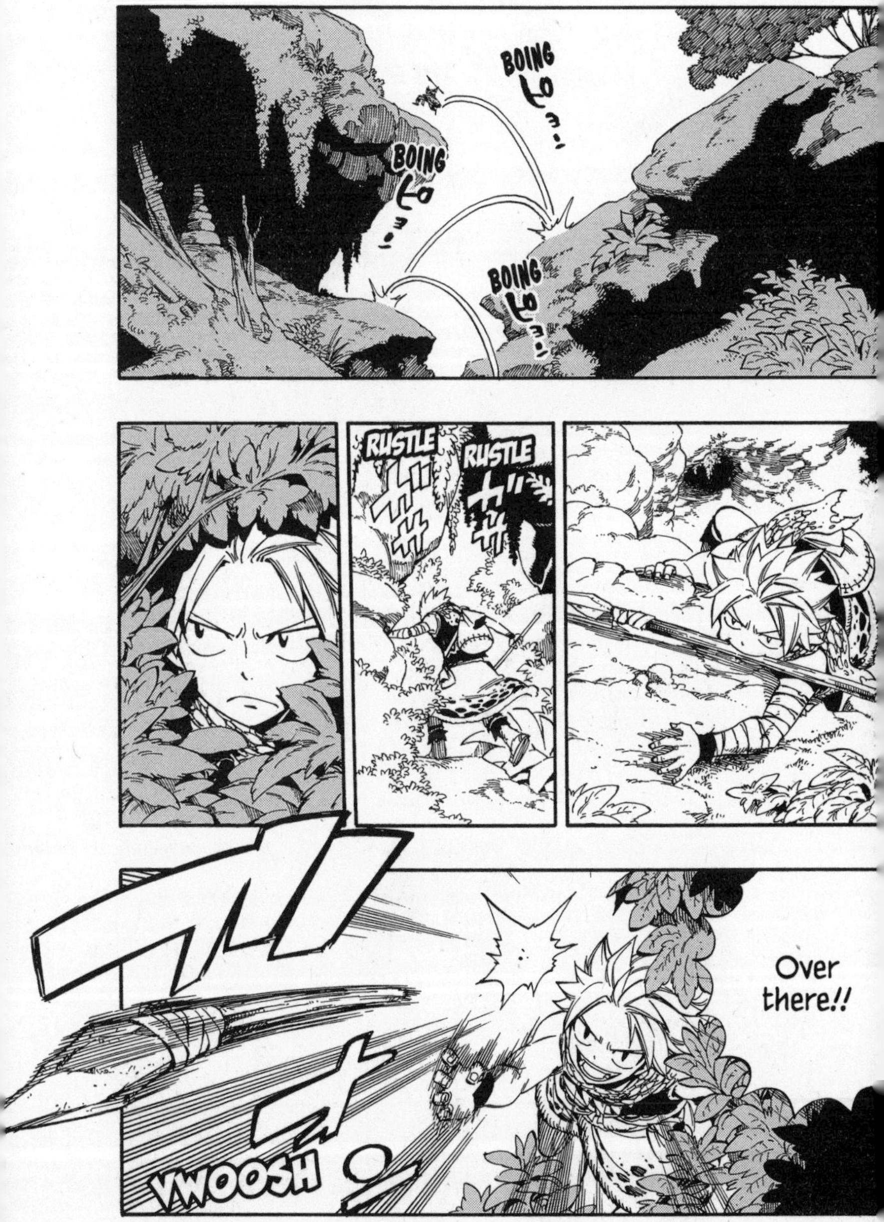
BOING
BOING
BOING
RUSTLE
RUSTLE
Over there!!
VWOOSH

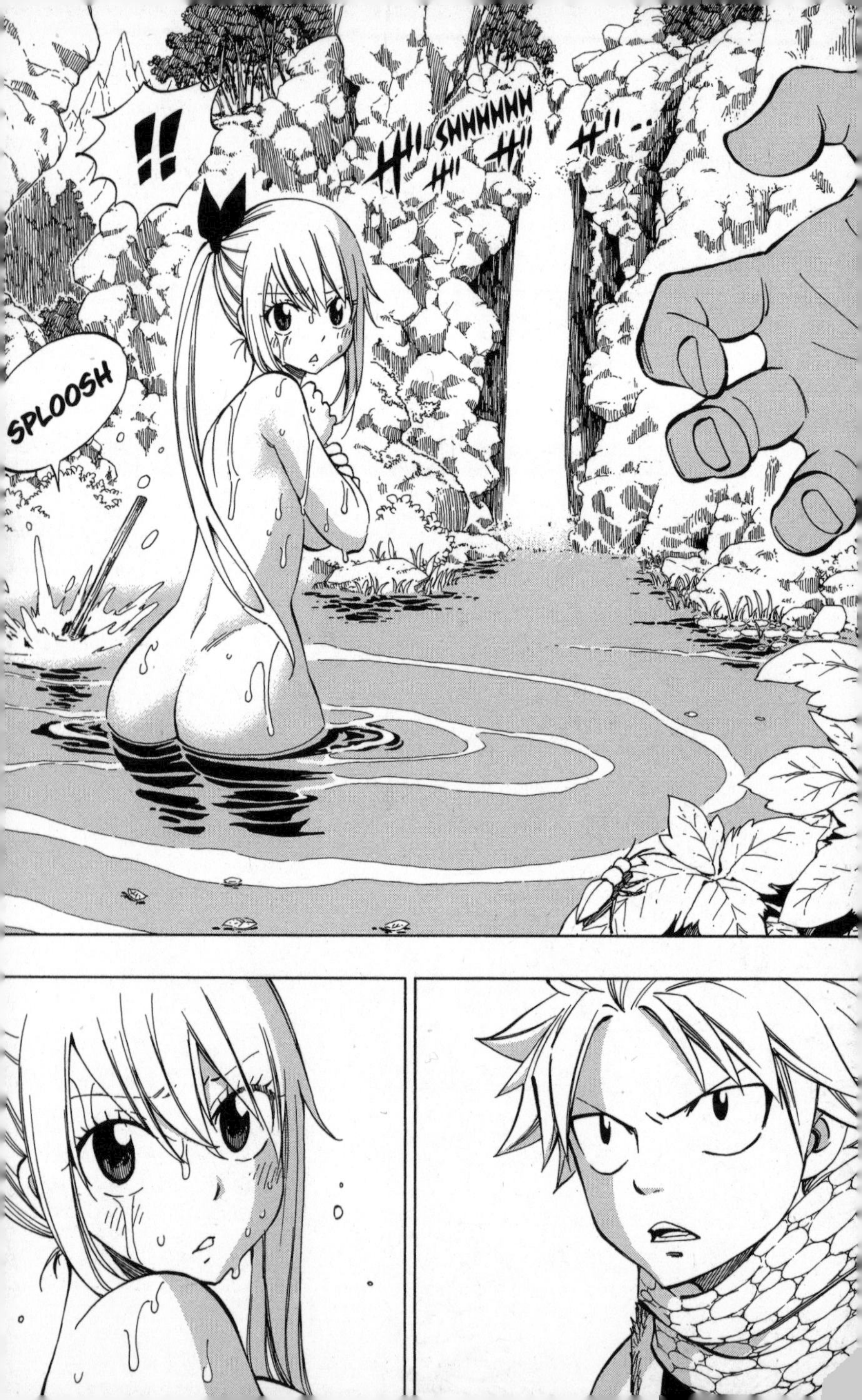
SHHHHHH
!!
SPLOOSH

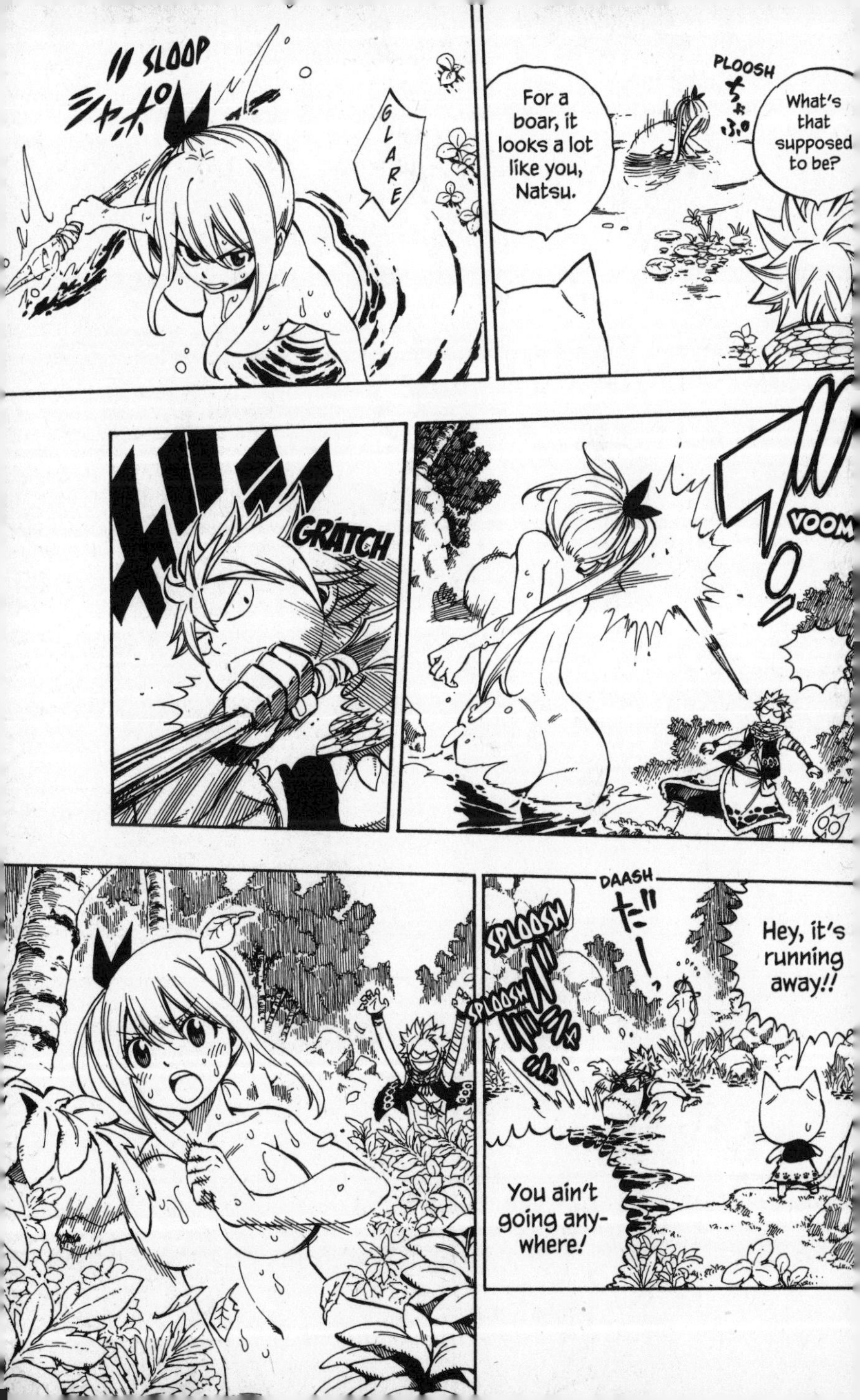
PLOOSH
ちゃぷ
What's that supposed to be?
For a boar, it looks a lot like you, Natsu.
SLOOP
シャポ
GLARE
VOOM
GRATCH
DAASH
だー
Hey, it's running away!!
SPLOOSH
SPLOOSH
You ain't going anywhere!

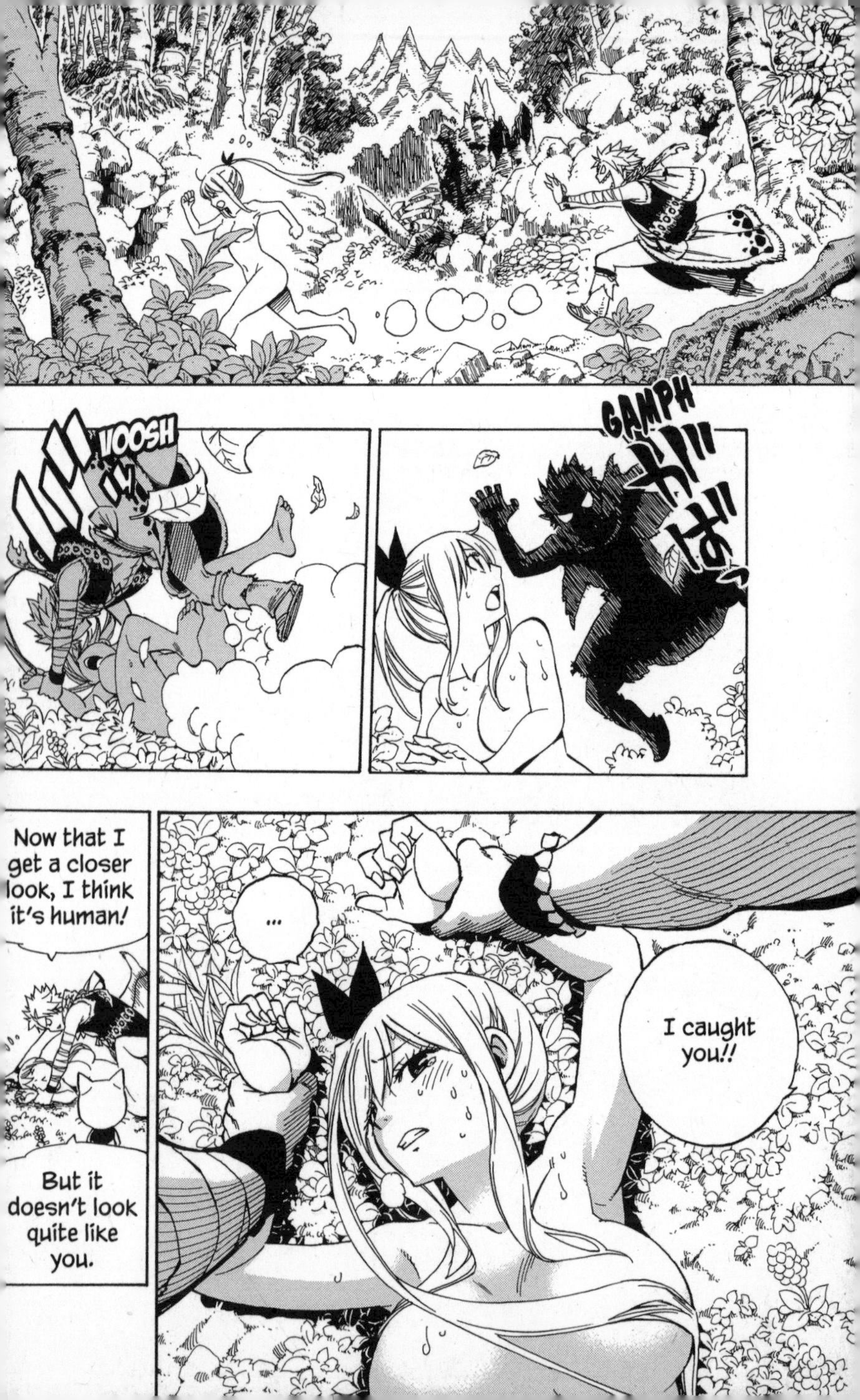

GAMPH
VOOSH
I caught you!!
...
Now that I get a closer look, I think it's human!
But it doesn't look quite like you.

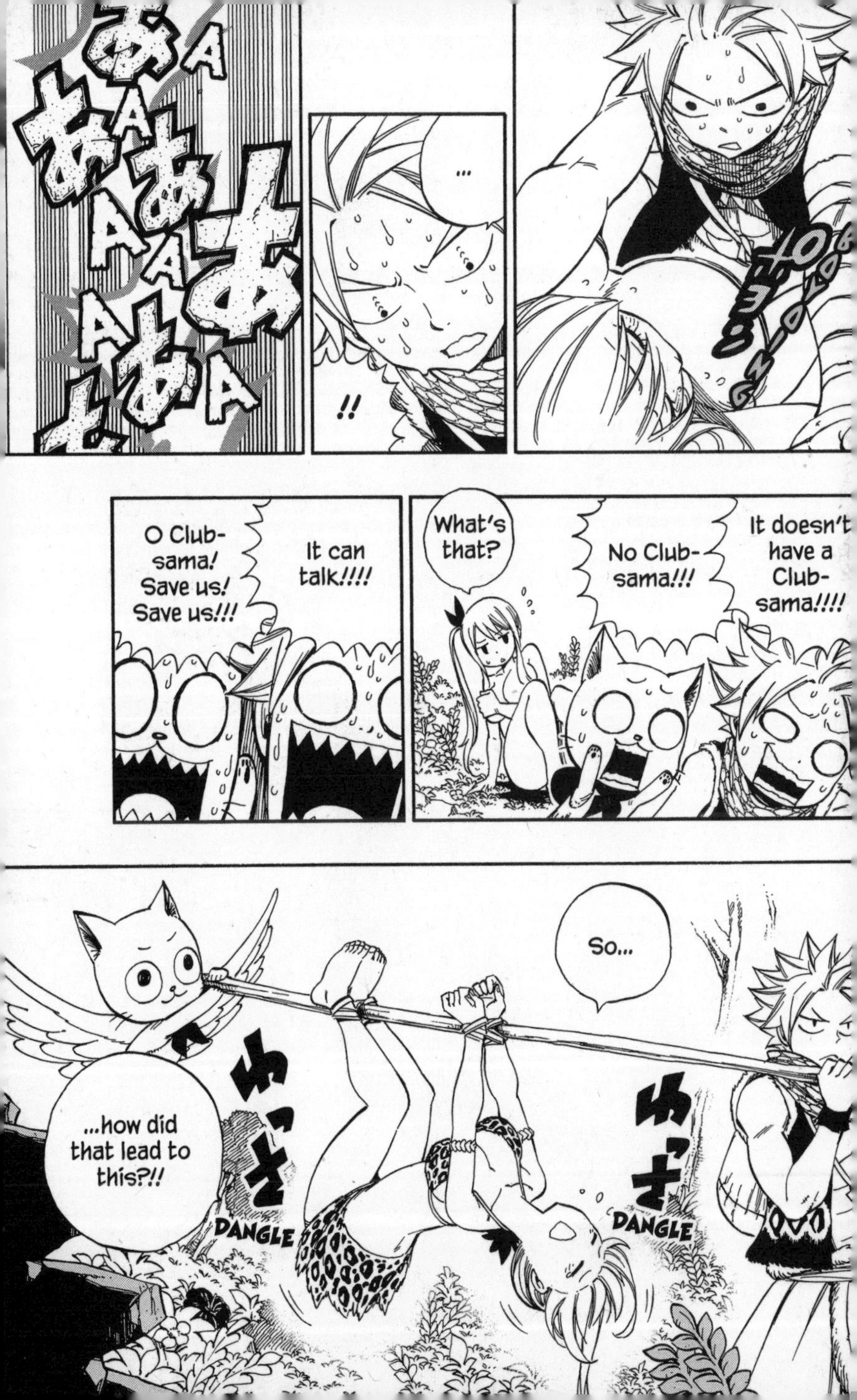
BOOOING
...
!!
It doesn't have a Club-sama!!!!
No Club-sama!!!
What's that?
It can talk!!!!
O Club-sama! Save us! Save us!!!
So...
DANGLE
DANGLE
...how did that lead to this?!!

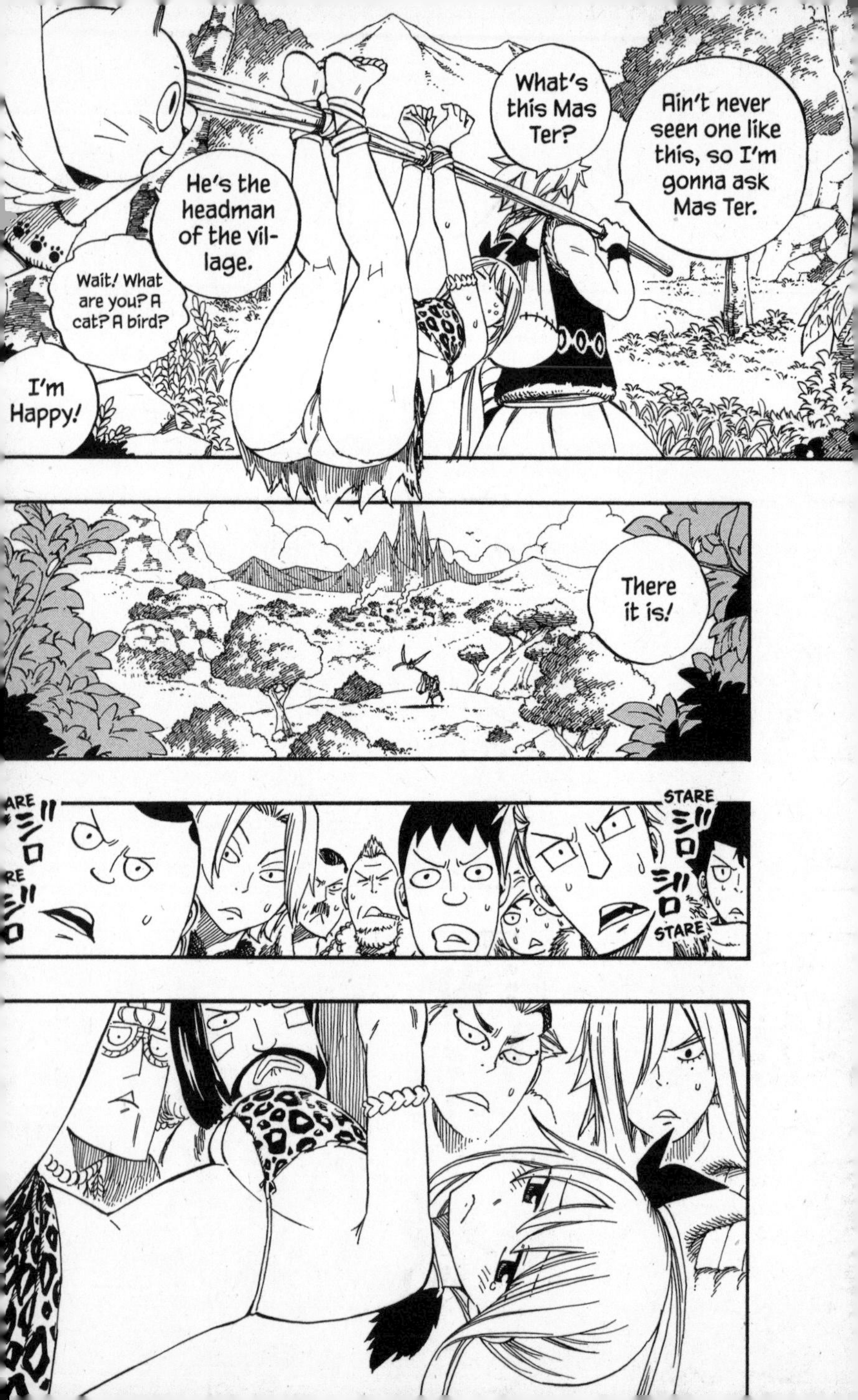
Ain't never seen one like this, so I'm gonna ask Mas Ter.
What's this Mas Ter?
He's the headman of the village.
Wait! What are you? A cat? A bird?
I'm Happy!
There it is!
STARE
STARE

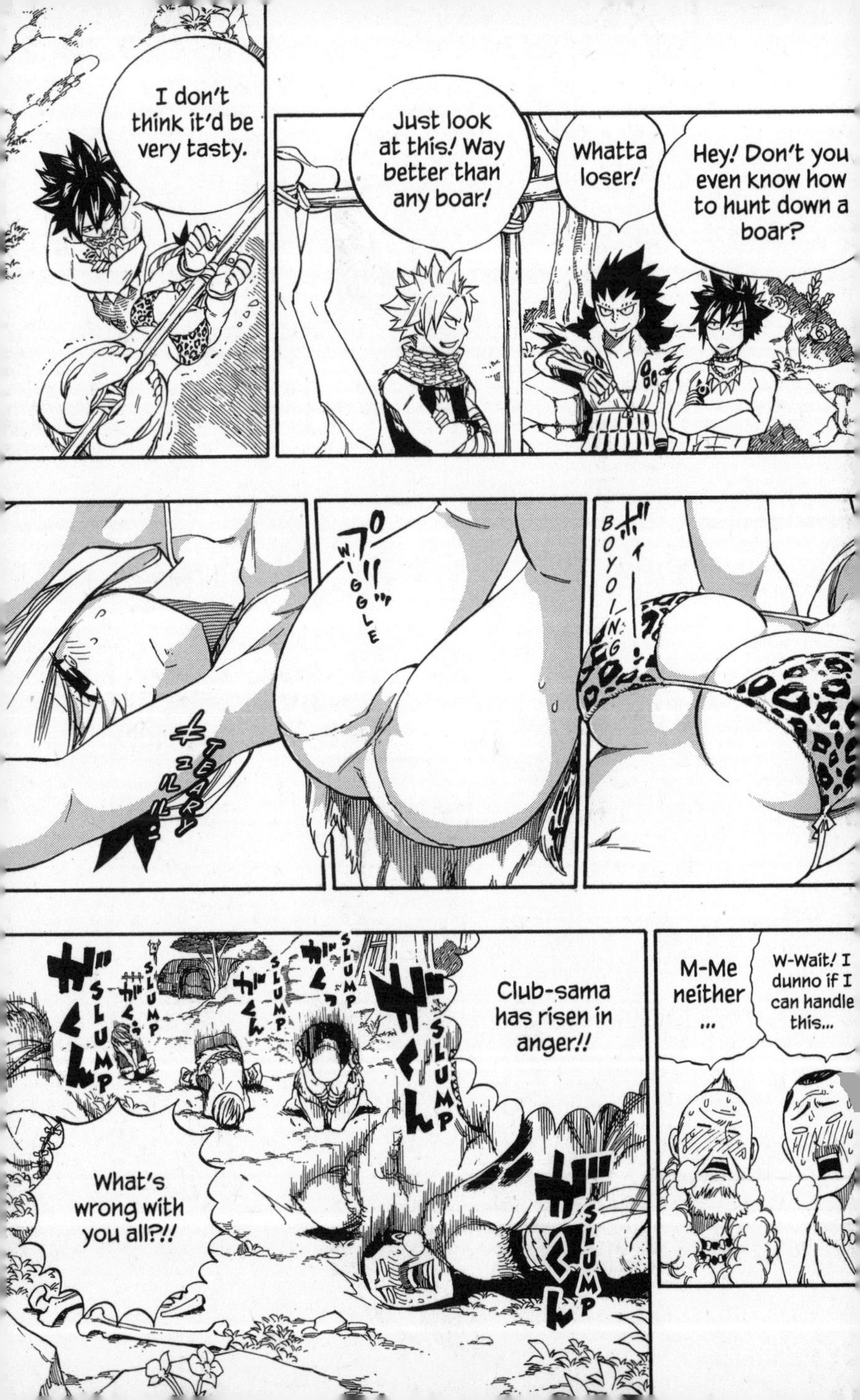
Hey! Don't you even know how to hunt down a boar?
Whatta loser!
Just look at this! Way better than any boar!
I don't think it'd be very tasty.
BOYOING
WIGGLE
TEARY
W-Wait! I dunno if I can handle this...
M-Me neither ...
Club-sama has risen in anger!!
SLUMP
SLUMP
SLUMP
SLUMP
SLUMP
SLUMP
What's wrong with you all?!!

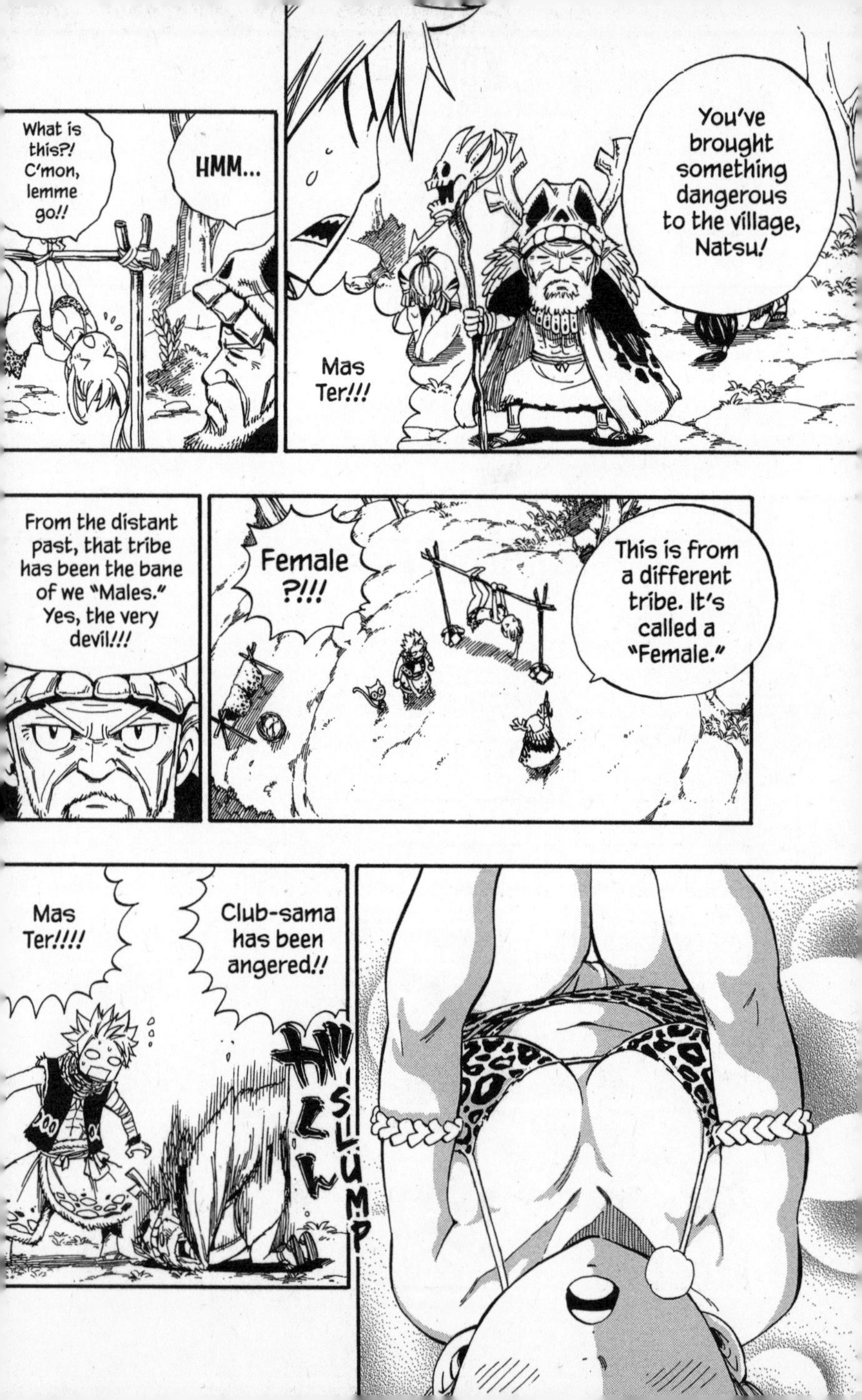
You've brought something dangerous to the village, Natsu!
Mas Ter!!!
HMM...
What is this?! C'mon, lemme go!!
This is from a different tribe. It's called a "Female."
Female ?!!!
From the distant past, that tribe has been the bane of we "Males." Yes, the very devil!!!
Club-sama has been angered!!
Mas Ter!!!!
SLUMP

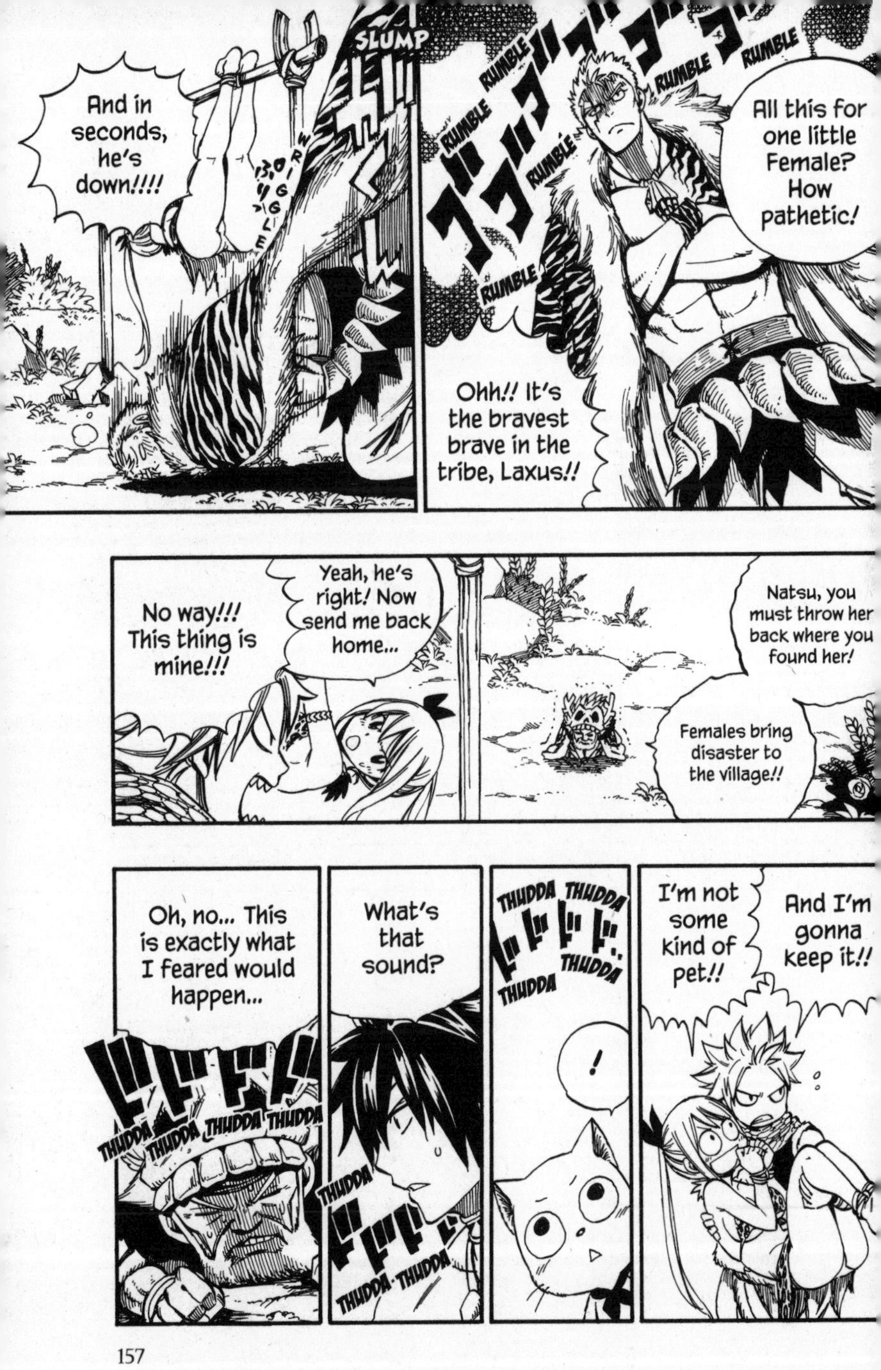

RUMBLE RUMBLE RUMBLE RUMBLE RUMBLE RUMBLE
All this for one little Female? How pathetic!
Ohh!! It's the bravest brave in the tribe, Laxus!!
SLUMP
And in seconds, he's down!!!!
WRIGGLE
Natsu, you must throw her back where you found her!
Females bring disaster to the village!!
Yeah, he's right! Now send me back home...
No way!!! This thing is mine!!!
And I'm gonna keep it!!
I'm not some kind of pet!!
THUDDA THUDDA THUDDA THUDDA
!
What's that sound?
THUDDA THUDDA THUDDA
Oh, no... This is exactly what I feared would happen...
THUDDA THUDDA THUDDA THUDDA

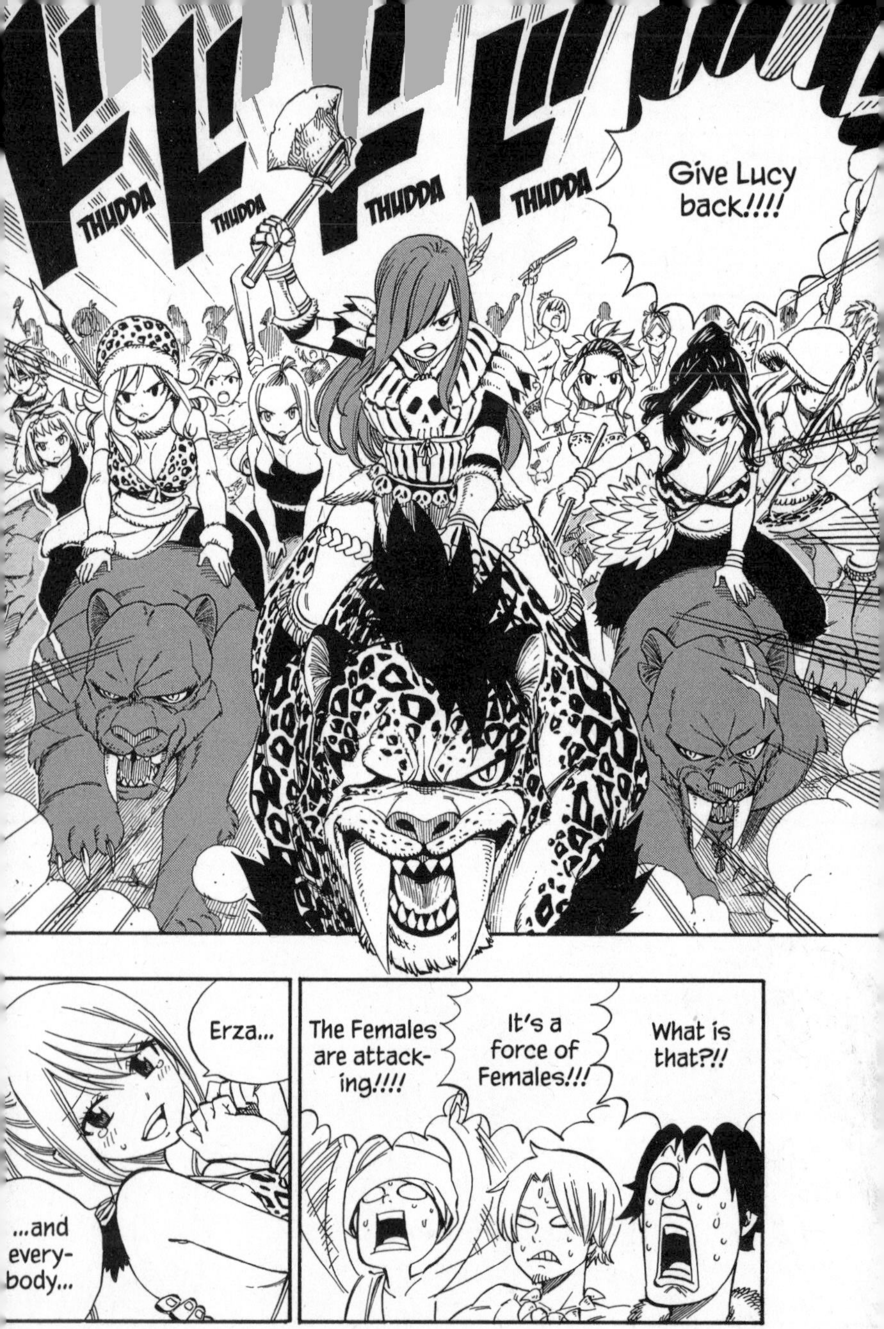

Give Lucy back!!!!
THUDDA
THUDDA
THUDDA
THUDDA
What is that?!!
It's a force of Females!!!
The Females are attack-ing!!!!
Erza...
...and every-body...

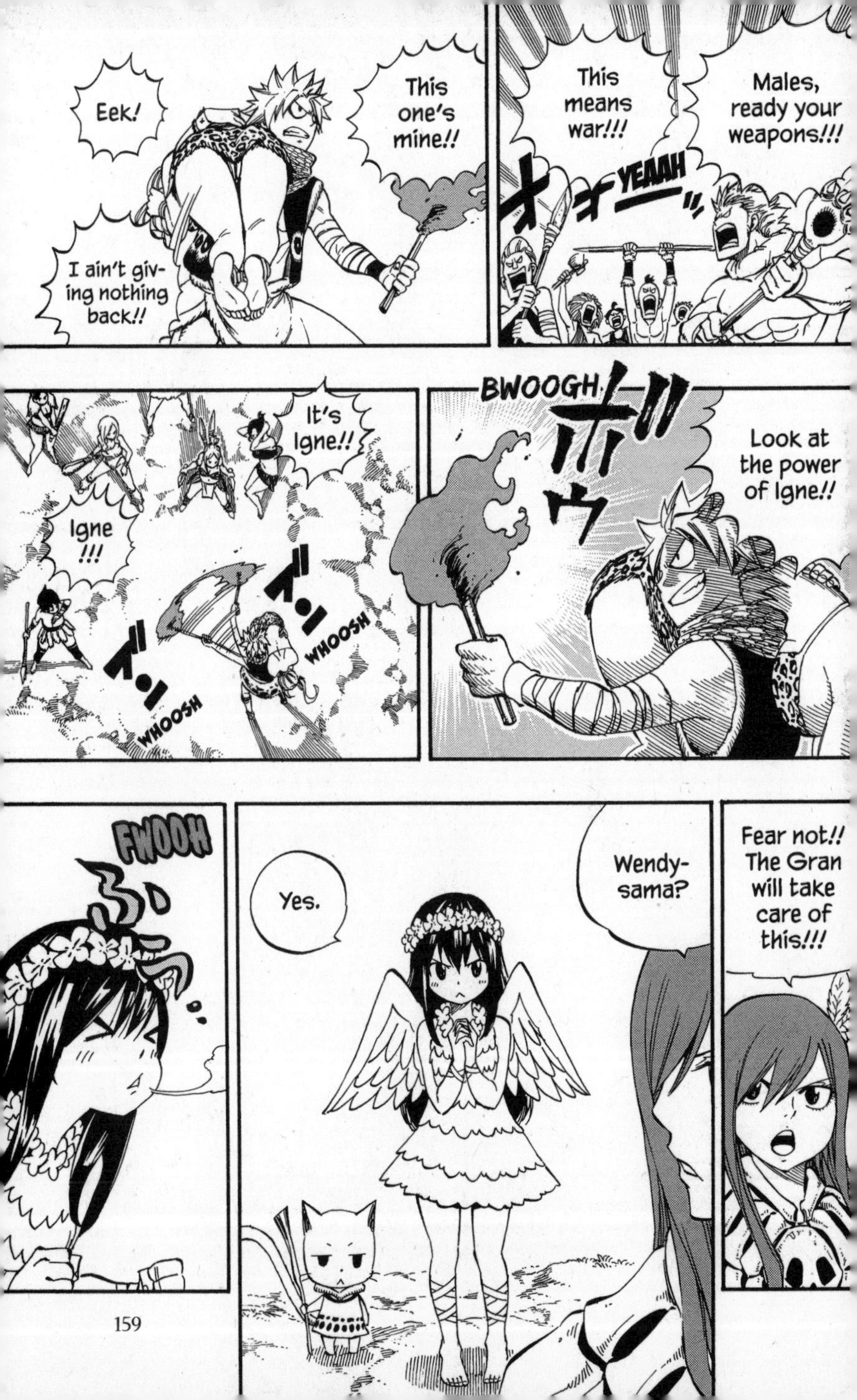
Males, ready your weapons!!!
This means war!!!
YEAAH
This one's mine!!
Eek!
I ain't giving nothing back!!
BWOOGH
Look at the power of Igne!!
It's Igne!!
Igne !!!
WHOOSH
WHOOSH
Fear not!! The Gran will take care of this!!!
Wendy-sama?
Yes.
FWOOH

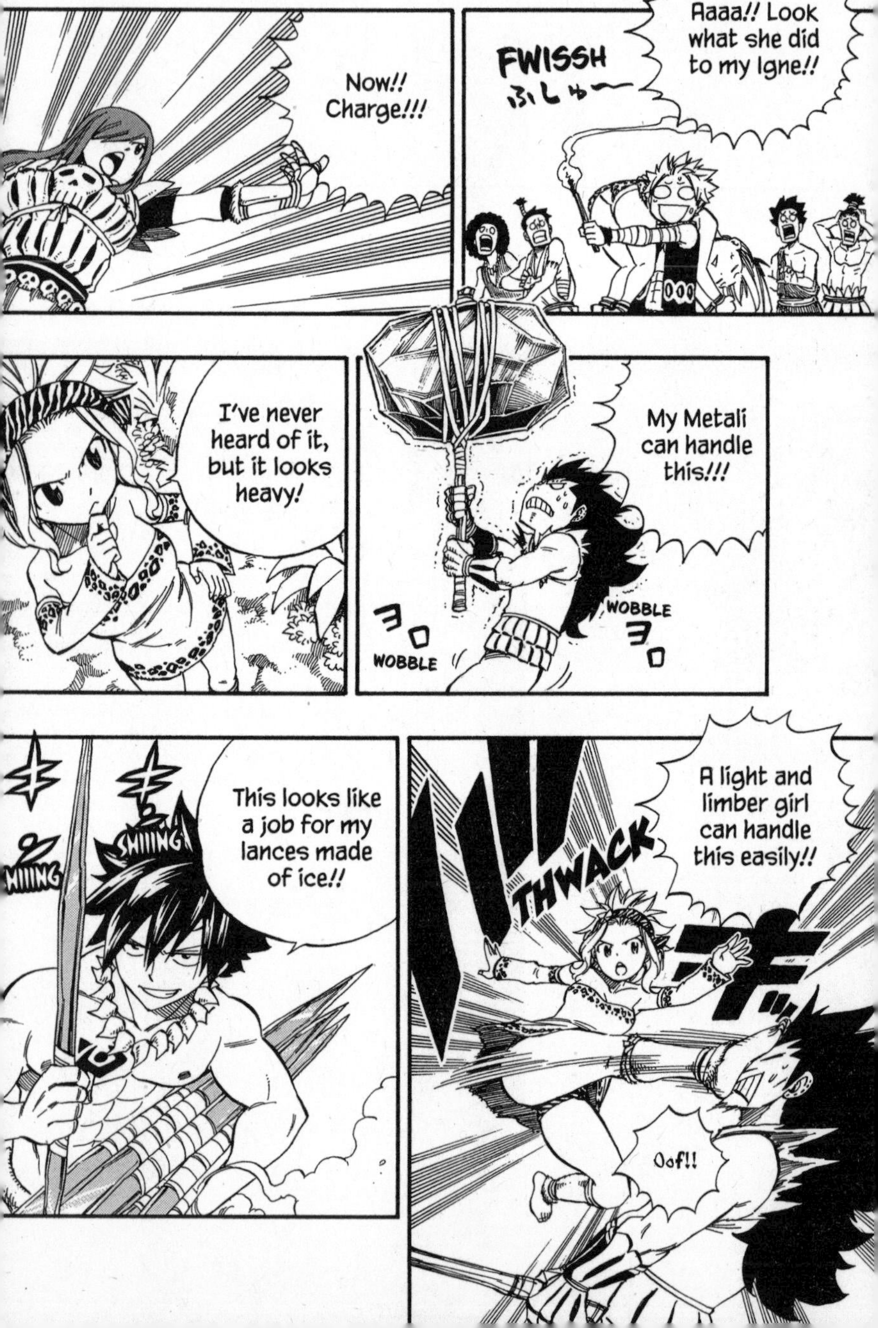
Aaaa!! Look what she did to my Igne!!
FWISSH
ふしゅ〜
Now!! Charge!!!
My Metali can handle this!!!
WOBBLE
ヨロ
ヨロ
WOBBLE
I've never heard of it, but it looks heavy!
A light and limber girl can handle this easily!!
THWACK
Oof!!
This looks like a job for my lances made of ice!!
SHIIING
HIIING

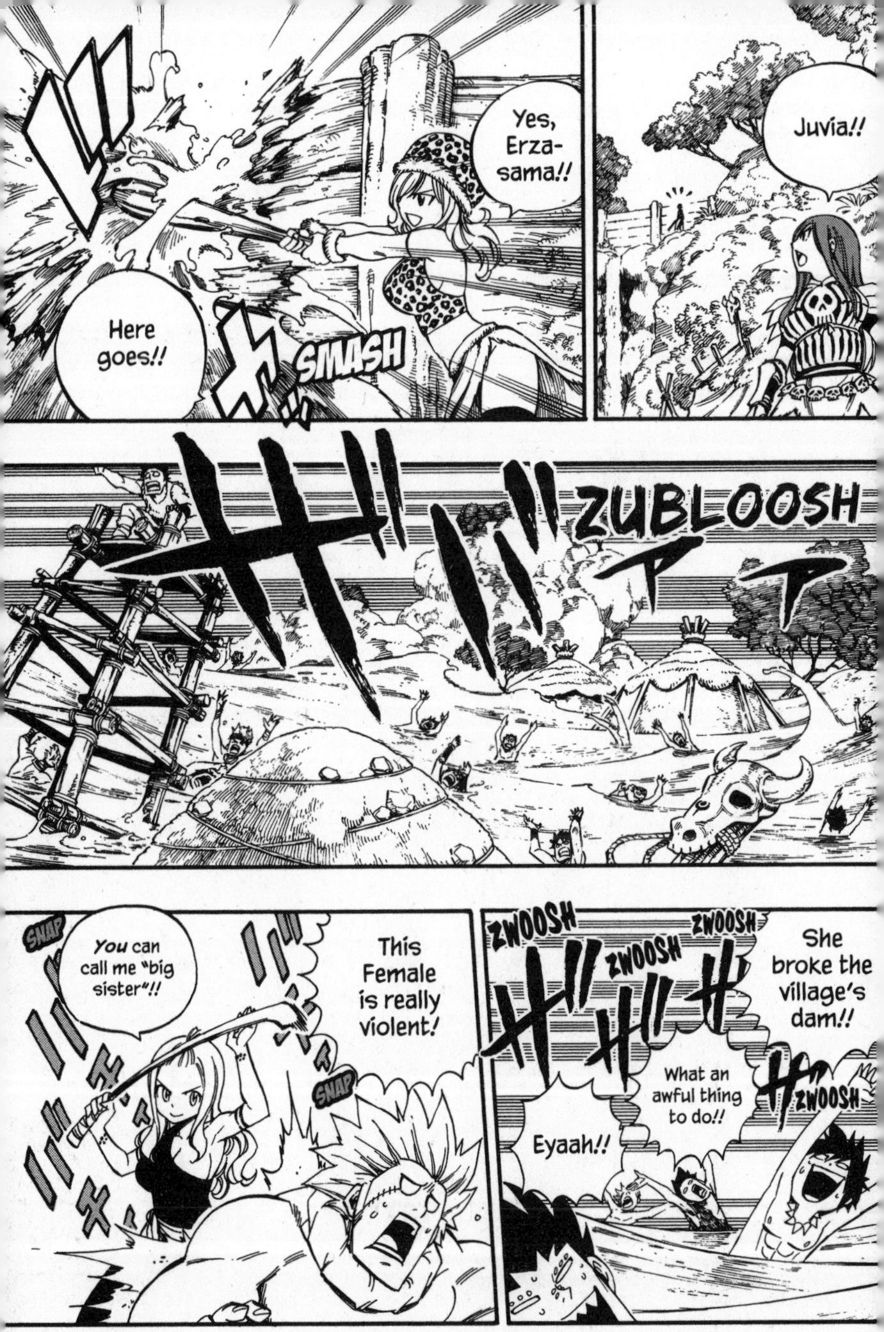
Juvia!!
Yes, Erza-sama!!
Here goes!!
SMASH
ZUBLOOSH
ZWOOSH
ZWOOSH
ZWOOSH
She broke the village's dam!!
What an awful thing to do!!
ZWOOSH
Eyaah!!
This Female is really violent!
SNAP
You can call me "big sister"!!
SNAP

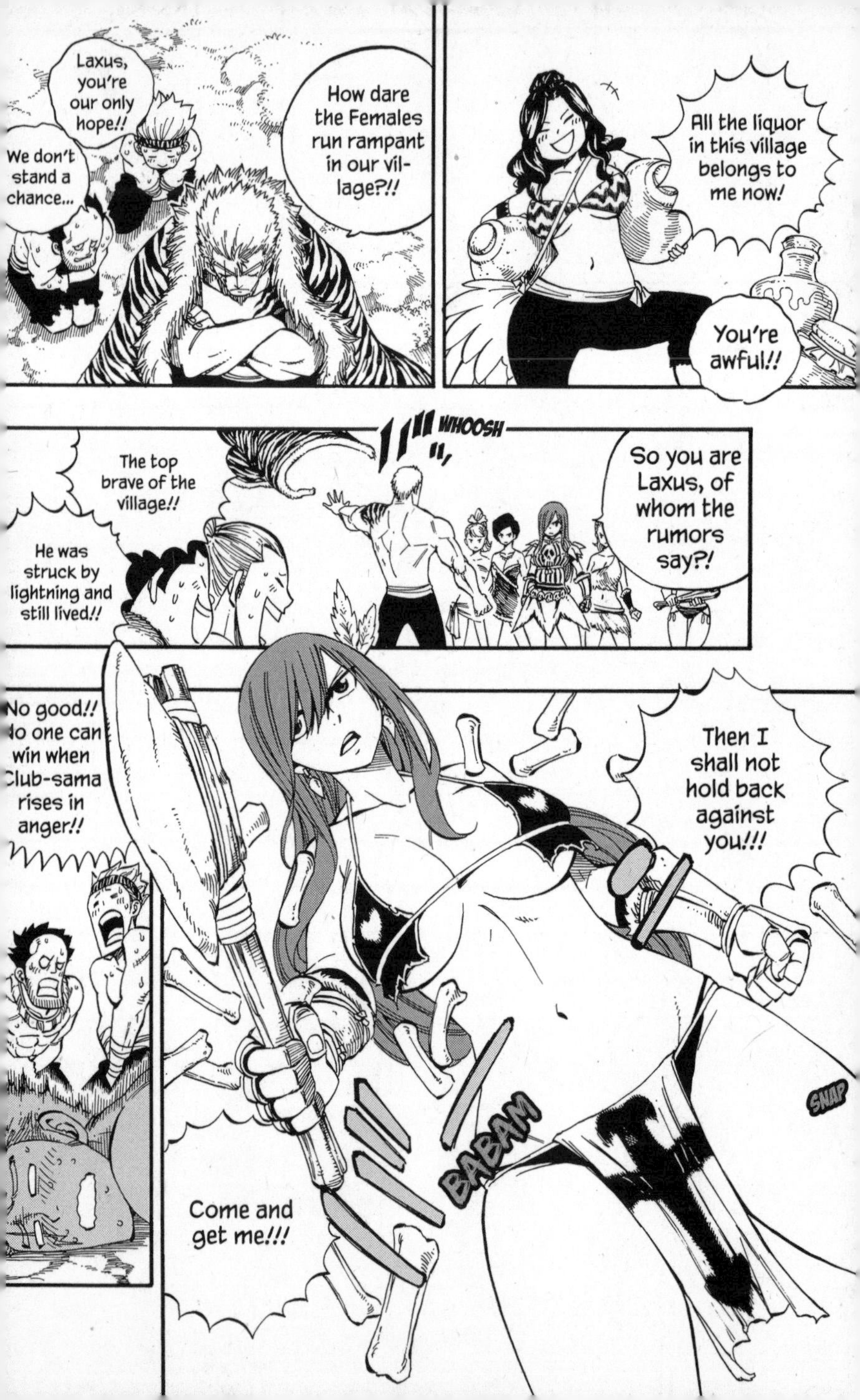
All the liquor in this village belongs to me now!
You're awful!!
How dare the Females run rampant in our vil-lage?!!
Laxus, you're our only hope!!
We don't stand a chance...
WHOOSH
So you are Laxus, of whom the rumors say?!
The top brave of the village!!
He was struck by lightning and still lived!!
Then I shall not hold back against you!!!
SNAP
BABAM
Come and get me!!!
No good!! No one can win when Club-sama rises in anger!!

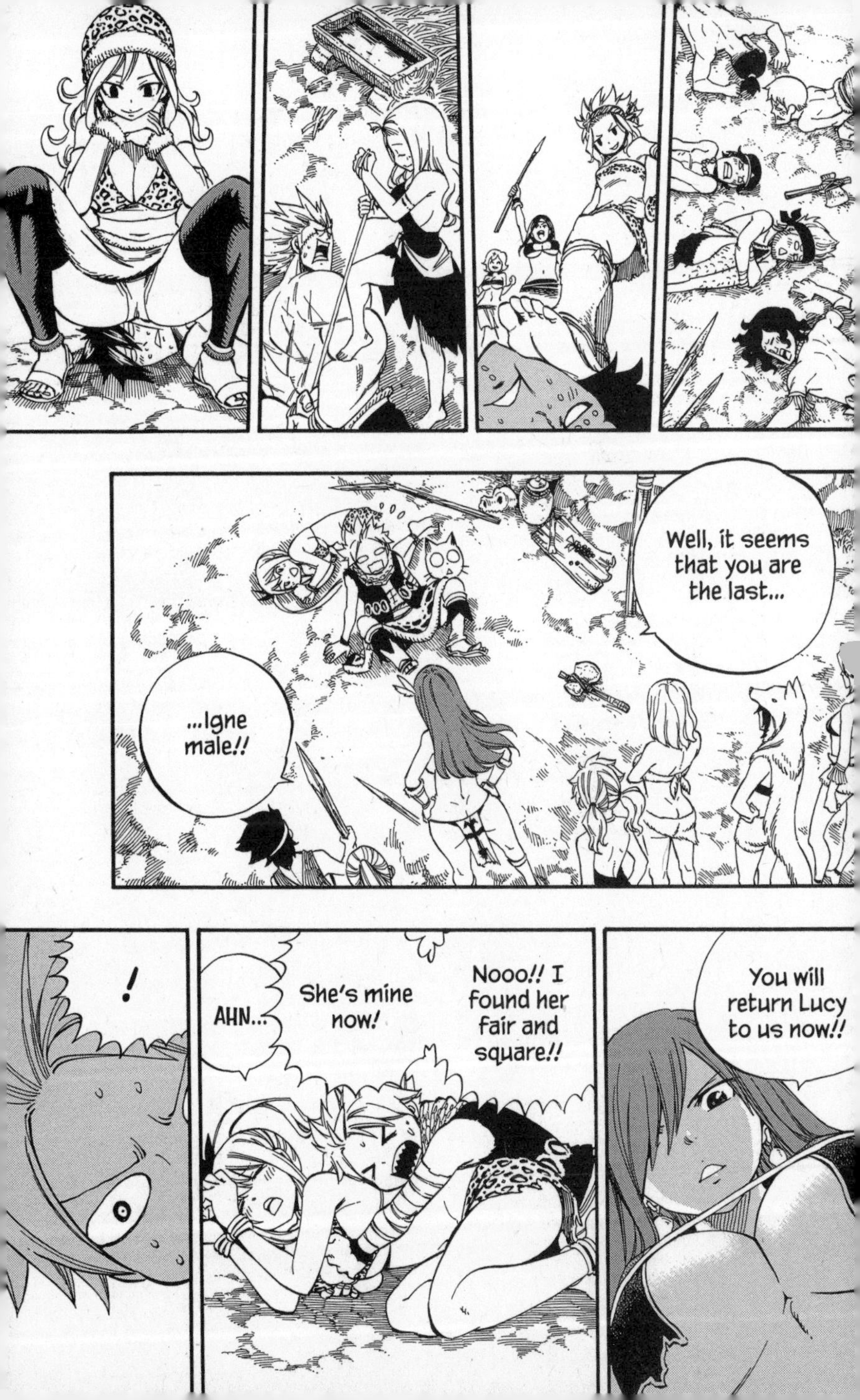
Well, it seems that you are the last...
...Igne male!!
You will return Lucy to us now!!
Nooo!! I found her fair and square!!
She's mine now!
AHN...
!

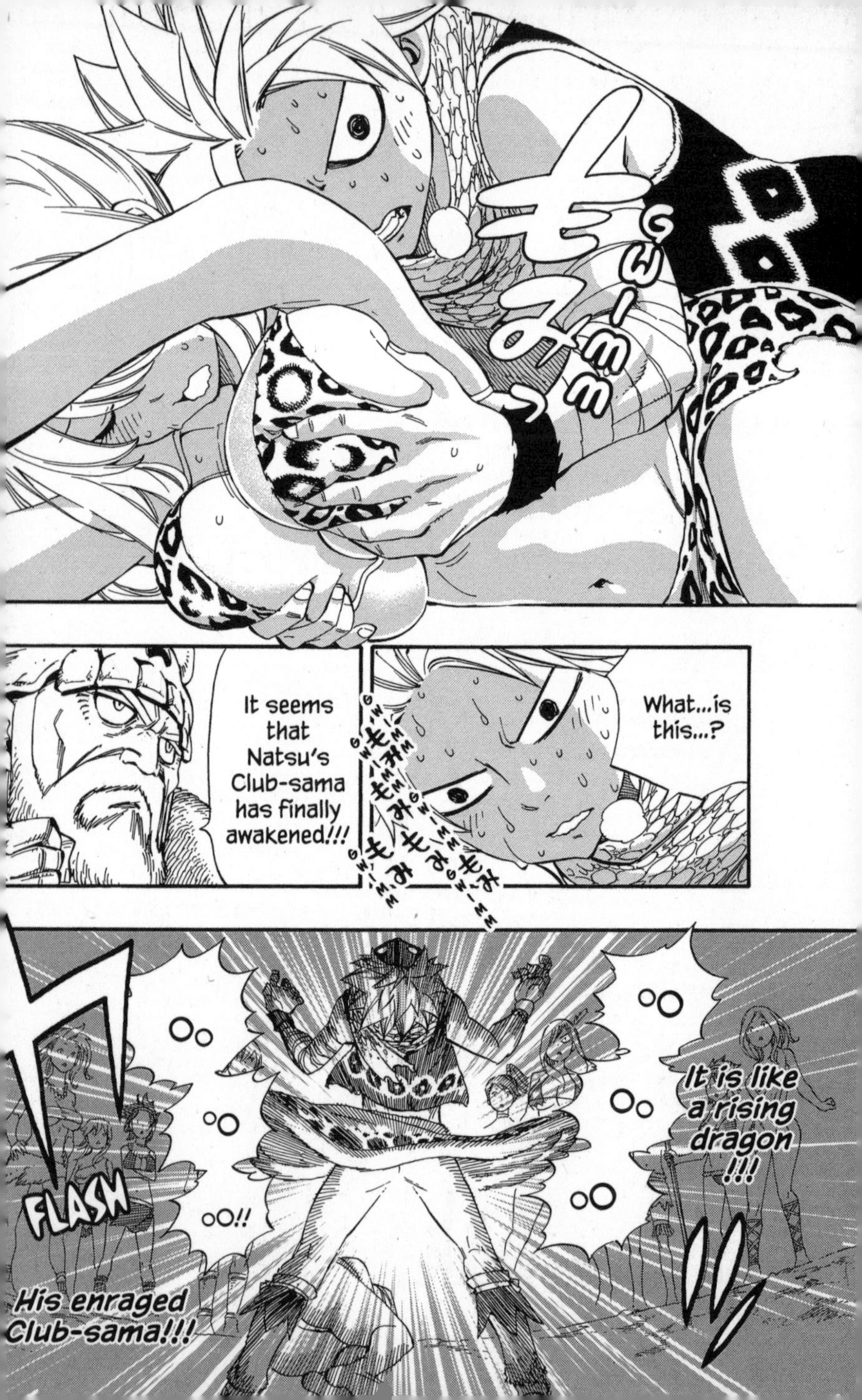
GWI-MMM
What...is this...?
GWI-MMM GWI-MMM GWI-MMM GWI-MMM
It seems that Natsu's Club-sama has finally awakened!!!
It is like a rising dragon!!!
oO!!
FLASH
His enraged Club-sama!!!

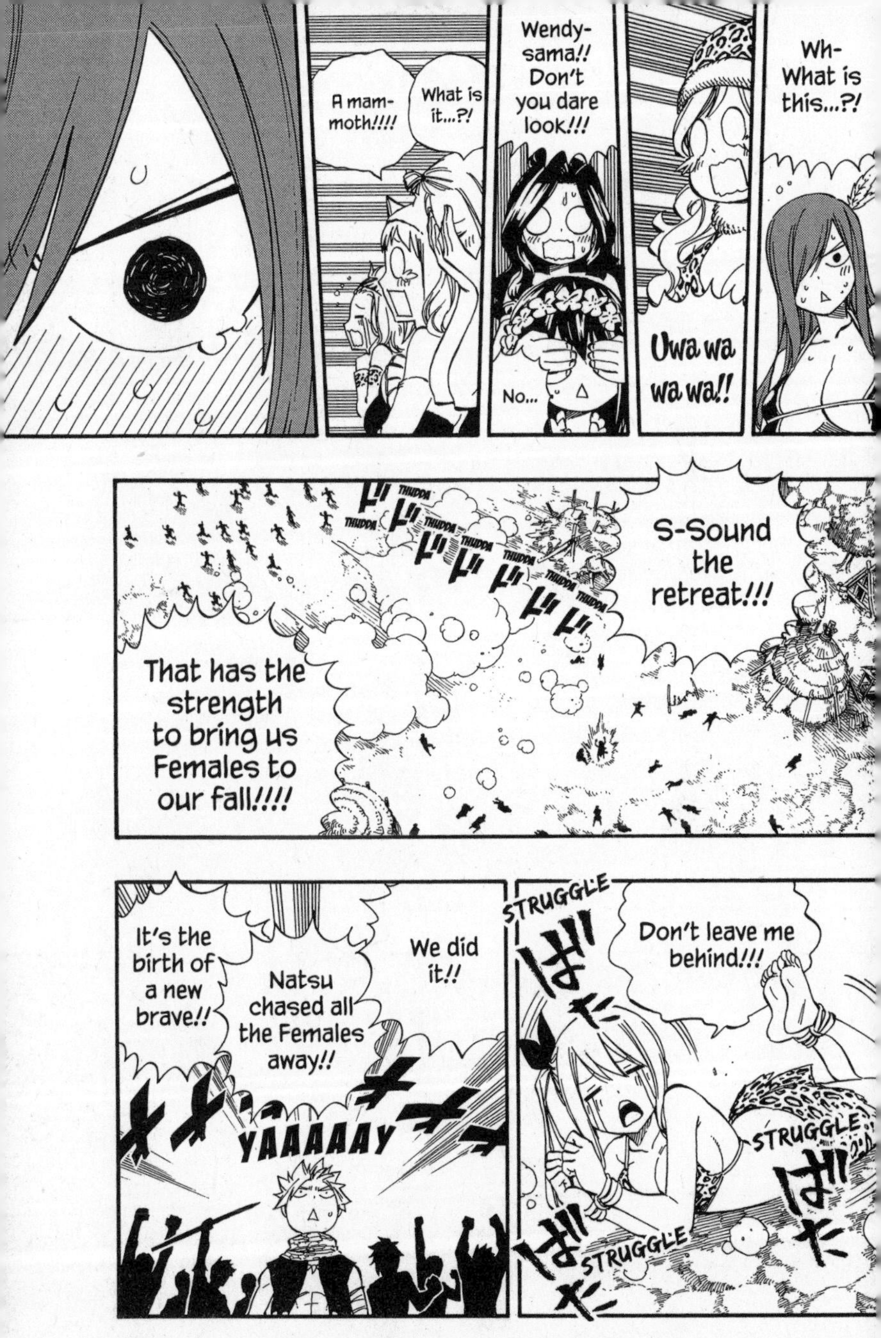
Wh- What is this...?!
Uwa wa wa wa!!
Wendy-sama!! Don't you dare look!!!
No...
What is it...?!
A mammoth!!!!
S-Sound the retreat!!!
THUDDA THUDDA THUDDA THUDDA THUDDA THUDDA THUDDA
That has the strength to bring us Females to our fall!!!!
Don't leave me behind!!!
STRUGGLE
STRUGGLE
STRUGGLE
We did it!!
Natsu chased all the Females away!!
It's the birth of a new brave!!
YAAAAAY

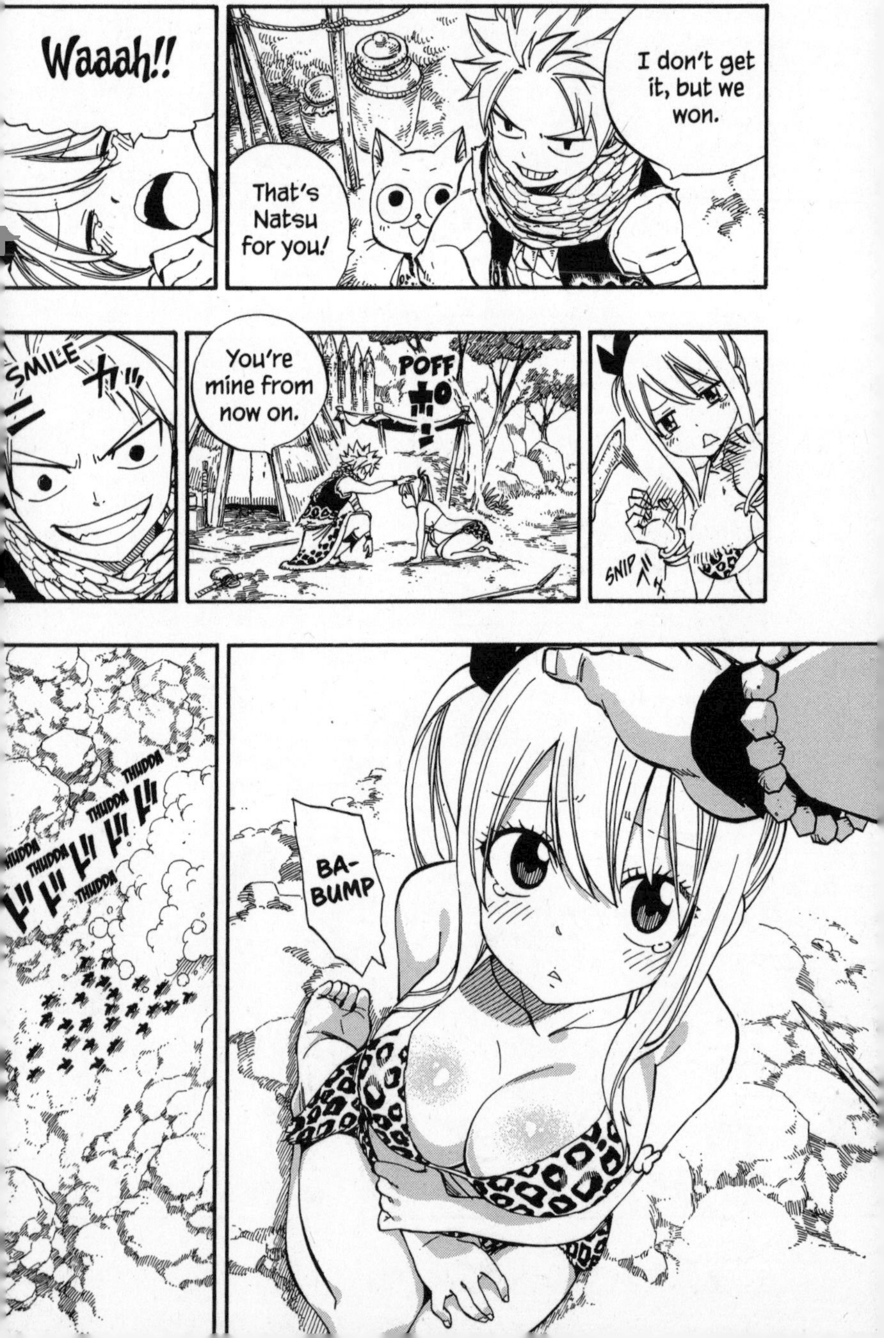
I don't get it, but we won.
That's Natsu for you!
Waaah!!
SNIP
POFF
You're mine from now on.
SMILE
BA-BUMP
THUDDA
THUDDA
THUDDA
THUDDA
THUDDA

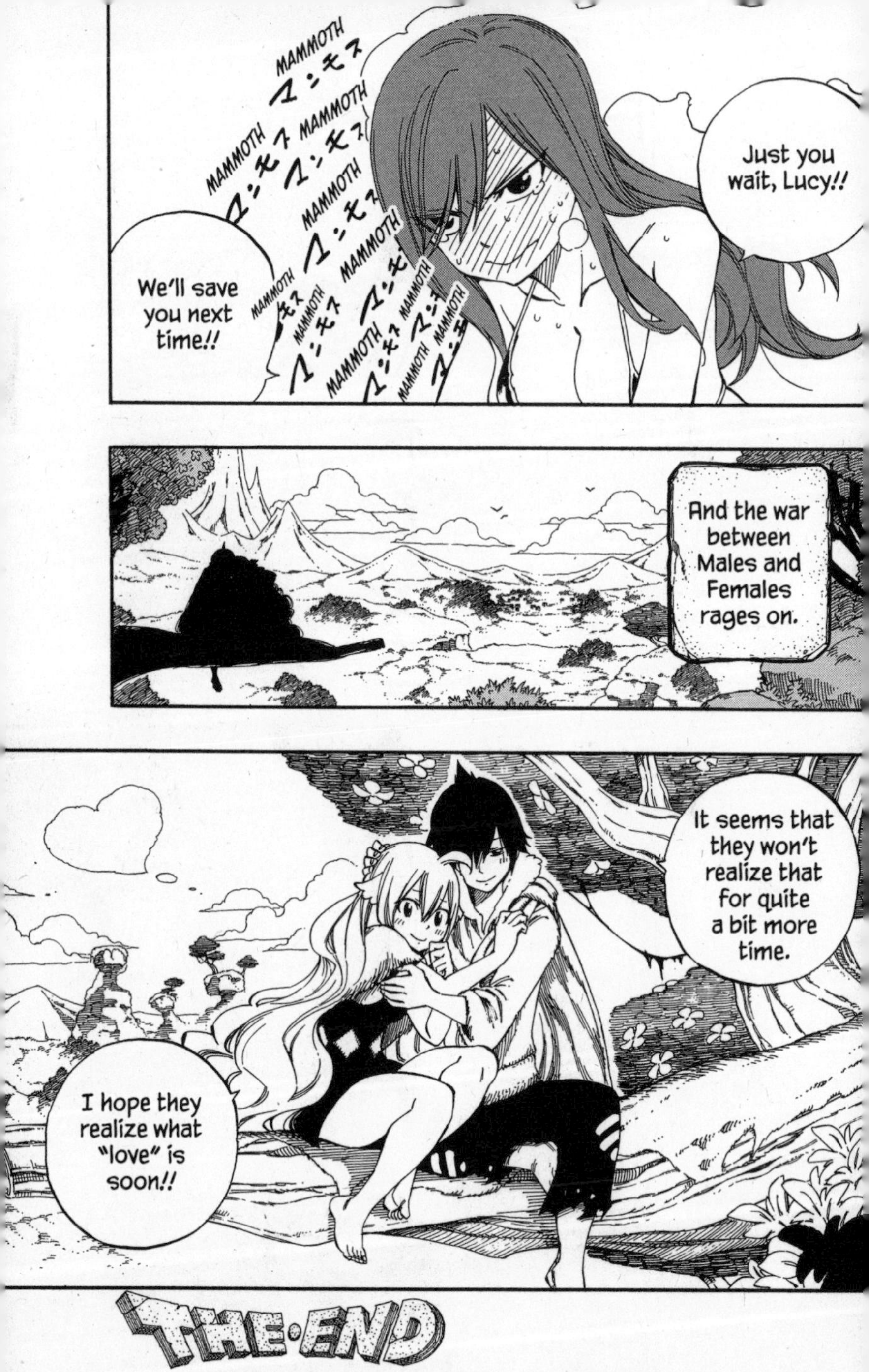

Just you wait, Lucy!!
MAMMOTH マンモス MAMMOTH マンモス MAMMOTH マンモス MAMMOTH マンモス MAMMOTH マンモス MAMMOTH マンモス MAMMOTH マンモス MAMMOTH マンモス MAMMOTH マンモス
We'll save you next time!!
And the war between Males and Females rages on.
It seems that they won't realize that for quite a bit more time.
I hope they realize what "love" is soon!!
THE·END

FT☆S

FAIRY TAILS

VOLUME 2

EXPLANATION & AFTERWORD by HIRO MASHIMA

WELCOME TO FAIRY HILLS

This is one of my earlier short stories that kept coming back to my mind. Even before the series was published, I had the idea of a girls' dorm for the guild, but who lived there, how it looked inside, and other concepts were developed as I was writing. This was the first story to become an original animated DVD (OAD), and I think it is especially popular among fans.
The dorm mother Hilda makes a brief appearance in the third OAD, so I encourage anyone interested to check it out.

GANGSTA GUYS AND GANGSTA GIRLS

I borrowed the Japanese title (*Yankee-kun to Yankee-chan*) from Miki Yoshikawa's manga *Yankee-kun to Megane-chan* ("Gansta Guy and Glasses Girl"). To use the slang term, it's *"genparo."* (a parody that takes SF/Fantasy characters and puts them into modern clothes and settings). It felt really natural to draw the *Fairy Tail* characters in school uniforms, and it turned out to be a lot of fun to draw. I had orginally wanted to include more characters if there were more pages but it already felt like there were too many characters for a short story. I worried a lot over how to characterize their magic, but in the end it wound up that real-world items became connected to their magic. For some reason, I never second-guessed my decision to make Happy their teacher.

FAIRY TAIL X RAVE MASTER

This one turned out to be a collaboration with myself in the form of my first series, *Rave Master*.

Since the series was over, I didn't want to go dredging it up again, but I suddenly had this, "I've got a great idea, so let's do a short story!" feeling.

Before I drew it, I thought that drawing it would overwhelm me with nostalgic feelings, but when I actually set pen to paper, I found that I had forgotten a lot of the characters' habits and speech patterns. So I had to rush through the artwork while reading the old graphic novels, and it wore me out.

I wrote this so that readers who never read *Rave Master* wouldn't complain about not being able to follow it. But still, if you read it with the idea that "these characters are out there too," I think it'll be fine.

RAINBOW CHERRY BLOSSOMS

This was originally released as a full-color manga.

I was worrying about whether I should do the colors myself, but at the time, there were conflicting deadlines in my schedule, so I wound up asking a coloring specialist to do it for me.

This person was able to capture even the most subtle quirks of my color work so at a quick glance, the quality is so good that you wouldn't notice the difference.

I thought that it would look wonderful to have these full-color, rainbow-colored cherry blossoms on a page, and that's how this story came about.

FAIRY WOMAN

Okay, why did I want to draw images you'd find in an American comic? Because I think that was the whole inspiration behind this story. It's only a six-page short story, but for some reason, it seems extremely popular overseas. I get the feeling that I've seen tons of Fairy Woman fan artwork.

NATSU AND ASUKA

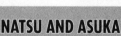

This one ran in *Monthly Shonen Magazine*. I had wanted to draw it with an eye towards having non-readers of *Fairy Tail* enjoy it, but about the time of planning the stories out, it was put forth to tie this story in to the "That Woman, Erza" short story. The idea was that the truth of the Moulin Rouge was revealed here, and the mystery behind this short story was revealed in Erza's short story. Then the plot turned out a lot more complicated than I had planned, and I figured first-time readers would just get confused, so I called a halt to that idea. And this is how it turned out.

By the way, apparently Tetsuya Chiba read this story, and he drew for me a sketch of Natsu and Asuka that I will treasure for the rest of my life.

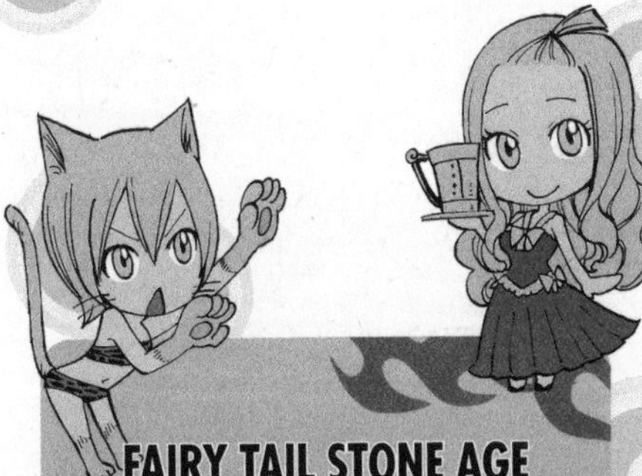

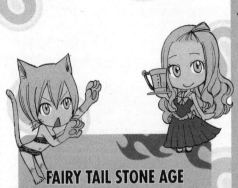

FAIRY TAIL STONE AGE

This was all triggered when I did a sketch just for fun of the Stone Age period, and posted it to Twitter.

I got many more ideas out of it than I expected, and I felt I could put it into a short story. But I never imagined for a second that the final story would turn out as dirty as it wound up being.

I basically drew it for an audience of male junior high school students, but this became one of the ways that I came to understand just how wide-ranging in age and gender the readers of *Fairy Tail* are.

There's no two ways about it: This story is dirty. But on a personal level, I enjoy it.

Especially Laxus. He was such a fool that I laughed when I was drawing my own pictures. I think he came out really cute.

LUCY AND MIGI

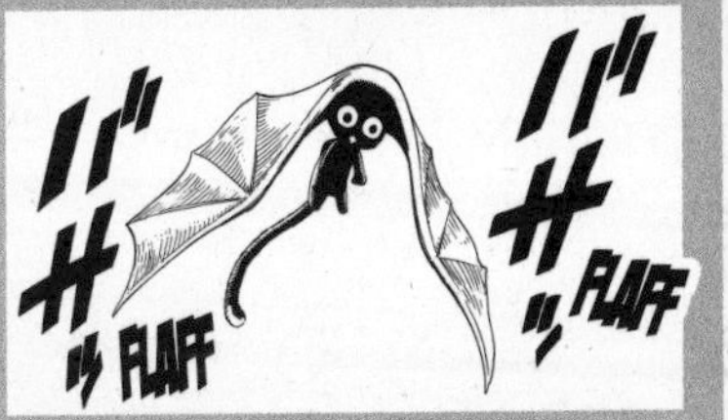

バサ
FLAFF
バサ
FLAFF

This is a collaboration manga with the manga *Parasyte*. During my junior high school days, I was so hooked on *Parasyte* that when the idea was barely touched on in a meeting, I agreed to do it without a second thought. But when it came to drawing it, I just couldn't come up with an idea that I felt comfortable with, so it basically became a parody of the manga's chapter two.

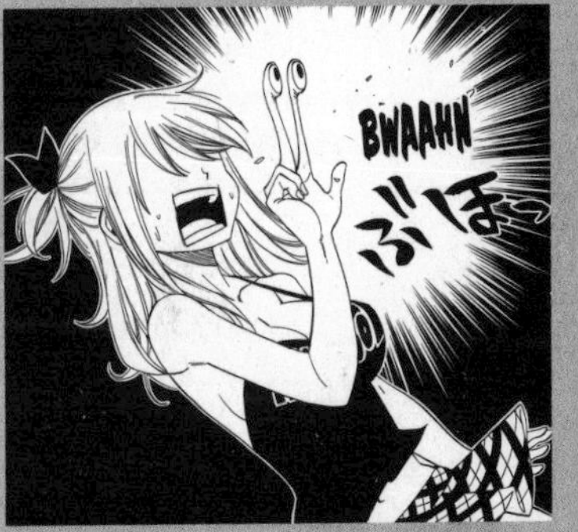

BWAAHN
ぶほっ

I think a lot of people know this already, but the voice actress for both Lucy and Migi is the famous Aya Hirano-san. But when I was submitting the *name** for this chapter, the voice actress for Migi had not yet been decided. I think fate can be kind of mysterious.

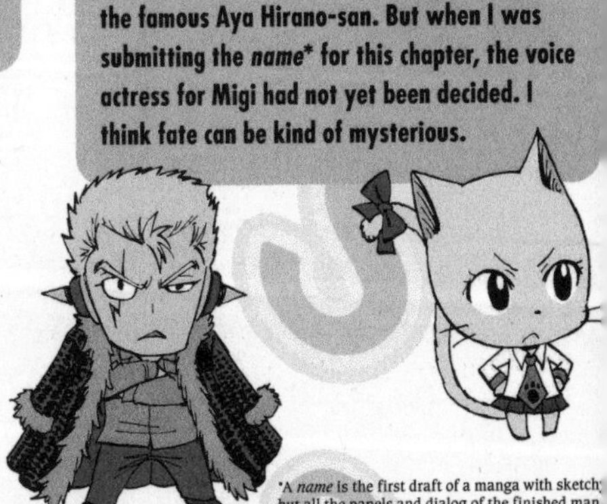

*A *name* is the first draft of a manga with sketchy but all the panels and dialog of the finished man

Translation Notes:

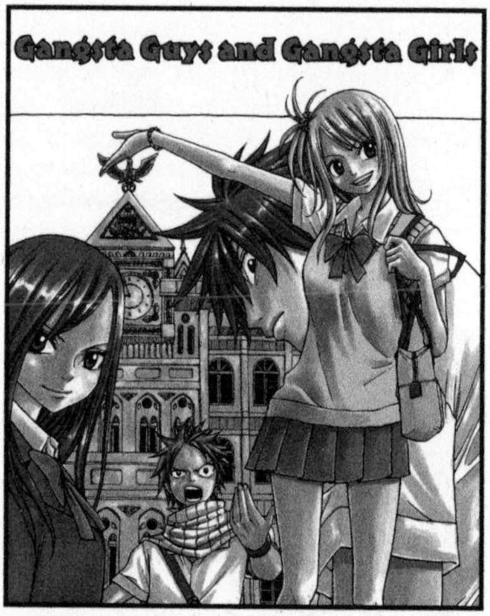
Gangsta Guys and Gangsta Girls

Page 4, Yankee

In most foreign countries, including Japan's neighbors such as China and South Korea, "Yankee" is a derogatory term for an American (such as in "Yankee go home"). But in Japan, the word has taken on a completely different meaning. In Japan the word "yankee" means a juvenile delinquent. The type of teenager who skips school, acts up in class, smokes, hangs with the "wrong" crowd, etc. The Japanese title for this chapter is "Yankee Guys and Yankee Girls."

Page 6, "How Do You Do"

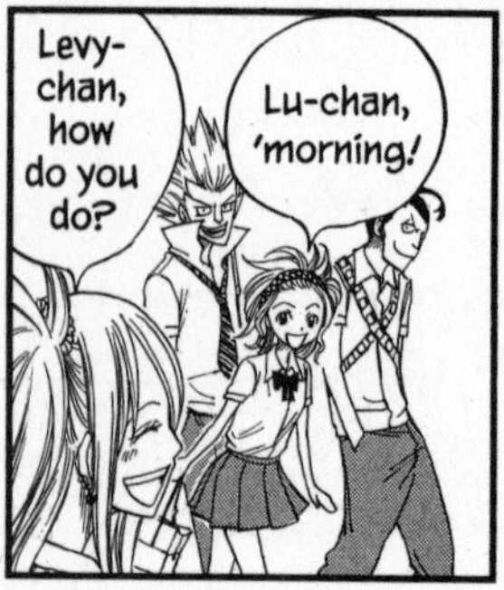
Lu-chan, 'morning!
Levy-chan, how do you do?

When arriving at school in Japan (particularly in manga more than in real life), everyone greets each other with some variation on the Japanese term for, "Good morning." But in elite girls' schools (especially in manga, but probably also influenced by real-life experience), the girls greet each other with a more formal greeting, *gokigenyou*, which translates to something like "How do you do?" in English.

Page 12, Loke being smooth

Loke sweet talking the girls is something one would expect more from a guy working in a host bar (a bar where male servers compliment and make conversation with women who pay premium prices to drink with handsome men) than a high school student.

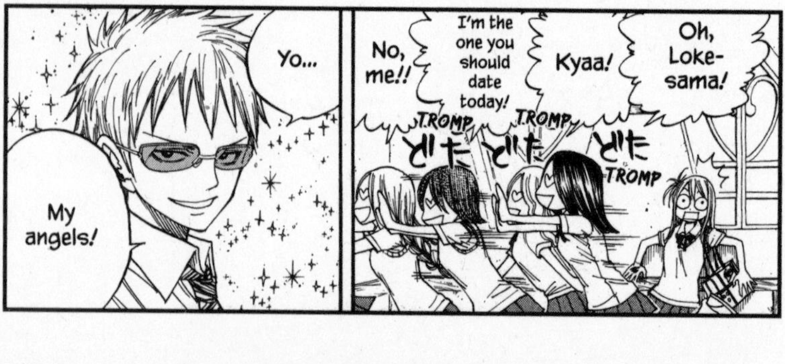
Oh, Loke-sama!
Kyaa!
I'm the one you should date today!
No, me!!
TROMP
TROMP
TROMP
Yo...
My angels!

Page 68, Flower-Viewing Party

There can be flower-viewing parties for different types of flowers but the most famous and popular type of flower-viewing party is in late March or early April to see the cherry blossoms. In many cases, flower-viewing parties are for a large number of people, all sitting in the same vicinity, sharing food, sweets, and especially alcohol (making it a perfect thing for the *Fairy Tail* guild to do together). In fact, the famous phrase, "*hana yori dango*" ("rice dumplings over flowers") comes from flower-viewing parties where the people there are more interested in the food than the flowers.

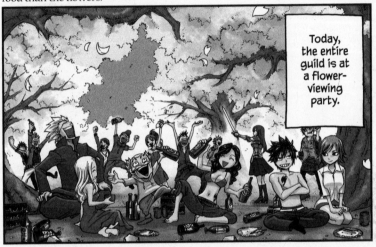

Today, the entire guild is at a flower-viewing party.

Page 81, Haru and Natsu

Haru means "spring" in Japanese, and Natsu means "summer." Fuyu (page 83) means "winter," and this comes into play when Natsu remembers that Haru is named after a season but he can't quite remember which one!

They call me Haru.
I'm Natsu.
Natsu of Fairy Tail.

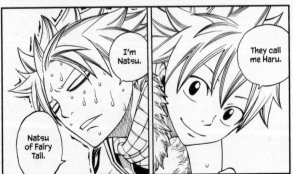

FAIRY TAIL ZERØ

We are happy to present you with a preview of Hiro Mashima's *Fairy Tail ZERØ*.

Mavis, the future first master of Fairy Tail, lives with her best friend Zera on Sirius Island. At six-years-old, Mavis is just a simple bookworm who dreams of meeting fairies someday. In the year X686, treasure hunters invade Sirius Island, forcing Mavis to take flight and embark on a fantastical adventure! She etches the joys and sorrowws of each new encounter and heartbreaking fare-well into her memory, and finally figures out her ultimate goal...

NOW AVAILABLE IN PRINT AND DIGITAL!

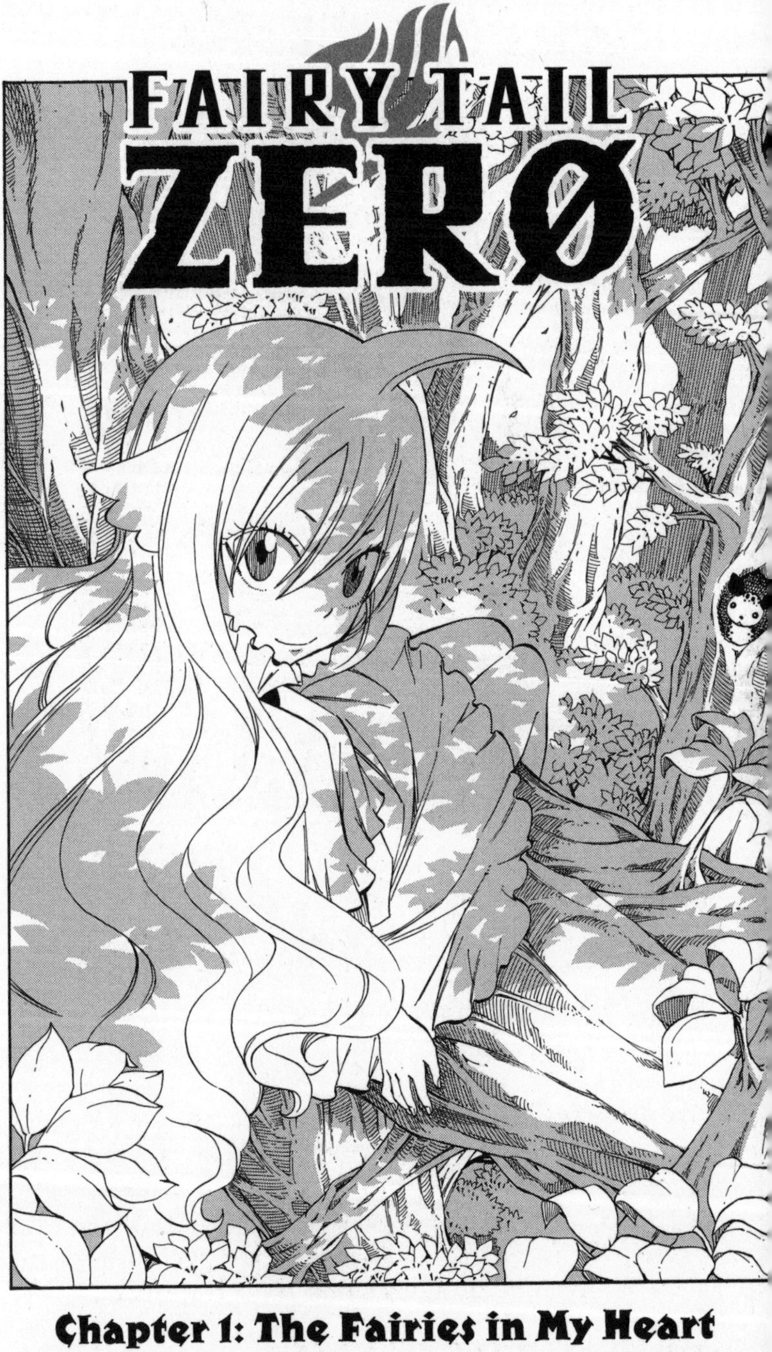
FAIRY TAIL
ZERØ

Chapter 1: The Fairies in My Heart

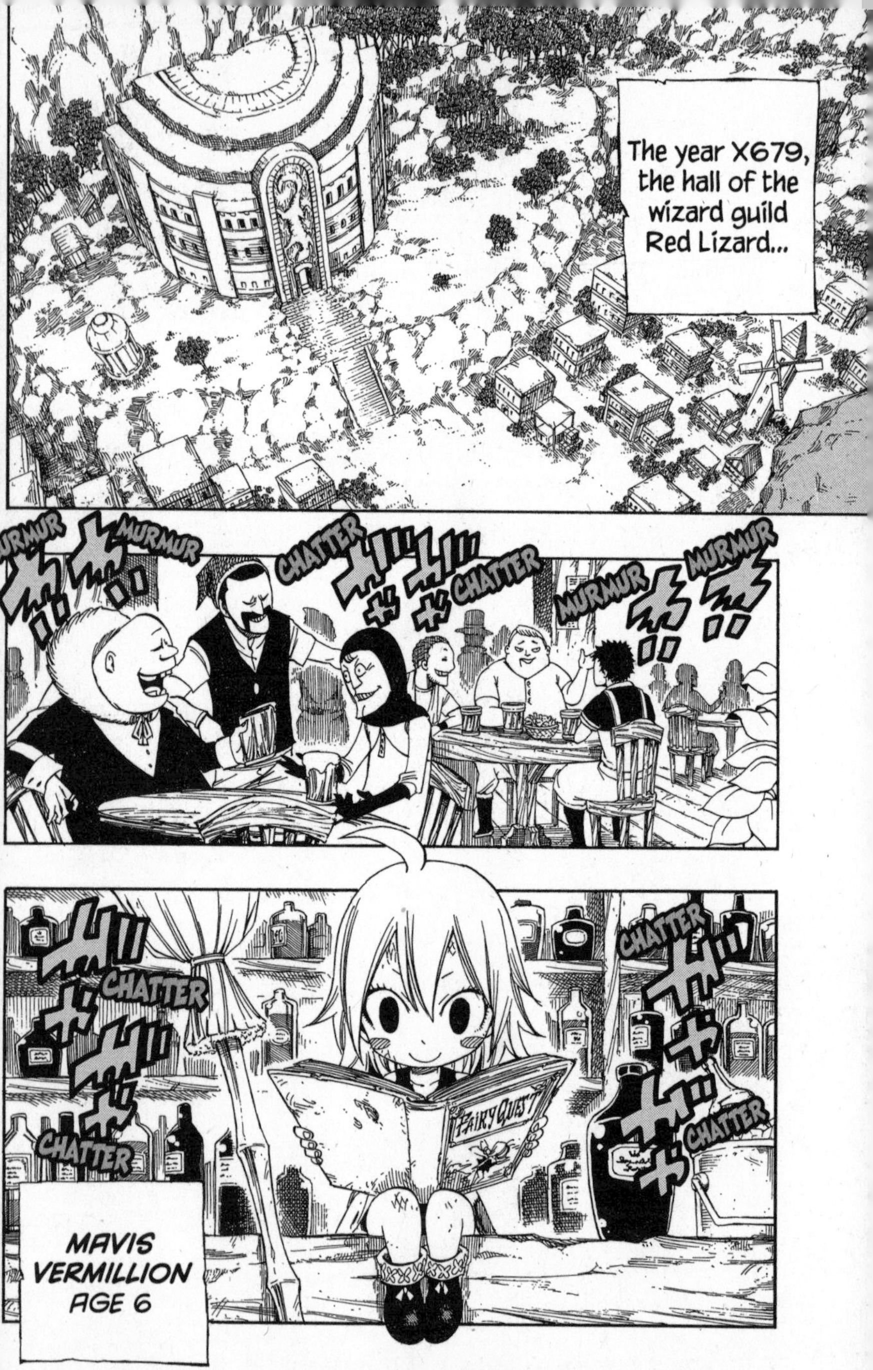
The year X679, the hall of the wizard guild Red Lizard...
MURMUR
MURMUR
CHATTER
CHATTER
MURMUR
MURMUR
CHATTER
CHATTER
CHATTER
CHATTER
MAVIS VERMILLION AGE 6

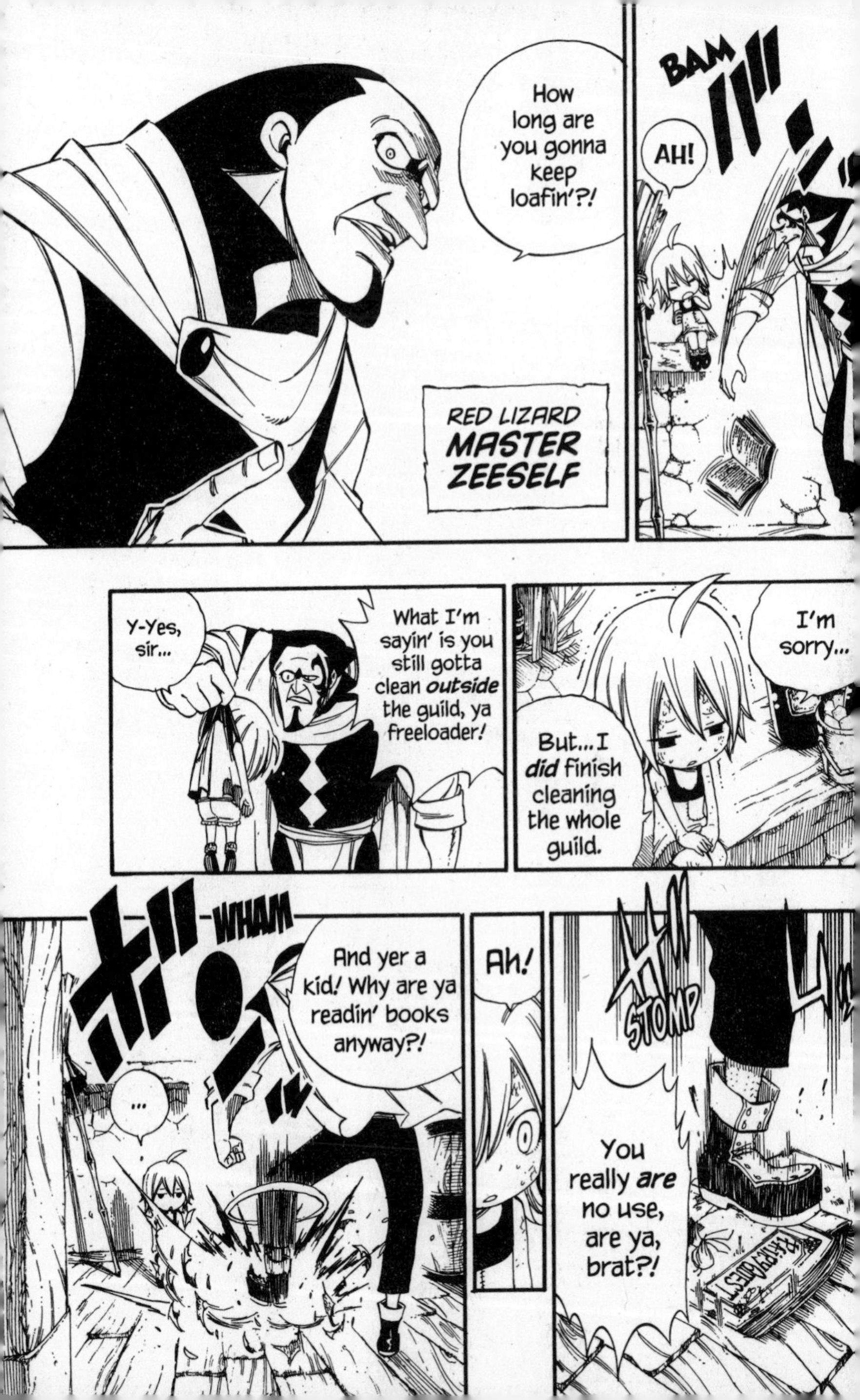
BAM
AH!
How long are you gonna keep loafin'?!
RED LIZARD MASTER ZEESELF
I'm sorry...
But...I *did* finish cleaning the whole guild.
What I'm sayin' is you still gotta clean *outside* the guild, ya freeloader!
Y-Yes, sir...
STOMP
You really *are* no use, are ya, brat?!
Ah!
And yer a kid! Why are ya readin' books anyway?!
WHAM
...

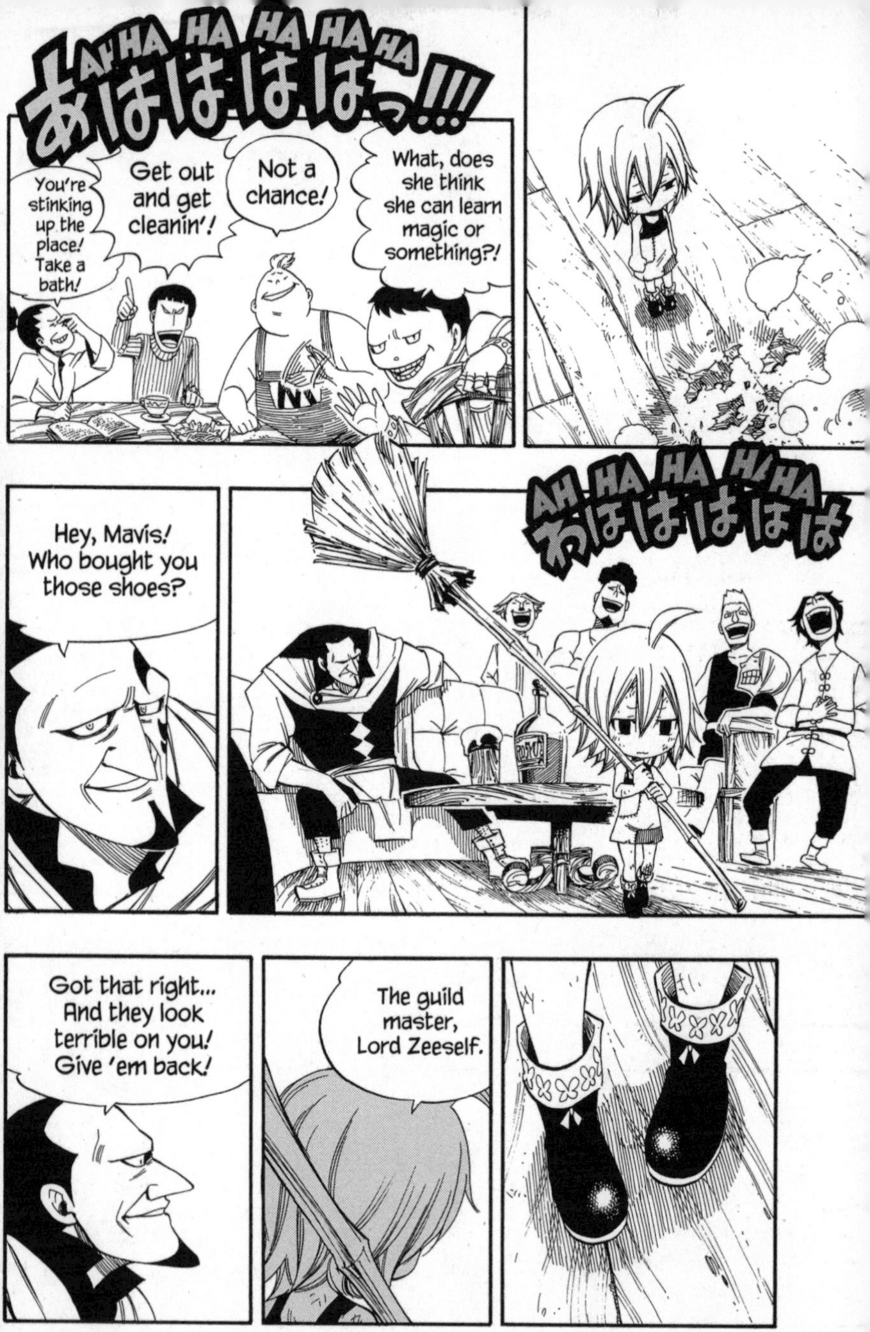
AH HA HA HA HA HA
あははははっ!!!
What, does she think she can learn magic or something?!
Not a chance!
Get out and get cleanin'!
You're stinking up the place! Take a bath!
AH HA HA HA HA
わははははは
Hey, Mavis! Who bought you those shoes?
The guild master, Lord Zeeself.
Got that right... And they look terrible on you! Give 'em back!

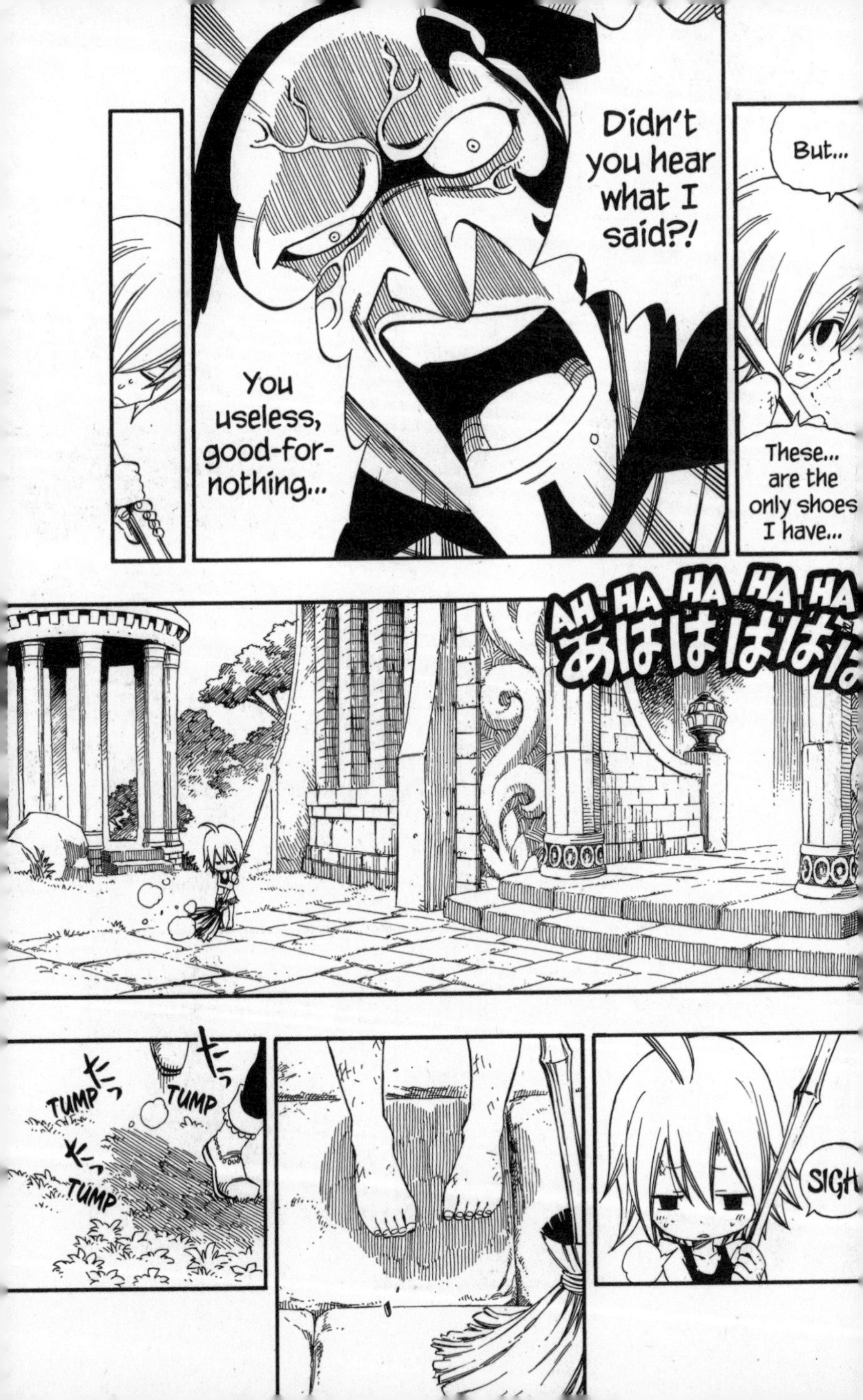

But...
These... are the only shoes I have...
Didn't you hear what I said?!
You useless, good-for-nothing...
AH HA HA HA HA
あはははは
SIGH
TUMP
TUMP
TUMP

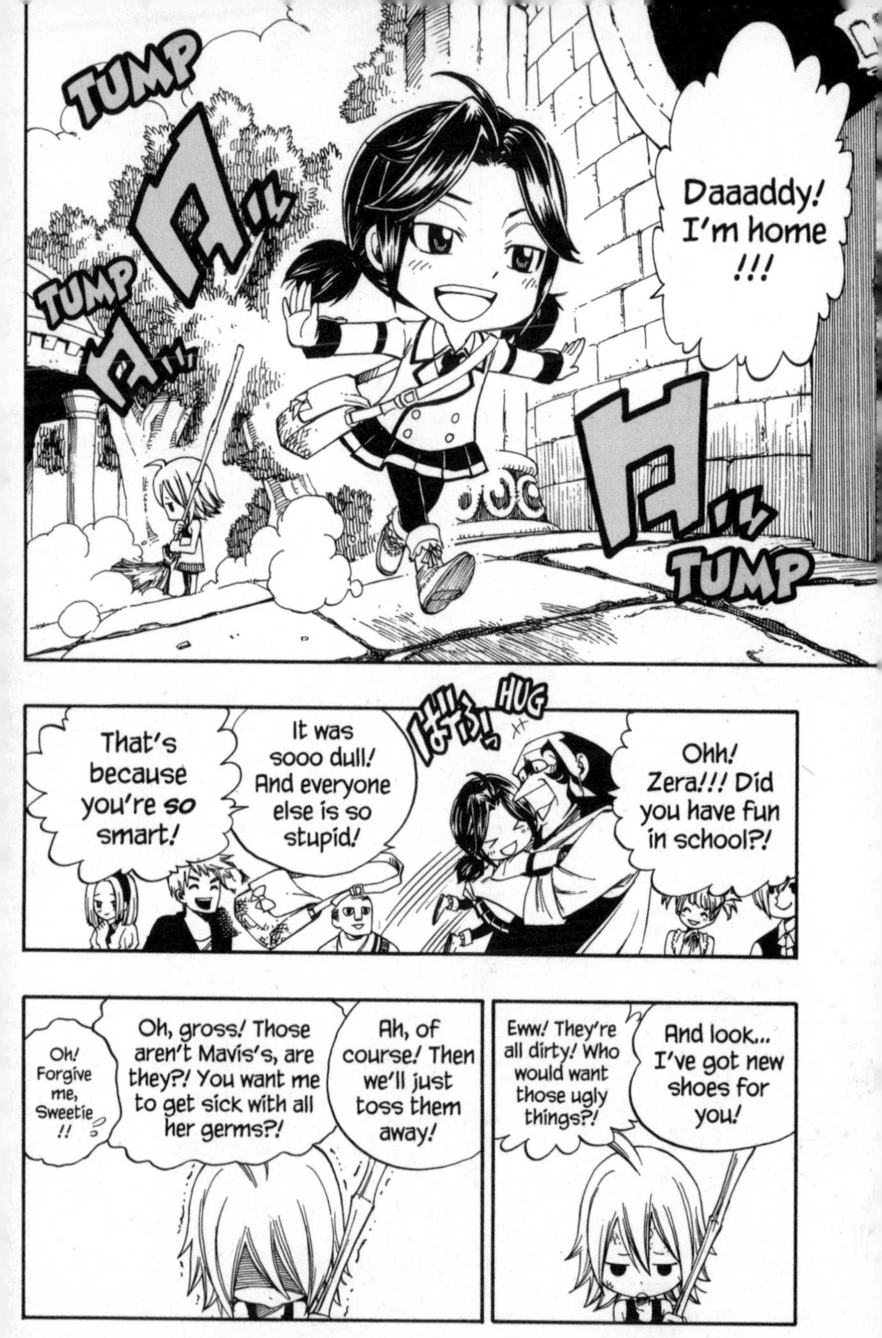
Daaaddy! I'm home !!!
A..
TUMP
TUMP
A..
TUMP
A..
Ohh! Zera!!! Did you have fun in school?!
HUG
It was sooo dull! And everyone else is so stupid!
That's because you're so smart!
And look... I've got new shoes for you!
Eww! They're all dirty! Who would want those ugly things?!
Ah, of course! Then we'll just toss them away!
Oh, gross! Those aren't Mavis's, are they?! You want me to get sick with all her germs?!
Oh! Forgive me, Sweetie !!

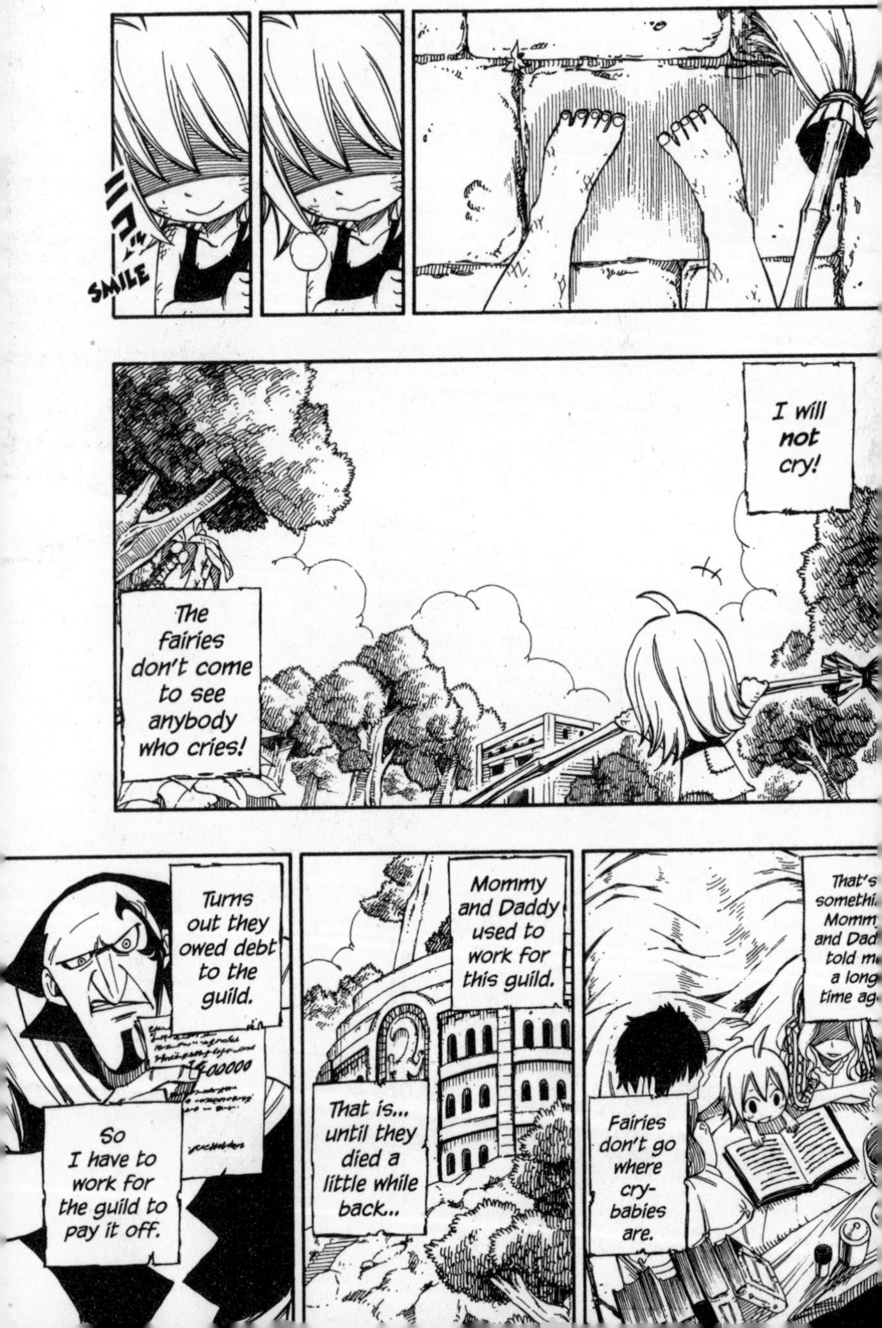
SMILE
I will not cry!
The fairies don't come to see anybody who cries!
That's somethi Momm and Dad told m a long time ag
Fairies don't go where cry-babies are.
Mommy and Daddy used to work for this guild.
That is... until they died a little while back...
Turns out they owed debt to the guild.
So I have to work for the guild to pay it off.

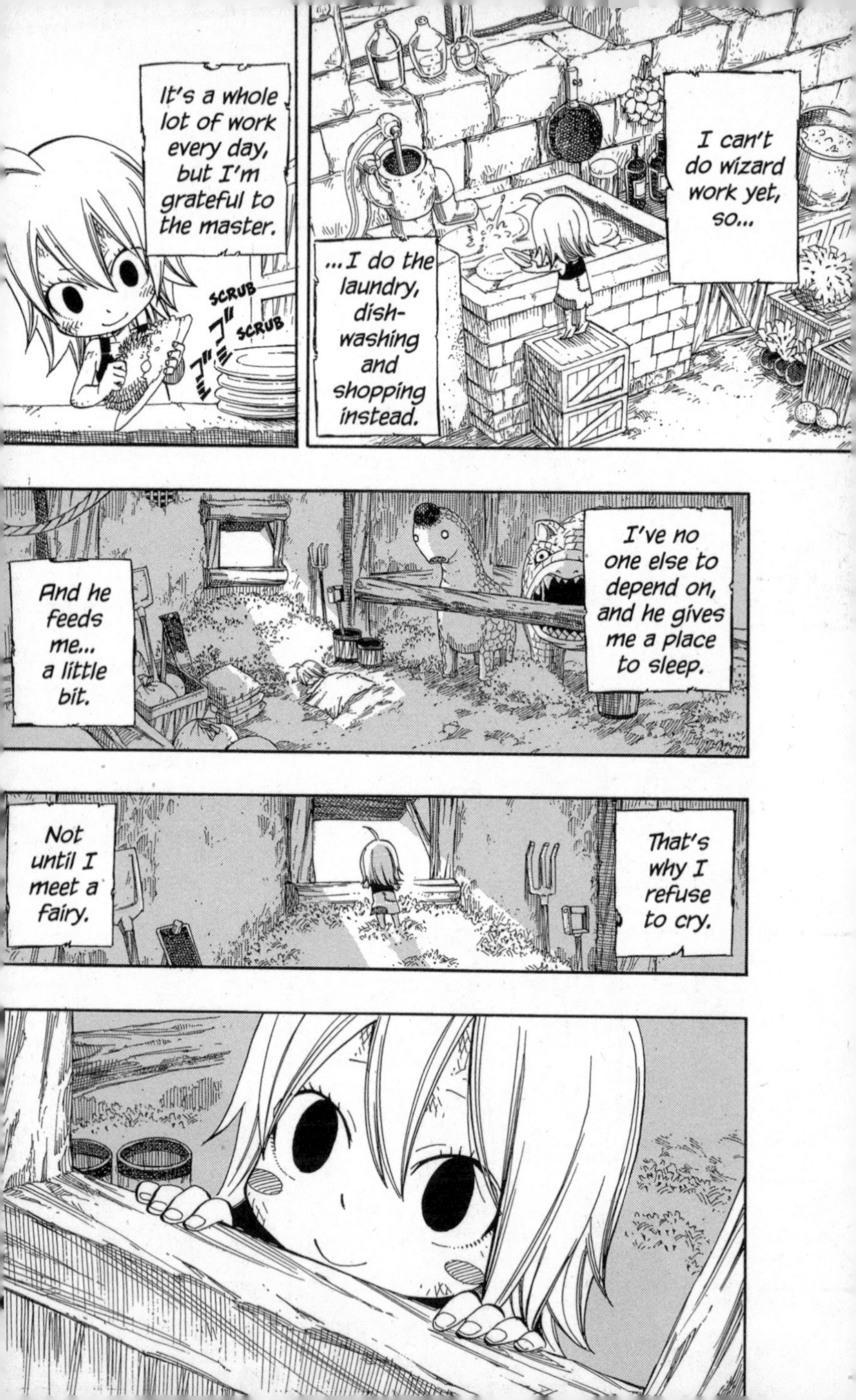
I can't do wizard work yet, so...
...I do the laundry, dish-washing and shopping instead.
It's a whole lot of work every day, but I'm grateful to the master.
SCRUB
SCRUB
I've no one else to depend on, and he gives me a place to sleep.
And he feeds me... a little bit.
That's why I refuse to cry.
Not until I meet a fairy.

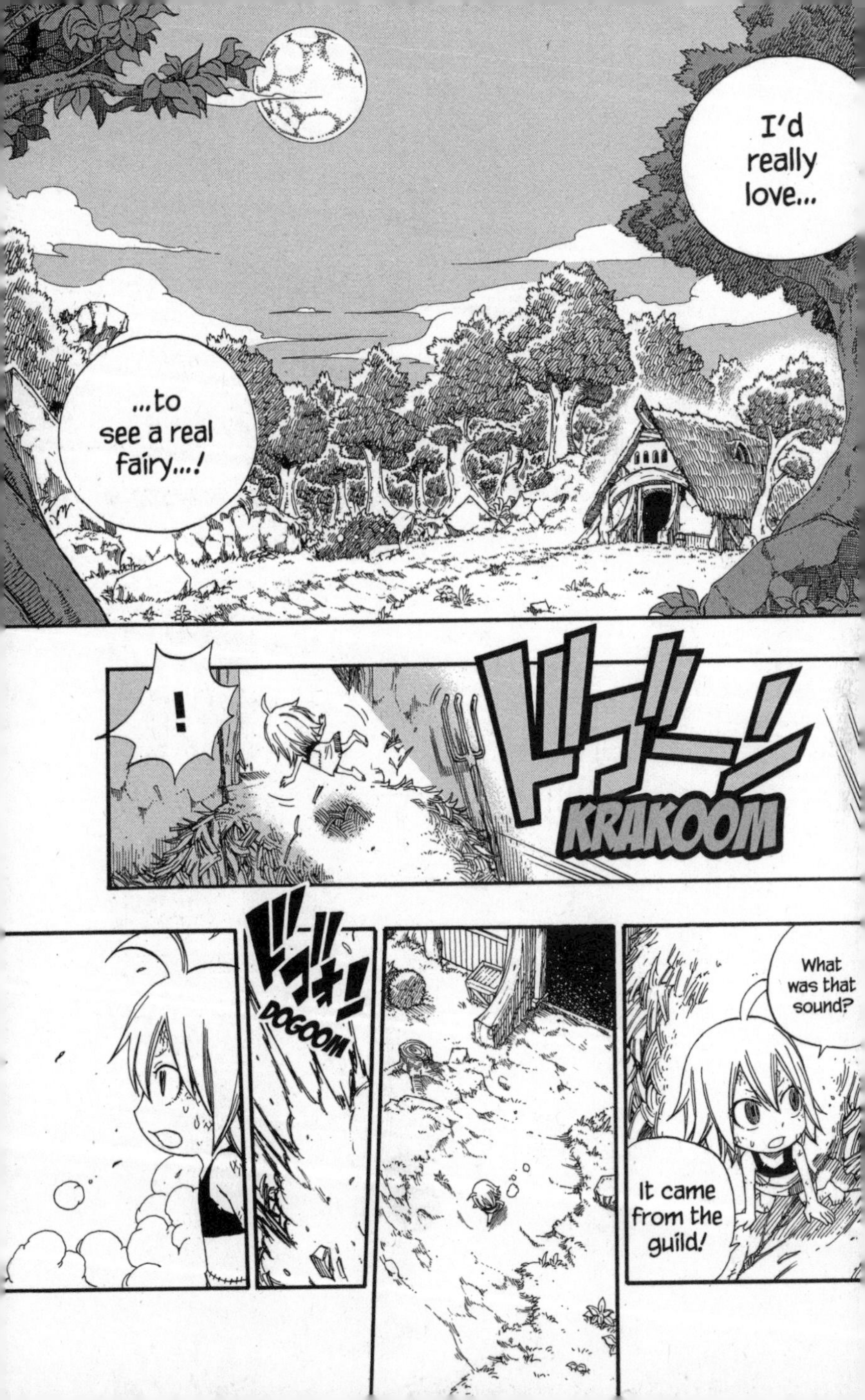
I'd really love...
...to see a real fairy...!
KRAKOOM
!
DOGOOM
What was that sound?
It came from the guild!

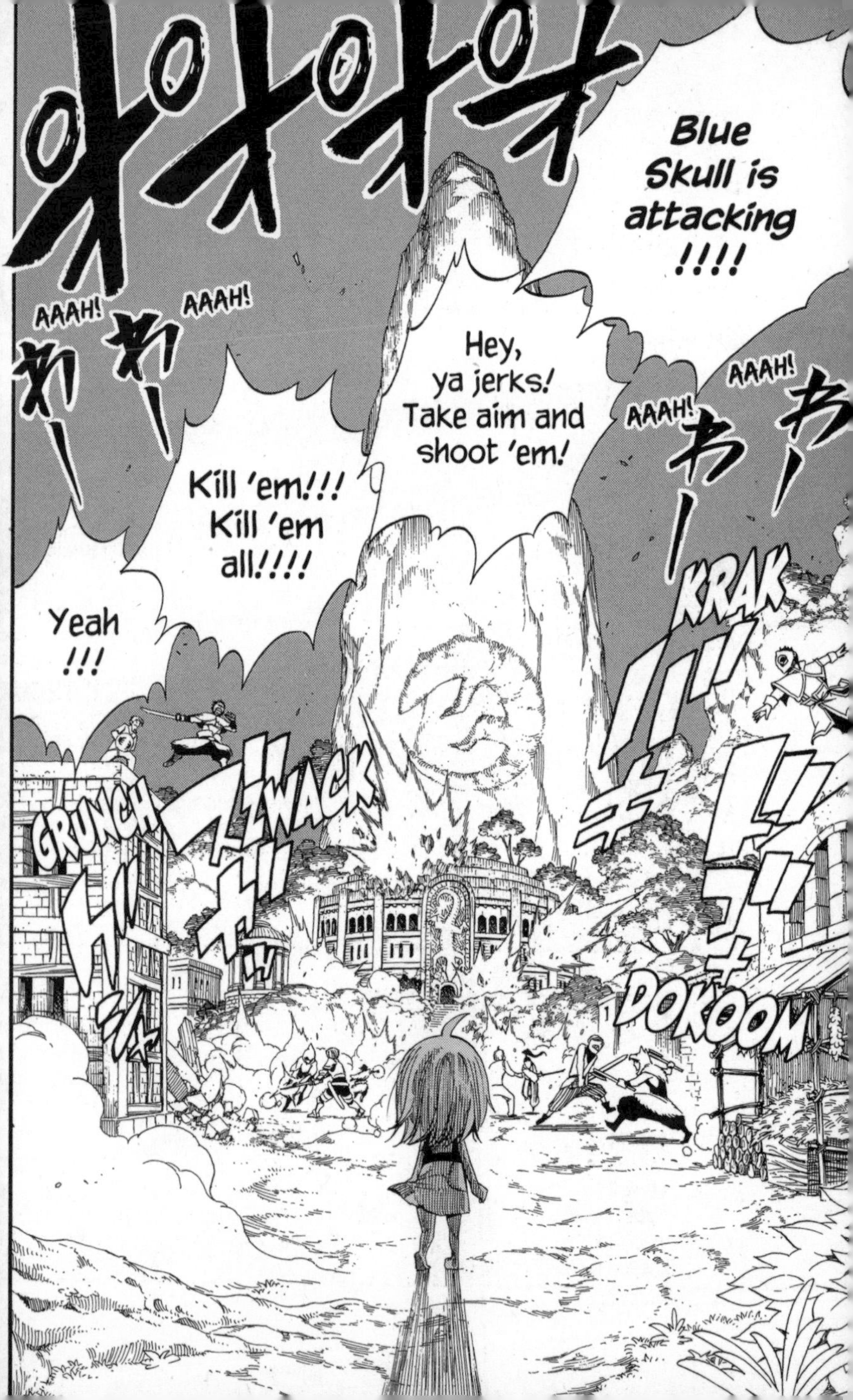
Blue Skull is attacking!!!!
AAAH!
AAAH!
Hey, ya jerks! Take aim and shoot 'em!
Kill 'em!!! Kill 'em all!!!!
AAAH!
AAAH!
Yeah!!!
KRAK
DOKOOM
ZWACK
GRUNCH

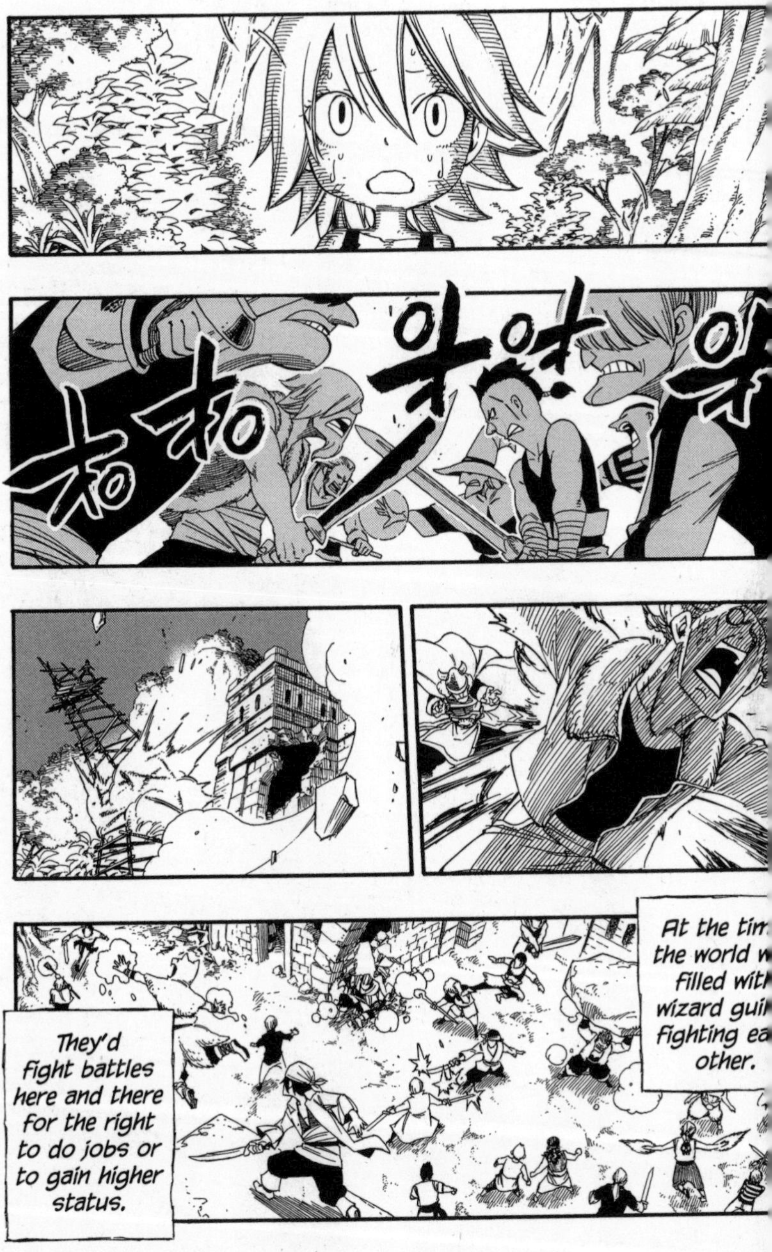
At the tim
the world w
filled wit
wizard gui
fighting ea
other.
They'd fight battles here and there for the right to do jobs or to gain higher status.

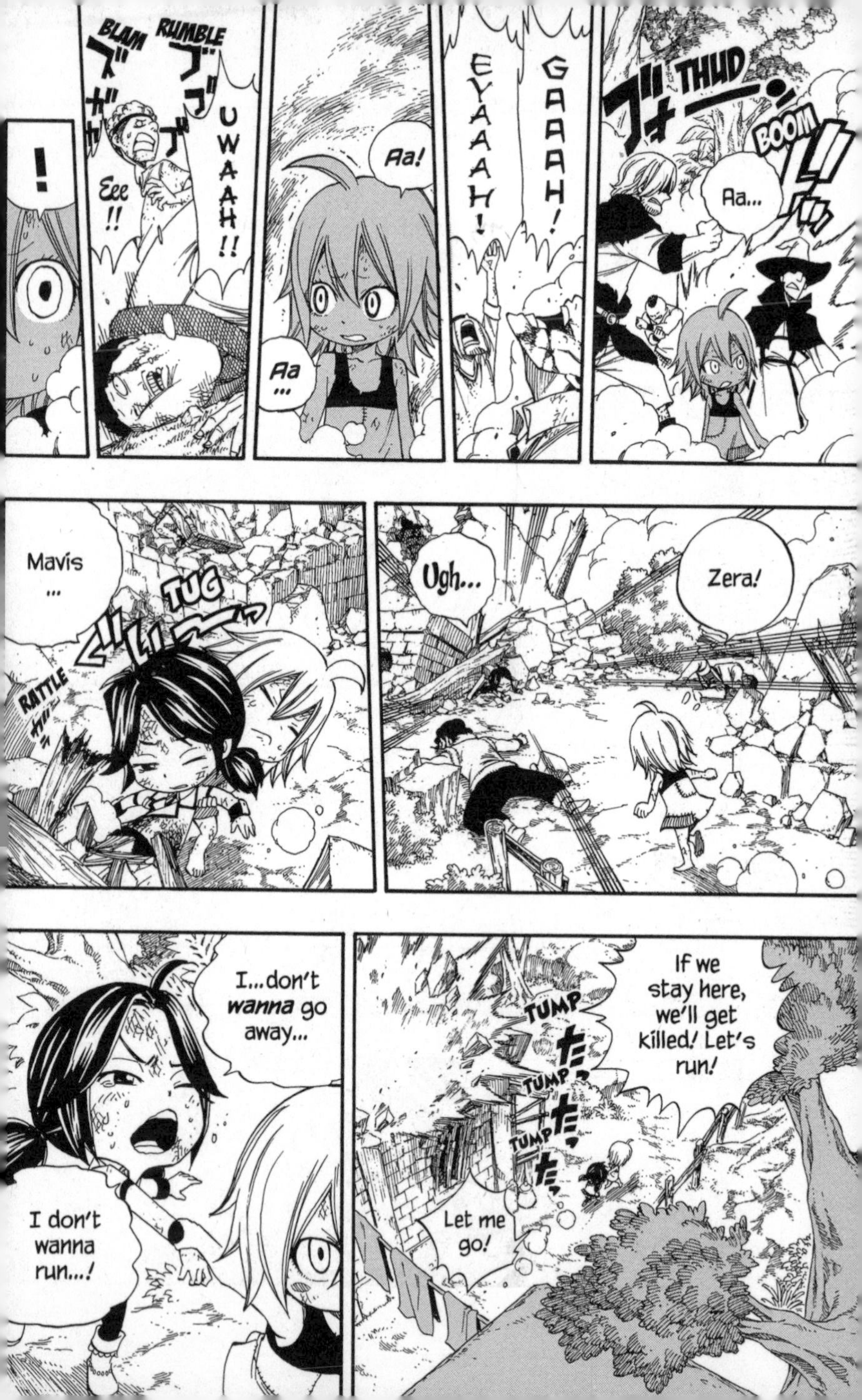
THUD
BOOM!!
Aa...
GAAAAH!
EYAAAAH!
Aa!
Aa...
RUMBLE
BLAM
UWAAH!!
Eee!!
!
Zera!
Ugh...
Mavis...
TUG
RATTLE
If we stay here, we'll get killed! Let's run!
TUMP
TUMP
TUMP
Let me go!
I...don't wanna go away...
I don't wanna run...!

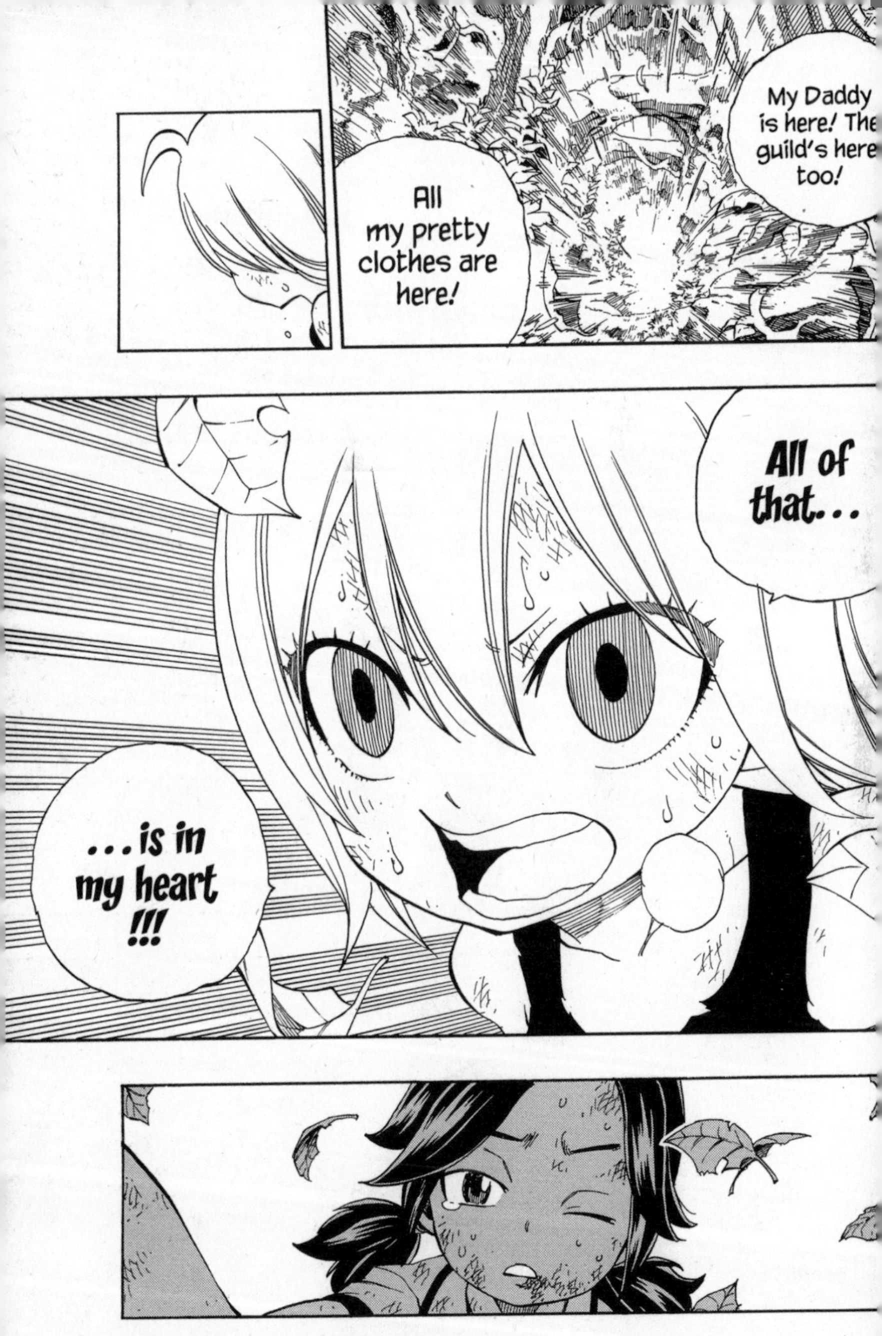
My Daddy is here! The guild's here too!
All my pretty clothes are here!
All of that...
...is in my heart!!!

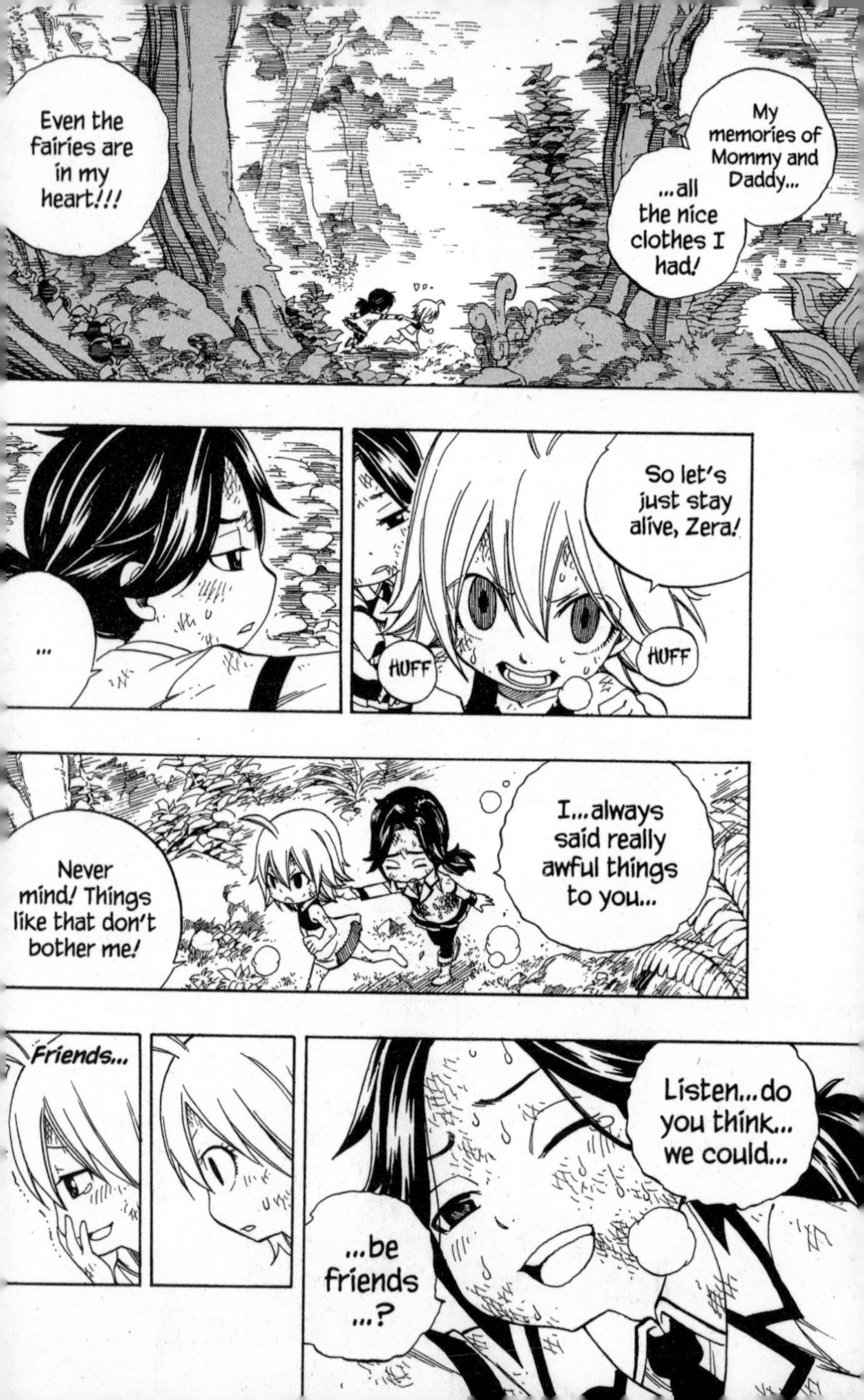
My memories of Mommy and Daddy...
...all the nice clothes I had!
Even the fairies are in my heart!!!
So let's just stay alive, Zera!
HUFF
HUFF
...
I...always said really awful things to you...
Never mind! Things like that don't bother me!
Listen...do you think... we could...
...be friends ...?
Friends...

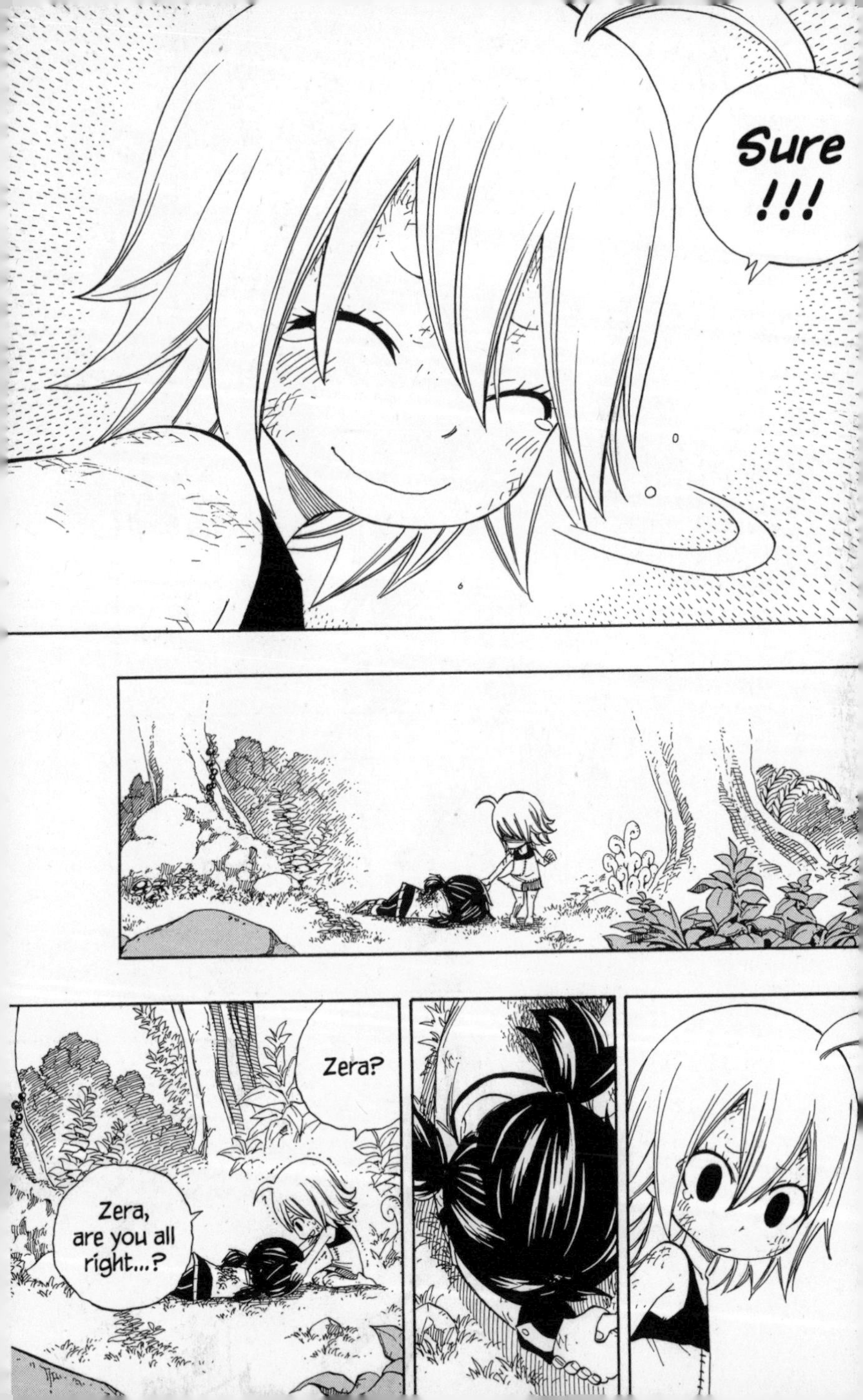
Sure!!!
Zera?
Zera, are you all right...?

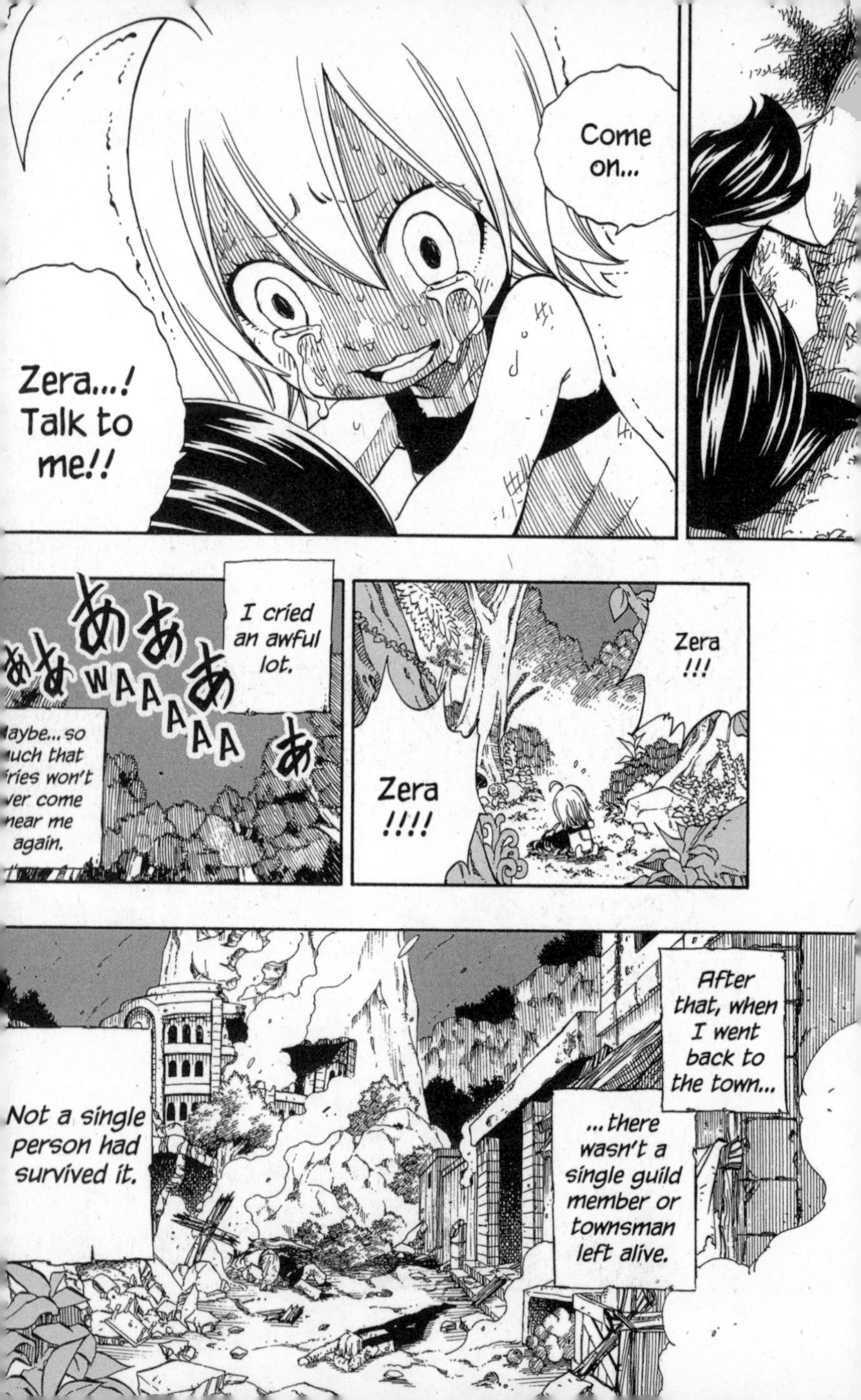

Come on...
Zera...! Talk to me!!
Zera !!!
Zera !!!!
I cried an awful lot.
あああ WAAAAAA あ
aybe... so uch that ries won't ver come near me again.
After that, when I went back to the town...
...there wasn't a single guild member or townsman left alive.
Not a single person had survived it.

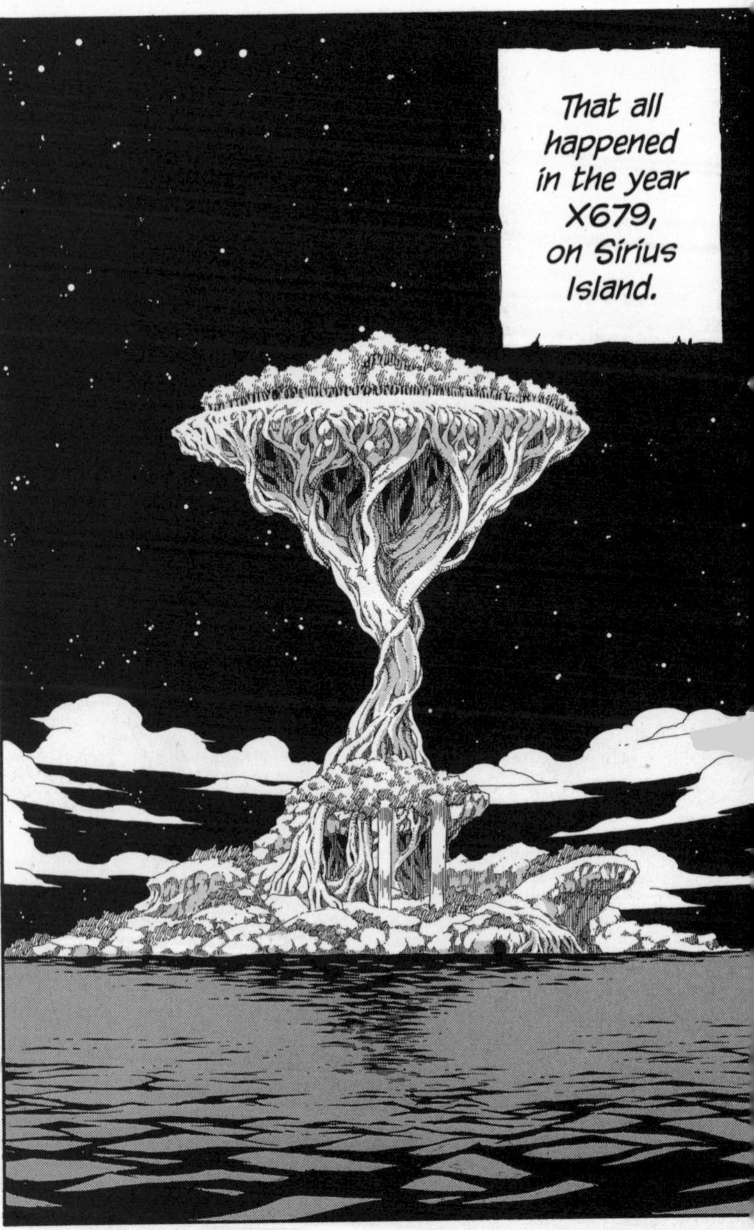
That all happened in the year X679, on Sirius Island.

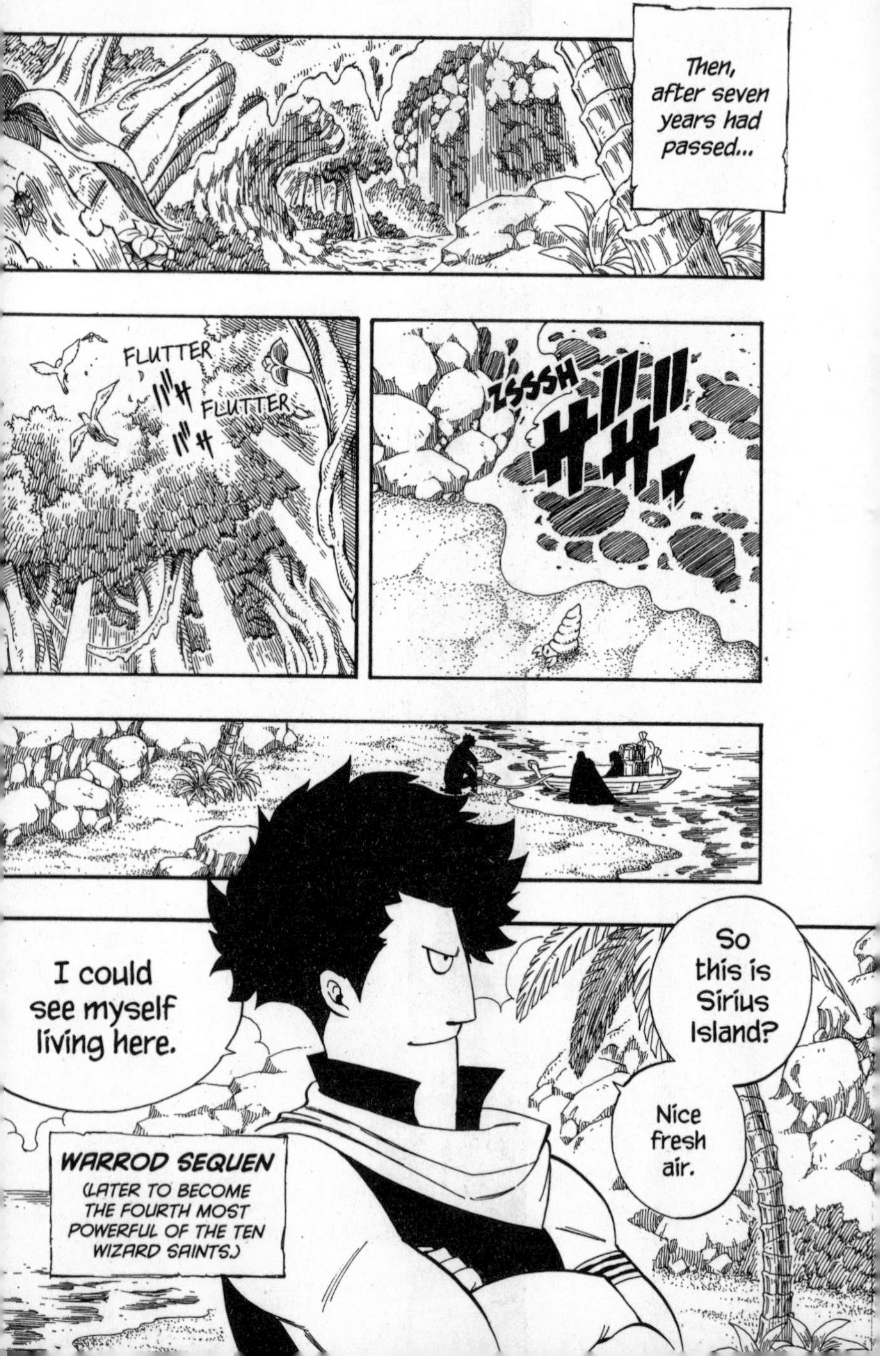
Then, after seven years had passed...
ZSSSH
FLUTTER
FLUTTER
So this is Sirius Island?
Nice fresh air.
I could see myself living here.
WARROD SEQUEN
(LATER TO BECOME THE FOURTH MOST POWERFUL OF THE TEN WIZARD SAINTS.)

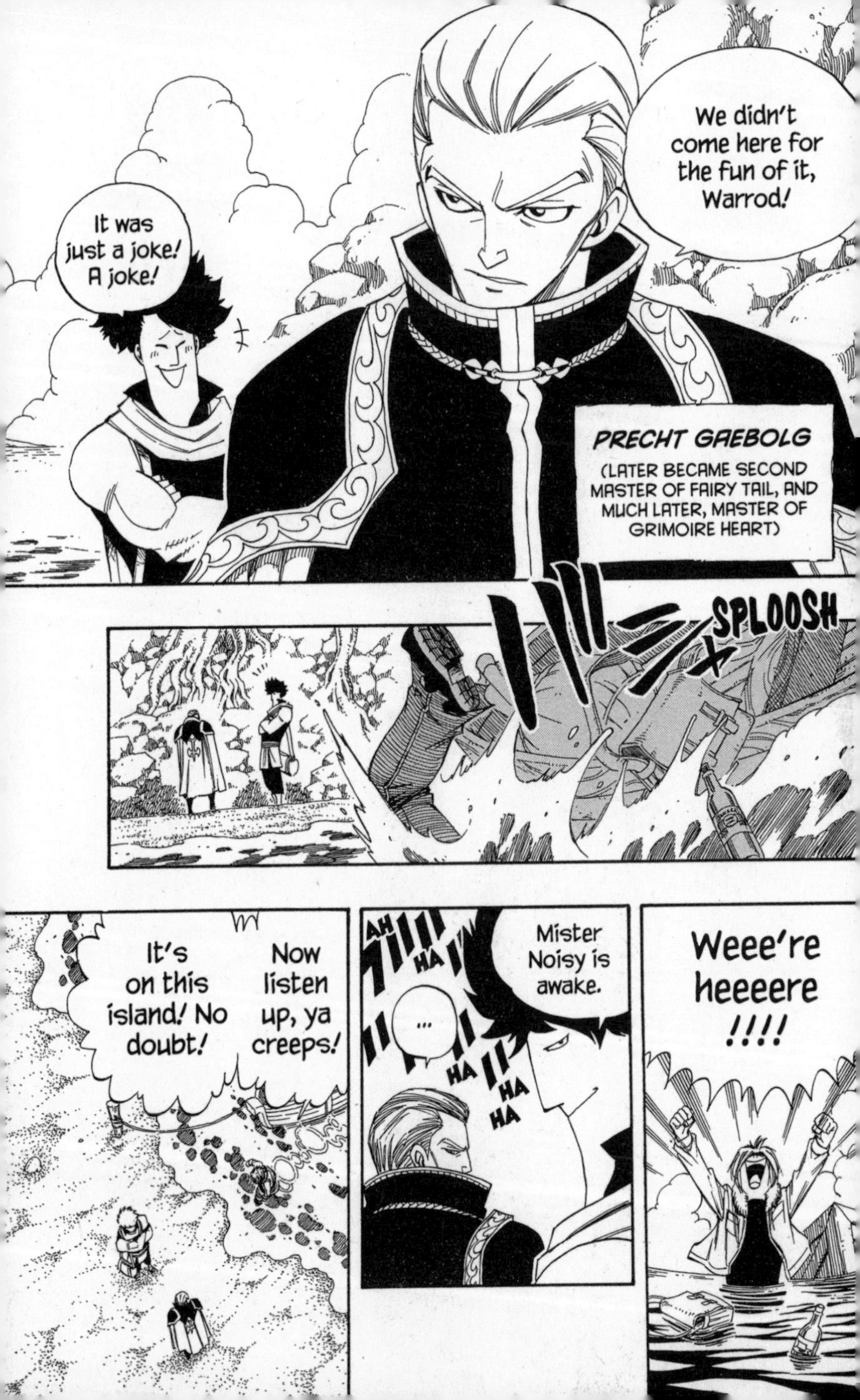
We didn't come here for the fun of it, Warrod!
PRECHT GAEBOLG
(LATER BECAME SECOND MASTER OF FAIRY TAIL, AND MUCH LATER, MASTER OF GRIMOIRE HEART)
It was just a joke! A joke!
SPLOOSH
Weee're heeeere !!!!
Mister Noisy is awake.
...
AH HA HA HA HA HA
Now listen up, ya creeps!
It's on this island! No doubt!

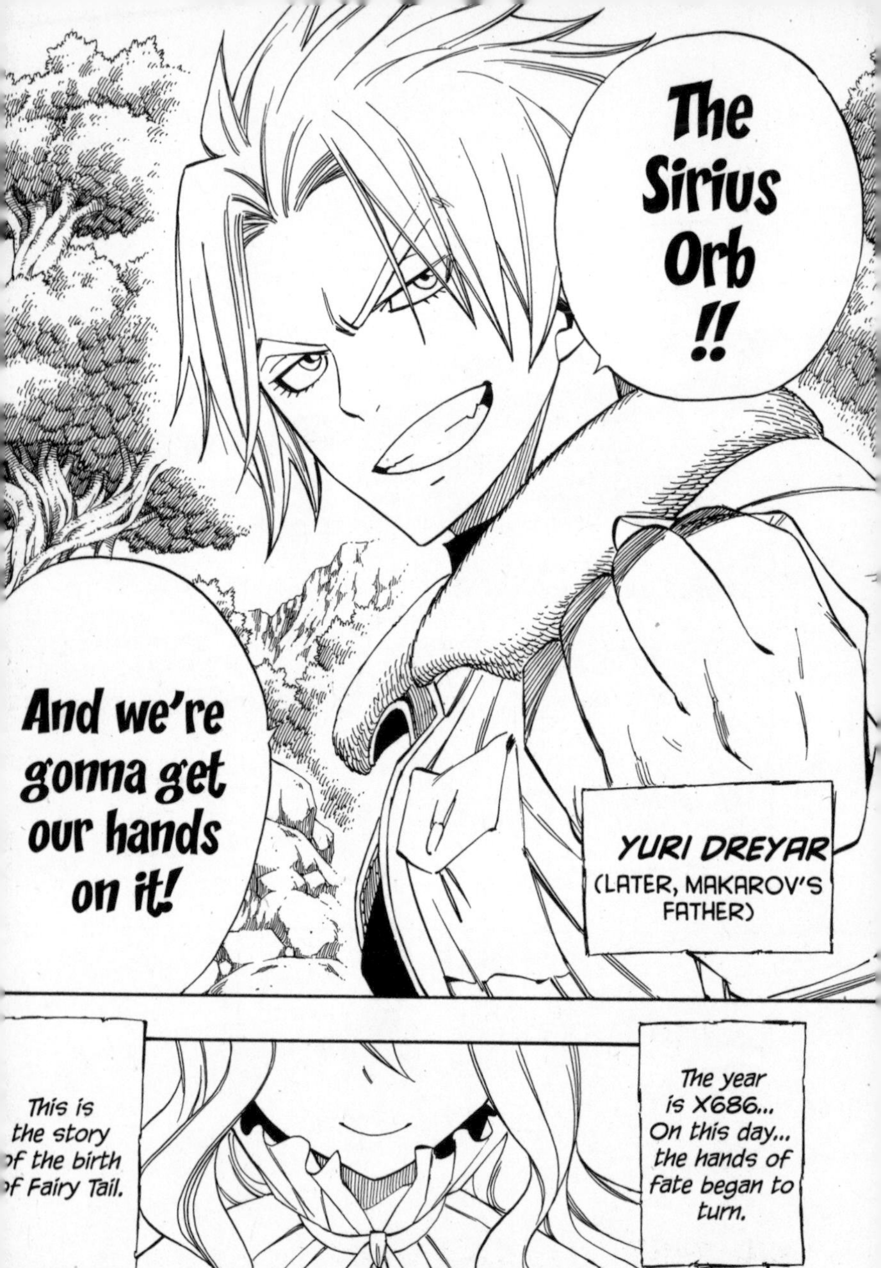
The Sirius Orb!!
And we're gonna get our hands on it!
YURI DREYAR (LATER, MAKAROV'S FATHER)
The year is X686... On this day... the hands of fate began to turn.
This is the story of the birth of Fairy Tail.

FT★S

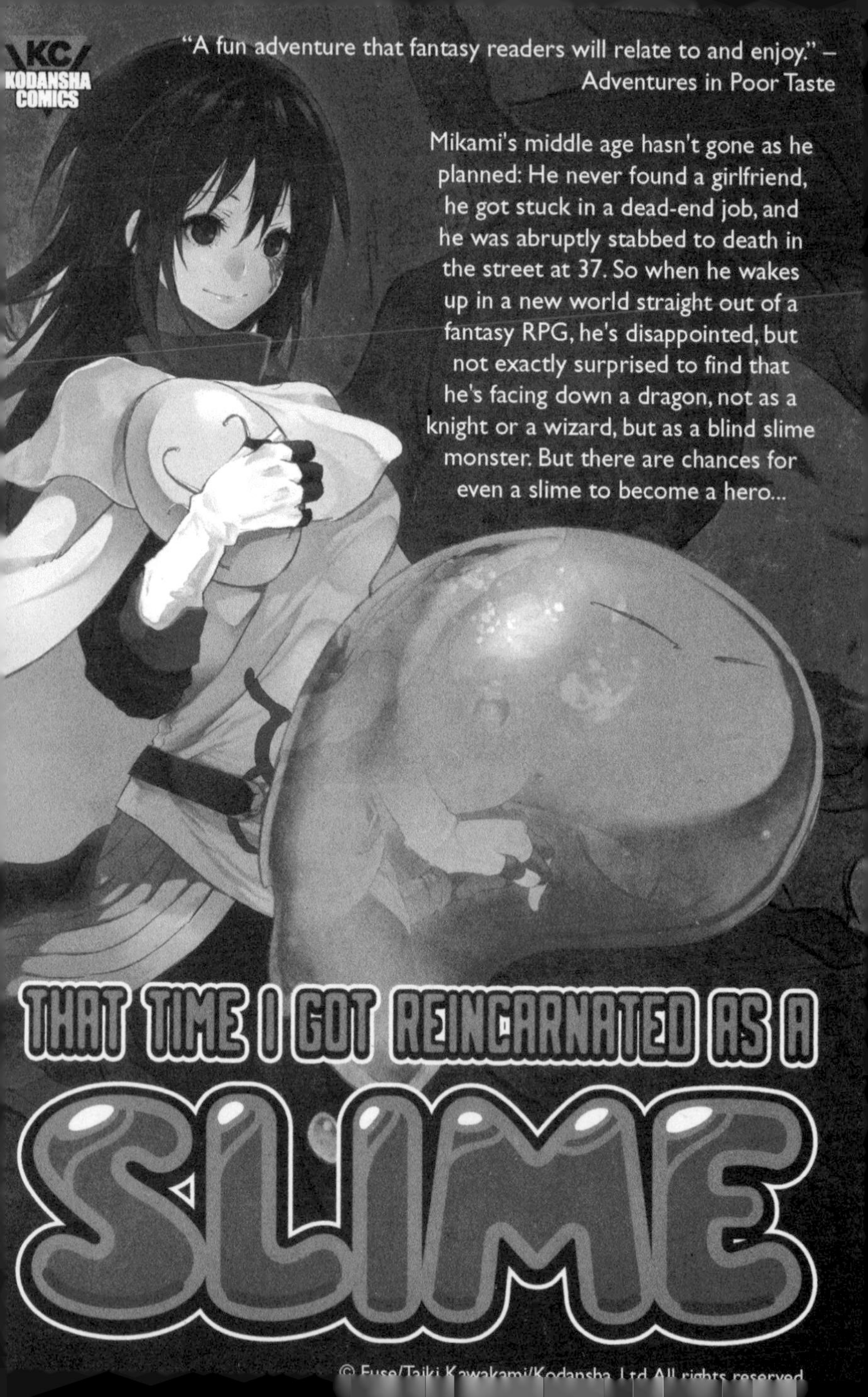
KC
KODANSHA COMICS
"A fun adventure that fantasy readers will relate to and enjoy." – Adventures in Poor Taste
Mikami's middle age hasn't gone as he planned: He never found a girlfriend, he got stuck in a dead-end job, and he was abruptly stabbed to death in the street at 37. So when he wakes up in a new world straight out of a fantasy RPG, he's disappointed, but not exactly surprised to find that he's facing down a dragon, not as a knight or a wizard, but as a blind slime monster. But there are chances for even a slime to become a hero...
THAT TIME I GOT REINCARNATED AS A
SLIME
© Fuse/Taiki Kawakami/Kodansha Ltd All rights reserved

H A P · P I N E S S
——ハピネス——
By **Shuzo Oshimi**

From the creator of *The Flowers of Evil*

Nothing interesting is happening in Makoto Ozaki's first year of high school. His life is a series of quiet humiliations: low-grade bullies, unreliable friends, and the constant frustration of his adolescent lust. But one night, a pale, thin girl knocks him to the ground in an alley and offers him a choice.

Now everything is different. Daylight is searingly bright. Food tastes awful. And worse than anything is the terrible, consuming thirst...

Praise for Shuzo Oshimi's *The Flowers of Evil*

"A shockingly readable story that vividly—one might even say queasily—evokes the fear and confusion of discovering one's own sexuality. Recommended." —The Manga Critic

"A page-turning tale of sordid middle school blackmail." —Otaku USA Magazine

"A stunning new horror manga." —Third Eye Comics

DISCOVER YOUR NEW FAVORITE FANTASY WITH TWO NEW TANTALIZING SERIES!

LAND OF THE LUSTROUS

A BEAUTIFULLY-DRAWN NEW ACTION MANGA FROM HARUKO ICHIKAWA, WINNER OF THE OSAMU TEZUKA CULTURAL PRIZE!

Kigurumi GUARDIANS

LILY HOSHINO, THE BELOVED ARTIST BEHIND *MAWARU PENGUINDRUM*, OFFERS HER CUTE AND TWISTED TAKE ON THE MAGICAL GIRL GENRE!

KC KODANSHA COMICS

In a world inhabited by crystalline life-forms called The Lustrous, every gem must fight for their life against the threat of Lunarians who would turn them into decorations. Phosphophyllite, the most fragile and brittle of gems, longs to join the battle. When Phos is instead assigned to complete a natural history of their world, it sounds like a dull and pointless task. But this new job brings Phos into contact with Cinnabar, a gem forced to live in isolation. Can Phos's seemingly mundane assignment lead both Phos and Cinnabar to the fulfillment they desire?

Hakka Sasakura's life is about to turn upside-down. She comes home from a day of admiring her student body president to discover that a mysterious creature resembling a man in an animal suit has taken up residence her home. What's more, she has been chosen to work with this strange being to fight off invaders from another dimension and save the world...and she has to kiss him to do so?!

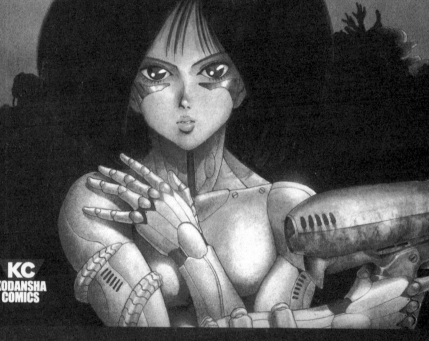

DELUXE EDITION

BATTLE ANGEL ALITA

After more than a decade out of print, the original cyberpunk action classic returns in glorious 400-page hardcover deluxe editions, featuring an all-new translation, color pages, and new cover designs!

KC
KODANSHA
COMICS

Far beneath the shimmering space-city of Zalem lie the trash-heaps of The Scrapyard... Here, cyber-doctor and bounty hunter Daisuke Ido finds the head and torso of an amnesiac cyborg girl. He names her Alita and vows to fill her life with beauty, but in a moment of desperation, a fragment of Alita's mysterious past awakens in her. She discovers that she possesses uncanny prowess in the legendary martial art known as panzerkunst. With her newfound skills, Alita decides to become a hunter-warrior - tracking down and taking out those who prey on the weak. But can she hold onto her humanity in the dark and gritty world of The Scrapyard?

"An emotional and artistic tour de force! We see incredible triumph, and crushing defeat... each panel [is] a thrill!"
—Anitay

"A journey that's instantly compelling."
—Anime News Network

WELCOME TO THE BALLROOM

By Tomo Takeuchi

Feckless high school student Tatara Fujita wants to be good a something—anything. Unfortunately, he's about as average as a slouch teen can be. The local bullies know this, and make it a habit to hit him u for cash, but all that changes when the debonair Kaname Sengoku send them packing. Sengoku's not the neighborhood watch, though. He's professional ballroom dancer. And once Tatara Fujita gets pulled into the world of ballroom, his life will never be the same.

KC
KODANSHA
COMICS

Based on the critically acclaimed classic horror manga

The first new *Parasyte* manga in over 20 years!

NEO PARASYTE f

ASUMIKO NAKAMURA, EMA TOYAMA, MIKI RINNO, LALAKO KOJIMA, KAORI YUKI, NKO KUZE, YUUKI OBATA, KASHIO, YUI KUROE, ASIA WATANABE, MIKIMAKI, KARU SURUGA, HAJIME SHINJO, RENJURO KINDAICHI, AND YURI NARUSHIMA

collection of chilling new *Parasyte* stories from Japan's top shojo artists!

rasites: shape-shifting aliens whose only purpose is to assimilate with and consume *e* human race... but do these monsters have a different side? A parasite becomes a *nce* to save his romance-obsessed female host from a dangerous stalker. Another *sts* a cooking show, in which the real monsters are revealed. These and 13 more *ries*, from some of the greatest shojo manga artists alive today, *gether* make up a chilling, funny, and entertaining tribute to one *manga's* horror classics!

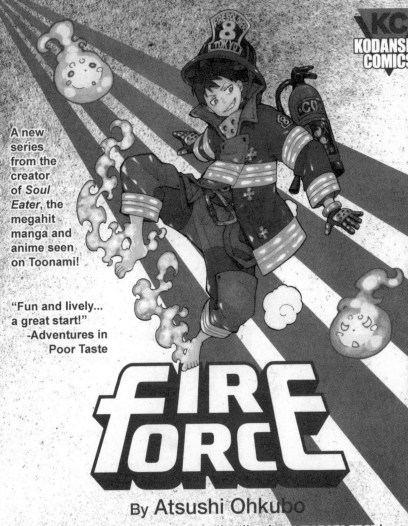

A new series from the creator of *Soul Eater*, the megahit manga and anime seen on Toonami!

"Fun and lively... a great start!"
-Adventures in Poor Taste

FIRE FORCE

By Atsushi Ohkubo

The city of Tokyo is plagued by a deadly phenomenon: spontaneo human combustion! Luckily, a special team is there to quench inferno: The Fire Force! The fire soldiers at Special Fire Cathedra are about to get a unique addition. Enter Shinra, a boy who possess the power to run at the speed of a rocket, leaving behind the famo "devil's footprints" (and destroying his shoes in the proces Can Shinra and his colleagues discover the source of this stran epidemic before the city burns to ashes?

New action series from Hiroyuki Takei, creator of the classic shonen franchise Shaman King!

In medieval Japan, a bell hanging on the collar is a sign that a cat has a master. Norachiyo's bell hangs from his katana sheath, but he is nonetheless a stray — a ronin. This one-eyed cat samurai travels across a dishonest world, cutting through pretense and deception with his blade.

NEKOGAHARA

STRAY CAT SAMURAI

By
Hiroyuki Takei

Japan's most powerful spirit medium delves into the ghost world's greatest mysteries!

Story by Kyo Shirodaira, famed author of mystery fiction and creator of *Spiral*, *Blast of Tempest*, and *The Record of a Fallen Vampire*.

Both touched by spirits called yôka Kotoko and Kurô have gained uniqu superhuman powers. But to gain h powers Kotoko has given up an ey and a leg, and Kurô's person life is in shambles. when Kotoko sugges they team up to de with renegades fro the spirit world, Ku doesn't have many oth choices, but Kotoko might ju have a few ulterior motives...

IN/SPECTRE

STORY BY KYO SHIRODAIR
ART BY CHASHIBA KATAS

The award-winning manga about what happens inside you!

"Far more entertaining than it ought to be... what kid doesn't want to think that every time they sneeze a torpedo shoots out their nose?"
—Anime News Network

Strep throat! Hay fever! Influenza! The world is a dangerous place for a red blood cell just trying to get her deliveries finished. Fortunately, she's not alone...she's got a whole human body's worth of cells ready to help out! The mysterious white blood cells, the buff and brash killer T cells, even the cute little platelets— everyone's got to come together if they want to keep you healthy!

Cells at Work!

はたらく細胞

By Akane Shimizu

From the creator of *The Ancient Magus' Bride* comes a supernatural action manga in the vein of *Fullmetal Alchemist*!

More than a century after an eccentric scholar made an infamous deal with a devil, the story of Faust has passed into legend. However, the true Faust is not the stuffy, professorial man known in fairy tales, but a charismatic, bespectacled woman named Johanna Faust, who happens to still be alive. Searching for pieces of her long-lost demon, Johanna passes through a provincial town, where she saves a young boy named Marion from a criminal's fate. In exchange, she asks a simple favor of Marion, but Marion soon finds himself intrigued by the peculiar Doctor Faust and joins her on her journey. Thus begins the strange and wonderful adventures of *Frau Faust*!

A Kodansha Comics Trade Paperback Original.

Fairy Tail S volume 2 copyright © 2016 Hiro Mashima
English translation copyright © 2018 Hiro Mashima

Fairy Tail ZERØ copyright © 2015 Hiro Mashima
English translation copyright © 2016 Hiro Mashima

Published in the United States by Kodansha Comics, an imprint of
Kodansha USA Publishing, LLC, New York.

Publication rights for this English edition arranged through Kodansha
Ltd., Tokyo.

First published in Japan in 2016 by Kodansha Ltd., Tokyo

ISBN 978-1-63236-610-8

Printed in the United States of America.

www.kodanshacomics.com

9 8 7 6 5 4 3 2 1

Translation: William Flanagan
Lettering: AndWorld Design
Editing: Tomoko Nagano
Kodansha Comics edition cover design: Phil Balsman